# THE EMERGENCE OF

## The Republic of Bolivia

CHARLES W. ARNADE

# THE EMERGENCE OF

# *The Republic of Bolivia*

*University of Florida Press*
*Gainesville - 1957*

*A University of Florida Press Book*

Copyright, 1957, University of Florida
All Rights Reserved
Library of Congress Catalogue Card No. 57-12879
Printed by the Rose Printing Company, Tallahassee, Florida

# CONTENTS

v

# PREFACE

*S*O FAR AS I CAN ASCERTAIN, THIS STUDY is the first
attempt in English to present a section of Bolivian
history with the help of primary sources. It is obvious that in such
a task I had to rely on the help of many people. Without their
cooperation and enthusiasm this book would have never seen print.

To the Henry L. and Grace Doherty Foundation I owe a special
word of thanks for awarding me a substantial grant which
enabled my family and me to go to Bolivia in search of sources.
I was able to remain for fourteen months in that fascinating country,
where I already had spent six years in my teens.

A small grant from the Florida State University Research
Council provided me with student help in the final preparation of
the manuscript.

All the Bolivian scholars I met received me with great enthusiasm. Don Gunnar Mendoza, the energetic director of the Archivo
y Biblioteca Nacional de Bolivia, was a constant source of help. He
provided me with a great deal of material with which I was unac-
quainted. Mr. Mendoza spent innumerable hours aiding me in my
research and in discussing the many phases of Bolivian history.
He is a good scholar and a splendid friend. To all other employees
of the Archivo y Biblioteca Nacional I am very grateful for their
patient help and their many attentions and courtesies.

Don Jorge Urioste, past president of the Sociedad Geográfica de
Sucre, also dedicated long hours to aiding me. Without any quali-
fications, he put the rich collection of the society at my disposal.
There are many more Bolivians in Sucre, La Paz, Cochabamba,

Potosí, and Oruro who gave me valuable assistance at one time or another. The list is long and space does not permit me to mention them. I will always remember them all with pleasant memories. But I cannot fail to mention the dynamic Bolivian historian, Dr. Humberto Vázquez-Machicado, of La Paz. His great generosity in making available his rare collections which took years to gather was a most unexpected and welcome gesture.

An equal number of people helped me in this country. Mrs. Margot de la Cruz, an instructor at the University of Puerto Rico, was helpful in pointing out many defects in grammar and style. To Dr. Donald E. Worcester of the University of Florida I owe equal thanks for his valuable comments and criticism. Drs. A. Curtis Wilgus, Raymond E. Crist, and Lyle N. McAlister of the University of Florida and Dr. Harris G. Warren of the University of Mississippi gave many suggestions. The reference staff of the University of Florida Library was extremely helpful in locating and providing me with printed sources that were unavailable in Bolivia. Professor Charles B. Varney of the University of Florida prepared the maps. His expert geographical knowledge was of great assistance.

It is no exaggeration to say that my wife, Marjorie, has spent as much time as I on this work. She checked and rechecked the manuscript, which she typed twice, and was my most severe critic. To her I owe more than to anyone else and she is as much the author of this book as I.

A last word of sincere appreciation goes to my four little boys, Frank, Carlos, Stephen, and Timothy, who have done the impossible, for in the three years of my preparing this book they have never destroyed a single page. Neither have they used pages of the manuscript as their scrap paper or scattered them in all directions. But I am sure this is just a coincidence. It is to Carlos that I dedicate this book because he was born in old Chuquisaca (today Sucre) while we were in Bolivia. The many events discussed in this book are part of the very history of his native town.

For errors of fact and interpretation I assume full responsibility. Unquestionably their number has been reduced by the helpful hands of my friends who showed a lively interest in this study. To all of them goes a most modest and simple *muchas gracias.*

CHARLES W. ARNADE

*Tallahassee, Florida*

# FOREWORD

$\mathscr{C}$ENTURIES BEFORE COLUMBUS sailed from the port of Palos, there dwelt in the central part of South America, high in the mountains, a people who worshiped the sun and revered Mother Earth, and who gradually extended their cultural and political influence from the shores of Lake Titicaca. They had developed a civilization which had managed to solve many of the problems that confound us today. They lived mostly by agriculture and they learned how to share production for the benefit of all; there was, therefore, little strife over what they had. It was enough, and almost everyone had a fair share.

These people had their problems, of course. The high altitude in which they lived made the raising and harvesting of crops difficult; they had problems about water. Yet they were energetic and resourceful. Since war was almost unknown, their energies could be devoted to the task of cultivating the soil. They knew that there was great mineral wealth around them. A large part of their economy was based on copper which they used for tools and utensils. Gold and silver had been discovered, but to them these metals did not mean wealth. They were symbols of the sun and the moon and were used for ornaments. They were pretty metals and were valued, but their possession did not give any individual power over his fellow man.

These same people were discovered by men from other continents who brought another civilization with them, a civilization that was harsh and powerful and which used weapons of iron and steel. However, while the real strength of such a civilization lay in iron, it used gold and silver as money. These were the media of exchange, and they gave their fortunate possessor great power which was often used to acquire still more power.

The agricultural civilization fell before the weapons of iron and steel, and peace vanished from the country of which I speak. The conquerors concentrated on the production of gold and silver. Farming was neglected. Shafts were sunk in the earth and the native population was forced to work in the mines. Billions of dollars' worth of gold and silver were sent overseas. The peoples were driven like animals to find and dig still more metal to be sent out of the country. Other minerals and metals were found. The conquerors discovered new uses for these minerals and metals. They searched for and mined them with the same feverish energy and greed which had distinguished the search for gold and silver. Power and wealth mounted but nothing remained in the hands of the natives. The people as a whole had only the privilege of working ceaselessly, living on little and dying at an early age, worn out and old before their time.

One day the imperial power that had been supporting such colonial domination crumbled under the impact of new spiritual and material forces: the North American and the French revolutions, the former based on the principle of self-determination, and the latter on the abolition of power based on privilege and class distinction.

Was the spreading of ideas of democracy, liberty, and self-government the main factor involved in the revolutionary movements among the Spanish Colonies? Did Great Britian expect to reconstruct its Colonial Empire in America at the expense of the Spanish Colonies? Was the invasion of the Iberic Peninsula by the Napoleonic forces the determining factor for the disintegration of the Spanish Colonial Empire? Was the independence won by the former colonies a complete or partial restoration of power to the descendants of the peoples of the ancient American culture? Why were the former provinces of the Spanish Colonial Empire unable to form a single Federation, similar to that of the United States of America? These questions are being answered by history.

Dr. Charles W. Arnade has worked on a very important chapter of the history of Bolivia and he finds the answers to some of the above-mentioned questions. His book is written with the precision of a true academic work of art, and to introduce it is not only an honor but a source of deep satisfaction.

Shakespeare saw the march of men as actors in this tremendous drama of life. It is possible to elaborate on that concept and see the immense theater, the earth; the eternal actor, man; the argument, history; and as spectators, the eternal things of the cosmos. Characters will change with the ages and the heroes will succeed each other, leading the chorus and the retinue. The scenery will also change from one point to another on the face of the earth, and in that drama the scenes, if repeated, are never with the same actors and the same setting. Each act of this eternal human drama seems to be represented as if it were the final act. The arrogance of the leading actors often does not let them admit that after them there will be other leaders, other events going on and on. That is why this moving drama is so tense, and it seems that each time and in each scene it is reaching the climax of a spectacular finale.

The emergence of Bolivia as an independent nation and as a consequence of the collapse of the Spanish Colonial Empire is one of the most touching scenes of that drama. Dr. Arnade not only brings to us a methodical and exhaustive account of the human struggle involved in the birth of a new nation, he also presents the necessary background for those who are interested in understanding the struggles of the modern Bolivia. As he summarizes with a masterful stroke: "On Saturday, August 6, 1825, Bolivia began her life as an independent nation; she was on the threshold of a terrible and frightening history."

VICTOR ANDRADE
*Ambassador of Bolivia*

*Washington, D.C.*

*Chapter 1*

# THE TWO SYLLOGISMS

*T*HE LANDS OF UPPER PERU, known in the great Inca Empire as Kollasuyo, became involved in the great struggle that lashed over Spanish South America soon after its conquest in the early decades of the sixteenth century. The various conquerors disputed their rich claims savagely and their armies had all the color of the great feudal wars of Europe, but in a geographical setting much richer and more difficult. Charcas, as the Spaniards began to call Upper Peru, had been a part of Diego de Almagro's claim but the Pizarros took possession of it. Yet with the defeat of the Pizarro brothers, unrest in the lands of Charcas continued unabated. In 1545 the richest mine ever known to exist was discovered in its soil. The silver hill of Potosí brought this majestic and mountainous region into great prominence. Already rival Spaniards from the newly settled Río de la Plata region and the forests of Paraguay were infiltrating Charcas to share the wealth. And the aggressive Portuguese adventurers were most anxious to push from the Brazilian plains to the tall mountain of Potosí.[1]

By 1551 the Council of the Indies saw it necessary to advise the establishment of an audiencia in Charcas.[2] An audiencia was a vital agency of Spanish rule in the colonies. It supposedly was the highest court of appeal, but it was much more than this; it was a "center of executive, administrative, and judicial action."[3] It came to acquire political, economic, legislative, ecclesiastic, and military attributes. Many times it wielded as much power or more than the viceroy. In the Laws of the Indies (*recopilaciones*) it was even stipulated that the audiencia should keep an eternal check

1

over the viceroys or presidents.[4] Here then we have a rudimentary
concept of checks and balances without a separation of power.
Viceroy and audiencia checked each other and both had executive
and legislative power, while the audiencia also had vast judicial
powers. When the audiencia was far away from the viceregal seat
its power was supreme by default. Such a mighty body was created
to govern the provinces of Charcas.

The same day that the royal cedula setting up the Audiencia
of Charcas in 1559 was issued, another cedula was released placing
the new body on an equal basis with that of Lima. When, two
years later, the Audiencia of Charcas began to function, it was
stipulated that it should have jurisdiction over a circle of one hundred leagues in radius (320 miles), with the town of La Plata
(Chuquisaca), the seat of the audiencia, as its center.[5] Small as
the audiencia's domain was, in subsequent years much new land
was added. Royal cedula after royal cedula came from Spain,
continually changing the jurisdiction of Charcas, usually adding
territory, occasionally withdrawing some land. Soon no one knew
where the precise limits of Charcas were. This gave rise in modern
times to many disputes between Bolivia and her neighbors, and
she became involved in war more than once.

The Audiencia of Charcas soon wielded power over what is
today Bolivia, Paraguay, Argentina, Uruguay, and parts of Peru,
Brazil, and Chile. Its domain extended from ocean to ocean; from
the Pacific shores of the Atacama Desert to the waters of the Atlan-
tic in the Plata estuary. In South America there was no other body
which possessed so much power over so much land. This audiencia,
removed from its greatest rival, the viceroy in Lima, became arrogant. It "appropriated the powers of the sovereign and laughed at
the orders of the viceroy."[6] To be chosen an *oidor* (a judge) of
the Audiencia of Charcas was a great honor which commanded
the respect of everyone. One had to greet its members with the
utmost dignity, and the *oidores* even began to refuse to kneel during
religious functions. When invited to participate at ceremonies the
members of the audiencia always purposely came late because it
was their belief that everyone had to wait for such an august body.
Not even the Sacred Host, the archbishop, the president, or the
faraway viceroy received respect from the audiencia. Indeed, the
*oidores* were the practical sovereigns of Charcas. Mariano Moreno,
who in his youth studied in Chuquisaca under the vigilance of the

audiencia, quite properly comments on the "Roman majesty" of the audiencia.[7] At the end of the eighteenth century this powerful body rallied all inhabitants of Spanish blood and hurled them with great power against the revolting Indians under the leadership of the Catari brothers and Tupac Amaru, thus crushing this native revolt mercilessly. The Audiencia of Charcas had reached the apex of its power. From then on this majestic and despotic body began to decline in power, stature, quality, and territory. Also, a new dynasty in Spain was aware of the need of basic reform of its empire.

In 1778 the huge Viceroyalty of Peru, to which Charcas had belonged from its beginning, was split into two viceroyalties, with the creation of the Viceroyalty of Río de la Plata. The Audiencia of Charcas became responsible to the new viceroy in Buenos Aires. Actually, this in itself caused no real damage to the power of the audiencia, since the new viceroy was as distant from Chuquisaca as was the one in Lima. But now each viceroyalty had less territory, and the task of supervision became easier. Besides, two more audiencias were carved out, one at Buenos Aires, and another at Cuzco, not too distant from Chuquisaca.[8] What really doomed the majestic rule of the Audiencia of Charcas was the political reform of 1782, creating intendancies. Eight such intendancies were created in the lands of Charcas. At the head of each was appointed an intendant who was responsible to the viceroy. Much power, especially of a political and administrative nature, was thus taken away from the audiencia, limiting its power more nearly to that of a court of appeal.[9] The beginning of the audiencias at Buenos Aires and Cuzco, plus the administrative reforms and the shifting of Charcas to a new viceroyalty, were the causes for the passing of the golden age of the Audiencia of Charcas; however, it was still an undeniably powerful body. But with the reduction of much of their authority the *oidores* began to feel even more arrogant. For example, they became very particular about correct etiquette to the point of absurdity. They would bow to no one, but they demanded that everyone bow respectfully to them; when they walked in the street, other inhabitants had to step down from the sidewalk. Once they even supported, with a judicial decision, a certain citizen who had refused to address an intendant by the accepted title of *Señoría*.[10] Their arrogant and punctilious behavior soon blinded them to more urgent matters, thereby making them unconsciously

the tool of subversive elements—a very small minority, to be sure—
that wanted to precipitate a separation from Spain. These radical
elements had developed their theories while studying at the University of Chuquisaca.

Chuquisaca, the seat of the audiencia, was also a university city;
six hundred students lived in town, and around seventy *doctores,*
mostly in law and theology, guided these students. More than five
hundred of the students came from all over the viceroyalty to study
and receive degrees at the Universidad Pontificia y Real de San
Francisco Xavier or the Real Academia Carolina, and about one
hundred were local residents.[11] Yet it was a small provincial town
in the midst of the Andes. It conformed to the wise advice of the
old Spanish code, the *siete partidas,* as stated in its first law, that
a house of studies should be in a "good place and beautiful sur-
roundings" so that the students might study in peace and the
teachers think in a refined, quiet atmosphere. There was plenty
of tranquillity in which to think and ponder, and some men took
full advantage of it; revolutionary ideas were born there.

The university was founded by a papal bull in 1621, confirmed
by a royal cedula the following year. Classes began on a very
limited scale in 1623, but the audiencia did not give its mark of
approval until 1624. The Jesuits were allowed the exclusive right
to guide the new university. The same year they wrote and received
approval of the charter for the new university. A glorious career
lay ahead for the institution.[12] But in 1767 the Jesuit era came to
an end with the expulsion of the order from Spanish America, and
the university passed through a critical period. It was turned over
to lay hands but the archbishop of Charcas became its chancellor;
however, because of the *vice-patronato,* the president of the audiencia did not hesitate to interfere often with the teaching and
administration of the university. The question of professorial appointments was a continual bone of contention. No defined line of
responsibility was adopted and the smooth functioning of the university depended on harmony between the archbishop, the president,
the audiencia, and the cloister of the university which directed the
immediate administration of the college. The problem of curriculum
was one of the hardest to solve, but the new order began to lay
less emphasis on theology and more on training in law.[13]

With this over-all reorganization of the university, following
the departure of the Jesuits, it was decided in 1776 to create a new

academy in which graduate students could intern in law before being admitted to the bar. The academy was called the Real Academia Carolina. The exact position of the academy in relation to the university and the audiencia is obscure. It is not even known in which building it functioned.[14] An advanced student of law intending to take his examination before the audiencia was required to practice before this body under the tutorship of an *oidor*. The academy was in charge of this kind of graduate internship. An *oidor* was always the master of the academy; the students were either enrolled in the university or graduates from it. Therefore the academy could be considered a graduate law school of the university administered by the audiencia. It was a place where the advanced law students gathered together, had their carrells, consulted specialized law volumes, and received their tutors' assignments and criticisms. Throughout the day advanced students and lawyers of the town gathered in the recreation hall of the academy to converse and to discuss the whole range of human knowledge. Many of these discussions were vigorous and sometimes attracted a wide audience; some were of a highly abstract nature. Many more hours were spent in discussion than in studying law or practicing law before the tribunal. It was in this hall of the academy that radical ideas began to develop during these private polemics. The academy, with no physical remains left today, was small, but within its halls were planted the seeds which brought doom to the Spanish empire in all of southern South America.

When these students and graduate lawyers began to develop ideas questioning the sanctity of the Spanish crown remains a matter of speculation. Just as they loved to argue in the hall of the academy or over drinks in the taverns, they were extremely fond, too, of writing anonymous sheets which they circulated and answered. These writings were of various types: sarcastic political essays, philosophical papers, satires, poems, love ballads, or pornographic prose or poetry. Writing was one of the favorite pastimes of the students. In Chuquisaca everyone seemed to debate about everything, either by word or in writing, and often the quill was as prolific as the mouth. These handwritten sheets were known as *libelos, caramillos,* or *pasquines,* and many of them were sent out from Chuquisaca to be circulated throughout all the audiencia and the viceroyalty.[15] In other towns much of the same thing took place, inspired by university alumni. Some of these sheets were satires about the Spanish regime. As early as 1780 some *pasquines* circulated in Upper Peru. One said that the Spanish public officials were "thieves," another called them "pirates." "Death to bad government and long live our monarch," read still another, and a sheet distributed in La Paz even demanded "death to the King of Spain."[16] Many were much more subtle, praising the benevolence of the Spanish system but with an implicit double meaning. These *doctores* were crafty and they argued the whole day and deep into the night, and they wrote abundantly.

One of the *pasquines* of a political nature, posted in 1794, proclaimed, "Long live France!" In a *caramillo* dialogue, written in 1807, the questioner asked whether his listener knew "this Franklin, the revolutionary philosopher who disturbed the monarch of Great Britain."[17] Does this prove that the radical *doctores* of Charcas were influenced by the new ideas from France, England, and the United States? Indeed it does; some of the liberal eighteenth-century treatises made their way to Chuquisaca; to what extent— and which titles—is not known. Matías Terrazas, secretary to the archbishop at the turn of the century, had a splendid library and since his high position exempted him from the Inquisition list of forbidden reading, the most modern works were on his shelves. Mariano Moreno received his indoctrination in the library of Terrazas and many students and *doctores* found ways to become acquainted with Terrazas' books.[18] A certain Upper Peruvian *doctor* translated *Common Sense* by Thomas Paine into Spanish, and conceivably might have even been the first to do so.[19] This same *doctor,* Vicente Pazos Kanki, in 1825 was so enthusiastic about American political science that he composed a history of the United States.[20] Bernardo Monteagudo, a main participant in the coming rebellion for independence in Charcas, was deeply affected by French and American liberalism.[21] But the foreign radical thoughts were not overly influential in the formation of the revolutionary *doctores of* Chuquisaca. They learned their radicalism mostly from their own university curriculum. It was mainly Roman Catholic philosophical thought, partially elaborated by a Spaniard, which brought them on the road of opposition to the colonial system.

No philosopher was studied more at San Francisco Xavier than Saint Thomas Aquinas. When the students graduated they knew the philosophy of Aquinas thoroughly and could recite it from memory. Aquinas' *Summa Theologica* was the bible of the students at the university and the academy. Naturally, other great Church Fathers were studied, too. Among these the famous Jesuit philosopher, Francisco Suárez, was the most outstanding and no student left the university without understanding the writings of Suárez. This was because San Francisco Xavier had been exclusively a Jesuit institution, and Jesuit thought permeated the curriculum as well as many of the books on the library shelves. These two men had a great intellectual influence on the generation of 1809 which precipitated the War of Independence in Charcas.[22]

The writings of Aquinas, directed mostly toward defending the papal claims in the great Battle of the Two Swords, were profoundly political in nature, too. In order to insure good and decent government every citizen should participate in its function. Should the ruler cease to govern for the maximum good of the people, government would degenerate into a tyranny and then it might become the people's right to depose the ruler and replace him with a new government. To Aquinas "rulership is an office of trust for the whole community."[23] Therefore resistance to a bad ruler was justified. Suárez, too, was primarily interested in developing the supremacy of the pope over the ruler; consequently his writings were also of a political vein. He concluded that government was to serve the physical needs of men. Should a ruler forget this basic responsibility it was within the rights of the people to replace him with one who would not ignore his duty. Aquinas and Suárez stood solidly for the papal supremacy, but they developed inherently some revolutionary thought. People had the right to turn against the king but never against God.

The radical *doctores* learned their revolutionary ideas from a study of the history of the papal conflicts and the philosophy propounded by the Church Fathers. And although radical eighteenth-century thought was only incidental, it certainly helped to strengthen their convictions. In order to become thoroughly acquainted with the great controversy of Church versus State they also read the works of Machiavelli. This Italian philosopher appealed to the personality traits of the Upper Peruvian intelligentsia which usually expressed itself in double talk. In Machiavelli they learned the many ways that might be taken to achieve a desired result.

But Church thought had developed from ancient Western philosophy, and Roman and Greek ideas were crucial. The law student at Chuquisaca studied the art of logic thoroughly and through it

was taught the importance of the syllogism. The intelligentsia of
Charcas debated either by pen or orally; arguing was their main
pastime. The syllogism was their most useful tool. As warriors
hold their swords ready to strike, so the *doctores* at the turn of the
century were always ready to use the syllogism to defend their
point. They handled it with great mastery.[24] Aquinas, Suárez,
Machiavelli, and the syllogism were four fundamental elements in
the movement of independence in Charcas. Could separation from
Spain be achieved?

Applying three—Aquinas, Suárez, and the syllogism—of these
four elements, the reasoning of the radicals ran more or less like
this: the king deserves the allegiance of the Americas as long as
he governs for their total benefit. But the king's regime is discriminatory against the Spaniards born in America; therefore their
obedience to the crown is void. Did the revolutionaries believe in
premise number one? Yes, since they were heavily indoctrinated
with Aquinas and Suárez and were profoundly religious. Did they
believe honestly in the second major premise? Yes, since this was
their main cause to dislike the regime. They studied mostly law,
they were trained before the audiencia, yet they could never
aspire to become *oidores* because they were not born in Spain.
One of them, Dr. Mariano Alejo Alvarez, a graduate of the university in Chuquisaca, intended to read an essay entitled "The Preference That the Americans Ought to Have in the Positions in
America" before the College of Lawyers at Lima.[25] The speech
was cancelled and the essay filed away.

But these radicals were a small minority. The masses would
not follow their banner of separation from the Spanish crown. The
Spanish regime in Charcas was respected and the king loved.
United, all the people fought against the great Indian rebellion at
the end of the century; and, united, all the people of Charcas stood
ready to help repel the English in case they were victorious in the
Buenos Aires area.[26] The Spanish government still stood on solid
ground in Charcas, and a handful of intellectual radicals who had
learned their ideas from standard texts used in the university could
hardly disturb the solidarity of the regime. Maybe that is why
Father Terrazas was so willing to let students and graduates read in
his splendid uncensored library. And the audiencia, highest Spanish
authority in Charcas, was too preoccupied with punctilious matters
to worry about private affairs of students and young lawyers.[27]

But these radicals had learned by reading Machiavelli that political action often requires patience and that the road to the final result must often lead through ways completely at odds with their beliefs. While in search for means which would weaken the crown by crafty subversions, unexpectedly the great chance to do so arrived. On August 21, 1808, news arrived from Viceroy Santiago de Liniers in Buenos Aires that the Spanish king, Charles IV, had abdicated in favor of his son, Ferdinand; that the powerful Manuel Godoy had fallen from power; and that the French armies were entering Spain. Hardly a month later, on September 17, further news arrived in Chuquisaca, telling of the captivity of the Spanish Bourbons and the coming to power of the Napoleonic dynasty in Madrid, plus the violent reaction of the Spanish people who had risen against this usurpation and formed juntas. The one in Seville requested the leadership of the whole nation to govern in the name of Ferdinand VII, and asked the Spanish colonies to give their allegiance to it rather than to the new French authorities in Madrid. The information also stated that a delegate of the supreme junta, by the name of José Manuel de Goyeneche, a native of Arequipa, was on his way to the Viceroyalty of Río de la Plata to formally request submission to the junta in Seville.[28]

The news was directed only to the authorities, which in Charcas meant the audiencia, the president, and because of his prestige and influence, the archbishop. These three offices represented the highest echelon in the Spanish hierarchy in Charcas. The *cabildo* and the university cloister were of inferior rank. Quick and united decisions, in view of the momentous news from Spain, depended upon harmony and understanding among the three authorities. Unfortunately the relationship between the president and the rest of the audiencia was extremely cold and since 1804 continual quarrels between them had taken place because of administrative jealousies.[29] The president in his loneliness had found a good friend in the archbishop, who had become extremely annoyed at the *oidores'* haughtiness. This dangerous split, along with the amazing news from Spain, prepared fertile ground for the few radical *doctores* to apply their fourth element (besides those of Aquinas, Suárez, and the syllogism)—the advice given by Machiavelli in political behavior and action. From August, 1808, to May, 1809, a great drama unfolded in Chuquisaca.

Don Ramón García León de Pizarro became president of Charcas in 1796. He was born in Spanish Africa of a good family, and had behind him a long governmental career in the Indies. Before coming to Chuquisaca he had been stationed in various capacities in Cartagena, Río Hacha, Mompós, Mainas, Quito, Guayaquil, and Salta. Pizarro was good-looking: tall, slender, with rosy cheeks. He was simply but well dressed, and his excellent breeding and manners inspired great sympathy. The president was open-minded, but not well-read, and rather a slow thinker. He was neither haughty nor stern, and mingled with all classes; anyone who wished to consult him had only to stop him on one of his many walks through the town. He loved to walk with his servant through the streets of Chuquisaca unprotected, stopping here and there to chat with bypassers or with storekeepers. He participated actively in the activities of the social classes of the town, and was always being happy and gay. He disliked rough talk or anything that even resembled a fight. Pizarro abhorred war and was very proud that he had never fought in a battle; he was a pacifist, the sight of any weapon nauseated him. Pizarro enthusiastically beautified Chuquisaca by creating many parks with shady trees and flowers. He believed that bread was the most vital food and he himself kept close watch that the bakers always had plenty of bread at a reasonable price and that they used the best flour. Everyone loved him with the exception of the bakers—to whom he was an eternal nuisance—and his fellow companions on the audiencia, the *oidores*. They considered this plain man weak, cowardly, and hardly intelligent. Pizarro was not fond of those haughty judges whose proud behavior he despised. His great friend was the archbishop.[30]

Don Benito María de Moxó y de Francolí also came from a distinguished Spanish family, and had an advanced education and had held high posts in the Church in Spain and America. He assumed the archbishopric in Chuquisaca in 1807, taking the place of the late José Antonio de San Alberto, an outstanding figure of the Enlightenment in the Perus. Moxó y Francolí was highly refined and well-read. Quite different from San Alberto, he loved luxuries and his food, dress, and furniture were the best. His table was renowned and always well attended. He had a large library and his gardens were well kept. The archbishop hated vulgarity, and he was extremely sensitive and afraid of every kind of physical pain. Any little problem could upset him and he would cry like a child. In his spare time he wrote sweet poetry which he would recite in his feminine voice. In demanding obedience from his subordinates he was stern and very exacting, and his clergy throughout the extensive archdiocese disliked him because of his sense of duty and his insistence upon strict devotion. His efforts to reform the degenerate clergy, especially in Cochabamba, met with tremendous resistance.[31] He was rather small, round, and jolly.[32] The archbishop was of superior intelligence, intellectually much more mature than Pizarro. His influence over the goodhearted president was extensive. Moxó y Francolí possessed a deep love for Spain and an even more intense fervor for the Spanish crown. God and crown were sacred to him. He hated and feared the English and French.

Indeed, the archbishop was extremely sentimental. He had the tender sensitivity of a girl in her middle teens. When in August, 1808, the news of the abdication of Charles IV and the invasion of Spain by the French reached Chuquisaca, Moxó, instead of maintaining silence, requested the people of the town to go to church to pray for the survival of Spain. He himself preached and cried for four days from the pulpit, inciting the people to more and more prayer. When the church proved too small he marched with them to the *Plaza de Toros* to continue the great rogation under the open sky. Looking toward heaven, he asked the people to kneel and pray to the Virgin, "Oh, Lady . . . do not permit that any country of this universe ever wrest us from the sweet authority of Spain under which our fathers lived so happily."[33] Pizarro, too, was happy over such enthusiastic fervor. Charcas belonged to Spain and she loved Spain: this is what the people wanted; so thought Moxó and Pizarro. The audiencia, well-versed in human nature and human weaknesses, was plainly disgusted. Why divulge to the people the critical news from Spain; this was dangerous, and one should never admit weakness. Were not Moxó and Pizarro playing with fire by telling people what was happening in Spain? And to pray was even a greater show of weakness, according to the *oidores*. They had wanted to ignore the news, not to publicize it, and show more strength and power than ever. They were thoroughly angry at the archbishop's doings.[34]

In September further bad news came from Spain, via Buenos Aires, containing the request for allegiance from Seville. In view of such grave news Pizarro requested the audiencia to meet immediately in *real acuerdo* (extraordinary administrative session). On

September 18, late in the afternoon, the audiencia met with Pizarro to consider the communications of Viceroy Liniers. Naturally Moxó was informed by his good friend of the news. Immediately, claiming the love and respect of the people of Charcas, he requested to be invited to the meeting of the audiencia. The *oidores* answered him that when they needed his aid they would call him. Moxó felt deeply injured by such a blunt rejection. The audiencia informed Pizarro that it was strictly against the law that a church representative be present at a *real acuerdo* and that Moxó's request was a breach of the gravest nature.[35] The break between the archbishop and the audiencia was now final and irreconcilable.

The session of the audiencia was stormy. Pizarro gave the audiencia the letters from Viceroy Liniers and the latter's request to submit to the junta in Seville and to receive with dignity the representative of the junta, Goyeneche, when he arrived in Charcas. Pizarro was in favor of following the advice of Liniers. To him the Spanish empire was in danger, and Seville was energetically assuming the leadership against the French invaders. Therefore it was in the interest of all colonies to follow the lead of Seville; if they did not, the empire might disintegrate into anarchy. The *oidores* and the *fiscal* were violently opposed to such a step. Sternly they examined the letters of Liniers and came to the conclusion that there was no proof that such grave events had taken place in the peninsula. After all, they reasoned, any town in Spain could ask for the colonies' allegiance, inventing news. They decided "to do nothing," waiting for royal orders.[36]

Six days later the mail brought further confirmation of the happenings in Spain. Goyeneche had arrived in Buenos Aires and Liniers was forwarding the news he had brought to Chuquisaca. Again Pizarro called the audiencia into *real acuerdo*. This time he thought that they would have to recognize that grave events had really taken place and that in the action of the Spanish people lay the only hope for the survival of Spain and her empire. But the *oidores* were hardly moved. They were set to follow their policy "to do nothing," or as they stated, *no hacer la menor novedad*. It was the *fiscal*, Miguel López Andreu, who this time spoke for the audiencia. He said that there was nothing in the documents brought by Goyeneche that was in accordance with the Spanish laws. They wished to see the king's order or a written document from the Council of the Indies, requesting them to swear allegiance to Seville. Pizarro was flabbergasted. How naïve could they be? The king was a prisoner and the Council of the Indies had become a tool of the usurping Napoleonic dynasty. But the audiencia, in view of the absence of a royal order, decided to continue its policy of doing nothing. The real reason for the audiencia's rejection of Seville was the *oidores'* autocratic royalist philosophy. Seville was the product of the rebellion by the people, and to recognize Seville was to approve the theory of popular revolt as exercised in the French Revolution.[37] Interestingly enough, by holding so tenaciously to this idea they innocently became the very tools of the radicals. Pizarro, Moxó, and Liniers were much more practical and saw clearly the danger to which the narrow-minded action of the audiencia might lead.

After the September twenty-third meeting the lines were clearly drawn. The audiencia, composed of Antonio Boeto, José de la Iglesia, José Agustín de Ussoz y Mozí, José Vásquez Ballesteros, Gaspar Ramírez de Laredo, and Miguel López Andreu, all *peninsulares*,[38] was determined to continue under all circumstances its policy of doing nothing. They wished to withhold the news of Spain from the people as much as possible. By insisting on a royal order to recognize Seville, which was an impossibility, they could forever postpone submission to the junta. President Pizarro was for the immediate recognition of the Junta of Seville in order to maintain the unity of the Spanish empire. Archbishop Moxó was fully in agreement with Pizarro but, considering himself the spiritual leader, he also favored inspiring the masses with a patriotic fervor, reminding them that in the hour of danger their religious duty was to come all out in defense of the Spanish monarchy. Moxó told the people that they must repeat and repeat, "If I could fight with our beloved battalion [in Spain] I would fight to break the chains of Ferdinand, but a huge ocean does not let me do this. But even so, from this faraway distance I shall never cease to serve you, O beloved fatherland."[39] This was obviously in direct opposition to the audiencia's policy of maintaining the populace in ignorance. The situation between the two forces was becoming explosive.

This was further aggravated when Moxó, in his great zeal to mobilize public opinion, demanded from his clergy that they swear allegiance to the Junta of Seville and declared that those who refused would be excommunicated. The audiencia then requested an explanation from Moxó for such a daring action. Moxó, when confronted by the audiencia, acted evasively and denied that he had threatened those who disobeyed with excommunication. He said that he had only given them "fatherly and healthy advice."[40] Yet in the minutes of the meeting held by Moxó with the clergy it states precisely that Moxó said, "I order under the penalty of secret excommunication *(excomunion mayor reservada)* that no one of this body should have doubts about the legality of the supreme Junta of Seville."[41] The audiencia was determined to force the archbishop out of office when the right opportunity came.[42] At this moment they could not yet act without precipitating a serious conflict. In the last days of September, 1808, the situation in Chuquisaca was tense. By then the people knew of the serious split among the Spanish authorities. Everyone expected that the rivalries might reach a climax when the delegate from Seville, Manuel Goyeneche, should arrive in Chuquisaca. But there was an even greater question, unknown to most people: what would the radical *doctores* do in view of the astounding event that had taken place in Chuquisaca?

The radicals had observed the clash between the audiencia, on the one hand, and the president supported by the archbishop, on the other, with great interest. They soon realized that they should close ranks with the archconservative *oidores*. It was now time to apply the theories of Machiavelli, since to support the audiencia, the very rock of Spanish power, was completely contrary to their hopes for everlasting separation from Spain. But the radicals realized immediately that to aid the pro-Seville forces would be to support those who wanted to maintain the unity of the Spanish empire in view of the grave dangers that confronted Spain. To support the audiencia would mean to bring quasi independence to Charcas under the leadership of the audiencia until the return of Ferdinand. The radicals were aware that the *oidores*, by refusing allegiance to Seville, were for all practical purposes separating Charcas under their leadership. If there was no allegiance to a single existent authority in Spain then the empire was in danger of breaking up. The *oidores* in their supercilious behavior were blinded to the real consequences of their action. Of this blindness the intelligent and dangerous radicals took advantage. It was to their interest to support the *oidores*. It was too doubtful whether Ferdinand would ever come back or whether he would be able to have a legal successor. They recognized that from the quasi independence under the not too astute audiencia to independence under the radicals was a short step. Chuquisaca, the intellectual center of the Viceroyalty of Río de la Plata, would lead the way to independence. This was their intimate thinking, but how could they rationalize their support of the audiencia? They again fell back upon the syllogism.

This time they used the syllogism to defend the legality of the crown. Their rightful king had been imprisoned and by sheer force obliged to abdicate in favor of a foreign dynasty. This was the minor premise. It was irrefutable, since it was confirmed by the mail in September. The major premise outlined the legality of the union of the crown and the Indies. It said that in the Laws of the Indies (recopilaciones) it was stated that the union of the American colonies was directly with the crown and that it constituted an insoluble bond. In this great code of law the Spanish crown said, "We shall promise and give our royal word of honor that we and our successors shall never alienate or separate part or all [of the Indies] . . . for any reason whatsoever. Should our successors alienate or separate [these lands] it shall be void, this we declare."[43] It meant that the Indies and the crown were united forever in an eternal allegiance. The colonies did not belong to Spain but to the crown, the crown of Castile and Aragon. The everlasting union could not be destroyed either by the king or by the Indies. Therefore the conclusion was that Ferdinand could not have given the Indies to a new foreign ruler nor could he have delegated his power over the Indies to a junta in Seville. The rulers in Seville might speak for the people of Spain, but the Indies were not part of Spain but belonged to the king. Their lawful sovereign was the king, who now was Ferdinand. It did not matter that he was in prison. He could abdicate only to the one who was in the rightful line of succession, and he had not done this. This was the syllogism of legality[44] which led to quasi independence. It stood squarely in contrast to the syllogism based on the right of the people to rebel as stated by Aquinas and Suárez, which the radicals believed but could not advocate as it would lead nowhere but to defeat. As one historian has put it, it was the *cara* versus the *careta* (the face versus the mask),[45] and the rebellious *doctores* decided to use the *careta* at the appropriate opportunity.

Meanwhile, the delegate from Seville, José Manuel de Goyeneche, left Buenos Aires for Charcas on September 20, 1808. In Chuquisaca Pizarro and Moxó were anxiously awaiting the representative, hoping that he might convince the audiencia to submit to Seville. Moxó, again defying the audiencia, and wishing to make himself acceptable to Goyeneche, issued a pastoral letter the day before Goyeneche's arrival, in which he glorified the Junta of Seville as "the liberator of the generous Spanish nation" and the "faithful depository of the [Spanish] throne."⁴⁶ He asked the people of Chuquisaca to receive Goyeneche with exuberant enthusiasm. Although Moxó had never met Goyeneche, he glorified the representative's personality. Pizarro, also wishing to gain the favor of the approaching Goyeneche, issued a public letter to the audiencia in which he said that he was in complete disagreement with the *real acuerdos* of that body ignoring the wishes of Seville and deciding to do nothing.⁴⁷ Before this, Pizarro had done his best to keep his disagreement with the *oidores* from the people as much as possible. Now he decided to follow the policy of Moxó and make public the tremendous split among the Spanish authorities; he also criticized the position of the *oidores*.

On November 11, Goyeneche reached Chuquisaca and was received with immense enthusiasm by the people, Moxó, and Pizarro. The audiencia was conspicuously absent. Moxó gave a pompous speech of welcome.⁴⁸ Goyeneche was immensely pleased with Moxó and Pizarro, and everyone was highly impressed with Goyeneche, a man who really was clever, shrewd, and deceptive. But the representative inspired great respect. He was tall, slender, and extremely good-looking. He dressed elegantly and neatly, in the latest French style.⁴⁹ His behavior was dignified and decorous, but any man with insight could have detected a certain haughtiness and a complete mechanization of gestures and phrases. But Moxó and Pizarro, not being experts in human nature, were overjoyed with Goyeneche, while he, a much shrewder observer, immediately detected the weaknesses of the archbishop and the president. He realized that Pizarro was of limited intelligence and that he relied heavily on the archbishop. In Moxó he detected an extreme sensitivity and a fanaticism for the Spanish crown.

When Goyeneche, Pizarro, and Moxó were alone, the delegate from Seville told the archbishop that the situation of the Spanish kings was dubious; it might even be considered hopeless. Moxó

then became overwrought, tears came into his eyes, and he inco-
herently muttered that he would prefer to die in the jungle from
the bites of snakes, lions, and tigers than to live under the cruel
regime of the French.[50] Goyeneche had anticipated this event. At
the precise psychological moment he removed from his pockets
two heavy letters and gave one to Pizarro and one to Moxó. When
the archbishop looked at the envelope he became joyful, blushed,
and his eyes brightened. It was a letter addressed to him, in her
own handwriting, from Carlota Joaquina of the House of Bourbon,
princess-regent of Portugal, who was then in Brazil, daughter of
Charles IV and sister of the imprisoned King Ferdinand VII. Moxó
could not believe it; was it possible that an immediate member of
the Spanish crown had condescended to write to him directly; what
an honor, what a delight![51]

Both Moxó and Pizarro held the unopened letters nervously.
Although consumed with curiosity they decided to return them to
Goyeneche. It was their opinion that it would be improper to open
in private letters that came from a foreign nation. It should be
done before the audiencia. The personal meeting then ended and it
was decided that the president should call the audiencia into
session the next day to introduce the representative of Seville. The
session was called in the late afternoon of November 12. At first
the *oidores* had refused to come, but Pizarro, this time using strong
words, ordered the members of the audiencia to attend; in addition
he insisted on the presence of the archbishop and two representatives of the *cabildo*.[52] Reluctantly the audiencia conceded. The
presence of Goyeneche was needed to give Pizarro a certain
strength he had lacked earlier.

The meeting took place in a room in the president's house. At
last the audiencia would meet this Goyeneche, the imposter, as
they thought him. As the members filed into the elaborately decorated room there was an air of tenseness. Hardly anyone talked;
each sat in his chair, avoiding looking at the others. Goyeneche,
immaculately dressed, was introduced by Pizarro. Immediately
the delegate from Seville addressed the assembly; his words were
the platitudes of etiquette. Then he handed his credentials to the
*regente-oidor*, Boeto, an old, distinguished-looking gentleman. Boeto
got up, and handing the credentials to the *fiscal*, said that since
there was no royal signature nor that of the Council of the Indies
he thought the credentials, and therefore the mission, of Goyeneche

were invalid and unacceptable. As if hit by lightning Goyeneche jumped up and furiously told Boeto that his naïveté and behavior were disloyal to the crown and insulting to the imprisoned King. Boeto, first pale, then red in his face, also jumped up and, beating his chest, screamed, "I, a traitor? I, a traitor? Impossible! Impossible!" To which Goyeneche shouted that he would imprison anyone who refused to obey the Junta of Seville. Then Boeto, more infuriated, beads of perspiration running down his scarlet face, pointed at Goyeneche and loosed a stream of angry vituperations, calling the delegate a "dirty adventurer, paper general, roving cashier without bail and guarantee," and adding obscene insults. Suddenly everyone was on his feet, rushing to avoid a fist fight between Boeto and Goyeneche. There was a long moment of confusion. Finally Moxó was able to placate Boeto, and Pizarro was successful in calming Goyeneche. Again silence prevailed. Any further debate was impossible. Moxó and Pizarro uttered some words about the need of harmony, and expressed the hope that the imprisoned king would come back soon. The members of the audiencia insisted that they would continue to uphold their *real acuerdos* to carry on their policy of doing nothing in regard to the constitutional problems of the crown.[53]

But there was one more item of business to be taken care of. For nearly twenty-four hours Moxó and Pizarro had waited anxiously for the opportunity to open the letters from Carlota. Before breaking up the meeting of the audiencia and notables, Goyeneche again handed the envelopes to the president and the archbishop. Both quickly opened the letters and, after reading them, showed them to the other members. There was a startled silence. The content of the letters was of a completely unexpected nature; it put the whole constitutional problem into a new perspective. The letter to Pizarro contained several proclamations[54] by Carlota in which she declared that since her father and brother were forced to abdicate the Spanish throne by the French forces she was the legal depository of the crown. Carlota wrote, "I think it is convenient and opportune to forward these proclamations in which I declare void the abdication or resignation that my father, the King, Charles IV, and other members of my royal family of Spain [Ferdinand VII] have made to the Emperor and General of the French. . . . I only consider myself as the depository and defender of those [royal rights] and I want to conserve them undamaged

and immune from the perversity of the French in order to turn them
back when possible to the legal representative of my august
family."[55]

The significance of this was that Carlota, in view of the imprisonment of Charles IV and Ferdinand VII, was claiming the Spanish
colonies. The letter to Moxó included that proclamation as well
as a personal salute from the princess. In the face of such momentous news the audiencia vacillated, but then insisted that since
these letters were directed to Pizarro and Moxó, they had little to
do with them. Thus ended the stormy meeting of November 12,
1808.[56] But everyone was aware that a completely new factor had
entered the tense picture of Charcas. And everyone must have
thought about another question: Why was Goyeneche, who was
supposed to represent the claims of Seville, carrying letters containing a rival claim? Handing over the letters, Goyeneche said
they were given to him in Buenos Aires by a British sea captain
who had come from Rio de Janeiro, who had asked him to carry
them to Charcas as a favor. But today it is known that the delegate
from Seville was really riding two horses; he was also the agent
for Carlota.[57]

The introduction of the Portuguese claim into the already complex picture in Chuquisaca made a final peaceful solution less
probable. Carlota's claim did not help the party of the president
at all, but did hasten his fall. The Portuguese letters became a
potent catalyst in accelerating events to their final violent conclusion; they were the immediate cause for the start of the War of
Independence in Charcas. Those proclamations gave the audiencia
a powerful weapon against the president and the archbishop. And
they forced the radical *doctores* to come out into the open and
take the lead against the presidential forces. Yet the *doctores* still
trapped the archconservative and royalist audiencia in their nearly
imperceptible web.

Goyeneche, realizing the futility of trying to persuade the
audiencia, but knowing that he had planted his seed successfully
with Moxó and Pizarro, soon left Charcas for La Paz and Lower
Peru. Since Moxó and Pizarro—true, though shortsighted, Spanish
patriots—were interested in preserving the unity of the Spanish
empire, the idea of Carlota appealed to them. To both it was
more practical and legal than the cause of Seville which they had
upheld. What they did not realize was that the Portuguese move

was calculated solely to absorb the Spanish colonies by taking advantage of the defeat of the Spanish Bourbons. It was not done because of a desire to help the hard-pressed Spanish crown. Moxó and Pizarro hoped that recognition of Carlota might be more appealing to those who had opposed Seville. After all, one of the objections to Seville was that it was created by the revolution of the people. But the claim of Carlota came from the nearest relative of the imprisoned kings (father and son). Again, what the president and the archbishop did not see was that by supporting the claims of Carlota they might be accused of infidelity, in insisting on giving allegiance to a foreign country which had long had an ambition to acquire more of the Spanish colonies.[58]

When the audiencia refused to recognize the Junta of Seville it simply insisted on its right to do what it pleased, giving as a legal excuse the theory that the radical *doctores* had worked out for them in their legal syllogism (the syllogism of the *careta*). But it could hardly accuse Pizarro and Moxó of any grave breach of the Spanish laws. At last it had an issue. Moreover, the president and the archbishop decided to answer the letters of Carlota in a vein that might be easily construed as favoring her dynastic claims.[59] The audiencia could accuse, as indeed it did, the president and the archbishop of treason.[60] Francisco de Viedma, the enlightened intendant of Cochabamba, which formed the vast eastern part of Charcas to the borders of Brazil, had also received a personal letter from Carlota. But Viedma had realized the intentions of the princess-regent and his answer, while polite, stated that he was not authorized "to submit to a foreign country although it claimed the title of regent"[61] until the Spanish Bourbons were freed. Such should have been the reply of Moxó and Pizarro. The naïveté of the presidential forces did have a grain of common sense. After all, Carlota was the nearest relative of the imprisoned royal father and royal son. Might not Carlota's claim be in accordance with the legalistic syllogism that the radical *doctores* had constructed to persuade the audiencia not to recognize Seville? What the audiencia, Moxó, and Pizarro could not realize, but the radical *doctores* of Charcas, always shrewd and alert, understood clearly, was that the new situation was a great threat to the final success of their Machiavellian move. It might demolish their hopes of making the audiencia an independent junta, from which they would later wrest the power. It was time to act.

The radicals' syllogisms of legality or *careta* were based on the theory that the colonies belonged to the Spanish crown. The king could never alienate these lands to someone else, as Ferdinand and his father Charles were forced to do. This is just what Carlota claimed. Since father and son were held by Napoleon, she, as the daughter of Charles IV and the sister of Ferdinand VII, was the guardian of the colonies until one of the two imprisoned kings could return to assume his usurped throne. Therefore, Carlota with her proclamations had demolished the usefulness of the syllogism of the *careta* so carefuly constructed by the radicals for the benefit of the archconservative audiencia. If the plans of the radicals to force out the president and the archbishop were intended to succeed, tempo and direction must be increased and changed at once.

The best way to check the ambitions of Carlota in Charcas was to exploit with energy the charge that those who favored her claim were traitors, as they intended to hand over the colonies to a foreign country. The radicals used this diligently to stir the masses and to force the audiencia to take a firm stand against the claim of Carlota. In December, 1808, a whispering campaign was started, accusing Moxó and Pizarro of wanting to give Charcas to the Portuguese. The audiencia concurred, branding the archbishop as having become a victim of the "seductive words" of Carlota, intending to "separate these colonies from our monarch," and saying that the president was "managed" by the archbishop.[62] It was a campaign of subversion. But the claims of Carlota could have been disputed by more honest means.

It was also said that Carlota was really disbarred from any claim to the Spanish throne by the Salic Law of Felipe V of 1713, which disqualified females from governing Spain. The abrogation of the law by Charles IV in 1789, kept secret by the royal family because of possible opposition, was known only by a handful of favorites of the crown. Archbishop Moxó was one of those very few since he was a personal friend of the powerful Manuel Godoy, Charles IV's great minister and the queen's paramour. Naturally the issue was brought up by the anti-Carlota forces. Moxó insisted that the Salic Law was void,[63] but his only proof was his argument that he had been favored with being told this carefully guarded secret. Yet the radicals preferred to exploit the treason charge to its full extent rather than use the Salic Law. It was much more effective and, after all, everyone in Charcas knew that Moxó was close to Godoy and that often he knew more of the intimate doings of the crown and its ministers than even the highest officials in the viceroyalty, including the viceroy. One thing was certain: the campaign against the presidential forces had to be increased.

It is difficult to know exactly what happened among the radicals, since their actions were *sub rosa*. The first phase had consisted of constructing for the audiencia the syllogism of legality in its opposition to Seville. The effectiveness of this syllogism was weakened by Carlota's unexpected claims. The second phase, the fight against the Portuguese claims, was directed at maintaining a grip on the narrow-minded audiencia and stirring up the people against the popular president and archbishop by circulating the rumor that both men were selling Charcas to Carlota. The immediate goal was to overthrow the presidential forces, thereby making the audiencia semi-independent. The ultimate goal was to eliminate the audiencia and to lead the forces of independence in Spanish South America. This was justified by the revolutionary syllogism to which they subscribed secretly.

Strictly speaking, the radicals did not have an accepted leader; they amounted to scarcely more than fifty persons.[64] But three men stand out. Jaime Zudañez, attorney of the audiencia in the department for the defense of the poor, was responsible for influencing the audiencia, which hardly suspected his revolutionary ideas. His brother, Manuel, occupied a key position in the *cabildo* and the university cloister, and led these important bodies to the antipresidential camp. The Zudañez brothers were in crucial places and credit for the success of the radicals' plan was due mostly to their brilliant maneuvers.[65] The third man, Bernardo Monteagudo, was a talented conspirator, writer, and theoretician of humble origin, and probably conducted the whispering campaign. He joined the attorneys staff of the audiencia in 1809, being assigned to the staff of the department for the defense of the poor. Monteagudo also was an influential member of the university cloister. He was graduated from the university and academy in 1808 and the vociferous *oidor*, Ussoz y Mozí, supervised his thesis.[66] All three, with the aid of their confreres, began to step up their conspiracy as the new year started. The plan was to force the president into a position in which, out of sheer anger, he would act with force against the audiencia, thereby justifying his removal. It was a campaign to needle the pacific president and the archbishop.

The conspirators began with good fortune. The *regente-oidor*, Boeto, who on November 12 had the verbal battle with Goyeneche and was still upset over the insults of the delegate, had soon afterward a heart attack of which he died on December 6.[67] Naturally the radicals did not lose time in beginning to whisper that Goyeneche, the man of duplicity and the friend of Pizarro and Moxó, was the real murderer of Boeto. The *regente's* death was a heavy blow to the audiencia and its allies. Pizarro and Moxó had enough common sense to realize that the Carlota question had slowly undermined their high reputations in Chuquisaca, but they still believed that any move that would cement the unity of the Spanish crown was the best defense against possible anarchy. In order to regain some support, they now looked to the powerful university. On January 12, Pizarro asked the university cloister to give him a vote of confidence. Forty-eight *doctores* gathered together, many of them radicals.[68] By an overwhelming vote led by the Zudañez brothers and Monteagudo the cloister rejected Pizarro's wishes and condemned in harsh words the maneuvers of Carlota of Portugal. On January 19 the cloister was again called into session, and the attendance of all the members was requested. This time, ninety-two *doctores* came and gave their signed approval to the minutes of the meeting held seven days earlier.[69] The presidential forces had suffered another defeat.

After this success, the radicals swung into greater action. Manuel Zudañez, through some of the discontented priests in Cochabamba who hated Moxó for his moral fervor, had gotten hold of a letter the archbishop had written to a faithful priest in Cochabamba. In this letter Moxó had complained about his trouble with some malicious elements in Chuquisaca whom he called "seductive hypocrites" engaged in "filthy intrigues."[70] In late April, Manuel Zudañez convinced the *cabildo* to request the audiencia to censure Moxó for such disrespect. In the first days of May the *fiscal* of the audiencia began to hear testimony to discover the validity of the charges.[71] The Zudañez brothers worked hand in hand. Again, in the middle of May, the *cabildo*, at the instigation of Manuel, requested the audiencia to investigate the president, since it had come to their attention that he was going to apprehend many people who were against him. The audiencia instructed *oidor* Ussoz y Mozí, the man who hated Pizarro most, [72] to investigate the case.[73]

Pizarro felt deeply insulted. Although a convinced pacifist, he realized that something had to be done. He could not continue his policy of appeasement. That was just what the radicals had waited for. On May 20 he had the minutes of the cloister confiscated and ripped out the pages referring to the meeting of January 12 during which the *doctores* had denied him a vote of confidence and had insulted Carlota. Permission to do this had already been granted in early April by the viceroy, but Pizarro had hesitated to take such a drastic step. Now Pizarro wanted to show that he could use energy to fight the opposition. May 20 marks the end of his policy of hesitation and appeasement. The next day, although it was a holiday, the Feast of Pentecost, Ussoz y Mozí publicly invited anyone who wished to appear before his one-man committee to accuse Pizarro of misconduct.[74] Besides, Pizarro was informed by his trusted friends that Colonel Juan Antonio Alvarez de Arenales, a pureblood Spaniard in charge of the Spanish militia in nearby Yamparáez, decided not to depart for his vacation to Salta. It was rumored that in case of a clash between the forces of the audiencia and the president, Arenales would support the audiencia.

In view of this grave news Pizarro, on May 23, decided to request the intendant of Potosí, Francisco Paula Sanz, to send him troops. This became known to the opposition on May 24 and it was considered of a serious nature. Therefore, that very night, the revolutionaries, made up of the audiencia, part of the university cloister, and the *cabildo,* met in an urgent meeting in the house of the *regente,* José de la Iglesia. It was decided that the united forces of the audiencia, *cabildo,* and cloister would arm themselves and patrol the town. It was also determined that the audiencia in *real acuerdo* would depose the president the next day.[75]

On the morning of May 25 Pizarro was informed of the open insurrection of the audiencia and its allies. He ordered the arrest of the executive staff of the audiencia, *oidores, regentes,* and the *fiscal,* plus the employed attorney for the poor, Jaime Zudañez. Seemingly Pizarro was aware that Jaime Zudañez was one of the moving spirits of the rebellion. Pizarro based his action on the contention that the audiencia had violated a certain section of the Laws of the Indies *(recopilaciones)* which forbade the audiencia to investigate the viceroy and the president.[76] The opposition was informed of the impending arrests, and went into hiding. By seven o'clock at night only Jaime Zudañez was located and arrested.

He was conducted by six soldiers and one officer through the streets to a barrack in the center of town. All along the road Zudañez was crying out loudly so that everyone in the street and the nearby streets could hear, "Citizens, they are taking me to the gallows."[77] Although Zudañez was not abused by the soldiers, his screaming was calculated to incite the people. It produced an astounding effect. Soon the streets of the small town of Chuquisaca became alive; the moon was full and as bright as day. In view of the agitation, Zudañez was taken to the president's house. The mob, loud, uncontrolled, some firing into the air, slowly began to march toward the president's house. The cry, "Viva Fernando! Viva Fernando!" resounded in many places. Suddenly the hidden members of the audiencia, *cabildo,* and cloister were found in the streets. The revolution had started. May 25, 1809, marks the beginning of the War of Independence in Charcas. Yet few who took part in the drama of that day realized it.

The mob yelled in front of the house of Pizarro. Evidently only a single shot was fired by a soldier who guarded the house. Furiously, the people forced the heavy gate, sacked the place, and apprehended the elderly president. Fortunately some radicals were able to wrest him from the wrath of the people and took him to a room at the university where he was put under arrest. The archbishop, after failing to calm tempers, became panicky and escaped toward the village of Yamparáez. He was terrified, trembling, and pale. Father Jorge Benavente, who accompanied Moxó in his escape, was forced to carry him on his shoulder. Feeling cold and tired, they stopped at an Indian hut where the Indian and his wife politely offered the two men some food and warm drinks. They ate some purée of red corn but Moxó, unaccustomed to such food, was unable to digest it and started to vomit. Since the corn was red, Moxó became panic-stricken because he believed that he was spitting blood.[78]

After deposing the president the audiencia assumed all powers in the name of Ferdinand VII, at four o'clock in the morning of May 26, 1809; they were only nominally responsible to the viceroy in Buenos Aires and directly responsible to the imprisoned king. Immediately, the new colonial government of the audiencia took several important steps. It appointed Colonel Arenales as the over-all commandant of Charcas, and requested him to organize a strong militia.[79] Arenales was a perplexing man. He was a *peninsular* but being less narrow-minded than the *oidores,* he realized that the War of Independence had started. Yet his thinking had nothing in common with that of the radicals, who wanted separation because of their inferior status as *criollos*. Seemingly, Arenales honestly believed that the independence of America was inevitable. He later established the most distinguished and the longest record as a veteran of sixteen years of fighting in the War of Independence.[80]

A further step by the audiencia was to invite Archbishop Moxó to return and assume his office. Arenales, who disliked Moxó, opposed this step. The audiencia realized that the people still loved him. The courier located the suffering Moxó abandoned in an Indian hamlet on his way to Potosí. He was delighted to return, and he kissed and embraced the courier.[81] But the most important step the audiencia took was to send delegates to the several larger cities in Charcas to forestall pro-Pizarro elements beginning a reactionary movement. As the audiencia was unaware that it was really in the hands of such cunning revolutionaries as the Zudañez brothers, it appointed the delegates proposed by these advisers. The delegates were all radical *doctores*. Monteagudo left for Potosí and Tupiza, Joaquín Lemoyne was sent to the vast province of Santa Cruz, a certain Manuel Arce went to Oruro, and Tomás de Alcérreca, in the company of a certain Pulido (first name unknown), went to Cochabamba.[82] In addition to carrying official instructions from the Spanish audiencia they had another mission given them by their revolutionary leaders. They were to incite other radicals in those places to repeat what had been done in Chuquisaca under the facade, or *careta*, of "Viva Fernando, the Audiencia is our junta, not Seville, down with Carlota and her traitors." This indicates that the radicals were dispersed all over the audiencia, and even beyond, as far as Buenos Aires. How they really acted, how they were organized precisely, remains unknown; only the general outline can be deduced from documents. But one thing is sure: their headquarters was in Chuquisaca and from there came the leadership. Their forces in other places were relatively weak, as all delegates failed in their secret mission with the exception of one city that rebelled.

The man appointed as delegate to go to La Paz was probably the most radical of the revolutionary cell in Chuquisaca. Mariano Michel, a graduate of San Francisco Xavier,[83] was of a rebellious nature, and had the gift of stirring the masses. He was not an advocate of complicated political theories. It is probable that the radical lawyers were divided into two factions: a moderate one which wished to continue at all costs the policy of the *careta* as long as it was advantageous, and a more aggressive section which wanted to abandon the legalistic syllogism as soon as possible and come out publicly for separation from Spain. One could suspect that the Zudañez brothers belonged to the moderate faction and that Monteagudo led the aggressive section. As a matter of fact, in January, 1809, another one of the anonymous *pasquines* or *caramillos* was circulated in Chuquisaca. This latest one purported to be a dialogue between Atahualpa, emperor of the Inca nation, and Ferdinand VII, who met on the Elysian Fields. Ferdinand complained bitterly about Napoleon's usurpation of his crown. To this Atahualpa answered that the French emperor was merely doing what Ferdinand's forefathers had done to him, Atahualpa. Both engaged in a long philosophical discussion. Ferdinand elaborated the syllogism of legality and Atahualpa spoke for the innate rights of the native Americans, thereby identifying his thoughts with the revolutionary syllogism. Throughout the pages of the dialogue Church dogma, philosophy, and Western revolutionary thoughts are well blended. The discussion of Atahualpa and Ferdinand is a perfect synthesis of the intellectual currents that motivated the unrest in Charcas in 1808 and 1809. Monteagudo is believed to be the author of the dialogue. The words of Atahualpa represent Monteagudo's real feelings and they portray a true radicalism. In one of his final sentences, Atahualpa said to Ferdinand, "If I could transmigrate from here to my Kingdom I would issue a proclamation saying: . . .Destroy the terrible chains of slavery and begin to enjoy the sweet pleasure of independence."[84] Monteagudo was a radical who wanted immediate action, to replace the *cara* for the *careta,* and who gathered around him few followers. Michel was one of them.

Michel's official mission was to inform the intendant of La Paz that if he knew of anyone favoring the claims of Carlota he should arrest him and send him to be judged before the Audiencia in Chuquisaca. His secret mission was to see whether he could convince the radical *doctores,* alumni of San Francisco, to repeat what had been done in Chuquisaca and apprehend the intendant, Tadeo Dávila, and the bishop, Remigio de la Santa y Ortega, accusing them of sympathy with Carlota's scheme.[85] Once successful, the *cabildo* should take over the power and recognize the absolute sovereignty of the audiencia as the depository of the power of the imprisoned king. In a word, they would play the *careta* all over again, using the *cabildo* as the front.

Michel immediately went to see his friend, José Antonio Medina, the parish priest of Sicasica, not far from La Paz. Medina was the most extreme radical of all the generation of 1809. He, too, was a graduate of San Francisco and had taught there for a time after his graduation. Young Monteagudo had been one of his favorite students.[86] Medina promised to see to it that the radicals in La Paz obeyed the instructions of Chuquisaca. He kept his promise. On July 16, 1809, the *cabildo* deposed the intendant and the bishop. A few days later the revolutionaries superseded the *cabildo* and created a new body called the Junta Tuitiva, of which Pedro Domingo Murillo, a more moderate and distinguished radical, was made president. The idea of creating a new government made up of the radicals was Medina's. He and his followers in one stroke had abolished the *careta* and the syllogism of legality and had come out openly for the revolutionary syllogism.[87] The proclamation of the junta constituted the first open demand for independence from Spain; it said, "It is now time to overthrow the [Spanish] yoke. . . . it is now time to organize a new government based on the interests of our fatherland. . . . it is now time to declare the principle of liberty in these miserable colonies acquired without any title and kept by tyranny and injustice."[88] The movement in La Paz had taken a different turn from the one in Chuquisaca. Medina and Michel, probably with the advice of Monteagudo, had quickly realized their goal and put aside the elaborate scheme of the *careta*. This proved to be the downfall of the whole generation of 1809.

It was a great mistake. The time was not yet ripe to announce publicly the desire for independence. The movement in La Paz collapsed due to the fact that it soon produced internal dissension; the moderates deserted the cause. The people were unwilling to follow the lead against Spain. And from Cuzco came Goyeneche, the newly appointed president of this audiencia, with an army, and crushed the revolt mercilessly. He took stern measures and many of the leaders were condemned to death. They were hanged in the middle of the square. Others were sentenced to the galleys or to hard labor in the mines. Hardly anyone escaped the mighty hand of Goyeneche. Murillo, the nominal head of the revolution, was hanged; Medina, the real leader, because of his status as a priest, got a life sentence. The elaborate scheme of the radical *doctores* was destroyed in a single stroke, by the single mistake of discarding too soon the *careta* for the *cara*. Michel, Medina, and perhaps Monteagudo were responsible for this. The Audiencia in Chuquisaca, caught in the web of the *careta*, finally saw its mistake.

In Chuquisaca the rule of the audiencia had continued. Arenales had raised an army of about one thousand men from the countryside.[89] The audiencia had been able, by a combination of threat and persuasion, to induce Intendant Sanz of Potosí to give up his idea of marching on Chuquisaca with the intention of restoring Pizarro to the presidency.[90] The audiencia and Arenales had wooed the new viceroy in Buenos Aires, Baltasár Hidalgo de Cisneros, to accept the new order in Charcas, accusing the ex-president of all kinds of crimes. But Cisneros appointed a new president, Vicente Nieto, to assume office in Charcas and investigate the strange events that had taken place. Arenales wanted to refuse to receive Nieto. As a matter of fact, Arenales wanted to march with his popular army toward Potosí, conquer the town, and then move into Salta and from there advance on Buenos Aires.[91]

But in view of the amazing news from La Paz the *oidores* began to see their mistakes, and realized that they had only been a tool of unscrupulous elements. Therefore, on September 27, 1809, the audiencia decided to receive Nieto with all honor. Pizarro was released from his prison and given permission to return to his house. On November 8 Nieto issued a proclamation from Jujuy, saying that he was coming to Chuquisaca with an army and hoped to have the necessary cooperation from the audiencia. On October 13 Arenales agreed reluctantly and ordered that his militia safeguard the entrance of Nieto's army. On December 21 Nieto announced from the village of Cuchiguasi that he and his five hundred men would enter Chuquisaca in two days, December 23.[92] Nieto was received without incident. There had been only one condition that the repentant *oidores* asked from Nieto when he was on his way to Chuquisaca: that Goyeneche, the man they had scorned, would not move with his formidable army from La Paz to Chuquisaca. Nieto agreed; and on November 10 he wrote a letter to Goyeneche in which he thanked him for his fine cooperation in suppressing the movement in La Paz. But at the same time, he informed him that his services were not needed in Chuquisaca or any other place in the Audiencia of Charcas, as he was assuming office as president of Charcas.[93]

Immediately, Nieto began to investigate the past events in Chuquisaca. He acted with much greater tact and moderation than Goyeneche had in La Paz. But even so, he asked permission from the viceroy to depose several *oidores* and expel them from Charcas. The viceroy approved the request. Seemingly only Ussoz y Mozí and Ballesteros were sent away. What happened to the rest of the *oidores* remains a mystery, since in 1810 the colonial Spanish government in Buenos Aires was overthrown.[94] It is known that Arenales was removed and sent to Lima for trial. Several of the radicals, including the Zudañez brothers and Monteagudo, were imprisoned. Manuel died in prison. Jaime and Monteagudo later escaped.[95] By the beginning of 1810 Goyeneche, with sternness, and Nieto, with moderation, had destroyed the whole generation of 1809. Yet not all was lost. On May 25, 1810, exactly one year after the imprisonment of Pizarro, the radicals in Buenos Aires, among whom was an alumnus of the University of San Francisco, Mariano Moreno, an early member of the radical generation born in Chuquisaca, repeated more or less what had been done in Chuquisaca. This time, however, it succeeded. Although the radical generation failed in its home town and home provinces, it was successful in Buenos Aires. From that city efforts would have to be made to free the birthplace of the ideas which had helped to liberate it. Could the victorious radicals in Buenos Aires do it? Unexpected help in Charcas would be forthcoming.

The unrest in Charcas had somewhat stirred the masses of Indians and mestizos. They were used for the advantage of both rival parties. Arenales had organized a militia with the people of the countryside, and so had the revolutionaries in La Paz. Such royalists as Goyeneche, Nieto, and Sanz had also used the indigenous elements to enlarge their armies of repression. With the defeat of the radicals at the hands of Goyeneche and Nieto calm returned to the provinces.

But with some groups, mostly *caciques* (Indian chieftains), small landlords, and village bureaucrats, the lust for adventure stirred by the agitated year of 1809 continued unabated. Arenales was able to escape from Peru. He went back to Charcas to live in hiding in the countryside, and with the help of these elements he began fighting the Spanish authorities as a sort of guerrilla leader.[96] When Paula Sanz, intendant of Potosí, was organizing an army to liberate Pizarro, he requested the help of the Indian *cacique*, Martín Herrera y Chairari of Chayanta, to come with his Indians to aid his army. But the Indians of Chayanta hated the cruel *cacique*. The *alcalde* of the village of Moromoro, a *criollo* by the name of Manuel Ascencio Padilla, who was a friend of Monteagudo's, and who had an extremely well-educated and aggressive wife, Doña Juana Azurduy de Padilla, stirred the Indians to disobey the *cacique's* order. The Indians decapitated Herrera y Chairari. The Padilla couple and their army of Indians supported the Arenales militia. When Nieto became president he ordered the arrest of Padilla. But he and his wife, together with the Indians, disappeared into the mountainous countryside.[97] Thus another irregular unit was born. These bands, unleashed by the unrest of 1809 and by punitive expeditions of Goyeneche and Nieto, were an unexpected inheritance begot by the generation of 1809. They came to be known as the guerrillas of the War of Independence. They maintained the fight for separation from Spain which started on May 25, 1809, in Chuquisaca.[98]

The long and intelligently prepared movement of 1809 collapsed as a result of the fiasco in La Paz. Most of its leaders died, a few were exiled to faraway lands. Yet their action was inherited by two new movements which kept alive the flame which was ignited by the Zudáñez brothers, Monteagudo, Medina, Michel, Murillo, and many others. The successful revolution in Buenos Aires was partly inspired by their example, and the guerrilla leaders were an unforeseen result of their action. The guerrillas and Buenos Aires would have to continue the fight against the Spanish authorities in Charcas.

*Chapter 2*

# THE ARMIES OF THE PARTISANS

*H*OW MANY GUERRILLA LEADERS FOUGHT in the war? One historian gives the exact number as one hundred and two.[1] Another Bolivian writer even goes so far as to say that two partisan leaders deserted during the fight and nine survived the war.[2] Any exact statistics are useless and really senseless. It is simply impossible to know the exact number of guerrilla leaders. But the serious Bartolomé Mitre has rightly pointed out six strong points which, under the leadership of six guerrillas, seriously jeopardized the Spanish hegemony in Upper Peru. These were the six most important and extensive *republiquetas*.[3]

Upper Peru in those days was accessible from two main directions: from Lower Peru or from northern Argentina. In the east were the impenetrable jungles of the Amazon Basin and the plains of Santa Cruz that merged into Brazil. In the west the Atacama Desert was an obstacle to reaching the Pacific coast. Therefore nearly all movement was north and south. In the heart of Charcas six towns flourished: Potosí, Chuquisaca, Oruro, La Paz, Cochabamba, and Santa Cruz. Of these Potosí was the most important for Spain because of its riches, and Chuquisaca was the capital where the audiencia was located. La Paz and Oruro were mining centers; Cochabamba and Santa Cruz were of agricultural importance. The six *republiquetas* were wedged between Charcas and the neighboring lands, and among the six important cities.

On the shores of Lake Titicaca the priest, Ildefonso de las Muñecas, obstructed communications between Upper and Lower Peru. He operated from the village of Ayata in the *partido* of

ROYAL HIGHWAY
AND
GUERRILLA AREAS
Royal Highway
Borders of Guerrilla Areas

C. B. VARNEY

Larecaja. In the south Vicente Camargo ruled another *republiqueta,* with headquarters in Cinti. This represented a threat to Cotagaita, one of the strongest fortresses in Upper Peru. This fortress protected Potosí from the southern route which the Argentine expeditionary forces took on their march to liberate Charcas. Camargo held the door open for these Argentinians as Muñecas closed the door to the Spanish armies from Lima, Cuzco, and Arequipa. Somewhat to the west of Camargo's jurisdiction was another large partisan republic lying between the Grande and Pilcomayo rivers.

Its center was Laguna,[4] and it obeyed the command of the Padilla couple. This *republiqueta* neutralized the capital, Chuquisaca, and kept a road open from Argentina to the capital. In the east was the most extensive *republiqueta*, that under the famous Ignacio Warnes, with its capital at Santa Cruz de la Sierra. Although the largest, this one was the least important from a strategic point of view. It neither guarded nor opened the entrance to anyone. Yet it protected the eastern flanks of almost all the other *republiquetas* and was a haven for escape and retreat for them in time of defeat.

In the center two fairly extensive *republiquetas* were like two emboli in the very heart of Upper Peru, putting the communications among the six big towns at their mercy. One was under the celebrated Arenales, with its center in Mizque and Vallegrande. This threatened and often cut off the roads connecting Cochabamba, Chuquisaca, and Santa Cruz. The other was the partisan republic of Ayopaya in the center of Bolivia's mountain region. From its confines the guerrilla forces could dominate the roads between Oruro, La Paz, and Cochabamba. The *montoneras* of both of these central regions had escape routes. From the Arenales domain it was easy to go to Warnes' republic, since the two were adjacent. The Ayopaya *republiqueta*, on its eastern frontier, lost itself in the dense jungles of Mojos.

These were the six great *republiquetas*. There was one more of great strategic importance but of unstable nature, and with no one outstanding commander. This was the factional jurisdiction of Chayanta which, when active, dominated the roads connecting Potosí, Oruro, Chuquisaca, and Cochabamba.[5] But since it was encircled by these four towns, strong points of the Spanish army, it had no escape route and therefore was only of a temporary nature, appearing and disappearing in accordance with the Loyalist impact upon its domain.

However, these were not the only guerrilla republics. There were many more of minor extent and importance. From Camargo's and the Padillas' jurisdictions down to Tarija numerous factions kept the line to the United Provinces open. In the neighborhood of the valley of Tarija important guerrilla commanders such as José Fernández Campero, Ramón and Manuel Rojas, Francisco Uriondo, and Eustaquio Méndez were actively in command of *republiquetas*.[6] In the eastern territories, in addition to Warnes, numerous partisan leaders were practically independent. It is as

impossible to determine where one *republiqueta* started and another
ended, as it is to determine the lines between Patriot and Loyalist
territory. Furthermore, there were smaller *republiquetas* within
larger ones. Sometimes minor factional leaders were under the
command of major guerrilla leaders, while at other times they
acted independently and drew together only in times of emergency.
Usually one leader did not know what the others were doing, and
cared little. Commander Arenales complained vociferously about
the neighboring commander, Warnes, who nearly always refused
to cooperate.[7] Yet the six major jurisdictions, or *republiquetas*,
gave the Spaniards the greatest trouble. They isolated Upper Peru
and dominated the communications among the main centers of
Charcas. In 1816 they had become a major threat to effective
Spanish domination of Upper Peru. The Royalists finally attained
their goal of destroying the *republiquetas* in 1816. Muñecas, Camargo, Padilla, and Warnes fell in battle, and Arenales had to flee
to Argentina. Only the *republiqueta* of Ayopaya survived the
impact and remained undefeated throughout the remainder of the
war. On January 29, 1825, the Ayopaya commander, Miguel Lanza,
occupied La Paz before Marshal Sucre and his liberating army
entered the town.

The epic of Ayopaya was extremely obscure. As this guerrilla
republic was isolated by lofty mountains and bordered by impenetrable jungles, little news of the events in it reached the outside.
Historians claimed that Ayopaya existed and was heroic because
of its leader, Miguel Lanza—known today as *pelayo boliviano*. He
created this partisan territory and from it fought until the very
end of the war. Lanza was given credit for having threatened the
roads to the cities of La Paz, Cochabamba, and Oruro.[8] Lanza
survived the war, was then integrated into the Bolivarian army,
and became a trusted lieutenant of President Sucre. He was the
sole guerrilla leader to take part in the foundation and consolidation
of Bolivia. He gave his life for Sucre in 1828, and was one of the
few associates and friends of Sucre who remained loyal to the last,
when the president was betrayed by unscrupulous supporters.

Lanza's career as a guerrilla is quite different from what it has
been generally believed to be. This can be ascertained from a
fascinating diary kept by a simple drummer of the Ayopaya guerrilla
unit.[9] When the soldier's narrative opens, in 1816, Miguel Lanza
was not in Ayopaya. Only on February 3, 1821, did he make his

appearance in the *republiqueta* with the appointment by his
superiors in Argentina as the "principal commander of the interior."[10]  In cold blood he killed the previous commander of the
republic, José Manuel Chinchilla, a close friend of his who had
fought the Spaniards valiantly for many years. The diary ends in
1821.[11] It must be assumed that from that time on Miguel Lanza
was the chief of the *republiqueta*. But to give him full credit, he
was not new to the Ayopaya region in 1821, and very likely had
been the original organizer of this factional territory. Already in
1812 he was engaged in fighting the Spaniards. On September 4,
1812, the audiencia condemned him to ten years imprisonment for
his revolutionary activities, "fighting against the King's army."[12]
In that same year Lanza was in jail together with Chinchilla, the
man he killed nine years later in order to take his place. Both
escaped; Lanza was naked, and his friend and fellow prisoner,
Chinchilla, provided him with clothes.[13] From 1812 to 1821 Lanza's
activities are quite obscure. It might be that in those years he
set the foundations for the guerrilla faction of Ayopaya. After the
defeat of the third auxiliary army under José Rondeau in 1815,
Lanza left Upper Peru with the retreating Argentineans, not to
return until six years later. During the most critical years of the
war, therefore, Lanza was not even in Upper Peru.[14] It was Eusebio
Lira, Santiago Farjado, and José Manuel Chinchilla who were
respectively the commanders of the Ayopaya republic.

The *republiqueta* of Ayopaya extended about 250 miles from
north to south and about 125 miles from east to west. The land
was unusually rough, varying in elevation from 3,300 feet at some
places to 18,000 feet at others.[15] No particular town served as permanent headquarters, but such small mountain villages as Palca,
Machaca, and Inquisivi were the core of the partisan republic.
Palca had only a single, muddy street and a few dilapidated houses,
but it did have a spacious church and its drinking water was good.[16]
Although small, such villages as these were the heart of the republic,
and from their confines the *montoneros* dashed to the very limits
of Oruro, Cochabamba, and La Paz. Indeed, Oruro once nearly
fell into partisan hands. The traveler who today flies from La Paz
to Cochabamba or vice versa—a well-established international air
lane—flies directly over what was the Ayopaya guerrilla country.
Those who have gone over it know that this is a most fascinating
and breath-taking flight. Underneath lies very rough, but most

beautiful, terrain. It includes sharp mountains, narrow, fertile valleys, the magnificence of the eternal snow-capped peaks of the Cordillera Real, and then the fearful drop into the jungles. In itself this region is like a microscopic reproduction of the whole world. Both everlasting snow and bananas are seen within its confines, and only at short distance from each other.[17] When the weather is clear and the plane lifts itself over the mountains instead of flying in the narrow passes, one can see snow and jungle at the same time. It was then, as it is now, a region where Indian blood flowed in everybody's veins. There were very few whites, many pure Indians that spoke Aymara or Quechua, and much mixed blood.[18] The people were hardy, for the roughness of the territory molded men to fit their environment. And the cleavages of the social classes had not penetrated into its midst.

Such was the place in which the guerrilla republic of Ayopaya existed, and about which only vague or erroneous information was available until the diary of Vargas, a soldier of that faction, was located. Why did he write this diary? He tells us simply because he "was curious to do this."[19] Vargas is a common name, and author Vargas does not tell his readers what his first name was. He was the main drummer, and he was a native of the region, from the little mountain village of Moosa (or Mohaza). It was a wretched little town of narrow and dirty streets, with an unattractive plaza and a run-down church, in the middle of a canyon. People in Moosa took their scanty produce to sell in distant Oruro.[20] Vargas was no Indian, but came from a fairly well-established mestizo family which had some land. One of his brothers was a priest. The discoverer of the drummer's diary, Gunnar Mendoza, has spent many hours searching documents of the early period of independence for a better identification of Vargas, since from the diary it can be inferred that he survived the war. Moreover, in his reading of Bolivian documents of 1825 to 1828 the present writer has also looked out for this particular Vargas, but has found no tangible evidence. It remains that the author of the best existing primary source of information about the War of Independence in Upper Peru is a Vargas from Moosa,[21] and that is all that is known about him.

Vargas knew how to write, but he probably had a very limited education. His diary is hard to read and difficult to translate. His vocabulary was extensive,[22] with all the colloquialisms of the region.

He was undoubtedly a brilliant man with a superb speaking ability, and he wrote just as he spoke. There is absolutely no syntax in his composition. His style is intimate and frank, and it fits into the whole milieu of the era, region, and fighting band.

There were no dull times in the life of the faction. It is therefore fitting that a certain section of the diary should be given here. In order to be true to the author, direct translation would be the most satisfactory way of passing on the diary. But because of the peculiarity of the style such is hardly possible, for it would mean writing without any syntax. A modernistic style would spoil the whole tone and setting of the diary. Therefore the following pages are not a translation but a sort of edited version, maintaining the tone and simplicity of the original.

The general opinion is that the faction was there to fight the Spaniards. Indeed this they did, but not all the time. The diary verifies this. On November 5, 1817, Captain Eugenio Moreno, with his company and about one hundred Indians, all of them stationed between Moosa and Leque, went to Paria. Moreno had not received any order to go there. Very early in the morning of November 17, they reached Paria and many of them went to the house of a respected citizen of the village, Eugenio Flores, whose birthday was being celebrated. Hearing all the noise that was being made, an honest citizen of the town, Anselmo Carpio, of "patriotic leaning," went to join the party since he had heard the toasts of "Long live the fatherland." But as soon as he entered they shot him and left him dead. Then the partisans left the party and took as prisoners whomever they found in the streets. The next day at nine o'clock the unit left the village, but not before the Indians had sacked and destroyed whatever they wished. The unit took fourteen prisoners with them—innocent people whom they had taken from the streets. On the way one of the prisoners requested permission from a sergeant to step out of line for a while. When Captain Moreno saw this he had the prisoner killed. On the way home Moreno ordered two more of the prisoners to be shot. But Laureano Choque kept close watch over the village mayor whom they had arrested, "very much an enemy of the fatherland and decorated by the King."[23] Choque sent him to Cabari where Commander Lira had him shot to death. On November 19 Moreno and his band returned to Leque. The next day the enemy, one hundred and fifty men strong from Oruro, met them. A little skirmish took place and the enemy had to retreat, burning some houses and killing five Indians.

During this time Commander Lira had seen to it that a certain Barrientos from the hacienda of Manata was captured and hanged because this individual had helped in the intrigue that had killed Lira's father. On December 1, Lira left Inquisivi and went to Machaca, accompanied by drummer Vargas, writer of the diary. Commander Lira ordered Moreno to appear and he reprimanded him very severely for having gone to Paria and sacked that town for absolutely no reason, and for having killed Carpio and three prisoners without even inquiring whether these people were Patriots or friends of the king. Lira asked Moreno to tell him who had ordered him to do all this, who had told him to sack the town, who had told him to take old people prisoners. The commander told Moreno that such behavior would make their "cause hateful" to the people, and if news of such behavior would reach the ears of the superior commanders in Salta and Buenos Aires, what would they think of them? Their superiors would say that Captain Moreno had gone to Paria without orders, that he had destroyed and killed, and that he had taken peaceful villagers prisoner. Commander Lira continued saying that he would not know how to explain to the people, to his superiors, and to the whole continent such behavior of his troops. Lira said that everybody might well say that they were not troops of "the fatherland," but a raving band.[24]

Commander Lira had Moreno put under heavy guard as a prisoner. He then called half of his grenadiers to Machaca, because he had gone there with only eight men. Lira also wished that no officer should come to Machaca because he knew they would press for the freedom of Moreno, who was a likable fellow. But even so a lot of people asked forgiveness for the prisoner. These included Colonel Buenaventura Zarate, Doctor Don Manuel Ampuero, the parish priest, and many others. There were many letters from the respectable citizens[25] of the neighborhood and from the officers. Lira's mistress,[26] Doña María Martínez, also interceded for Moreno. Lira would not agree with them because he thought that his honor, the honor of his unit, and "lastly, the cause of the fatherland" had been injured.

On December 5, at four o'clock in the morning, Moreno disappeared. Lira had put him in a room, forbidden visitors, tightly closed the door, and put a heavy guard before it. The prisoner escaped with the help of his *padrinos* and Lira's mistress. They had helped him through an old stone-filled window. When Commander Lira heard of the break he was so upset that he "nearly killed himself." He was very angry at everybody and wept. Then he took his horse and galloped away to the house of his mother in Moosa, about thirty miles away. At night he returned and called for the guards, but they had escaped too. Angrier than ever, he left for Palca. He was so furious, he would not eat. On December 7, he reappeared in a somewhat better mood and requested food. Then the commander decided to call a staff meeting of all the officers and available friends. The *padrinos* of Moreno told Lira that everything should be resolved with reflection and with the thought in mind of "Thou shalt love thy neighbor." They added that everybody knew that Lira was not responsible for the Paria massacre, that Moreno had gone there on his own without any superior orders. The parish priest[27] then added that everything was governed by God, that He had made everything, and that God has everything happen because He wants it so. He continued that since God had permitted Moreno to escape He must have had a reason, and one day God would punish him for his deeds. He then terminated his speech by saying that Lira should leave the punishment of Moreno to God alone.

Following the address of the pastor everybody remained reflective. Then everyone in the meeting supported the words and thoughts of Don Ampuero, the priest. After a period of tense quietness Lira gave a huge sigh and said that he was very sorry that Moreno had been able to escape but that he, Commander Lira, had learned a lesson. From then on he would not throw into prison anyone who had committed a crime. He would instead catch him and put the delinquent immediately before a firing squad; he would forget all about putting them in prison, calling a jury, putting them in the death cell, commuting the sentence, and all such needless prolongations. Lira continued, saying that all those who escape do the same nasty thing that Moreno would do: they go over to the enemy, and the final consequence is that there is one more enemy to fight. He thought Moreno would tell the armies of the King everything about his unit, its strength, and what he wanted to do.

When Lira had terminated his address Colonel Zarate asked if Lira knew that the accused Moreno had not gone over to the enemy, but rather was hiding in the territory of this partisan unit.

If Moreno of his own free will would come into the open and ask forgiveness, would he, Commander Lira, pardon Moreno? Lira became somewhat thoughtful and then gravely responded that he would forgive him in "the name of the fatherland."[28] Lira thought that in doing this Moreno would not go over to the enemy. He, Lira, was convinced, as everybody had assured him, that the people and his superiors would know that he was not responsible for the massacre of Paria. The priest then suggested that all this be put into writing immediately. Commander Lira had to sign a sworn testimony twice, and then again swear before the Holy Cross to fulfill his words: that Moreno be pardoned, but that he be retired from the service, and that ex-Captain Moreno not be permitted to leave the territory of the partisan republic of Ayopaya. Then Colonel Zarate offered to vouch for Moreno. After this happy settlement the grenadiers were called and everybody gave loud hails to the fatherland and more cheers to the commander for his generosity. Vargas took his drum from the box which he always carried with him and beat it to announce the great and happy event.

Then the pardoned man, Moreno, crawled out from beneath the bed of the priest where he had listened to the whole debate. Lira told him of the pardon and Moreno, with tears in his eyes, and kneeling, kissed the commander's hand. He then promised to return some of the remaining part of the stolen belongings to Paria, and said, too, that he would tell the names of the soldiers and Indians who had committed most of the crimes at Paria. Lira gently shook Moreno's hand, lifted him up, and asked him where he wished to reside, to which Moreno responded that he preferred Palca. Everybody then left Machaca for Palca. Moreno went to the house of Major Marquina, his good friend. On December 9 the whole corps of officers of the unit went to visit the home of the commander to express their thanks for his having pardoned one of their fellow officers. They said that everyone thought that Lira was a very prudent commander. After this Lira accompanied his officers to the barracks. Major Marquina had the entire division form a review line, and when Commander Lira entered the camp Marquina stepped forward and ordered all the soldiers to hail the great commander and the fatherland. After this everybody dispersed in a jovial and happy mood.

The night of December 14, 1817, around midnight, Major Pedro Marquina,[29] Captain Agustín Contreras, Lieutenants Santiago

Morales and Pedro Graneros, ex-Captain Eugenio Moreno, First Lieutenant Antonio Pacheco, and a soldier of the guard of Commander Lira by the name of José María Torres, entered the barracks. They ordered the whole unit to get up, they relieved the guards, Morales had his infantry unit so stationed that nobody could get out and no one was able to get in, and guards were put all around the barracks and the horse stables. Once the division was lined up, Major Marquina pulled out a piece of paper and gave the assembled unit a hard-hitting speech. He called the soldiers "companions in arms" and reminded them of their obligation to defend the fatherland with their own blood and their own lives. Marquina told the guerrilla force that they had served without pay, working extremely hard, many times suffering hunger, defeat, and heavy casualties. He said that he had never heard complaints from the troops, and this was rightly expected of them because they had joined "the sacred cause of our beloved fatherland, independence, and liberty." He continued that they had lived up to their obligation and that because of their faith the whole continent now knew that here, in these regions, were men "devoted to the common cause of the fatherland." The orator then said bluntly that they were all fighting for the welfare of the future and not for their own well-being or adventure, and that probably all those present in the service of their country would never see "the total triumph of our sacred opinion." He thought that the sons of those who were fighting, persecuting, and committing cruelties would enjoy the "fruit of the tree of liberty"[30] for which their unit was fighting. After this the officer added gravely that the commander under whom they fought was creating their ruin, that he was destroying their work, that this man would send them all to the grave, and he, Marquina, and those who had come to speak to them at this late hour, would prove this.

Then addressing all the sergeants, corporals, and privates who knew how to read, the speaker showed them a paper and asked them if they knew the signature. Everybody glanced tensely at the paper and all said that it was the handwriting and signature of their commander, Lira. Then the major read in a loud voice a letter addressed to Colonel José Manuel Rolando of the king's army; it was dated December 14, 1817, at Palca, county seat of the district of Ayopaya. The letter said that the writer, Commander Lira, had ordered that on the twenty-fifth of December, 1817, Commanders José Domingo Candarillas[31] and José Manuel Chinchilla should attend a meeting in Tapacarí. The writer continued that on the twenty-sixth he would fulfill the stipulated treaty made with the viceroy, taking upon himself the responsibility that all resistance in these regions by his unit and his subordinates would cease, and that no more partisan units would jeopardize the king's army. And then Lira would be only too glad to give Colonel Rolando an embrace and greet him as a "loyal vassal of the King." From then on Lira too would become a faithful servant, as he had intended to do for a long time, but, since an early defection would end in failure, he had not taken such a step. Now the time was ripe and Lira emphasized that Rolando should not doubt for a minute that he was ready for the defection and surrender which he had promised a long time ago to the governor of the district, Juan Oblitas, as well as to the governor of Sicasica, Francisco España, even though they had lately persecuted him frequently. The commander then suggested that the king's forces should be stationed in the villages of Calliri or Caraca; and that after this they could meet at an appropriate point between, on neutral territory, to conclude the final surrender. The writer of the letter then reassured Colonel Rolando that he would proceed as promised "on his word of honor." He requested that the letter be forwarded to the intendant of Cochabamba. The communication was signed "Eusebio Lira."[32]

When the reading of this amazing letter was terminated everyone was stunned, as if a bomb had dropped in their midst. Many wished to read the letter several times. Vargas was there too, and he said that in the very moment of confusion when everybody was discussing this surprise First Sergeant Manuel Branes took him, Vargas, to one side and whispered, "This signature is falsified. It is not the handwriting of Lira."[33] Vargas rushed to see the letter again, and then mustered courage to approach Major Marquina and ask him bluntly how he had got hold of this letter. Marquina said that it was the soldier, Torres, of the honor guard of Commander Lira, who had given him the letter. Torres jumped up and said that when Lira was changing his coat the letter had fallen out of the pocket, and that he, Torres, picked it up in order to hand it to Lira. Then he saw the insignia of the Spanish army on the envelope and quickly decided to keep it and take it to Marquina. Again there was silence, and then everybody insisted that the commander should be arrested and face the accusation. Some soldiers wept, and wanted to kill him immediately for his treason. Others, also crying, said that Lira was honest and incapable of committing such a base deed, and insisted on a quick clarification of the abominable accusation.

Vargas, seeing the tumult, called aside his little friend, the small drummer from Tapacarí, "the smartest of all drummers," according to Vargas. He told him to slip out through the back wall of the stables and rush over to the commander's house, and explain everything to him so that he would be warned of what he would have to face. The little fellow did as told, went out unseen by the guards, and rushed over to Lira's residence, three blocks away. But time was short, and when he reached the house he already saw a crowd moving from the barracks toward the residence. He hurriedly explained to the commander, in an incoherent way, the unfortunate news. Lira apparently did not understand the real significance of it, scolded the little drummer for having left the barracks, and sternly ordered him to return and go to bed, where he should have been at that very late hour.

In the meanwhile, it had been decided at the barracks that a selected platoon with its leader, Don Ramón Rivera, go to arrest the commander. Some officers opposed this procedure, and confusion reigned. Captain Moreno, whom Lira had pardoned for his massacre of Paria, now insisted that he go with the soldiers himself. Moreno won his point. At two o'clock in the morning he and Sergeant Manuel Miranda, an intimate friend of the captain, and the platoon left the barracks for Lira's residence in order to apprehend him. The house of Lira, a dilapidated single-story building three blocks away from the quarters, was located just across from the priest's residence. Moreno knocked on the door. From the inside a voice, that of the commander, responded, "Go to sleep, let me sleep, don't disturb me." Moreno answered, "Get up, Commander, you are arrested." Again from the inside Lira replied, "Arrested, who has ordered this?" Moreno shouted through the door, "By the order of the whole officer corps and all the troops." Again Lira put a question, "Do you have armed men with you to apprehend me?" "Yes, I have half of the grenadiers with me," responded Moreno. Then Lira said, "Let's see you prove to me that you have armed soldiers with you." Moreno ordered his men to fire two shots into the air. The door then opened, and Lira stepped out and said calmly, "Ha, you are making a revolution, you smart *cusqueños*.[34] I want to ask you not to kill me without letting me go to confession."[35] Lira was wide awake and dressed in a poncho which concealed his saber. Then Moreno explained that this was not a revolution, but that they had found a paper with Lira's signature, and that the reason for the commander's arrest was simply to prove or disprove the authenticity of the signature.

Lira was taken to a nearby store where the trial was scheduled to take place immediately. The store was closed, and while they tried to open it the captured commander sat down on a bench in front of the store. The platoon of soldiers surrounded him. Once the store was opened Moreno asked Lira to enter. At the moment that the commander stepped into the store someone from behind fired a shot. It hit Lira. Moreno turned around and yelled, "Who has shot, from where did it come, who has shot?" The bullet had penetrated from behind into the ribs. There was confusion. Moreno ordered Vargas to sound a general alarm. The drummer and the band left for the village square to fulfill Moreno's order. On his way back to the store he saw that the village had been thrown into an uproar. Those soldiers and officers who had remained in the barracks had rushed out. The village inhabitants who had been peacefully sleeping at that very early hour, unaware of the coup that was taking place in the guerrilla unit stationed in their town, had been awakened by the noise and were wandering in confusion in the dark streets. Moreno was frantic. He was swearing and continually mumbling and repeating, "I don't know who has shot the commander." The wounded Lira was painfully and nervously pacing in the dark in the store.

Vargas approached the store because he wanted to see Lira and be with him in his critical hour. When the wounded commander saw him he shook his hand then spoke in sad words to his faithful subordinate, the drummer. He reminded him that Vargas had been his companion from the very start of the struggle, that together they had traveled extensively and worked very hard, that the drummer had been a faithful witness of everything, and that he had been a devoted comrade and defender of the fatherland. He complained that bad people had forged the letter and falsified his signature. The dying Lira was bitter against Moreno and Marquina, who, he said, were "good soldiers of the King." He believed they had seduced his troops. Lira emphasized that he never would have committed the crime of which they had accused him. He wondered why he would have wanted to surrender when his troops were stronger than ever, and when he had fought bravely against the enemy at a time when he had had only six or eight rifles. He was sure that none of the division believed this fraud. He ended in a tone of desperation saying, "Everything has been fraud, rivalry, envy, and this [coup] is [only] ambition for power." He then repeated, "This is not my signature, I never thought of this."[36] The deposed commander then asked his friend Vargas to go to the barracks and tell the army of his innocence.

Vargas did as requested by Lira. But when he reached the quarters they were empty, with the exception of a few officers who had been arrested, probably because they had voiced allegiance to the wounded commander. The drummer was also arrested and jailed with these officers. Later they were all freed and taken to an assembly room. There Santiago Farjado, father-in-law of Marquina, was the first to address the meeting. He said that history was full of such incidents, but what he lamented most was that a courageous and fine leader had been murdered in cold blood. Farjado wondered what the superiors in Buenos Aires would think about this, and what excuse they could give them for such a barbarous act. He was concerned, too, about what the Patriots would say of such a scandal, and the way this unit did its business. Farjado was wondering how they could cleanse their name. As Lira in his speech to Vargas, so Farjado, the man who soon would take the place of Lira, in his speech to the assembly, ended on a note of sadness and skepticism. He thought that he would have been better off if he had remained a disinterested citizen instead of becoming a Patriot. He added that if he had the means[37] he would leave these lands in order not to witness these rivalries among the Patriots.

Marquina, the son-in-law of Farjado and the man who had first publicized the original charges against Lira, said to the meeting that this eventful day had produced two important incidents. The first was the loss of a "brave, sagacious, prudent, and meritorious commander," and the second, the awareness that someone had wanted to start a great intrigue with the intention of destroying the unity and faith of this partisan unit. He thought that nobody was responsible for the death of Lira, who incidentally had not yet died, but that it was due to the wishes of "the god of the warriors,"[38] who is the one who holds in his hands the destiny of all fighters.

He thought that the most important thing to do was to name a new commander in order to avoid further anarchy. Everybody present agreed with this need. Farjado was quickly and unanimously elected as the new commander of the partisan unit. At first he refused the honor but then gave in. The new leader then swore to uphold the cause of the Patriots, and afterwards all the other members at the meeting offered allegiance to Farjado and swore to obey strictly his orders and judgments.

Immediately four members[39] raised the question about the false signature, and wanted it to be cleared up. They were of the opinion that the letter was false and that the signature was forged, and demanded that a committee be set up to investigate this scandalous case. They emphasized that it was most urgent to come to a conclusion, since in the future the same kind of trick could be played with the new commander. But already most members at the meeting advanced the opinion that the signature was forged by Lieutenant Antonio Pacheco. Farjado ordered that Pacheco be arrested for inquiry and if enough evidence was available he should be put before a military court.

Meanwhile, the disorder in the village streets had not yet subsided. Soldiers were roving in the streets, shouting, "Long live the fatherland, death to bad government." At nine o'clock the dying Lira requested that Vargas be with him in his last moments. Farjado consented to this wish. The ex-commander, in a coma, lay on the bed, very pale, with a wooden crucifix in his hand. The county commissioner (*subdelegado*) held him in his arms; a priest stood at the other side. No one else was in the room. Four heavily armed guards stood outside, not letting anyone in. Vargas embraced the dying man with tears in his eyes. In a shaking voice he told him that he was greatly moved, that he felt so very bad that Lira was paying dearly for his uninterruped work for the Patriotic cause. Lira was unable to answer, but only held up the crucifix, pointing to Christ as if he wanted to say that in Christ he had found peace. Vargas was completely overwhelmed by his emotions, as were the priest and the commissioner.

It was indeed a pathetic moment. Then Lira suddenly rallied strength, took some water, and said quite clearly, "Where are all my companions, why do they leave me alone in this moment? Are they already dead? Where are they? Without doubt dead or prisoners." Rallying more strength, he embraced Vargas and whispered,

"Good-by, my friend." He was painfully hurt that no one else besides Vargas had come. Whispering still, he said that he was dying but that he had worked always for the cause of the Patriots, that he had worked very hard, and in gratitude his troops had now killed him. Lira advised Vargas to commit suicide or go to the enemy. He thought the enemy would take him and free him, and then Vargas would be free of all this nonsense. But it might be, although he did not think so, that the enemy would put him before a firing squad. But then he would die in honor for the fatherland "in a public square, well provided for, and with the formalities of the occasion." At least Vargas would not finish as miserably as he, Lira, had. He became agitated, fell back, and was unable to continue. Again he mustered strength, put his hand in the wound, tore out a piece of bone, and handed it to a second priest, who had just entered, saying, "I'm dying innocent, I die innocent, they have betrayed me. I die as a Patriot, I die as a Catholic." He then mumbled some prayers very weakly, holding the crucifix tightly. Lira was in his very last moments. At ten-thirty in the morning of December 15, 1817, one more guerrilla leader passed away.[40]

With Lira's death and Farjado's election unrest did not cease; instead, a period of anarchy and internal strife followed. Nobody thought of fighting the Spaniards. How much jurisdiction Lira had or how extensive his *republiqueta* had been is vague. But it certainly extended beyond the limits of his headquarters. He had commanded the allegiance of faraway villages, and the Indians had loved him since he had their blood in his veins.[41] Once he was dead, thousands and thousands of Indians and minor guerrilla leaders converged upon Palca and Machaca. They wished to know who had killed their beloved leader and hero. The picture then took a dramatic turn. The Indians threatened and besieged the Farjado force. They demanded that Moreno, Marquina, Miranda, and others be turned over to them to be tried for the death of their *caudillo*.[42] Farjado vacillated and negotiated, and small skirmishes took place. Then the new commander decided to turn over the wanted ones. Moreno and his band resisted, and fought the Indians bitterly. Farjado was helpless. It was a war among the factions. Moreno and Marquina were accused by their own fellow officers of having been soldiers of the king. It was said that Marquina was responsible for the death of the great guerrilla

Muñecas. Farjado, a peacemaker with no ambition but to lead a simple life, wanted to resign and turn over his command to a council composed of all the antagonistic factions. His son-in-law, Marquina, and his followers refused to let him do this, for it would have meant the end for them. But finally a junta composed of all important members of the factions, including such Indian and mestizo leaders as Copitas, Calderón, Chinchilla, Quispe, and Zúñiga, was set up and Farjado resigned. The sole function of this junta was to supervise an election of a new over-all commander. Then the voting took place. It is not clear who could vote and who could not, but it resembled a sincere show of grass-roots democracy. Village mayors and Indian *caciques* were there for the election. The voting was secret. The honest, but uninterested, Farjado was re-elected, and Chinchilla, the favorite of the Indians, became second in command. The members who had engineered the coup against Lira remained unpunished.

But peace was not yet established among the factions. Again in the early part of 1818, another crisis arose. Under the influence of alcohol, Marquina and Moreno accused each other of planning the death of Lira. Later they decided to desert to the enemy, but the news leaked out. Marquina killed Moreno. Then he defended himself against arrest, with the help of his unit. Finally, the Indians, who had not yet forgotten their beloved Lira, captured Marquina, and "shot him, cut off his head, and put it on a post." Farjado, who had let those who had killed Lira go unpunished, then wished to retire. In a grandiose manifestation the Indians and other soldiers elected Chinchilla as their commander. From then on more unity was achieved and Chinchilla distinguished himself as an active fighter against the king's army. The Ayopaya guerrilla republic remained united until the end of the war.[43]

What are the deductions or conclusions that one can make from this account of the intimate life of the most successful guerrilla unit of the War of Independence in Upper Peru? The existence of the partisan republic was due to the war, but was enmity and hatred of the Spaniards the incentive for fighting? The point is unquestionably debatable. The patriotic sentiments of the Bolivian historians do not permit them even to consider any other cause.[44] To them the guerrilla is a heroic being. One distinguished Bolivian historian has severely criticized another for not pointing out that the qualities of the Upper Peruvian guerrilla leaders were superior to those of the gaucho guerrillas of the United Provinces.[45] But would not the spirit of adventure be a rather potent factor for the existence of those factions? Clear-cut points of grievance against the Spanish domination, such as the generation of 1809 published and used as the platform for their rebellion, were not considered by the guerrillas.[46] They spoke against the crown in vague terms, such as freeing themselves from the Spanish yoke. Indeed isolated cases of sincere anti-Spanish hatred and complete dedication to the cause of freedom are known, such as the guerrilla soldier, Pedro Loaysa, of the Ayopaya unit, who refused to surrender to the Spaniards and threw himself over a precipice rather than fall into the hands of the hated enemy. But these are exceptions. Desertion was very common. Even the great fighter Lira was many times in contact with the Spaniards,[47] although the accusation which was used as an excuse to kill him was absolutely false. There was constant intercourse between the enemies. Soldiers and officers passed over from one side to the other, whenever the other side offered better conditions, or when their positions in their unit had become threatened because they had committed some misdemeanor. Each side accepted the enemy's deserters with great pleasure. The War of Independence offered a wonderful opportunity for adventure, a free and loose life, and living outside the law. Around a few honest people with clear-cut convictions, such as Chinchilla and Padilla, a huge group of adventure-loving people gathered. To them it did not matter for what they fought, but only that they were able to fight.

In order to put up a successful fight, manpower was needed. The great Indian masses offered a large reservoir of able fighting men. The Indians constituted one of the most complex aspects of the War of Independence in Upper Peru. They were the *materia prima* for both sides, and both of the contending parties of the war siphoned off this source of supply as extensively as possible. The Indian, far more than the mestizo, was very ignorant of the issues and reasons for the war,[48] and therefore became an extremely dangerous element, because he shifted allegiance at the slightest provocation. In some instances when he deserted to the opposition, he took with him the heads of some soldiers or officers to gain acceptance with the other side.[49] The Indian was needed and feared,[50] but he was nothing more than reservoir material. The natives knew little of the issues involved; they cared only that their services were needed. It is hardly possible to say that the great bulk of Indians were in favor of the Spaniards or were sympathetic to the Patriots. They fought for whichever side was more convenient. The partisan leaders had an advantage over the Loyalist officials because most of them had Indian blood and the ability to make themselves more acceptable to the Indians. Also, the guerrillas operated mostly in the countryside which had a heavier Indian concentration. It was natural that the Indians fought for whoever was dominant in their district. They constituted a great power in the Ayopaya republic, and when Lira was assassinated they were responsible for raising their favorite, Chinchilla, to the command.

There were, however, some Indians and Indian *caciques* who were staunchly loyal to either the Patriots or the Spaniards.[51] It often happened that the Spaniards treated the natives much better than the American whites did. The *criollos* and the mestizos felt a certain disdain for the Indians. During the great Indian rebellions of the late eighteenth century in Upper Peru, it was the *criollos* and mestizos who frantically mobilized resistance against the Indian threat.[52] In Upper Peru's capital, Chuquisaca, the *criollos* more than anyone else were responsible for the public hangings of some captured rebels in the city's parks and main square.[53] Several Indian *caciques* might have still remembered those days, and probably were fearful that the *criollos* would win the War of Independence. Of the two evils, the Spaniards represented the lesser. To *cacique* Manuel Cáceres the ideal solution was the elimination of both contingents. In the midst of the war he and his Indians revolted, with the aim of re-establishing the Inca empire.[54] He shrewdly offered support to both the Patriots and the Loyalists, with the idea of waiting for the opportune moment to do away with both of them. He failed completely. Of interest are the various proclamations in Quechua by the Spanish and Argentine authorities, trying to persuade the Indians to join their side, promising them in vague terms many privileges that they never intended to give. Both sides called the natives "brothers" and offered to "consider them as equals."[55] The Indians were a huge pool of manpower which could not be ignored. They represented an amorphous mass to be used freely by the Loyalists and the Patriots.[56] Neither the generation of 1809 nor the guerrilla leaders ever thought of emancipating them.[57]

The guerrilla units represented a more democratic front solely because they were of a wider cross section of society. None of the Patriots fought for an independent Upper Peru, but only for freedom from the Spaniards, for personal ambition, adventure, and loot. Surely not all of them were stimulated by simple material reasons, but those who fought for an ideal did so because they disliked the "tyranny of the Spanish government" and the "Spanish cupidity."[58] Beyond these incidental and vague expressions of protest against the crown, nothing of a more definite nature, such as a declaration of grievances, is ever known to have been formulated by any guerrilla.

There is one single word which is mentioned over and over. They fought for the *Patria*, the fatherland. When guerrilla Padilla sent his record of experiences to his superiors in the United Provinces, he called it a résumé of his services "in defense of the sacred rights of the *Patria*." Drummer Vargas in his diary uses the word *Patria* innumerable times. The partisans called their units "armies of the *Patria*." Those who fought against the Spaniards are known today as *patriotas*, to distinguish them from the Loyalists, known in the annals of history as *Realistas*, or Royalists. The war was between *Patriotas* and *Realistas*.[59] And *Patriotas* means those who fought for the *Patria*.

What was the *Patria?* Once a country with its definite boundaries exists, then it is that country. But such was not the case at that time. There had been only administrative units within the Spanish colonial empire. Upper Peru was part of the Audiencia of Charcas.[60] The audiencia, at the time of the beginning of the war in 1809, had been part of the Viceroyalty of Río de la Plata. When Buenos Aires, in all practicality, broke loose from the empire in 1810, the Loyalist authorities in Upper Peru annexed the Audiencia of Charcas to the Viceroyalty of Lima. What was the *Patria* then: the Audiencia of Charcas, the Viceroyalty of Río de la Plata or Lima? Or was the *Patria* each little guerrilla republic? No definite answer can be given. The partisan leaders never did define what they considered the fatherland. Drummer Vargas tells us that the "*Patria* is the soil on which we step and on which we live; *Patria* is the real cause which we must defend at all costs; for the *Patria* we must sacrifice our interests and our lives."[61]

Vargas probably expressed very well what the average guerrilla believed the *Patria* to be. It did not mean any defined jurisdiction, but the longing for freedom was predominant in their minds and it meant freedom for their soil; as the great *montonero*, Padilla, expressed it, "We love our soil with all our hearts."[62] The concept of freedom was ambiguously amalgamated with the notion of the *Patria*. Any more definite elaboration of this fusion was not available. The Bolivian historian, Humberto Guzmán, has summarized this amalgamation very well when he wrote that "the attachment to the soil inspired the origin and meaning of *Patria*."[63] Upper Peru was then still occupied by the Loyalists, but the United Provinces were free, and from those free provinces aid came and more might come. Therefore the guerrilla units looked to them for guidance, and attached their divisions to the command of the forces in the United Provinces. The authorities of the free territory never once doubted that Upper Peru was part of their jurisdiction. They called them the "internal provinces"[64] which still were occupied by the enemy. If the term *Patria* at the time of the high point of the guerrilla operations had any jurisdictional connotation, one could make a better case for the Viceroyalty of Río de la Plata.[65]

The diary of Vargas portrays one evident factor, the strict allegiance of the commander of the unit to the United Provinces.[66] When Captain Moreno sacked Paria, the commander's first worry was how to explain this insubordination in his unit to his superiors in Argentina. Again, when Commander Lira was killed the newly appointed commander, Farjado, was greatly worried about "what the principal chiefs in Buenos Aires would say and how they would excuse such an atrocious act" committed in the Ayopaya division. Any thought of acting independently of the United Provinces was inconceivable. As the word *Patria* was used repeatedly, so the references to the superiors in Buenos Aires and Salta are abundant. This alone is a potent proof that there was no idea of pursuing the fight for the purpose of creating an independent Upper Peru.

The Ayopaya partisan republic is not the only case that illustrates this important point. When the various auxiliary armies from the United Provinces invaded Upper Peru, the guerrilla units always tried to gear their actions to the movements of the invading army. As a matter of fact, the commanding general of the auxiliary army automatically became the over-all commander of the Patriot forces in Charcas.[67] Of the few available records of the guerrilla leaders,[68] all show that these partisan commanders expected their orders from, and reported their movements, if possible, to the general of the liberating army. When Rondeau's army was defeated

in 1815, upon his arrival in Jujuy he received from practically all
of the guerrillas reports of how they intended to maintain the War
of Independence in Charcas.[69] Even Muñecas, who operated along
the shores of Lake Titicaca, within view of Lower Peru, held himself responsible to the United Provinces. Drummer Vargas tells
us about an Indian who had gone to Salta to receive instructions
or orders to deliver to Lira. It is known that Warnes used as his
flag the blue and white colors of the United Provinces, and supposedly Arenales and Warnes always played the national anthem
of the free provinces.[70] It is patent that Upper Peru was actually,
in the minds of the guerrillas at least, a part of the United Provinces.
That this sentiment of unity was later destroyed was clearly the
fault of the free United Provinces. The failure of the auxiliary
armies, their cruel behavior, and finally, their abandonment of the
internal provinces that constituted Upper Peru stimulated the
desire for an independent Charcas.[71]

Much is made of a letter written in 1815 by the partisan Padilla
to the Argentine general Rondeau, in which the guerrilla leader
chastises the general in rough words about the Argentine failure
and his unbecoming behavior in Upper Peru.[72] This letter is often
considered the beginning of a strong feeling for an independent
Charcas.[73] If one wishes to determine the exact date at which, for
the first time, a vague expression for an autonomous Upper Peru
is available in a document, this letter no doubt could serve the
purpose. But one single letter, written probably under emotional
strain by a single guerrilla, although indeed a very important one,
is not very conclusive. Vargas' diary points out that obedience to
the United Provinces was still strong in 1821.

In that year Chinchilla was still the commander of the Ayopaya
partisan republic. On February 3, 1821, Miguel Lanza, without any
previous notice, showed up in the guerrilla republic.[74] Lanza probably had been the founder of this guerrilla faction. After the
disastrous defeat of the third auxiliary army from Argentina in
1815, he retreated with the army into the United Provinces. From
1815 to 1821 Ayopaya managed its own affairs and continued the
partisan warfare without further thought of Lanza. Then in 1821
he appeared, appointed by the superior in Argentina as the new
commander of the interior. Chinchilla accepted this arrangement.
But Lanza immediately accused the ex-commander of having cooperated with the enemy, just as Lira had been accused in 1817.

Without any trial, Chinchilla was put before a firing squad,[75] and in this way Lanza killed a close friend who in 1811 had helped him escape from a Spanish jail.[76]

What justification did Lanza have to do what he did? Chinchilla had been his early companion, he had been elected commander of the whole unit by the soldiers and Indians of the partisan republic. He had maintained the *republiqueta* in those critical years when all other important partisan *republiquetas* were unable to withstand the Spanish offensive of 1816. Chinchilla had the faithful support of the Indians, who loved him. When the Indian leader, Quispe, who fought under the banner of Chinchilla, requested an explanation from Lanza for his behavior, Lanza responded: "I come to investigate all the acts of Commander Chinchilla by order of the chief commander in Buenos Aires, and to punish him if he deserves it, or to praise him if not." When the author Vargas, who came to like Lanza's efficiency and enthusiasm, but hated injustice, later asked Lanza many times why he had killed Chinchilla, the commander angrily evaded the question or stated he had strict orders from the superior in Salta to kill Chinchilla.[77] Lanza thought that dissatisfied officers under Chinchilla had communicated wrong impressions to Salta. After Chinchilla's death Lanza streamlined and reorganized the guerrilla unit.[78] He fought bravely until the end of the war.

It is certain that Lanza did not kill Chinchilla simply because of personal ambition, but rather because he had instructions from superiors in the United Provinces. Argentina was still the source of authority and the guerrillas did not dispute this right. The idea of an autonomous Upper Peru that Padilla, in a moment of disgust, had hinted at, had not yet caught on. The guerrillas still fought for the ambiguous *Patria,* for freedom, for adventure, and for their own petty ambitions.

It was petty ambitions that were responsible for the deaths of Commanders Lira and Chinchilla. Farjado had enough sense to retire at the right time. The prime purpose of the factions was to fight the enemy, the Spanish forces, but often this became a secondary aim. There were always squabbles among the members of a faction. Perhaps the most significant facet of the history of Ayopaya is that this guerrilla republic shows an amazing similarity to the later history of Bolivia. The history of this *republiqueta* represents a microscopic prelude to the history of Bolivia. The internal warfare and miniature revolutions of this guerrilla unit presaged the political pattern of the country, which became "a hurricane of changes and vicissitudes."[79]

Was this all not begot in a period before autonomy? The guerrillas were an integral part of Bolivian history and an important link to independence, but they were not the creators of autonomous Bolivia. The independence of Upper Peru was due, among other factors, to two antagonistic but important causes: resentment against Argentina because of her failure to liberate the interior provinces from Spanish rule, and the later intrigues of some Loyalists who, when seeing their cause lost, came out for the second-best alternative, the independence of Upper Peru, which then would continue to serve as the base for their enterprises, free from any outside interference.

*Chapter 3*

# THE ARMIES OF DOOM

*I*N THE CREATION OF THE REPUBLIC of Bolivia in 1825 the guerrillas represented a small factor because of their lack of a precise goal, because the majority had gone down to defeat, and because the remaining number were ignored and outsmarted by more politically subtle elements. But the guerrilla warfare had not been the sole militancy against the Royalists. The war was fought by two kinds of forces: "The everlasting battle of *montoneros . . .* and a series of strategic campaigns between armies of faraway origins."[1] This second struggle was the clash of the Spanish and Patriot armies. The Spanish legions were directed from the Viceroyalty of Lima, and the rebels came up from the Plata region with the purpose of liberating the upper provinces, which they considered an integral part of the Viceroyalty of Buenos Aires. Once freed the internal provinces could be used as a springboard to invade the Viceroyalty of Lima. The contingents sent from Argentina were known as the auxiliary armies.

By 1810 the battle lines were drawn. When the war started in Upper Peru in 1809 that region, organized as the Audiencia of Charcas, belonged to the Viceroyalty of Río de la Plata. When in 1810 Buenos Aires, for all practical purposes, severed her relations with the Spanish empire, the faithful Royalist officials in Upper Peru, who had successfully suppressed the revolts in 1809, delivered the Audiencia of Charcas to the Viceroyalty of Lima.[2] The authorities in Buenos Aires never recognized this switch, and from their point of view the upper provinces constituted an integral part of the new order within the Viceroyalty of Buenos Aires.

The upper provinces were occupied by the enemy; to liberate them was the immediate purpose of the auxiliary armies. Buenos Aires wished to consolidate her independence and a Royal Upper Peru was a threat to this fulfillment. From a juridical point of view Upper Peru was in the state of flux.[3] The Patriots looked to Buenos Aires for help and considered themselves part of the Viceroyalty of Buenos Aires, as had been the case before the war. The Loyalists approved the secession from Buenos Aires because of the spirit of revolt which was then prevalent in the Viceroyalty of Río de la Plata, and they looked to Lima for protection and guidance. In their view Charcas had reverted to Lima, to which it had belonged before the creation of the Viceroyalty of Río de la Plata. If the Patriots should win the war, the integration of the upper provinces within the jurisdiction of Buenos Aires would be expected.[4] The spirit of isolation and the wish to separate which were prevalent in Paraguay and the Banda Oriental were at first absent in the upper provinces.

The units or armies which marched into Upper Peru from Buenos Aires with the specific purpose of freeing those provinces achieved the opposite result. Their military failure and undignified behavior created resentment which became the basis of the desire for separation from Buenos Aires. The brilliant and patently nationalistic Argentine writer, Bautista Alberdi, has frankly admitted, in speaking of his nation's armies, that they "soon exasperated the people because of their violence, and those lands turned against the Patriots with more intensity than against the Spaniards."[5] Alberdi was correct. A well-led Argentine army, with reasonable military success, good coordination with the guerrillas, proper behavior, and a polished propaganda apparatus could have liberated the Upper Provinces, and the problem of separation would have never become acute.

The first auxiliary army to enter the upper provinces was under the command of a lawyer by the name of Juan José Castelli, who in his youth had been a student at the famous University of San Francisco Xavier in Chuquisaca. His force entered Upper Peru in October, 1810. Before crossing the border of the internal provinces Castelli's army, on instruction from Buenos Aires, had already committed a serious mistake. Ex-Viceroy Liniers and some of his associates were put before a firing squad by the auxiliary army, an action which was not well received in Charcas. Liniers was a great hero in the minds and hearts of the people of Charcas. The English invasions in 1806 had produced a tremendous shock and fear throughout the whole Audiencia of Charcas.[6] Everybody was solemnly united against those "hateful islanders," as Archbishop Benito María Moxó had classified them. Everyone wished the defeat of this "gang of schismatics and heretics," and in his pastoral letters Moxó infused still more fear, suspicion, and hatred for the English.[7] When the English troops of General Beresford were defeated everyone felt relieved. It was Liniers who had saved them from those soldiers who the provincial people of Charcas, isolated in their mountains and jungles, thought would want to impose on them the hateful "revolutionary doctrine of Calvin."[8] Liniers had become the idol of all the people of Charcas, and now he had been condemned to death for treason. Without question the high esteem with which Upper Peru regarded Liniers had not completely vanished. And Castelli, who had carried out the death sentence, was on his way to Charcas to liberate them. Indeed a very bad start.

On November 25, 1810, after an initial defeat and then a surprising victory, the Argentine army entered Potosí, the most important town of Upper Peru.[9] After the victory of Suipacha the pro-Patriot element inside Potosí had taken over the town and Castelli's victorious army entered in the midst of cheering partisans. Perhaps the first Argentine mistake was forgotten, and with tact and intelligence Castelli could have easily improved his favorable position. Chuquisaca, the capital of the audiencia, had only days before pronounced itself for Buenos Aires. The guerrillas had liberated Cochabamba, and La Paz too came out in favor of Buenos Aires. The Spanish army retreated to the outskirts of La Paz. It looked as if the upper provinces were free and had accepted the new order of the Viceroyalty of Río de la Plata. But Castelli proved to be the wrong man, for he "had the soul of a tyrant."[10]

Castelli committed another blunder, bloodier than his first one. He arrested the president of the Audiencia of Charcas, Vicente Nieto, and condemned him to death together with the venerable intendant of Potosí, Francisco Paula Sanz, and the Royalist general, José de Córdova. Although all three were Royalists, none of them was hated by the people, and the death sentence was unnecessarily severe. Paula Sanz was the most beloved figure in Charcas. He had governed Potosí for twenty-two years, and his behavior during his many years in office had been irreproachable. President Nieto's ten months of service in Upper Peru had not been enlightened and his rule was quite arbitrary, but he had not caused any terror.[11] From Chuquisaca Archbishop Moxó wrote Castelli, asking him why these three men had been sentenced to death, and requesting their liberty in the name of the whole city.[12] Castelli ignored every request. On Saturday, September 15, 1810, at twenty minutes to ten in the morning, in the main square of Potosí in full view of the terrified inhabitants of the *Villa Imperial*, the three prisoners were executed. The only crime the condemned men had committed was that of having remained loyal to the Royalist cause and of not having recognized the governing junta of Buenos Aires. Castelli had accused them of deliberately dismembering the Viceroyalty of Río de la Plata when Nieto and Sanz had united Charcas with Lima. For this he convicted them, with the ultimate penalty. No court judged them, and the sentence was Castelli's word alone. He reported to Buenos Aires that the execution was impressive because of "its military appearance, punctuality, and obedience."[13]

In addition, the auxiliary army behaved more as a cruel victor than as a liberating ally. At night the soldiers roamed freely in Potosí's dark and narrow streets, showing no respect for the town's citizens. One night Francisco Lacoa was killed by some soldiers who took a fancy to his elegant cloak and wished to own it. A Mrs. Terán was robbed of everything she possessed when some Argentineans came to search her house. A certain Faustino Velarde was attacked in the middle of the street, and once dead he was robbed of everything, disrobed, and his naked corpse left in the street. Another citizen was put to death in cold blood with a saber, for no reason at all. The soldiers of the auxiliary unit showed little respect for the women of Potosí, and whoever came to their defense was shot down mercilessly. Potosí came to fear and hate the Argentineans and when, on December 22, 1810, Castelli and his army left the town for Chuquisaca, the people of the City of Silver felt deep relief because a dreadful nightmare had come to an end.[14] The seeds of everlasting hatred for the Argentineans had been sown.

Castelli's and his army's behavior in Chuquisaca was also irresponsible. Although rumors of his preposterous conduct in Potosí had reached the capital, and the assassination of Nieto, Sanz, and Córdova was looked upon with abhorrence, still the auxiliary army was received splendidly. Yet Castelli lost not a moment in subjecting the town to his arbitrary rule. He immediately interfered in the town's government by naming a *cabildo* of his own choice. He decided who would occupy all important positions. On January 5, 1811, Castelli issued a stern proclamation in which he restricted all political and judicial guarantees. Everyone who opposed the auxiliary army would be declared a traitor and liable to court-martial. No one could speak against the government of Buenos Aires; to do so would be a "crime of the first magnitude."[15] Anyone who denounced those who voiced an opinion against the government and the Argentine army would be rewarded. Because of this many distinguished citizens were arrested and shipped to Argentina. Not satisfied with this, on February 8, the Argentine commander issued an even sterner proclamation in which he promised that anyone who opposed the government in word or action would be militarily convicted of the highest crime and executed. The Argentine nightmare had gone from Potosí to Chuquisaca. Castelli also announced some radical political and social reforms which were advanced for that time. Castelli wanted honestly to improve the lot of the Indians and free them from all bondage.[16]

To the relief of the capital Castelli and his army left Chuquisaca in March to push the advance north to the border of the Viceroyalty of Lima. He took Oruro and La Paz. In the latter city he and his secretary, Bernardo Monteagudo, outraged the deep religious feelings of the inhabitants by ignoring the observance of Holy Week.[17] Afterwards Castelli signed a forty-day armistice with the Royalist general, José Manuel de Goyeneche, stopping the lines of battle more or less along the border separating the two viceroyalties. But Castelli was not true to his word and slowly, in defiance of the armistice, pushed the line farther north. Goyeneche answered with a surprise attack and completely routed the auxiliary army at Huaqui (or Guaqui) on June 20, 1811. Castelli and his defeated army fled in panic toward Oruro. They had to bypass Oruro because its inhabitants were ready to finish off the hated auxiliaries, an indication that Castelli had repeated his performance of Potosí and Chuquisaca in that mining town. Goyeneche was taken by surprise at the easy victory. Being a careful soldier, he avoided haste and did not pursue the routed enemy. He cared for the wounded of both sides and treated the many prisoners decently.[18]

The auxiliary army dispersed in complete disorder toward Cochabamba, Chuquisaca, and Potosí. In most instances the retreating units plundered towns and villages as they passed. La Paz had some agonizing moments when part of the defeated army came through there. There was absolutely no contact among the retreating units, but most of them took the road toward Potosí, the strongest fortress of Charcas. Castelli went to Chuquisaca. Again the Imperial City was the host of the Argentine army, which this time used the town to reorganize its decimated ranks. The residents of Potosí were by then violently opposed to the Argentineans; memories of the previous year were still vivid, and while the army had been north an ugly incident had occurred between the people of Potosí and the little Argentine garrison left behind.

On February 4, 1811, the people of Potosí were celebrating the Feast of the Purification of Mary, as was the custom. Among the high points of the festival was an afternoon bullfight. The Argentine officers were seated in a balcony of honor, and the auxiliary soldiers were dispersed among the people, some taking part in the bullfight. At the moment when the main bull of the arena was passing underneath the balcony of honor an Argentine lieutenant jumped up, took out his sword, and tried to stick it into the bull from above. Because of a last second sharp movement of the animal he missed, and his sword hit the empty air. The officer lost his equilibrium and in a most ludicrous somersault fell from the balcony into the ring. General laughter rang through the arena. The lieutenant sprang up, picked up his saber, and swinging it around furiously, wounded some Indians who were taken by surprise. Several people who tried to restrain the officer were also struck by the weapon. A sudden and unanimous protest arose among the spectators, who spontaneously fell upon the auxiliaries. Armed with "sticks, rocks, and knives"[19] they pursued the panic-stricken soldiers and officers, who ran in haste to their quarters to fetch their arms. Tempers ran high. The auxiliary commander ordered his unit to open fire if the people should attack the barracks. The *potosinos* meanwhile were advancing in fury toward the soldiers' quarters. Everything was set for a terrific massacre. Only a last minute intervention by a citizen named José Guzmán led both sides to lay down their arms. Bloodshed had been averted, but tempers were higher than ever and any slight provocation on the part of the auxiliaries would have produced a second incident.[20]

And then in June and July of 1811, the rest of the auxiliary army, completely defeated and demoralized, returned to Potosí. The situation was explosive, and everybody felt that a second

February fourth was quite possible. On Monday, August 5, 1811, a drunken Negro auxiliary soldier interrupted a peaceful conversation of some citizens in one of the plazas. When they ignored him he took his knife and furiously attacked them. A fight ensued. The news spread quickly, and the drunken soldier received help from some of his comrades. The other side was reinforced by more and more *potosinos*. The auxiliary soldier was killed. The Argentineans ran to their quarters for their weapons. Armed, they advanced upon the people and opened fire, but the civilians increased their ranks to such a number that the auxiliaries again started to retreat. The people brought out all kinds of weapons and the casualties of the auxiliaries were heavy. From all sides the townspeople harassed them. Many fell wounded but the fury of the *potosinos* had reached unreasonable heights. They fell upon the wounded soldiers, beating them to death. The frenzy of the people knew no bounds, and they now directed their attack against those civilians who had shown favor to the auxiliaries. The Argentineans were no longer fighting in a unit, but each was fighting to save his own life.

The battle of Huaqui had been mild compared with this massacre. A priest by the name of Arechabala wanted to intervene and stop the slaughter, but was shot to death. Through the whole night the battle continued. Throughout her history Potosí had seen many bloody scenes, but she had never witnessed another such as this. Even with the coming of morning the struggle did not abate. Many citizens were looking frantically for hidden auxiliaries, while other soldiers fought valiantly to keep the masses away from them. To fall into their hands meant sure death. The people of Potosí were determined to be finished with the auxiliary army. By midday the few *potosinos* who had remained calm hit upon a last resort to terminate the massacre. They took the images of the Virgin of the Rosary and of Vera Cruz from the churches of Santo Domingo and San Francisco and organized a procession through the streets where the heaviest fighting continued. It had a smashing effect. The fight subsided, and an ominous quietness settled over the Imperial City. One hundred and forty-five soldiers had been killed, but only nine civilians had lost their lives.[21] The resentment against the Argentine army's abuses, which had accumulated for nearly a year, had caused an explosion much worse than the people had expected.

In the absence of Castelli the auxiliary commander was Juan Martín de Pueyrredón, who prior to Castelli's defeat had been named president of the audiencia. Pueyrredón acted with caution and seemingly good will, even though the *potosinos* had massacred his unit. He undertook to reconcile the opposing explosive tempers. On the next day he ordered his army to dress in gala uniforms and march to the main square. At the same time he invited all the citizens to come to the plaza. Then the auxiliary commander urged both soldiers and townspeople to make peace, forget the past, and unite against the common enemy. A real comedy took place; whereas only a day before a furious battled raged in the Imperial City's narrow streets, an air of festivity now reigned. Auxiliaries and *potosinos* fell into each other's arms, embraced each other, and swore to forgive all past unpleasantness. From that time on they would be friends and allies. More than a hundred and fifty men had perished, apparently for nothing. But such a theatrical scene was nothing more than an expression of "hypocrisy."[22] Pueyrredón had without question done what he honestly believed was necessary to restore peace. But simply calling everyone to the plaza and then asking that each one should embrace a rival was no real remedy for the deep-seated antagonism caused by the auxiliary army. An investigation was started to determine the cause of the tragedy of August 5.[23] The Argentineans who conducted the inquiry came to the conclusion that the city's priests were responsible for what Pueyrredón called the "revolution of August 5 and 6."[24] They were accused of inciting the masses to a counterrevolution in favor of Lima. Four priests were arrested and ordered away from Potosí. It is hardly possible that Pueyrredón's conclusion as to the cause of the tragedy was even close to the truth.[25]

In the meanwhile the Peruvian army, under the capable Goyeneche, was advancing toward the south. In a battle at Amiraya it completely defeated the auxiliary contingent which had been reorganized in Cochabamba. Pueyrredón, afraid that this news would encourage the *potosinos* to further acts, boldly announced that Díaz Vélez, the auxiliary commander in the Cochabamba district, had won a splendid victory. The church bells announced the hoax to the Imperial City. But the dishonesty was soon discovered when a Franciscan friar received from a friend, an officer in the Goyeneche army, a detailed account of the battle of Amiraya. The letter further told of the great magnanimity with which Goyeneche had treated the people of Cochabamba. The news spread like a flash, and tempers again ran high against the auxiliaries. Soon after this Díaz Vélez entered Potosí with his defeated unit, proving that the friar's letter had been only too true. It was then advisable for the Argentine army to evacuate Potosí.

Díaz Vélez, rightly fearing that his defeated unit would only stir up more hostile feelings, and realizing the impossibility of defending Potosí with a disorganized army and an unfriendly town, decided to leave the Imperial City and retreat to Argentina. Pueyrredón and some selected crack units were to remain in town as long as possible. He wanted nothing more than to get hold of the plentiful funds deposited in the famous Casa de Moneda, the San Carlos Bank, and other fiscal agencies.[26] He requested from the *potosinos* four hundred mules to carry the spoils.[27] A unanimous protest arose among the irate citizens. Pueyrredón tried to calm tempers by saying that he had no intention of carrying the funds to Argentina, but he wished to take them to the Upper Peruvian village of Tupiza so that those valuables would not fall into the enemy's hands. But the commander had overreached himself. The town's hostility against his small unit became more acute and the position of the remaining auxiliary contingent was exceedingly precarious. Pueyrredón decided to leave town during the dark of the night without telling anyone. He gave the impression that he was postponing his departure. It was planned that the night of August 25 was the propitious time to make the escape. Everything was set, when at seven-thirty of that night his best and most trusted unit mutinied. The commander decided that he and the remaining forty-five auxiliaries must take to the road immediately. If in the morning the *potosinos* realized that part of his troops had deserted, the people would take advantage of his desperate position and liquidate him and his faithful soldiers. It was midnight when the commander and the rest of the auxiliaries entered the Casa de Moneda to load the mules with silver. From twelve until four o'clock they loaded the animals with the silver bars, working in absolute silence. Then at four-thirty, very carefully, they moved quietly through the deserted streets with the hope of reaching the open road. Each one was tense, his nerves on edge; it was just like the escape of a thief after a successful robbery. At dawn they had reached the open space and had flanked the majestic silver mountain.[28]

When the people awoke they realized that they had been duped. The auxiliaries had left and had taken with them the stored riches of their Imperial City. The alarm was sounded, church bells were rung, the people organized hastily, looking frantically for weapons. Then, like a furious avalanche, they rushed out of town in hot pursuit of the auxiliaries. The people's army reached the Argentine unit and a wild skirmish ensued. Pueyrredón estimated that two thousand townspeople attacked him, but they were poorly armed and had no guidance or organization. The Argentine commander had placed his unit in a strategic position and this, plus his far superior weapons, forced the people to retreat toward the Cerro Rico. Pueyrredón again started his march and again the *potosinos* pursued him. The previous scene was repeated, with identical results. This kind of mobile skirmish continued throughout the whole day until nightfall drove the pursuers back to Potosí. While many of the people had been trying to catch the auxiliaries, the Royalist, or pro-Lima, faction had quietly taken over Potosí.[29]

In the meanwhile the rest of what once constituted the proud first auxiliary army continued its retreat toward Argentina. Yet even though it had beaten off its pursuers, the retreating contingents had no easy road. The news had spread and the unit was harassed from all sides in its march through the countryside. Pueyrredón chose secondary roads to escape assaults.[30] He hoped to reach Tarija, the gateway to the lower provinces, as soon as possible. In June, 1810, the peaceful and delightful town of Tarija had come out with great enthusiasm in favor of the Buenos Aires junta.[31] When the auxiliary army had come up into the upper provinces six hundred *tarijeños* joined the ranks of the Argentine contingent and fought valiantly in the victory of Suipacha, that opened the gates of Potosí and Chuquisaca to Castelli. After this victory three hundred of the Tarija volunteers followed Castelli to Potosí and marched north with him. They asked no pay for their services. But the Argentine commander placed them in unimportant and inferior positions. The soldiers of Tarija became indignant at such a discriminatory policy, and after protesting they returned to their native town.[32] The same resentment that grew in Potosí sprang up in Tarija once the volunteers had returned. Tarija did not want anything more to do with the auxiliary army.

When Díaz Vélez abandoned Potosí earlier, he, too, took the

road to Tarija and was obliged to take the city by storm. A battle for Tarija developed and an estimated four hundred people perished.[33] Obviously, Pueyrredón could not expect to find a friendly reception there. The people of Tarija had heard that the Argentine commander was carrying the silver of the Casa de Moneda with him and they were determined to wrest it from him. Because of a last minute truce between Tarija and Pueyrredón, about which little is known,[34] this was not done and Pueyrredón continued on his way to the lower provinces. So ended the inglorious history of the first auxiliary army.

In Potosí enthusiastic preparations were made to receive General Goyeneche, the Royalist victor over the first auxiliary army. Triumphal arches were erected, the city was cleaned, and the balconies were adorned with rich tapestries and palms. It was a gala day, September 20, 1811, when finally the Spanish general and his army entered the Imperial City. People showered him with lovely flowers and exotic perfumes. Then the patricians of the town offered a sumptuous reception, just as they had done when Castelli had come for the first time. The main contingent of the army under the command of General Pío Tristán continued its advance south in hope of reaching, as soon as possible, the border separating the lower from the upper provinces. Goyeneche had to remain in Upper Peru because of a serious guerrilla threat at the rear of his army which was becoming acute and dangerous, especially in and around Cochabamba.[35] The montoneros were the only ones who maintained the fight against the pro-Lima army. Fighting in the countryside and isolated from the auxiliary army, they had not been subjected to the abuses of the Argentineans.

Having freed Upper Peru from the invading army, General Tristán crossed the border and invaded the lower provinces of the Viceroyalty of Río de la Plata. The coin had been turned. The Royalist army overran Salta and Jujuy and was enthusiastically pushing forward to conquer Tucumán. But Tristán overextended his lines. He was never able to take Tucumán and victory suddenly turned to defeat. A brilliant Argentine general, the famous Manuel Belgrano, had been put in charge of the defense. Just as Castelli's victory in the north had been converted by Goyeneche into a complete defeat, so Belgrano routed the invading Royalist army in the glorious battle of Salta on February 20, 1813. The victory was complete. Tristán's disorganized bands took the road of defeat north. Goyeneche, surprised by this upset, decided to evacuate Potosí and march north.

Belgrano, in pursuit of the routed army, entered Upper Peru. This was the second time that the lower provinces invaded the upper provinces, and this force has passed into history as the second auxiliary army. On May 7, 1813, at three-thirty in the afternoon, Belgrano and his army were in full view of the famous silver hill of Cerro Rico at Potosí. Again the inhabitants of that city erected triumphal arches and hung from their balconies the same tapestries that had been used for Goyeneche's entrance. It seemed as if Potosí had become accustomed to the glorious entries of victorious armies, only to see them leave ingloriously. By then the town had systematized its welcome fairly well: up went the arches and out of the chests came the tapestries. Seemingly, nobody cared anymore whether it was friend or foe. Among the officers of Belgrano was a young captain by the name of José María Paz, whose excellent character, quick mind, and delightful disposition would bring him future fame. He was a keen observer and a first-class writer. In his splendid memoirs[36] he tells that he felt that the apparently enthusiastic reception of the *potosinos* was only a farce and a façade behind which the fear of the people was detectable.

Belgrano ruled quite differently from Castelli, and his disciplined army behaved correctly. Unfortunately the Argentine commander's military fortunes were no better than those of his predecessors. The Spanish command had passed to a capable new general by the name of Joaquín de la Pezuela, who quickly decided that the best way to stop Belgrano was to start a counteroffensive. With a refreshed army he marched toward Potosí, forcing Belgrano into the open. The Argentine general was not disturbed about this since he was eager to leave the city and start his march north. He requested all nearby guerrilla units to work in harmony with his strategy. But the auxiliary army was unaccustomed to rough mountain fighting, and Pezuela inflicted upon Belgrano a resounding defeat on the plains of Vilcapugio on October 1, 1813. The decimated army of Belgrano and his lieutenant, Díaz Vélez, who had participated previously in the defeats of Huaqui and Amiraya, took the road back to Potosí. Pezuela did not pursue the routed army, and because of this and the absence of hostility in the town, which was due to the auxiliary army's good behavior, Belgrano decided to hold Potosí and not retreat. The Spanish commander again forced Belgrano into the open and defeated him for a second time on the plains of Ayohuma on November 14. This was a far more severe defeat than Vilcapugio. Again the auxiliary army retreated to safety in Potosí, where the people received the disorganized army calmly. José María Paz, the chronicler of the happenings in Potosí,[37] was deeply impressed by the "urbanity" of the welcome, and he writes that he "liked very much the reception which was given us, because it was grave, sad, official, and sympathetic . . . nobody feared disturbances and hostility." Paz then rightly states that the *potosinos* had changed their attitude toward the Argentineans because of the second auxiliary army's correct behavior.[38] Belgrano's force had been decimated and Pezuela was pressing hard and beginning a flanking movement, so that the only solution for Belgrano was to evacuate Potosí and retreat south. The Argentine commander wisely distributed among the people of Potosí, especially the poor, the stores of his army which would have been too heavy to carry on a quick retreat.[39]

On November 18, 1813, the army was ready to leave the Imperial City. At two o'clock in the afternoon the troops were in formation in the plaza and the adjacent streets. One hour later Belgrano and the cavalry departed. The infantry was to follow. Naturally people had come to the main square and lined the streets to see the auxiliary army leave. But then something happened. Paz, who had remained behind with the infantry unit, says that they suddenly felt an air of mystery which he could not explain. The people in the streets and the plaza were ordered to leave and go home. Everyone wondered why. The spectators disobeyed and the Argentine soldiers were commanded to disperse them. But this was to no avail, and the onlookers ran from one street to another. The soldiers, the people, and most of the officers were baffled by this strange order. Then suddenly a new command was given, ordering that everyone living on the plaza and in the houses near the Casa de Moneda should immediately evacuate their lodgings and retire to at least twenty blocks away. They refused, after which they were told that should they not obey, their lives would be in danger. This too had no effect. Then finally it was decided to tell them the truth, to clear up the mystery: the Casa de Moneda was going to be blown up. Momentary consternation overtook the confused people and it was impossible for them to comprehend such a horrifying action. The crowd still refused to move. The great amount of dynamite was already in its place.

Díaz Vélez had remained behind with his infantry unit in order to light the fuse. Disregarding the stubbornness of the inhabitants, it was now decided to light the fuse anyway. This was done and the heavy gates were closed, but then the huge keys to lock the gates were missing. Frantically the Argentineans searched for the keys; someone had hidden them. Time was short; the fuse was burning and with every second the flame was coming closer to the explosives. There was no more time to lose. Without finding the key, the Argentineans started on their rush out of town in order to be out of danger when the huge and massive building would go up into the air. But the auxiliaries ran into barricades; the streets were blocked. At an earlier time Belgrano had wanted to hold Potosí and the army had closed the streets. Although the plan was abandoned, the barricades had never been removed. The auxiliaries were frantic. They rushed back to the plaza in search of an open street. It was a race against time. At any moment the Casa de Moneda would explode and bury the center of town and its inhabitants under the heavy blocks. Luck was with the army, though, and it found an exit, raced to the outskirts, and didn't stop until it had reached the silver hill.

Then they realized that nothing had happened. The explosion had not taken place. Most probably the people of Potosí, seeing that the gates had not been locked, rushed into the Casa and had put out the fuse. Whoever had hidden the key knew that the dynamiting would take place, and to avoid it had made the key disappear. A terrible catastrophe and probably the complete destruction of the main part of Potosí had been averted. A captain by the name of Juan Luna offered to take twenty-five soldiers and ride back to town and light the fuse again. It was a daring plan, but when he reached the outskirts of town he realized the impossibility of his raid. The furious *potosinos* would have torn him and his soldiers to pieces. The people of Potosí were raging against Belgrano, who had wanted to destroy their city. It is probable that they would have pursued the auxiliary army as they had done with Pueyrredón, but for their efforts to save the Casa de Moneda and to see to it that nobody tried to light the dynamite again. The captain and his unit turned around.

The man who had concealed the key was a trusted auxiliary

officer by the name of Anglada, who was close to Belgrano and whom the general had appointed commander of Potosí. This Anglada had fallen under the influence of a lady from Potosí with Royalist sympathies, who probably persuaded him to betray Belgrano. Once his task was accomplished Anglada deserted to the Royalist side. Although he was a traitor, this officer saved Potosí from a grave disaster.[40]

The idea of dynamiting the Casa de Moneda was a monstrous plan; it was a first-class blunder. Mitre, in his excellent biography of Belgrano, which undoubtedly is sympathetic to the general, admits that it was a "barbarous project whose fulfillment would have done more damage to the prestige of the revolution than to the enemy."[41] Mitre is right. But many Argentineans hated Potosí and had not forgotten the massacre of 1811. To them the blowing up of the Casa de Moneda would not only have deprived the enemy of this important source of money, but it would have destroyed Potosí and its inhabitants. When a distinguished Argentine army officer referred to the *potosinos* as those "idiotic and bloodthirsty people," he only expressed the true feeling of many of his compatriots.[42] Without question, however, Belgrano had been ill advised. The general had done much to heal the wounds left by Castelli's behavior and Pueyrredón's thoughtless actions. Of course, his military campaign had been a total failure, too, but the good conduct and stern discipline of the second auxiliary army had favorably impressed the people of Potosí and Upper Peru. At the last minute, by wanting to dynamite the most important source of wealth of the internal provinces and thereby endangering the lives of every inhabitant in Potosí, Belgrano had ripped wide open the wounds which he had so successfully healed.

The defeated army crossed into the lower provinces and the Royalist force invaded the Upper Provinces for a second time. In Upper Peru only the guerrilla units continued their fight with ever-increasing tempo. But slowly the situation of the Patriots improved, and with the coming of 1815 everything took a turn for the better. The insurrection against the Royalists had spread to Lower Peru, the very heart of the Viceroyalty of Lima. Guerrilla warfare in Upper Peru had intensified, and such *montoneros* as Warnes, Padilla, Arenales, Lanza, and many others were seriously threatening the hegemony of the Royalists. San Martín, as the new commander of the northern army of the United Provinces, had successfully checked Pezuela around Tucumán. The guerrilla threat in both Perus and San Martín's able operations forced Pezuela to retreat into the inner provinces. In the meantime the United Provinces had finally conquered Montevideo. To everyone a strike into Upper Peru seemed opportune. Only San Martín, with clear vision and shrewd military instinct, was aware that the road through Upper Peru to Lima was a futile one. He was already thinking of conquering Lower Peru via Chile.[43] He left his command with the hope of organizing an expeditionary army into Chile. But to less-enlightened officers the route through Upper Peru looked better than ever. General José Rondeau was chosen to command the third auxiliary army. He was a simple man, honest, unambitious, and not well qualified as a soldier.

Rondeau lost valuable time by staying near the border and showing no enterprise in starting the offensive north. The severe discipline which Belgrano and San Martín had imposed on the army of the north went to pieces under the affable Rondeau. He wished to be moderate and liked by everyone. His troops and officers called him a "good Joe" or "mama." Finally in April, 1815, the army started its advance, and on the seventeenth defeated the enemy in a place called Puesto del Marqués, located about thirteen miles south of the village of La Quiaca, which is today on the border between Bolivia and Argentina. The victorious troops, instead of pursuing the enemy, celebrated the victory by consuming a great quantity of liquor found in the enemy's camp. Captain José María Paz, who was again an eyewitness of this event, wrote that he "had never seen a more disgusting picture . . . nor more complete drunkenness."[44] Pezuela and his subordinate colonel, Pedro Antonio de Olañeta, who soon played a key role in the creation of Bolivia, decided to retreat far north, evacuating Potosí and Chuquisaca and concentrating their forces in the centrally located Oruro. The guerrillas Zarate and Pedro Betanzos, with their Indian units, occupied Potosí on April 28, where they committed some minor misdemeanors. Guerrilla Padilla occupied Chuquisaca. On May 1 the third auxiliary army entered Potosí and was given the usual reception accorded to any army. Colonel Martín Rodríguez and Captain José María Paz were sent to take over Chuquisaca.

Castelli had been a tyrant and the people had feared him. Belgrano had been a thorough general, and had won the inhabitants' admiration, which he lost when he applied the military

principle that the end justifies any means. General José Rondeau
was quite different from both. He was good-natured but of weak
character, and as a consequence his troops and officers committed
all kinds of abuses which irritated the people. In Potosí the army
organized a commission of recovery, whose job it was to locate
and confiscate the money and goods of the Royalists who had
escaped town. The commission distinguished itself by its gross
corruption. Captain Paz, who loved honesty and decency, recounts
that a fellow captain by the name of Ferreira told him that one
day when he, the friend, stepped into the room of the commission,
its president, Colonel Quintana, was counting the money.[45] Quintana looked up, and then with no inhibition, said to him, "Ferreira,
why don't you take some of these pesos?" Ferreira, astonished at
the proposal, filled both of his hands with pesos. The colonel then
said to Ferreira, "What are you going to do with this? Go ahead
and take more." The captain took out his handkerchief and filled
it with silver coins. Probably Quintana showed the same generosity
to all his friends. Obviously all the employees of the commission
had the first opportunity to loot. Captain Paz thinks that even the
peons shared heavily in the spoils. However, Rondeau showed some
tact and shrewdness when he ordered his troops to camp outside
Potosí on nearby farms.

In Chuquisaca the same dishonesty took place. Commander
Rodríguez also searched for money and valuable goods with the
hope of confiscating them, using as an excuse that they were owned
by Royalists. Captain Paz reports that soldiers and officers were
spending huge sums of money far beyond their salaries. Soldiers
whose pay was low, or at best moderate, suddenly appeared dressed
in rich attire. Officers discarded their sabers and had new ones
made of pure silver. Everybody took part in the plunder, and
lived luxuriously. Only the frantic efforts of three honest officers[46]
lessened to some extent the immense corruption. It is said by one
chronicler that Commander Rodríguez fostered his ambitions and
vanity by forcing the Intendancy of Chuquisaca to adopt the federal
system of the United Provinces. He then had himself proclaimed
Supreme Director of the province of Chuquisaca, giving a sumptuous festival at this inauguration.[47]

Rondeau was losing valuable time by remaining in Chuquisaca
and Potosí. Furthermore, the morale of his army was practically
going to pieces. The Royalist commander, Pezuela, took advantage

of the breathing spell by reorganizing his army and putting down the rebellions in Lower Peru, thereby cleaning up his own back yard and acquiring more troops. If General Rondeau had continued his advance immediately after his capture of Potosí and Chuquisaca, he might have accomplished what the other two expeditionary armies had failed to do, namely, to occupy the whole of Upper Peru and perhaps penetrate into Lower Peru. But he lost his chance. Finally, in September the Argentine commander decided to open an offensive with the hope of conquering Oruro. Captain Paz writes that the departure from Chuquisaca was scandalous. Everyone including the commander had attended farewell parties. The march out of town was a parade of drunk soldiers and officers. Paz, bewildered and disgusted, remarked to some of his sober friends that "it would be impossible to win." His presentiment was correct.[48]

Pezuela was a capable general and his army succeeded in blocking the advance of the auxiliary expedition. The offensive bogged down and the Patriots suffered a minor defeat at Venta Media. Consequently Rondeau gave up the idea of marching on Oruro and turned to advance toward Cochabamba. But Pezuela was at his best in rough mountain territory, and he raced ahead of Rondeau. The Royalist general then swung around in front of Rondeau before reaching Cochabamba, which meant that the Argentine army ran straight into the Royalists in its march on that city. Rondeau either had to fight or turn around and retreat over rough territory to Potosí or Chuquisaca. The Argentine general decided to fight.

On November 29, 1815, the armies opened battle on the plains of Sipe Sipe.[49] Rondeau was completely routed. It was the worst defeat the Patriots suffered during the whole war. The entire Argentine expedition was torn to pieces and retreated in complete confusion. Each soldier took his own road, to wherever he thought was best. The auxiliary army of General Rondeau vanished from the battlefield. The general behaved valiantly, and to the end showed courage and calmness. He walked with two or three officers, having no contact with his troops, from the battlefield to Chuquisaca. Rondeau covered two hundred and sixty miles in eighteen days and arrived at the capital alone. Then he realized that his army had nearly vanished. But in Chuquisaca the general was successful in gathering some soldiers who had taken the same road. With this fragmentary force he began his march back to the

United Provinces, bypassing Potosí and Tarija. No auxiliary army
had ever returned in such bad shape. Castelli and Belgrano had
been defeated, but had returned home carrying the riches of Potosí.
The Royalists by one shrewd stroke, thanks to the ability of General
Pezuela, had reconquered all of Upper Peru. However they showed
a wise reluctance to invade the United Provinces. Again only the
guerrillas remained to maintain the war. The continuous defeats
of the expeditionary forces caused the guerrillas to lose confidence
in them, and disrespect for the Argentineans became noticeable.

On his retreat Rondeau wrote to the guerrilla leader Padilla,
requesting him to continue the fighting and to harass the enemy
whenever possible, and promised that his army would return. The
Argentine commander finished his letter by asking Padilla to double
his efforts and to use all available means in fighting the enemy.[50]
Padilla was annoyed with the request and on December 21, 1815,
from Laguna, he answered Rondeau in an angry letter which constitutes a landmark in Bolivian history.[51] The letter was cruel and
frank; it showed with perfect clarity Padilla's annoyance which had
accumulated slowly over a period of time. The guerrilla leader
started his letter by saying, "You order me to attack the enemy,
from whose hand you have received a most shameful defeat."
Padilla then continued, saying that surely he would go on fighting
the enemy as he had done for more than five years. He reminded
Rondeau that all the people in Upper Peru had fought and suffered,
too, for many years, but that this was not their only misfortune,
since they had to witness the "infamy and mockery of the armies
of Buenos Aires."

Padilla continued by saying that these armies had not only
ignored the merits of the Upper Peruvian Patriots, but even worse,
they had ridiculed and insulted them. The guerrilla from Laguna
stated that "thousands of examples of horror could be cited which
had irritated the people," and which had been caused by the
expeditionaries. Then the fearless writer enumerated some of them.
From the very beginning rivalries had existed between the guerrilla
units and the auxiliary armies. Such *montoneros* as Centeno,
Cárdenas, and he, Padilla, at one time or other had been arrested
by the Argentineans. Padilla thought that the real reason for these
arrests was nothing more than the jealousy of the Argentine commanders and officers. The partisan leader continued his irate letter
by saying emphatically that "the government of Buenos Aires has

shown only a filthy distrust for our people which has hurt the honor of the inhabitants," and the consequence of this abominable behavior was that the Argentine occupation was as bad as or worse than the Spanish rule. The guerrilla called attention to the fact that whenever the expeditionary forces were able to occupy Upper Peruvian territory, it was because of the decisive help they had received from its inhabitants. But instead of being grateful, the expeditionaries had sacked their homes and cities.

The dean of the Charcas *montoneros* continued his answer with many more harsh lines. He reminded Rondeau especially that although the Argentineans were then running away, they were so bold as to request the guerrillas to come out and fight the enemy in order to protect "the cowardliness of your army." And Padilla assured the Argentine commander "that the enemy shall not have a moment of rest." The final lines were of a conciliatory mood in which the writer reminded his correspondent that the guerrillas and people of Charcas were honest and of a forgiving nature, and were very willing to forget past excesses. Padilla stated that he did not doubt that when the Argentineans came back they would be received with open arms. Yet he bluntly advised the Argentine general to impress upon his government that the next time it sent an army, it should respect the people's customs, have good and decent authority, and under no circumstances bring officers who wished to steal, and were proud or cowardly. If this advice were followed the guerrilla leader thought that all the provinces could be united in one big *Patria*. The writer concluded his letter by saying "there is still time for remedy . . . but if not, then . . . ." With the word "then" and the four dots the letter ends.

What Padilla meant was that if his advice were not followed, the inner provinces would depart from the Plata union and take a different road. That is what finally happened. The guerrilla leader proved by this letter to be a sharp observer. Among the partisans of Charcas he was probably the most enlightened and intellectually best equipped.[52] He clearly foresaw the creation of an independent Upper Peru, if the free provinces continued their unintelligent policy with regard to the occupied inner provinces. But since Padilla was ahead of his time he was well aware that the sentiment for separation was not yet prevalent, and therefore his classic remark, "There is still time for remedy." In his letter the partisan commander also showed that he did not want a separate

Upper Peru. Although in the first part he cruelly enumerated the past abuses of the Argentineans, in the latter part of the letter he practically pleaded with the general to see to it that all this be remedied, because if not, it would be impossible to avoid the consequences. Padilla wanted to thwart what he probably thought would be a tragic event: the splitting up of the upper and lower provinces. Consequently the guerrilla from Laguna was not "the precursor of the Bolivian nation," as one Bolivian historian has interpreted this letter,[53] but rather a shrewd observer who was the first Upper Peruvian to foresee the course that the inner provinces might be forced to take.

The battle of Sipe Sipe was definitely a turning point in the history of Charcas. Before Sipe Sipe it is hardly possible to detect sentiments, or even one voice, in favor of the separation and independence of Upper Peru. Rondeau's defeat marks the beginning of this desire to part ways. Padilla felt it, as did the great San Martín. The Bolivian chronicler, Manuel María Urculla, cofounder of Bolivia, and the great Argentine leader and historian, Bartolomé Mitre, were well aware of it.[54] But the wish for independence was not overwhelming; only isolated seeds had been planted and even they had not yet germinated. The great number of guerrillas still looked to the free provinces for help and inspiration. The majority of these partisans had not even come in contact with the auxiliary armies, and were fighting their own private war. The well-to-do classes were inclined to favor the Royalists rather than the Patriots. Many sincere Patriots had emigrated from the upper provinces and had gone to the free provinces where they fell under the influence of the Argentine system. The lower classes, Indians especially, were inert or of changing allegiance. A well-equipped and victorious fourth auxiliary army under a popular general, such as San Martín, could have wiped out the separatist and anti-Argentine sentiment. But after Rondeau's enormous defeat no expeditionary army came up again, and from 1816 until the end of the war the inner provinces were left to their own resources. In 1816 the Royalist army began its great sweep to wipe out the guerrillas. Aid from Argentina was not forthcoming even in that critical year.

The year 1816 marks the beginning of the great anarchy in the United Provinces, an anarchy which made it impossible to organize a new campaign into the occupied inner provinces. Besides, it was then thought, in view of the continual defeats of the auxiliary armies, that the road via Chile into Lower Peru was more suitable, as indeed it proved to be. Because of these cumulative factors the army of the north, also known as the army of Upper Peru, again under the command of Belgrano, never started its offensive against Charcas, but rather was on the defensive under the impact of the renewed invasions of the Royalist army from Upper Peru. Only once, in 1817, did a small contingent of about a hundred and fifty men, under the adventurous Colonel Gregorio Aráoz de la Madrid, execute a raid behind the Spanish lines into the upper provinces. La Madrid, a daring soldier with absolutely no ability for military strategy, disobeyed his orders and decided to make an epic march. He surprised Tarija and then sneaked up to Chuquisaca, where he halted his small contingent at the very door of the presidential house of the Audiencia of Charcas. But the president, obviously astonished to see an Argentine unit in the midst of the capital, quickly recovered and forced La Madrid to leave Chuquisaca and retreat all the way back to northern Argentina.[55] This was hardly an assault, but only a disjointed raid,[56] which added nothing to Argentine prestige, except to show that another unqualified Argentine commander went on a foolish, useless rampage, merely to write an epic and glorify his name.

Not until 1820 did Salta and Tucumán demand vehemently the organization of a new auxiliary army with the hope of avoiding further Spanish invasions from Charcas.[57] Since the beginning of the war, armies from that area had penetrated the free provinces nine times.[58] But nothing definite was done, and when the army was finally ready to move in 1825, it was far too late[59] since the Bolivarian army under Marshal Sucre had already defeated the last remnants of the Spanish legions.

The abuses of the three auxiliary armies and the abandonment of the inner provinces were the main causes of Charcas' separation from the Argentine union. From 1809 until 1825 Upper Peru fought a bitter war against the Spanish forces. Argentine aid until 1816 was no help, and its armies turned out to be one more enemy instead of an ally. For the next nine years the occupied provinces were abandoned to their own fate, and alone they had to fight the war against the Spanish enemy. Once victorious, they also wanted to guide their destiny alone. The spirit of independence was created during the war. If the United Provinces had liberated their inner occupied provinces during the early or middle stages of the war, an independent Bolivia would never have emerged. But the failure to do this in addition to the behavior of the expeditionary forces killed any chance of a reunion of the lower and inner provinces. The history of the auxiliary armies constitutes a vital link in the creation of Bolivia.[60]

*Chapter 4*

## DOS CARAS

HUQUISACA, CALLED LA PLATA by the Royalists, was the capital of the vast Audiencia of Charcas. It was a proud and picturesque town, isolated from the stream of world events. Chuquisaca had been founded in 1539[1] by a distinguished conquistador with a delightful name, Pedro Anzúrez de Camporendondo. When the fabulous mines of Potosí began to deliver their prodigious wealth, the prosperous miners settled in nearby Chuquisaca. The city became the seat of an audiencia and an archdiocese, and, in 1624, the university was established there. Chuquisaca is located in mountainous territory, surrounded by a beautiful landscape that shows neither the aridness of Potosí nor the opulence of Cochabamba. The climate is mild and pleasantly dry. The city, situated at the foot of two steep hills, is long and narrow, and has many churches, pretty houses, and a wide and spacious plaza. After Mexico City and Lima it had more "colossal fortunes"[2] than any other city in the colonies. It considered itself the guardian and garden of Potosí, and Potosí was Spain's pride. Chuquisaca was a haughty town because its people thought that it was especially commanded by the king to preserve and stimulate the imperial city of Potosí. No other town in the Spanish colonies was more proud and conceited than Chuquisaca. Its audiencia ignored and even scorned the viceroys in Lima and Buenos Aires, and felt completely self-sufficient, responsible only to God and the king.[3]

Approximately 13,000 inhabitants lived in Chuquisaca at the end of the eighteenth century. Of these 4,000 were Spaniard,

3,000 mestizo, 4,500 Indian, and 1,500 Negro and mulatto.⁴ The Spaniards were either *gachupines* (those born in Spain) or *criollos*. They lived pleasantly, effortlessly, and uneventfully. They formed part of the bureaucratic apparatus always present at the seat of an audiencia, of the elaborate ecclesiastic hierachy existent in the capital of an archdiocese, and of the university, faculty and students. Some were active in the *cabildo*, others managed their estates, while not a few took continual delight in fighting lawsuits, the favorite pastime of Chuquisaca. There was an abundance of lawyers. It was an arrogant group, extremely conservative and provincial. All maintained that they came from distinguished families in Spain. This was the inner core of Chuquisaca, but it was neither united nor homogeneous, for there were the usual differences between the *peninsulares* and *criollos*. The core was divided into many strata, each looking with disdain on the ones beneath.⁵ The whites formed an isolated group in an isolated town, and there was a complete absence of new blood. The only newcomers to the town were the many students from throughout the viceroyalty, and it was they who brought the spirit of revolution. The narrow provincialism of Chuquisaca created what is known as the *mentalidad altoperuana*, Upper Peruvian mentality, or as one author has put it, the "collective psychology of Upper Peru."⁶ This characteristic was more pronounced in Chuquisaca than in any other place in Charcas.

It is difficult to enumerate the characteristics of this mentality. Gabriel René-Moreno, Bolivia's superb and only great historian, was unfortunately a dedicated racist.⁷ To him it was "a perverse tendency toward scheming and quarrels" and represented a love for "gossip and mischievous lies."⁸ He believed that the reason for this lay in the fact that the mixture between Indians and Spaniards was a bad one and resulted in individuals with false personalities. His basic belief was the "unquestionable superiority of the white race."⁹ The Indian was false and the whites, either through Indian blood or through close contact, had absorbed his duplicity. Even to the leftist writer, Tristán Marof, the racial aspect is the vital cause of this morbid mentality.¹⁰ The communist writer, Roberto Alvarado, prefers an economic explanation: that the inhabitants did not expend their natural energies in the profitable and healthy occupations such as tilling the soil.¹¹ The nationalist writer, Carlos Montenegro, attributes the psychology of the Upper Peruvians to extreme individuality.¹² The modern poet of Sucre, Joaquín Gantier, himself a patrician and a product of conservative Chuquisaca, admits that "unquestionably the Upper Peruvian was deceitful, false, shrewd, and intricate," but that on the other hand he also was "extremely sentimental."[13]

The Upper Peruvian mentality seems to be more the result of an extreme provincialism, caused by the "Andean enclosure"[14] of Chuquisaca, and aggravated by a false and distorted feeling of the importance of their town, together with the lack of any profitable economic enterprise. This gave rise to a peculiar character, given to loose play with ambiguous words and phrases in which the individual rarely came straight out for one or the other side, but rather manipulated all beliefs, never deciding for anyone. The classic appraisal of René-Moreno, calling it *dos caras* (two-faced),[15] has much truth in it. The elementary explanation of Simón Rodríguez (the brilliant teacher who went to Chuquisaca to establish a model school and failed) that it was an extreme egoism is an oversimplification.[16] The racist expositions of René-Moreno and Alcides Arguedas make little sense today. René-Moreno's sketch of the Upper Peruvian mentality is correct and sincere, but his reasons for it are erroneous. In brief, the society of Chuquisaca was sophistical and motivated by an unhealthy conservatism.

A member of this conservative and unenterprising society at the end of the eighteenth century was a certain gentleman by the name of Miguel de Olañeta. He was an *ultramarino*,[17] from overseas, a *peninsular*. Miguel's brother Pedro Antonio, lived in Salta. Miguel and Pedro[18] came from distinguished stock of the village of Elqueta in the Spanish province of Guipuscoa. Don Miguel's mother came from the same region, belonging to the Marquiegui family. Miguel, proud of his Spanish nativity, went to Spain in search of a wife,[19] but he came back empty-handed. He then married a *criolla*, Doña Rafaela de Güemes of La Plata, daughter of Francisco de Güemes of Burgos, Spain, and Doña Antonia Prudencia Martierena of the town of Yavi in the province of Chichas, near Potosí. Don Miguel's newly acquired mother-in-law was the daughter of the local Marquis of Toxo.[20] Don Miguel and his wife, Doña Rafaela, had only Spanish blood in their veins and had avoided the mixture of Indian blood. Their life in Chuquisaca was uneventful, and they did not have to worry about earning a living. Neither husband nor wife knew what hard work meant. The wife's family was wealthy and Doña Rafaela inherited most of the fortune of her parents.[21] Don Miguel became a *regidor* of the *ayuntamiento*,[22] which represented the average ambition of any distinguished citizen. Naturally his position on the *cabildo* did not absorb all his time, and he dedicated some of his spare hours to business ventures in La Plata and Potosí.[23] Many lawsuits and the management of nearby farms helped him break the monotony.[24] Miguel de Olañeta and his wife were the very picture of the typical aristocracy of Chuquisaca. From patrician families, trying to maintain their pure blood, and with no financial worries, they acquired whatever means they had not through private enterprise but rather through inheritance. His post on the *ayuntamiento* gave him stature and prestige; he did a little business and as a side line he supervised estates. Like him and his wife were many others in Chuquisaca and all over the colony.

On March 3, 1795, about ten years after their marriage, a very fragile son was born to the Olañetas, and it was feared that he would not see the light of the world for many hours or days. He survived, but two days after his birth his mother, Doña Rafaela, died. Her death certificate says "she died suddenly without receiving the sacraments." She must have been a sick woman with a presentiment of her death. On January 22, only a month before her son's birth, she made her will "in case I do not survive the birth of my forthcoming son or daughter."[25]

The baby grew strong, and on April 7 was baptized by the famous archbishop, San Alberto, and was given the name of Josef Joaquín Casimiro.[26] He was Casimiro Olañeta, to become one of Bolivia's greatest and most powerful figures. Casimiro spent his youth in his native Chuquisaca and little is known about those years. Although he later acquired a powerful pen, he never wrote the story of his life, and even if he had it might be of little value since he was a master in lying and boasting.

Young Casimiro who was not sent by his father to the University of San Francisco Xavier in Chuquisaca, which was the most famous institution in the Viceroyalty of Río de la Plata, but to the Colegio Real Convictorio de Nuestra Señora de Montserrat at Córdoba (Argentina). At the time this was a conservative school. As was customary in the colonies, one had to prove that one was a Christian, "clean of Jewish and Moorish race, not convicted by the Holy Office, and of legitimate matrimony," in order to enter. This was strictly enforced at Montserrat. Casimiro entered Montserrat in

1809, the year the War of Independence started in Charcas. Why his father sent him to Córdoba, instead of entering him at San Francisco in their own home town, remains a matter of speculation. One Bolivian author believes that the Olañeta family was aware of the radical spirit that was becoming noticeable at San Francisco in the first decade of the new century. They were determined not to send Casimiro into this nest of subversives. Therefore the conservative school at Córdoba was chosen as being better suited to their philosophy.[27] Besides, Casimiro's uncle, Pedro Antonio de Olañeta, had settled in Salta where he had become a successful and respectable businessman.

Montserrat had some excellent teachers, such as the venerable Dean Funes.[28] Among the fellow students of Casimiro were the sons of Viceroy Liniers, the son of the Royalist General José de Córdova, and José María Paz.[29] Liniers and Córdova were shot by Castelli in 1810 and undoubtedly Casimiro witnessed the plight and sadness of their sons. The students at the college saw the imprisoned leaders of the La Paz revolt when they were brought through Córdoba on the way to Buenos Aires. The real feelings of the student Casimiro Olañeta are not known. By 1810 the faculty at the college was sharply divided between the Royalists and the Patriots. Casimiro Olañeta's later identification with the Royalist cause would seem to indicate that he had little sympathy for the Patriots. In later years when Olañeta, then the most powerful politician in Bolivia, was accused of having been a "*godo pertinaz*,"[30] he defended himself by saying that when he was at Córdoba, "at the age of fifteen I was so fanatic for the liberty of my country that any kind of persecution of the Spaniards did not satisfy my desire. I did not admit weakness in this matter."[31] But Olañeta was a master prevaricator, and the fact that he emphasized his early patriotism so much is a good indication that he was the very opposite.

Later Casimiro returned to his native Chuquisaca. Probably his father requested that he leave the college, which, after 1810, was located in the free provinces and accepted the new order. Casimiro himself said that he went back to Chuquisaca after the victory of Salta won by Belgrano in 1813. But in the next line he stated that Belgrano imprisoned him, his sole crime being that of his name.[32]

His father fled Chuquisaca when the second auxiliary army was on its march to occupy the capital. After Belgrano's retreat,

Casimiro enrolled at the University of San Francisco which by then
had been cleansed of the subversive elements. In March, 1814,
Casimiro received his bachelor's degree in canon law.[33] Two months
later, on May 24, he entered the Carolina Academy, which was
the "forum of Upper Peru,"[34] where graduates were trained in law
to prepare them especially to work before or with the audiencia.
To enroll, one had to pass a difficult entrance examination and
swear loyalty to the King and the Catholic religion. At the time
that Casimiro entered the academy its headmaster was the famous,
able, shrewd, archconservative Pedro Vicente Cañete. Cañete
was a thorough Royalist, although he was a *criollo* born in Asun-
ción.[35] Undoubtedly he would not have tolerated any pupil at the
academy about whom he had even the slightest suspicion of
allegiance to the Patriot cause. Only known Royalists could enter
this conservative school. Casimiro Olañeta passed the entrance
examination in good standing. He was questioned for half an hour
about chapter two, title nine, book two, of the Justinian code of
law. He knew it thoroughly.[36]

Casimiro's training was interrupted when the third auxiliary
army under Rondeau occupied the capital. He fled to the Royalist
headquarters at Oruro. There resided the commander, General
Pezuela, and his lieutenant, Colonel Pedro Antonio Olañeta, who
were reorganizing the Spanish army. Colonel Olañeta was Casimiro's father's brother, the cunning businessman who had lived in
Salta, shipping all kinds of goods to and from Upper Peru, especially between Potosí and Buenos Aires. When the war had started
Pedro Antonio, a man of great physical ability and a fanatic conservative, had offered his services to the Royalist army.[37] Because
of his great knowledge of Upper Peru, his extraordinary contacts,
and his sharp mind he moved up in the army quickly. He showed
excellent military talent, especially for organization and logistics.
Casimiro joined his uncle who probably provided him with a job.
When Rondeau's army was completely defeated, Casimiro Olañeta
returned to Chuquisaca to continue his training at the Academy.
He petitioned the audiencia for an assistantship in order that he
might engage in legal practice and observe the workings of that
body, and his application was approved. Casimiro must have been
an able student and a smooth worker, since he was soon named
secretary of the academy,[38] the highest honor which a student in
Charcas could achieve. Everything seemed to indicate that the

young graduate student was destined for a brilliant career.

In 1817 Casimiro felt that he had acquired enough legal experience and requested admission to the final bar examination, which was granted. On May 19 he took his oral examination and was assigned to debate a minor inheritance case before the audiencia as his test question. He passed the examination "faultlessly and successfully."[39] Once admitted as a candidate for a degree, he then had to take an oath of allegiance to the Catholic religion and pay the necessary graduation fee. After this he was given his diploma of law and became a full-fledged lawyer.[40] After receiving his degree Casimiro Olañeta dedicated himself to his law career with enthusiasm, proficiency, and extreme shrewdness, He made a phenomenal rise in the conservative and exceedingly suspicious audiencia. In 1818 Olañeta became criminal attorney of the audiencia, and soon was given more responsible positions, such as associate judge, civil attorney, attorney in the office of Indian protection, as well as attorney in the census office.[41] These were positions which usually went to established and experienced lawyers.

Five letters of recommendation in the Olañeta files, from high Spanish administrative officials,[42] show that he was admired and respected and that everyone thought that he had extraordinary talents and a pleasant personality, and that he was a faithful servant of the Spanish crown. One official thought that he was "prudent, sagacious, and political," and that in his work he was "quick and clever."[43] Another wrote that he was an "excelling individual" and that he was "zealous in the cause of His Majesty and the nation," and that because of his extraordinary qualities Casimiro Olañeta had obtained the best positions which usually go to a man with much more service.[44] In 1820 Casimiro Olañeta requested a leave of absence from the audiencia in order to rejoin his uncle,[45] Pedro Antonio de Olañeta, who had been promoted to general and who was the new Royalist commander in Upper Peru. Casimiro seemingly left for Tupiza where General Olañeta had his headquarters.[46] From 1820 until 1824 very little is known about Casimiro Olañeta. He maintained his position on the audiencia but he also began his career of conspiracy and backstage politics and treason, which he kept up until his death in 1860.

Until 1820 nothing in Casimiro's career indicates a single breath of sympathy for the cause of the Patriots, although he later stated that when he was fifteen years old he was fanatic for the cause of freedom and the Patriots. As a matter of fact, his behavior and statements showed an absolute allegiance to and partisanship toward the Royalists. There is not a word, sentence, or any other evidence of concern for the fate of the native guerrillas. As one modern biographer of Olañeta rightly stated, "To the aristocratic Olañeta the native guerrillas were of no worth; they were poor and ignorant."[47] Casimiro Olañeta was no soldier nor hero of the war. He was a thorough Royalist, from a conservative family. His father's brother was the Royalist commander of Upper Peru. But Casimiro Olañeta was a genius in shrewdness, an unsurpassed intriguer, and a man with remarkable foresight.

In view of his later career of continuous plotting,[48] a pattern of behavior becomes noticeable. First of all, he had made himself acceptable to the people, next he brought the key person under his influence, and finally he dominated and manipulated him. With his phenomenal foresightedness he knew exactly when the cause or person he was supporting was losing popularity. When discontent was still in an embryonic stage he opened relations with the opposition from behind the scenes. At the appropriate time he betrayed the cause he had supported and swung to full support of its enemies. Olañeta then repeated the same game, over and over.[49] Later he not only acted in the realm of national politics, but was so unscrupulous as to make contact with foreign powers and invite them to attack Bolivia.[50] At the right moment, when the invaders lost popularity, he waved the Bolivian flag again. In this way he brought to power almost all Bolivian presidents who held office during his lifetime; at the same time he organized most of the revolutions against them, and twice he invited Peru to invade Bolivia. He always worked in the background, and wrote little, so that no definite proof could be used against him and he could deny any charge.[51] When someone accused him he came back with his famous *Exposiciones* and *Folletos*,[52] his sole writings. In them he showed that his accusers had nothing to prove and could only make intangible accusations, and then he paraded one extravagant lie after the other. His model was Talleyrand, whose name he could not even spell.[53]

By 1820 the Royalist cause was weakening. In the next year a definite crisis was noticeable. Before that time the Spanish army had been in firm control in both Perus. The threat from Argentina had been repelled, anarchy was prevalent in the Plata provinces, and the guerrilla threat in Upper Peru had been checked. There was little reason to doubt that the doom of the Patriots was likely. Casimiro Olañeta had no reason at all not to be a Royalist. His background and the favorable situation of the Spaniards made this course profitable. The surprising victory of San Martín in Chile changed the whole picture. From there the war was carried into Lower Peru, the great sanctuary of the Royalists. Military defeat resulted in dissatisfaction within the Spanish army, whose command until then had been thought to be efficient. A group of young officers rebelled against the old guard. In 1821 they deposed the viceroy, Pezuela, whose early military victories had been rewarded with the viceregal post. Yet everything was unchanged in Upper Peru, and the sense of security that the Royalists experienced in Charcas since the defeat of the auxiliary army was in no way abating. In Upper Peru the control of the Spaniards was stronger than in any place else. However, although few people realized it, the situation in Upper Peru was precarious. The fate of this region was completely tied to that of Lower Peru. If the heart of the Viceroyalty of Lima were lost, then the fall of Charcas would be only a question of time. Doubtless Casimiro Olañeta understood this and was well aware of the change taking place; he realized that the Royalist cause was no longer secure, as the local picture indicated, but rather, that it was weakening fast.

In all probability Casimiro Olañeta began to open contacts with the Patriots about 1820. The young lawyer started his double-faced career. In his first *Exposición* he wrote that he joined the revolution before the battle of Maypú and Chacabuco,[54] which is without question a gross exaggeration, since in 1818 he was rising fast in the audiencia. Then he stated that the president of Charcas, Rafael Maroto, prosecuted him for sympathizing with the enemy. No document in the complete files of the audiencia or in Olañeta's university file indicates anything of this nature. If this had been the case he would never have kept his position in the audiencia, which he did until 1824.

Olañeta went even further; he had the temerity to write that when San Martín landed in Peru, he wanted to help the invading forces from Chuquisaca, but lacked the means. He affirmed that he did distribute Patriot propaganda sent to him from Lima via Tacna.[55] Again he stated that Maroto wanted to bring him to trial, but that he escaped and went to his uncle's headquarters in

Tupiza. This is very strange: he was accused by the president of the Audiencia of Charcas of subversion, and in order to avoid trial ran away to the Spanish commander of Upper Peru. If he was sincere, why did he not join the native guerrilla force or escape to the free provinces or make his way to the invading forces in Lower Peru? He cited more examples, all very vague, of his efforts in behalf of the cause of independence after Maypú. Casimiro flatly stated that he sent secret messages to the expeditionary force in Lower Peru, informing them of the strength of the Royalist army.[56] Casimiro also wrote that when the Royalists found out that one of their young *criollo* officers, Agustín Gamarra, future president of Peru, was conspiring for the Patriots, he used his influence with his uncle to dismiss the case and therefore saved Gamarra's life.[57] But what really happened was that Gamarra had confided his doings to Casimiro Olañeta, who had given the appearance of being interested in joining him. Yet Casimiro immediately denounced Gamarra before the Royalist authorities and therefore was responsible for Gamarra's arrest.[58] After this he gave the outside appearance of wanting to help this turncoat officer at all costs.[59]

Because of his relationship with his uncle he had access to vital restricted information. If Olañeta was telling the truth, he was admittedly a traitor. All this is probably another exaggeration. If he had sent information he would have been the most formidable spy in the Peru, because of his intimate family contact with the commander of the Spanish army, and later Patriot sources would have mentioned such an invaluable agent. Such is not the case. Casimiro Olañeta never lost his position in the audiencia. All that he wrote about his trial appears completely false.

Furthermore, in 1822, another great honor was bestowed upon him when he was named representative to the Spanish Cortes.[60] For some unknown reason he did not go. In 1824 he was still criminal attorney of the audiencia and was responsible for dismissing one of the most sensational trials in Chuquisaca, a case against two women accused of being witches. He stated that this was a matter of the twelfth and fourteenth centuries, but not of modern times.[61] This demonstrated that the young lawyer did not have a provincial outlook. Everything considered, it would indicate that Olañeta remained a Royalist until the last moment. Once the Spanish cause was completely doomed he made a spectacular change to the enemy's side in grand style. His statement that he joined the cause of independence before the battles of Maypú and Chaca-buco, however, are fantastic exaggerations and defy historical evidence. As the Royalist cause became more and more precarious the young and brilliant lawyer probably began to look to the other side, making valuable contacts in a most careful and disguised manner. It is quite possible that he slipped some minor information to the enemy, so that if the time of a Patriot victory ever arrived, he had a ready-made case for himself. As the outlook for independ-ence improved, Olañeta proportionally increased his contacts. Finally in 1824 he pulled the great master stroke which catapulted him into becoming the most important person in Charcas. It was the plan and work of a true genius.[62]

For those who consider the Upper Peruvian mentality dishonest, with a tendency toward intrigue, Casimiro Olañeta must represent the quintessence of this complex behavior,[63] which René-Moreno has immortalized as *dos caras*. But the existence of only one figure as the prototype could weaken one's case. Besides, René-Moreno was an excellent historian, but he also was a profound stylist;[64] he was professor of rhetoric in Santiago, Chile, rather than a teacher of history. He was painstaking about his style and was a superb artist in this field. René-Moreno created two prototypes of *dos caras*, because one would not emphasize his point enough, and also because he could write a more beautiful sentence; to him *los Olañetas y los Urcullus*[65] sounded melodic. He used it over and over, he made them *compadres*.[66] To Casimiro Olañeta, René-Moreno added Manuel María Urcullu as the other example and master of intrigue and treason. The choice is indeed quite good, although Urcullu never acquired the stature and technique of Olañeta, but rather became a faithful assistant who imitated his young master.

But both played the same game. René-Moreno located the right person when he searched in historical annals, covering the period of the creation of Bolivia, for a second figure who would match Casimiro Olañeta. Urcullu was chosen because he too jumped on the Bolivarian bandwagon at the last moment and became a "creator of Bolivia." The main criterion of René-Moreno for elevating Manuel María Urcullu to the rank of master of double dealings was that he passed on to posterity the notion that Casimiro Olañeta was an "exalted Patriot."[67] Urcullu became the only Upper Peruvian chronicler of the War of Independence, and many later mediocre Bolivian historians, and indeed many foreign ones, used the book by Urcullu as the only source, instead of consulting other documents.[68] Urcullu not only made Olañeta a dedicated Patriot but also made him father and creator of Bolivia, an honor that should belong to Antonio José de Sucre. The chronicler, Urcullu, entitled his work *Annotations of the History of the Revolution of Upper Peru, Today's Bolivia, by Some Patriots.* Urcullu assumed that he was a Patriot and he was determined, by becoming a Patriot historian, to create an even greater Patriot, Casimiro Olañeta. Then he went even further and made his young master the father of the independent Upper Peruvian nation. Olañeta, a stern Royalist, a great civil servant of the King, who became a Patriot at the last minute, was written into the pages of history as a perpetual Patriot just before the deadline. During the early part of the war Urcullu had been Olañeta's teacher and superior. What a pair of shrewd *compadres!* But was Urcullu's early background that of an exalted Royalist? René-Moreno has very little proof. He talks about the well-known fact that in 1824 Casimiro Olañeta took Urcullu with him into the services of his uncle, General Pedro Antonio de Olañeta. But at that time even Bolívar had the idea that the general had become a Patriot, merely because he had a disagreement with the viceroy.[69]

No biography of Urcullu has been written. He is simply one of the cases in history, who was well known in his country's annals, but whose career and life remain vague, mainly because documents are lacking or have not been located. Manuel María Urcullu was born in Chuquisaca on July 16, 1785,[70] ten years before Casimiro Olañeta. He came from a distinguished family; his father was a *peninsular* from Viscaya. In school he was a dedicated student. Since he studied in a Catholic seminary, he concentrated on philosophy, theology, and Spanish grammar. He had to memorize the *Institutas* of Justinian. After this Urcullu followed a career similar to that of Casimiro Olañeta a decade later. He entered the University of San Francisco Xavier and then became a student of the Carolina Academy. In 1806 he took his written examination, and the next year his orals before the audiencia, having to handle a minor civil case as was the usual custom.

He then began his legal career holding various positions, similar to those of Casimiro Olañeta at the audiencia, such as that of associate judge, criminal attorney, and other attorneyships in the various departments of the audiencia. Apparently he became a professor at the Carolina Academy.[71] Being ten years ahead of Olañeta, he was undoubtedly his instructor at the academy and his senior in the audiencia. At this time Urcullu was master and Olañeta disciple, roles that were later reversed. Urcullu held many other administrative jobs and whenever there was need of a good lawyer and efficient public servant for a temporary task or investigation, he was called because of his "astounding knowledge of law," as one royal official put it.[72] He was recognized as the "most skillful and most studious lawyer" in the capital. In January, 1816, he was named assessor of the treasury, an eagerly desired position in the colonies. It is stated that Urcullu was chosen for this post because "he had not any doubtful spot on his record in regard to his loyalty to the King."[73] Urcullu also was a member of the *cabildo*, to which he was named in 1812 as assessor, and in 1815 he became *regidor*.

In 1816 the guerrillas in Charcas doubled their efforts to keep the War of Independence alive in the inner provinces, after the disastrous defeat of Rondeau's expeditionary army. Guerrilla Padilla, especially, was vigorously hammering at the Spaniards in order to make them realize that the war had not come to a victorious end because of their perfect victory in the battle of Sipe Sipe. Padilla, his wife, and a host of other notable guerrillas such as Jacinto Cueto, Pedro Calisaya, Agustín Ravelo, Ildefonso Carrillo, Prudencio Miranda, Esteban Fernándes, and Marcelino Torres, under the leadership of Padilla, had rallied together and were daringly attacking Chuquisaca in February, 1816. The capital was seriously threatened by their intrepid assault.[74] The patricians of the town decided to organize a unit in order to aid in the fight against those ignorant guerrillas, whose forces had rebelled against the crown. This was known as the regiment of the "notables" or of the "distinguished *vecinos*."[75] Manuel María Urcullu organized this regiment, and until a professional army officer was procured, commanded the outfit. Urcullu, as later certified by his superior officer, fought bravely against the attacking partisan forces. At one point he was put in charge of a patrol that had to go behind the enemy's lines.[76] The guerrilla army was forced to retreat and its attack ended in complete failure. Urcullu, because of his enterprise and courage, was decorated with a medal which had the inscription, "To the defenders of the right of the King."[77]

The next year, 1817, the capital was again the target of a surprise attack when the temerarious Argentine colonel, Aráoz de la Madrid, and his little contingent, penetrated to the very center of Chuquisaca without being noticed. The regiments of the patricians again went into action and Urcullu once more left the bench to take up arms for the King's defense. He fought bravely against the invaders. The commander of the regiment of nobles, Francisco Maruri, stated that he saw Urcullu fighting in the front lines, directly in the enemy's line of fire.[78] Because of the decisive defense of the city La Madrid had to retreat and give up his reckless project. And Urcullu said that he was a Patriot! Perhaps he was really a Patriot in Royalist disguise!

On January 1, 1818, the *cabildo* of Chuquisaca, as was customary, held elections for town officials. In this election Manuel María Urcullu was again chosen assessor of the *cabildo* with seven votes, against four for his nearest opponent, José Ygnacio Mendoza. Don Mariano Enrique Calvo was elected *regidor* with nine votes, against three for his opponent.[79] Calvo was another Royalist *criollo*, of the same breed as Olañeta and Urcullu. He later became vice-president of Bolivia and Santa Cruz's most important and influential official.[80] The list of those elected or re-elected was, in accordance with the usual procedure, presented to the president of the audiencia, Don José Pasqual de Vivero. In an astounding and unprecedented move Vivero did not consent to the election of Urcullu and Calvo. He certified their nearest opponents instead. The president threatened the royal notary with dismissal if he, on his own, should certify the election of Urcullu and Calvo.

It was sensational news. Vivero accused Urcullu and Calvo of having been disloyal to the Spanish cause and of having cooperated in the past with the Patriots whenever they had occupied the town. The *cabildo*, with Casimiro Olañeta as its most influential member, felt injured and thought that Vivero had invaded the prerogatives of that body. Urcullu and Calvo protested loudly because they had been accused of "being devoted to the infernal system of the revolution,"[81] to put it in the words of Mariano Calvo. Later Urcullu and Calvo became high officials in this infernal system. But at that time they decided to take the issue before the audiencia in order to vindicate themselves against such "malicious information" which went against their "reputation and honor."[82] Both had the support of the *cabildo* whose members were all friends and neighbors. Besides, the *cabildo* felt that Vivero had surpassed his authority by restricting the free will of that body. A common colonial problem of overlapping jurisdiction of governmental bodies had arisen. The case was taken before the audiencia and it became one of those long and complicated law cases so abundant in the Spanish colonies. *Regidores, regentes, escribanos, asesores, letrados, fiscal, procurador, president,* and *intendente* debated on paper the case of the loyalty of Urcullu and Calvo, and whether or not the president of the audiencia had the right to disapprove the election of the *cabildo*.

Out of the forty-three folios of statements and discussion it becomes quite clear that Urcullu and Calvo had shown a lack of political conviction and honesty. It was a clear and palpable example of *dos caras.* Each had cooperated with the Patriots when they had the upper hand, and when the Royalist army recaptured the capital, both again became staunch supporters of the crown, violently insulting the Patriots.

In 1813 the Spanish general, Juan Ramírez, had evacuated Chuquisaca because the second auxiliary army under Belgrano had taken Potosí. When the expeditionary forces had entered the capital Urcullu and Calvo had remained in the city and offered their services to the Patriot authorities. Urcullu had been appointed criminal attorney for the audiencia, and Calvo had been named *regidor* of the revolutionary *cabildo*. But both had miscalculated the situation; the auxiliary army was defeated and the Royalist forces reoccupied Chuquisaca. Then Urcullu and Calvo had enthusiastically waved the king's flag. A committee had been formed whose purpose it was to investigate those who had cooperated with the enemy (*Junta de Purificación*). Neither Calvo nor Urcullu had been called before the examining board. Probably they had pulled wires behind the scenes to avoid a public appearance. Casimiro Olañeta, who defended both men in 1818, insisted that this meant that both accused had not cooperated with the "infamous revolutionaries."[83] (Olañeta in 1826 affirmed that he had always been an enthusiastic and fanatic Patriot, but when he defended Urcullu and Calvo and tried to show that his clients had been honest Royalists, he called the Patriots "infamous.")

Urcullu and Calvo had been re-employed by the Spaniards later. The former received a responsible job in the royal treasury and the latter was named defense attorney for the poor, and became a candidate for the delicate position of assessor of the city of Potosí. Calvo had failed to obtain this position but had been appointed associate judge of the audiencia. Two years later, in 1815, the third auxiliary army had invaded Upper Peru. General Rondeau had named Martín Rodríguez as president of Charcas. Urcullu and Calvo had repeated the game all over. Calvo again had become *regidor* of the Patriot *cabildo* and his companion, Urcullu, had been named, of all things, secretary to Martín Rodríguez. Again the expeditionary forces had suffered defeat at the hands of the Royalist army and had had to depart from Chuquisaca. And again the two lawyers had changed their flag and had begun to unfurl the Spanish banner. Calvo defended his actions by stating that he had been forced to accept the position on the *cabildo,* and that he had wanted to resign. Since he had been told not to submit his resignation, he had left for the country in order to be away from the council's deliberations. Calvo insisted that he had never taken part in any meetings of the *cabildo,* but then he admitted that the Argentine authorities had appointed him *regidor* for a second time because they could find no one else to name to the council. This time, Calvo stated, he had gone before the *cabildo* to publicly announce that "he despised his appointment."[84] Calvo was unable to present witnesses who would corroborate his assertions.

Urcullu, after the retreat of the third auxiliary army, had been unable to convince the royal authorities that he was really a sincere Royalist. The Spanish officials had ordered him into exile. Urcullu had appealed and had written a pathetic letter to the Royalist commander of the Upper Peruvian army, General Ramírez.[85] He introduced this letter during the trial.[86] Urcullu had written the general that he was addressing this letter from "the dark corner in which I am, full of sadness and humbly prostrated at the feet of Your Excellency." He had said that he wished that justice and clemency, for which the commander was so well known, should be given him. Urcullu had recounted that he had gone back to his work in the royal treasury after the reoccupation of the capital by the Royalist forces. Then, suddenly, the new Spanish commander of Chuquisaca, General Miguel Tacón, had dismissed him, had wanted to arrest him, and had sent out an order for his exile. Urcullu wrote that he had gone into hiding. He asked Commander Ramírez in his letter why General Tacón wanted to send him into exile when he, Urcullu, had shown more loyalty than anyone else. He asked why this should be so, when he had been an efficient servant and had fulfilled his job conscientiously. Then the humble Urcullu ventured to answer his own questions. He thought that probably someone who hated him and had wanted to do damage to him might have slandered him before Tacón. Urcullu thought that if General Tacón had inquired of honest citizens of the capital, they would have given him a good recommendation. Besides, if he, Urcullu, could have talked personally with Tacón, the general would have become aware of his mistake and would have rescinded his order. So far, Manuel Urcullu had not mentioned a word about his cooperation with the enemy and the fact that he had become the private secretary to the revolutionary president, Martín Rodríguez.

In the next paragraph of the letter Urcullu had written that it was true that "when the infamous Martín Rodríguez usurped the government of this city [Chuquisaca] he obligated me to serve as his secretary, notwithstanding my repugnance and excuses." To Urcullu, his behavior and the facts that he had despised Rodríguez, that the revolutionaries had insulted him, and that he had escaped had been so well known in town there had not been any reason to detail it in the letter. Besides, Urcullu had reminded Commander Ramírez, that he himself, Ramírez, after the victory of Sipe Sipe, had occupied Chuquisaca and Urcullu had been given back his job in the royal treasury. Then Ramírez had been elevated to the post of commander of the Royalist army in Upper Peru, because General Pezuela had become viceroy. The new commander of Chuquisaca, General Tacón, had then dismissed Urcullu and had even wanted to exile him. Tacón had fired him from the job to which Commander Rodríguez had appointed him. Again Urcullu had written that most probably Tacón had been misinformed by some elements that had wanted to ruin his good reputation. General Ramírez had acceded to the request and had suggested to Tacón that he reinstate Urcullu. So ended the letter of Urcullu which had been introduced during the trial.

President Vivero was not impressed by the defense of Calvo and Urcullu before the audiencia and still refused to certify their election to the *cabildo*. Meanwhile, Vivero was transferred and a new general by the name of Rafael Maroto took his place as Spanish commander of Chuquisaca and president of the Audiencia of Charcas. Maroto concurred with his predecessor. The audiencia was sharply divided on the issue and ventured no decision. Maroto then issued the final judgment. He affirmed that the defense of Urcullu and Calvo before the audiencia had not proved their point, but had clearly indicated "that they really had served the revolutionary government." The new general and president concluded that "they shall be punished."[87] Therefore, he did not confirm their elections to the *cabildo* of January 1, 1818. General Maroto signed his decree on January 21, 1819. The attempt of Manuel Urcullu and Enrique Calvo to regain their positions on the *cabildo* had failed.

Three years earlier Urcullu had begun to realize that his actions of 1813 and 1815, when he had cooperated with the revolutionary governments probably because he thought they had a winning chance, were becoming dangerous to him and his reputation as a Royalist. After the battle of Sipe Sipe, when the auxiliary forces had suffered a gigantic defeat, Urcullu became an enthusiastic Royalist. He fought bravely in the front line of defense against the Patriots' attacks of 1816 and 1817, although in 1813 and 1815 he cooperated with the invading Patriots. But things looked different at different periods. In 1813 and 1815 it had appeared that the auxiliary armies of Belgrano and Rondeau would be victorious. They had occupied half of Upper Peru and had the Spanish army on the run. The shrewd lawyer, Urcullu, gambled on the expeditionaries' triumph, and lost. The revolutionary attacks of 1816 and 1817 were of a guerrilla nature, with no over-all plan, and were doomed to failure. Naturally Urcullu had stuck by the Spaniards to make good his miscalculations of 1813 and 1815.

Strangely enough, Urcullu did not mention in his defense before the audiencia, which took place in 1818, the fact that he fought like any soldier in the battle line against the attacking revolutionaries. Could it be that the audiencia admitted testimony only directly relating to the events under judgment? That would mean that he could not use as testimony his behavior of 1816 and 1817 to defend his actions of 1813 and 1815. Or did Urcullu and Olañeta, who rallied to his defense, purposely fail to bring up his later actions, because to any sensible and intelligent observer the implication of fickleness would be clear? Urcullu's intervention in the four events of 1813, 1815, 1816, and 1817 were twice in favor of the Patriots and twice in favor of the Royalists. A simple analysis shows that he supported whichever side had better prospects. To

bring in his behavior of 1816 and 1817, instead of strengthening his
case, might have weakened it. Very probably the shrewd Olañeta
and the intelligent Urcullu realized this quite well.

On January 21, 1819, President Maroto issued the final decision
that Urcullu and Calvo could not assume their elected positions
in the *cabildo* because they had cooperated with the enemy in 1813
and 1815. On February 18 of the same year, exactly twenty-eight
days later, President Maroto, at the request of Viceroy Pezuela,
decorated Manuel María Urcullu with a medal of the highest order,
a medal of solid gold.[88] This was awarded to him because of his
heroic behavior in the fight against the Argentine raid of Colonel
Aráoz de la Madrid. It was the play of *dos caras* in its most extreme
form. The Royalist authorities were defenseless against this
subtle intrigue. The president of Charcas condemned Urcullu for
his cooperation with the enemy in 1813 and 1815, and the viceroy
in Lima decorated him for his services to the king's cause in 1817.
In the jungle of Spanish colonial bureaucracy, where one hand
knew little of what the other was doing, a man who wanted to
play the game of *dos caras* had a wide field of action.

From 1819 to 1824 Urcullu disappears into unknown history.
But what has been said for Casimiro Olañeta for that time was
probably valid for Urcullu too. As the tide was again turning in
1820, so Urcullu, who had a less international outlook than Casimiro
Olañeta, was turning too, probably stimulated by Olañeta. They
were neither Royalists, as they affirmed staunchly when accused
of having cooperated with the Patriots, nor Patriots, as they energetically insisted later when accused of being Royalists. They had
no political conviction, to them politics was anything that would
lead to their own aggrandizement. They would have served the
devil if it had been to their advantage. Slowly, in the early twenties,
both came to realize, particularly Olañeta, who excelled Urcullu
in cleverness and ambition, that neither under the Royalists nor
under the regime of Buenos Aires could they climb the ladder to
complete mastery of Charcas. But if Upper Peru were independent,
free from Buenos Aires and free from Royalist control, perhaps
they could rule it. This impulse was not motivated by a desire
for the well-being of Charcas, but was a scheme to foster their
own personal ambitions.[89] How could they make Upper Peru independent? Anti-Argentine feeling was already deep-rooted. But
the problem of overthrowing the Spaniards when the Patriots,

guerrillas, and auxiliary armies had failed for more than a decade was more than difficult. They decided that they did not need armies or guerrillas. As a pair of clever manipulators they might pull a trick. This strategy could bring doom to the Spaniards. After all, Casimiro Olañeta's uncle, over whom he had tremendous influence, was the commander of the Royalist army in Upper Peru.

*Chapter 5*

# THE GREAT INTRIGUE

*T*HE FIRST SPANISH COMMANDER during the War of
Independence in Upper Peru was General José
Manuel de Goyeneche. He occupied this post until 1813, when he
resigned in the face of mounting difficulties and criticism. He had
failed in his invasion of the lower provinces and his army had been
seriously beaten by Belgrano before the walls of Tucumán. His
punitive expedition against Cochabamba in 1812, where Goyeneche
seemingly lost his temper, had discredited his policy of moderation.
The man chosen to succeed him was General Joaquín de la Pezuela,
a man of honesty and efficiency. He had a strict military mind, and
was well qualified to fight in rough mountainous territory. Pezuela
was unpolished, conservative, a strict disciplinarian, and of no
intellectual stature. His three main associates, General Juan Ramírez, and Colonels Pedro Antonio de Olañeta and Francisco Aguilera
were of the same timbre as their commanding general. Pezuela relied
heavily on Pedro Olañeta, especially in his campaign in southern
Charcas. This colonel, a businessman from Salta, knew the southern
region of Upper Peru and the northern fringes of the lower provinces as well as he knew his own hand. He had been a ruthless
merchant with a huge army of *peones,* trading goods between
Potosí and Buenos Aires. Because of this he fitted well into the
army picture. His army of *peones,* his contacts, and his knowledge
of the terrain were invaluable. Olañeta's ruthlessness made him
a first-class soldier. He was an archconservative, narrow-minded,
rough, but unwaveringly faithful, the last general to engage the
Patriots. He never surrendered, preferring to die in battle in 1825.

100

Colonel Aguilera operated in the spaciousness of eastern Charcas, Santa Cruz de la Sierra. He was native to the region and had qualities similar to those of Olañeta. Deep in his heart he was a staunch Royalist and in 1828, three years after the end of the War of Independence, in the most daring episode ever known in Bolivian history, he proclaimed the end of the republic of Bolivia and the renewal of Charcas as provinces belonging to the Spanish crown.[1] His bold plan almost succeeded. No other Royalist officers in all the colonies were more fanatic, absolute supporters of the Spanish crown than Olañeta and Aguilera, both from Upper Peru. The third officer in the Pezuela circle was General Ramírez. He was more polished than the others, sociable and a good politician. Yet he was merciless with his enemies. The staff of General Joaquín de la Pezuela was strictly militarily minded, unpolished, sometimes fanatic, ruthless, and honest. There was a remarkable homogeneity, perfect understanding, a clear-cut line of responsibility, strict obedience, and admirable discipline. All were convinced Royalists with no thought of changing allegiance. They were complete Absolutists who despised the Spanish constitution of 1812, and were suspicious of new ideas or changes.[2] Most of the officers on the staff were either American natives or were old veterans in the colonies. They lacked the experience of the Napoleonic wars in Europe. The viceregal seat in Lima was occupied by the venerable Marquis of Concordia, Fernando de Abascal. He held Pezuela and his staff in high esteem.

But Abascal was getting quite old and soon somebody would have to take his place. When Pezuela achieved his greatest victory at Sipe Sipe in 1815, he was rewarded with the viceregal chair. On April 15, 1816, he left his headquarters at Cotagaita, the great Charcas fortress which protected Potosí and Chuquisaca, for Lima. In the past three years he had won innumerable victories and he had just prepared to open a decisive campaign against the great guerrilla *republiquetas*. The second in charge, General Juan Ramírez, was named acting commander until a new commanding general was picked for this vital Spanish colony. Ramírez did not lose time, and instructed Aguilera to wipe out the two most dangerous guerrillas, Padilla and Warnes, which he did.

Starting in 1815, because of the vital importance of both Perus, new contingents of army officers arrived from Spain and other theaters of war in America. In September of that year such qualified officers as Mariano Ricarfort, Baldomero Espartero, Andrés García Camba, and José de Carratalá were transferred from northern South America.[3] The next year a new group arrived from Spain, led by Generals José de la Serna and José Canterac and Colonel Jerónimo Valdés, all veterans of the Napoleonic wars. La Serna was appointed to the post of commander of Upper Peru. He and his staff arrived in Cotagaita on November 12, 1816.[4] Acting Commander Ramírez was transferred to the presidency of the Audiencia of Quito. Colonel Jerónimo Valdés, a man who had fought with General Wellington, became acting chief of staff.[5] In 1818 another contingent was brought to Upper Peru, under the leadership of General Canterac. Canterac became chief of staff under La Serna, and Colonel Valdés was appointed chief administrative officer.[6]

All these new officers, especially the three great ones, La Serna, Canterac, and Valdés, represented a completely new school. They were younger and had fought in the Napoleonic wars, serving under the great European generals. They believed in new tactics and showed admiration for the French and English armies. They had a liberal outlook and were well versed in English liberal thought and the streamlined French administration. The new officers abhorred tyranny and absolutism and believed that the War of Independence was the consequence of misdirected Spanish policy. All of them were outspoken partisans of the Spanish constitution of 1812 and felt strongly that only sincere liberalism could save Spain from losing her colonies. These officers and their soldiers were Spaniards from Spain, but were eager and enthusiastic to change tactics, reorganize the army units, and modernize the administration. In a word, the policy of this diverse new element which had come to the Perus was diametrically opposed to that of Pezuela.[7] But Joaquín de la Pezuela was the viceroy and they were under his leadership. The unity and homogeneity of the Abascal and Pezuela regimes were torn to pieces, and a dangerous rift was in the making. In addition, the new viceroy was a military man, lacking political insight and tact.

General Pedro Antonio de Olañeta, who had got along so well with Pezuela, felt deeply antagonistic toward his new commanding officers. To him they were young radicals who lacked the experience of being part of the land. He regarded their ideas with extreme suspicion. Olañeta was ambitious and had hoped to become the supreme commander of Upper Peru, but instead he was being pushed aside by La Serna, Canterac, and Valdés. These officers looked upon Olañeta as a man who was useful because of his qualifications and his superb knowledge of the terrain and the people, yet they never accepted him as their equal. He was not a career soldier, but an amateur who had been a merchant. He had neither come from a distinguished school nor had he fought in the European theater of war. Colonel Aguilera felt the same way as Olañeta, but since he operated in a distant territory he was able to act more independently.

By 1820 the Royalist situation had become very critical. Viceroy Pezuela, who had enjoyed many brilliant victories in Upper Peru, was presiding over the defeat of the Spanish armies in Chile and Lower Peru. The important province of Chile was lost and the army of San Martín was fighting in the heart of the viceroyalty. The strategic importance of Upper Peru was vanishing. Commander La Serna, who had become intensely dissatisfied with the viceroy's command, tendered his resignation and requested to be returned to Europe. The Spanish crown recalled him. Before San Martín landed at Pisco, La Serna left Upper Peru for Lima, en route to Spain. But when he arrived in Lower Peru the Argentineans and Chileans had landed and La Serna's ability was urgently needed. He decided to remain because of the extreme emergency. General Ramírez was recalled from Quito and was appointed commander of the Spanish army of Upper Peru for a second time, but this time with permanent rank.

Since Upper Peru had lost its military importance as a result of the invasion of Lower Peru via Chile instead of via Charcas, it was decided to send most of the experienced troops to reinforce the hard-pressed army in Lower Peru. Colonel Valdés and General Canterac rushed to Lima with the cream of the Upper Peruvian army. Then it was decided to transfer the headquarters of the Upper Peruvian contingent to Puno, and General Ramírez left Charcas, too. When the situation became even more critical in Lower Peru, Ramírez was transferred to Arequipa. The only general that remained in Upper Peru was Pedro Antonio de Olañeta. By default he became commander of the Royalist army of Charcas, a post he had desired for so long. Theoretically he was still under the command of General Ramírez, but in practice he was left to act quite independently. Ramírez was forced to operate in Lower Peru, but soon became sick. Olañeta's dream had been fulfilled. He was the commander, and the three disturbing officers, La Serna, Canterac, and Valdés, had left Upper Peru. His friend Pezuela was still viceroy.

The situation in Lower Peru was becoming more precarious every day. San Martín was threatening the viceregal capital. The Royalist army was affected by a feeling of gloom and dejection. Desertion was on the increase and many trusted officers joined the enemy. An entire battalion deserted to the other side.[8] The guerrillas behind the lines increased their activities. Upper Peru had been severely exposed and weakened by pulling out most of the troops there. In Upper Peru, too, the guerrillas became more belligerent, especially Lanza who had just arrived from the lower provinces and was reorganizing the Ayopaya *republiqueta*. If the La Plata provinces would not have been in a state of anarchy, especially the northern provinces, another auxiliary army might have finished the Spanish forces in Charcas. Now was the time, but the United Provinces did not act. The Spanish position in both Perus, but particularly in Lower Peru, had reached a very critical point. Viceroy Pezuela, who had shown good qualities as a general, now vacillated, negotiated, gave orders, then counterorders, and trusted no one.

The bulk of the Spanish army with its commanding officers, especially the Upper Peruvian contingents, was concentrated in the village of Aznapuquio. Here were La Serna, Canterac, Valdés, Ramírez, Camba, and others. These officers had become disgusted with the behavior of the viceroy. The new element, especially Canterac and Valdés, had never liked the narrow and old-fashioned attitude of Pezuela. La Serna was too much of a gentleman to express an open opinion. Others, including Ramírez, who had belonged to the Pezuela school, were now disturbed about the viceroy's indecision. The only way to save the situation was to act fast. Pezuela had to go. General Canterac and Colonel Valdés were the main spokesmen for this sentiment. On January 29, 1821, nineteen officers[9] sent a stringent ultimatum from Aznapuquio to Viceroy Pezuela, requesting him to leave his office within twenty-four hours and adding, "You shall make the sacrifice, in considering the general welfare before your own pride; this will avoid a division or civil war, the consequence of which we would hold you responsible for before God, the government, and the people."[10] They gave him four hours to answer their ultimatum and offered his family and him all guarantees of safety. The rebellious officers demanded that Pezuela and his family go aboard the English boat *Andromaca*, which would continue her voyage to Panama. Pezuela, protesting violently, was forced to acquiesce.[11] The revolutionary officers under the leadership of Canterac and Valdés then named La Serna viceroy, and requested confirmation from the crown, which came promptly.[12]

The liberal element had won. The new viceroy named Canterac as over-all commander of both Perus, and Valdés as the chief of staff. Somewhat later La Serna promoted Valdés to general and divided the army into the army of the north under the leadership of Canterac and the army of the south under Valdés. Thus he got rid of General Ramírez, who had been a Pezuela man.[13] The new army of the south, under General Valdés, included Charcas and part of southern Lower Peru. The three companions, La Serna, Canterac, and Valdés, who earlier had fought together in Charcas and who had represented a minority reform wing, had suddenly become the absolute rulers of the Perus. Almost all subordinate officers accepted the new order. La Serna, a distinguished gentleman, was very popular.[14]

Because of the Riego revolt in Spain, Ferdinand VII was forced in 1820 to readopt the constitution of 1812, which he had annulled upon his return from French captivity. The liberal element of the Royalist army in Peru felt encouraged by this news and undoubtedly it gave them the much-needed incentive to materialize the overthrow of Pezuela, which they had contemplated earlier. Pezuela had been a thorough Absolutist. Pedro Antonio de Olañeta was dismayed at the promulgation of the constitution,[15] which he hated more than anything else, but he had to swallow the news. Then came the deposition of his beloved and respected superior, Pezuela. This was a terrific blow to Olañeta. La Serna and the liberals were then his superiors, and the radical Valdés his direct commander. This was an even worse misfortune. Valdés was the very opposite of Pezuela.

Pezuela was a man of impressive stature. His height and his silvery-gray hair gave him dignity, and his impassive stony face inspired deep respect, even fear, but no sympathy. He made his dominating and cold character felt with a fearful impact. His orders were listened to and obeyed, never discussed. He always was immaculately dressed. His jacket was adorned with beautiful embroidery, many decorations, and long, wide braid. He always wore a gold sword and handled his elegant cane proudly. Behind the lines he wore fancy silk stockings and expensive shoes from the best shops in Madrid. His campaign uniform was martial, with impressive boots, a wide, dark mantle over his shoulders, and a three-cornered black hat with cords and blood-red feathers. Indeed, everything about him seemed impressive and haughty.[16] Pedro Olañeta like him and his pomp.

General Jerónimo Valdés was always nervous and unceasingly restless. He moved with an amazing swiftness, rushing from one place to another. The general was small, thin, and somewhat bent. He spoke fast and intimately, and his eyes sparkled with enthusiasm. He magnetized people with his frank personality. His clothes were always ragged, he wore an old vicuña hat and dirty boots. He ate rapidly and disliked fancy food, and he always had his meals with his soldiers. The general despised comfort and always slept outside on the ground, with only two ponchos for blankets. Nobody recognized him as the commanding general and he was often mistaken for a common soldier. His soldiers venerated him and his officers respected him.[17] His enemies thought that he was the most able Spanish general,[18] and Marshal Sucre had immense respect for Valdés.[19] How could General Olañeta, who believed in strict social divisions, like this very plain general? Valdés was the very antithesis of Pezuela and Olañeta.

In the face of the popularity of the Aznapuquio coup Olañeta did nothing to dispute the accession of La Serna to the viceregal chair. He accepted the new order without a word, for opposition was useless. The new viceroy and his associates did not harbor any ill feelings toward Olañeta, whom they considered an able general, and he was left in command of Charcas, subject only to the commander of the army of the south, General Jerónimo Valdés. For three years Olañeta nurtured a hatred against the liberals, but La Serna and Valdés were unaware of it. But General Olañeta's shrewd nephew, Casimiro Olañeta, realized it. Casimiro knew that this might be to his own advantage, and in his mind a diabolical plan slowly began to take shape. From 1821 to 1823 the main part of the fighting took place in Lower Peru, and Upper Peru became a theater of minor importance. The United Provinces could have achieved with little effort what they were unable to accomplish after many and costly attempts at an earlier period, when three expeditionary armies failed miserably. But the free provinces had become the prey of a vicious anarchy, and powerful, egocentric, and commercial Buenos Aires opposed any extension of the provincial territory. The free provinces abandoned the inner provinces to their own fate, even though liberation would have been very easy in view of Spain's critical position in Lower Peru.[20]

But if military action decreased, behind-the-scenes intrigues and plots increased. The *dos caristas* saw quite clearly that the Spanish cause was losing ground and that the United Provinces' claim was a matter of the past. The loose La Plata union could never again expect to reintegrate the inner provinces within its political jurisdiction. Early abuses and failures and their recent inactivity had shut the door to any eventual hope that Charcas, when free from the Royalists, would want to join their nation. Casimiro Olañeta, as the leader of the Machiavellists, began to attract a group of men such as José María Urcullu, Mariano Enrique Calvo, Leandro Usín, Mariano Calvimontes, Mariano Callejo, José Antequera, José Santos Cavero, the four Moscoso brothers (Angel Mariano, José Eustaquio, José Antonio, and Rudecindo), and others,[21] all graduates of the Carolina Academy and *criollo* officials of the audiencia.[22] The time had come when they thought that perhaps they could dispense with the Spanish power and take its place. They became a sort of *dos caras* lodge.[23]

Many Upper Peruvian Patriots, because of the occupation of their home provinces by Spanish forces, had moved to the free provinces. Some had made their homes in the new country and become absorbed into its society. Others had become figures in Argentine politics with no wish to return. But some had remained in the northern provinces, especially Salta and Tucumán, with the hope of returning as soon as the revolutionary cause triumphed in Charcas. The latter were strong partisans of the United Provinces and naturally thought that if Charcas were freed by the armies of Argentina, then they would return and be put in charge of the administration in Upper Peru.[24] The most important figure of this group was a certain José Mariano Serrano, a man who had the same background and education as Casimiro Olañeta, but who in his youthful enthusiasm is said to have joined, as a very minor figure, the generation of 1809.[25] With the failure of the 1809 plot he was forced to leave for the free provinces. He was a man of dubious character, with no sincere political philosophy but rather of a fanatic personal ambition.[26] While Casimiro Olañeta was a Royalist *dos caras,* Serrano was a Patriot *dos caras.*[27] Indeed he was very eloquent, and it was Serrano who probably wrote the declaration of independence of the United Provinces in 1816.[28] Later, in 1825, he wrote the Bolivian declaration of independence, thereby becoming the intellectual father of Bolivia. In northern Argentina Serrano was watchful of whoever was winning, and in the early twenties it is said that he became a spy for the Spaniards. He was then secretary to the governor of Salta and from this confidential position reported important information to General Olañeta.[29] Another Upper Peruvian active in the United Provinces was Colonel José María Pérez de Urdininea, later the acting president of Bolivia, who was a close friend of San Martín. He had been named commander of the new auxiliary army which wanted to liberate Upper Peru in a fourth invasion (or fifth, if the raid of La Madrid is counted), but who never moved because of anarchy, opposition of Buenos Aires, and the incapacity of Urdininea, whom René-Moreno called "lead feet."[30]

Serrano, Urdininea, and others realized that in view of the impossibility of liberating Charcas with Argentine armies and the antagonism which had developed against Buenos Aires in Upper Peru, it was imperative to separate Charcas as an independent unit. This would be the best alternative to integration, which would have meant excellent jobs for them. Since integration was impossible, it was time to look for another possibility. There developed in the northern free provinces a lodge similar to the one in Chuquisaca.[31] The latter was directed by the Royalist intriguer, Casimiro Olañeta, the former by the Patriot intriguer, Serrano. Both had identical purposes: the independence of Upper Peru as an outcome second best to a Royalist victory, as envisaged by Olañeta, or an integration of Charcas into the United Provinces, as desired by Serrano. Really, this new choice was not bad at all; the Machiavellian Royalists and Patriots would then become the masters of the new country and would no longer be highly paid servants of the crown or the United Provinces. Suddenly the idea of independence became appealing. The aims of the two lodges coincided, although their origins were different and in distant places. Somehow they established contact, very probably through their leaders, since Serrano was allegedly a spy for General Olañeta, and Casimiro was with his uncle in the early twenties.[32] One of the two intriguers, probably Casimiro Olañeta, developed a daring plan, which took advantage of his uncle's hatred for the new viceroy and his liberal officers.

From Casimiro Olañeta's own words it is quite clear that in 1823 he was with his uncle, General Pedro Antonio de Olañeta.[33] It is probable that in this same year he opened his contacts with Serrano, laying the plan for the overthrow of the Spanish authorities. But, something unexpected happened. Colombian troops, full of enthusiasm from their victories in the north, landed at Callao under the command of General Sucre. These troops dominated the whole coast. A contingent under General Andrés Santa Cruz, with General Agustín Gamarra as second in charge, took Arica and started its march east toward the Desaguadero River, the border between the two Perus. Sucre was advancing in central Peru. For the first time since the raid of Colonel Aráoz de la Madrid in 1817, six years earlier, an army was invading Upper Peru. Sucre, who never liked Santa Cruz, a Royalist officer who at the right time had changed allegiance, did not agree with his precipitous march into Charcas. Viceroy La Serna and General Valdés rushed south to check the invading army. General Olañeta marched north to meet the enemy. Santa Cruz and Gamarra were aided by the strong guerrilla force of Ayopaya under Lanza, and the invading army took La Paz on August 8, 1823. General Valdés presented battle at Zepita but was defeated by Santa Cruz. The revolutionary army marched south and was able to conquer Oruro, the mining city well inside Upper Peru.[34]

Casimiro Olañeta realized that a new element had entered the complex picture with the unexpected and seemingly successful invasion of Santa Cruz and Gamarra. He acted fast and committed outright treason in company with his colleague, Usín; he later boasted about it as proof of his Patriot leanings. He forwarded information about the Spanish army, with which his uncle had entrusted him, to Gamarra, the man he had betrayed a few years earlier.[35] Then suddenly, without having been defeated, Santa Cruz turned around and retreated with such speed that it became a complete rout, leaving behind important material and wounded soldiers. He went back to the Desaguadero River and crossed it with his disintegrated and demoralized army. Lanza was left abandoned, and on his dash back to his partisan republic he was intercepted and thoroughly defeated.

Why did Santa Cruz practically run for his life when not even beaten in battle? It remains an enigma, and the words of a United Provinces editor, "Who knows why?"[36] are still appropriate. Santa Cruz had probably been confident that the stagnant auxiliary army of Colonel Urdininea would move from Salta north into Charcas.[37] But this did not happen. The division of Urdininea was more on paper than in the barracks,[38] and the opposition of Buenos Aires made it difficult for Urdininea to take the road to Upper Peru. Besides, it is said that José Mariano Serrano was instrumental in pulling strings which put all kinds of obstacles in Urdininea's way in case he tried to march.[39] It is still not known whether this is true. But to Casimiro Olañeta and José Mariano Serrano the sudden appearance of a man hopeful of becoming a liberator, the *dos caras* soldier, Santa Cruz, was none too pleasing. Santa Cruz, with his slick personality, had moved into Charcas to foster his own political ambitions, undertaking a dangerous political campaign. General Sucre understood well the true nature of Santa Cruz' intention and he expressed it quite frankly to Bolívar.[40] The honest and straightforward Sucre was unhappy about this campaign.

Casimiro Olañeta saw that a threatening rival, with a personality somewhat similar to his, had appeared in the picture and he was afraid that Santa Cruz's campaign might be successful. Therefore, he wanted to make himself acceptable to the invading general. He supplied him with information about the Royalist army. It is possible that Casimiro Olañeta and Serrano realized well that Santa Cruz could not win without the opening of a second front from the United Provinces, to be undertaken by Colonel Urdininea. For years the Royalist authorities had lived with the nightmare that an invasion of Charcas from the north and south might take place simultaneously, catching them in the middle. If Urdininea marched, even with a reduced contingent, the victory of General Andrés Santa Cruz was certain and he—the mestizo from La Paz, a Royalist soldier who rose through the ranks and then became a Patriot because he was sure that the Spaniards would lose—would become the liberator of Charcas. From there Santa Cruz could liberate Lower Peru and become another, or even greater, Bolívar. Santa Cruz could not be permitted to win, and it may be assumed that Casimiro urgently requested Serrano to do everything possible to prevent Urdininea's moving. Then Santa Cruz's expedition, with already overextended lines and harassed by three able generals, including the viceroy, would be doomed. As a matter of fact, during the days when Urdininea should have departed he was put under arrest and sent to Tucumán to be court-martialed, because in a fight he had hurt slightly a subordinate Upper Peruvian officer, an offense that in those rough days was quite common and hardly a reason for court-martialing.[41] Apparently someone wanted to see Urdininea away from his division. And the man who wrote most vitriolicly against the Urdininea division, mobilizing public opinion against a new expedition into Upper Peru, was the editor of the *Correo de las Provincias* of Buenos Aires, Fortunato Lemoine, an Upper Peruvian emigrant from Chuquisaca.[42] It seems more than a coincidence that José Mariano Serrano was also an emigrant from Chuquisaca.

Santa Cruz was an able and intelligent soldier; he would not have turned around and run for his life, giving up a brilliant ambition, just for a trifle. But he realized that without support he could not win, and rather than be encircled he retreated hastily. Urdininea did not march, perhaps because of Argentine apathy, or more probably because of the shrewd intrigues of the Upper Peruvian schemers.

Another auxiliary expedition, this time from the north, had failed, and as a result had made an aspirant for the title of liberator look foolish. Furthermore, the Argentine failure to move, when victory or defeat depended on them, had once more shown that the United Provinces had abandoned their interior provinces, and public opinion in Charcas now became more belligerent toward Buenos Aires. To Casimiro Olañeta and his colleagues the prospects seemed brighter than ever. The game of *dos caras* had worked quite well, but this time it was really *tres caras*. Casimiro had stuck to his uncle as his confidential aide; at the same time he supplied the enemy, Santa Cruz, with military secrets. Yet behind the scenes he mobilized a shrewd intrigue which would see to it that Urdininea's army, the only hope of success for Santa Cruz, would not march, therefore obliging the Upper Peruvian general to abandon Charcas. The Santa Cruz interlude, which had nearly doomed the intriguer's ambitions, had been weathered successfully, and afterwards the sun looked brighter than ever. However, it had set back the timetable of the great intrigue.

General Olañeta had cooperated faithfully in the defense of Charcas, hindering the advance of Santa Cruz and Gamarra, yet inside himself he was still harboring hate for the viceroy and his officers; this feeling grew stronger and assumed distorted proportions. It all became a senseless obsession which took the aspect of a persecution complex. He came to despise the Spanish constitutional system even more, and believed that his beloved king had become a prisoner of the constitutional liberals in Spain. General Olañeta believed himself to be the only faithful servant of Ferdinand in the Perus. He later spoke of the "insults" of the liberals.[43] To him the viceroy, Valdés, and Canterac had become the enemies and jailers of the king. General Pedro Olañeta really suffered because he was sure that the king too suffered. At the same time he was sure that once Ferdinand had freed himself from the shackles of the constitution and its supporters he would make him, his companion in pain, the viceroy of Peru. This amalgamation of a true fanatic loyalty and his personal ambition made him believe that La Serna had held him back in his military advancement and rank, that his letters to Spain had been intercepted and censored, and that he was being isolated in Upper Peru. As he kept all these impressions to himself they increased, so that he finally thought that the liberal trio contemplated killing him.[44] It reached a very absurd stage when the general received a copy of the newspaper, *El Depositario* of Cuzco, in which its editor, Gaspar Rico, published a badly done anachronistic poem in which La Serna was being made the king of the Peruvian empire from "Tupiza to Tumbes."[45] Since the viceroy used this paper in Cuzco to publish his announcements, edicts, and official correspondence, Olañeta was convinced that La Serna and his associates wanted to separate the Perus from Spain and make the viceroy king of this new empire.[46]

These ideas were creations of Olañeta's troubled mind. Neither the affable viceroy nor the simple Valdés, who appreciated a good soldier, nursed any bad feelings against Olañeta who, odd as he was, was a useful man. The trio was completely unaware of the psychological problem of General Olañeta since he as yet had given no outward sign. Nor had La Serna any ambition or idea of becoming emperor of the Perus. Busy with his multiple duties and worries he had never even seen the unimportant poem. It was a joke by the editor who loved filthy words and later wrote another poem in which he buried Bolívar in human excrement.[47] General Pedro de Olañeta had become a truly psychopathic case, although he was still a good soldier. He was intensely worried about Spain's fate.

In the years 1822 and 1823 Spain was in the midst of a civil war between the Absolutists and the Constitutionalists. The enemies of the constitution had organized in the castle of Urgel "the supreme regency of Spain during the captivity of Ferdinand VII."[48] By his captivity they meant his surrender to the liberals. The Urgel rebels wanted to free the king from his forced capitulation to the *Cortes*. The ideas of the Urgel faction were identical with the hopes and aspirations of General Olañeta. Yet the general had not openly expressed his accumulated feelings of contempt for the constitutional trio of Peru, La Serna, Canterac, and Valdés, his direct superiors. Apparently he had entrusted his private thoughts to the only man whom he appreciated in his isolation, his brilliant young nephew, Casimiro. He had made him his personal secretary. Casimiro had lost no time and had provided a job in the Olañeta army for his friend, Urcullu, who became treasurer. He got Doctor Usín, another Machiavellist, a position too.[49] The general fell under the spell of his scheming nephew, whom he looked upon as a smart and well-prepared man with good manners. He thought that he, a rough soldier and ex-merchant, needed someone who had more intellectual maturity than he and that Casimiro filled this role.

Casimiro began to stimulate his uncle's hatred for the liberal trio more and more, with the hope of building it up to such a point that it would finally force the general to rebel and thus incite civil war within the Spanish army in the Perus. The stage had been set with the hope of pulling this coup in 1823. To incite the general to action, the schemers had carefully spaded the ground and falsified a letter supposedly written by the regency of Urgel, whose belief coincided with the general's, requesting him to abolish the constitution in Peru and then offering Olañeta the viceregal chair of Buenos Aires. The letter has never been located. The only one who ever cites it is Urcullu.[50] Casimiro Olañeta admitted that in the town of Yotala he had falsified a letter to his uncle, which was the incentive for the rebellion of the general.[51] But the invasion of Santa Cruz nearly spoiled their shrewd plan, and the intriguers hurriedly had to restrain the general from rebelling until Santa Cruz was defeated. Therefore, the Peruvian expedition retarded the Olañeta mutiny by about one year. The general became even more convinced that in order to serve his master better he had to abolish the constitution and obey the falsified mandates of the regency of Urgel. When one of his subordinate officers requested a better position from General Olañeta, he told him that he should have patience because in three months he, General Olañeta would be viceroy.[52] The conspirators had tricked the general and had led him unsuspecting into their trap.

That his young nephew had this diabolically clever plan of forcing his uncle to rebel, therefore hoping to bring doom to the Spanish cause, is well documented, but has passed quite unnoticed. Casimiro boasted about it.[53] He was hardly lying this time, except that he turned things around somewhat, trying to prove his unshaken enthusiasm, sincerity, and fidelity to the revolutionary cause. This was not the case. When his uncle's army entered La Paz victoriously in 1823, Casimiro, in an intimate conversation in the municipality, expressed with daring frankness that since the army of Santa Cruz was defeated, "we must now work to introduce disunity among the Spanish chiefs to make America happy." Then he added with more emphasis that "since the devil has taken the Santa Cruz expedition we must create anarchy and unrest in the army of the King."[54] Later, when Casimiro was on an obscure mission for his uncle in Buenos Aires and Montevideo, he boasted at a party, after having drunk heavily, that it had been necessary to create "the germs of discord." When asked why he was fighting with the absolutist faction, he answered that "it does not matter what different roads are taken, but the important thing is to reach the same destiny."[55] Strangely, he expressed these feelings freely before Royalists, who passed on the information to their superiors. But nobody took this talkative and boastful young man seriously. As one Royalist witness said later, he thought it was only "bragging without any substance."[56] Too late the viceroy realized that General Olañeta had fallen under the spell of his nephew. When there was no longer a chance for remedy, Valdés said that "this foolish Olañeta has become a victim of his nephew, Urcullu, Usín, and others."[57] By then the germ of disunity planted by Casimiro Olañeta had grown to catastrophic proportions, causing the collapse and defeat of the Spanish armies in the Perus, and with it the Spanish cause in America.

In the meanwhile armed action in Upper Peru had practically come to a standstill, with one exception. The commander of the Ayopaya republic, Miguel Lanza, had come out of his impregnable *republiqueta* to join forces with Santa Cruz. Although Lanza was a harsh individual he was never a *dos caras*. When Santa Cruz retreated to Lower Peru in haste, Lanza was left abandoned with the route back to his Ayopaya republic blocked. He then retreated from Oruro to Cochabamba, the most Patriot-minded town in Charcas. With the help of its inhabitants he took possession of the city. General Olañeta left La Paz and marched upon Cochabamba. He sent Casimiro to offer Lanza surrender terms; Lanza refused. He and his *cochabambino* supporters met General Olañeta on the plains of Falsuri, thirteen miles from the town. In a savage battle on October 16, 1823, the Spanish general defeated the genuine revolutionary army. Lanza and his routed guerrillas, in an astounding operation, were able to climb the sharp and abrupt mountains and enter their republic, thereby escaping capture. Patriot historians say that Olañeta behaved cruelly in conquered Cochabamba.[58] His nephew wrote, vainly as always, that it was only because of his influence that his uncle did not harm the Patriots.[59] The storm of 1823 had passed and Charcas was quiet again. General Olañeta left with his army for his headquarters in Oruro. General Valdés was preoccupied with the fight in Lower Peru. General Olañeta had been left to himself again as virtual ruler of Upper Peru. It was time to act; the great intrigue was about to materialize.

*Chapter 6*

## A HOUSE DIVIDED

*B*Y THE END OF 1823 THE SITUATION in the Perus looked more optimistic for the Royalists. The ambitious expedition of Santa Cruz had been stopped without any great battle. The near loss of Upper Peru had been avoided, and the movement of encirclement with Argentine aid had not materialized. General Sucre was forced to retreat far north. The revolutionaries in Peru had split into factions, with Simón Bolívar, José de la Riva Agüero, and José Bernardo Torre Tagle competing for supreme leadership. The Patriots had lost Lima and Callao was surrounded. This harbor constituted an enclave in Royalist territory. Everything seemed to indicate that the able Spanish trio of La Serna, Canterac, and Valdés, whose intimate friendship was valuable in avoiding petty rivalries, could win a decisive victory over the divided enemy. La Serna was ready to start an offensive, with the hope of pushing the enemy into Colombia.[1]

The army of the north under Canterac, with its headquarters in Huancayo, had eight thousand troops. The viceroy in Cuzco had one thousand soldiers under his direct command to guard the temporary viceregal capital. General Valdés in Arequipa, as commander of the army of the south, had three thousand men under his personal order, watching southern Peru. General Olañeta commanded four thousand men with whom he maintained the Spanish hegemony over Upper Peru. His center was in Oruro. Theoretically, he was part of the army of the south and was responsible to Valdés in Arequipa, but because of the isolation of Charcas he acted quite independently. It had been decided that once the rains came to an end, in April or May, the great push against the revolutionary army in northern Peru could start. Canterac was to lead the march with his army, but Valdés with his three thousand men would be transferred north to augment the army of Canterac. Olañeta would move north, too, and take his position along the Desaguadero River, the border between the Perus. There he would remain and watch southern Lower Peru and Upper Peru in case the enemy wanted to land behind Spanish lines. Olañeta would become the vital vanguard of the Royalist army. The whole plan was a shift of all three army units north. A preliminary offensive would take Callao.[2] The plan was good and success was very possible. Everything depended on good discipline and strict obedience on the part of the three units, plus perfect coordination. But in the very last days of 1823 something unexpected happened that shattered the Royalist design and opened the door for a push south by Bolívar.

Five days before New Year's General Olañeta, with his army, munitions, stores, and money, evacuated Oruro and instead of marching north, turned south. From Challapata he wrote the viceroy that he was moving to Chichas because of the danger of an Argentine invasion. He then continued to Potosí and entered that city on January 4, 1824. Its commander, General José Santos de la Hera, was just ready to dispatch some troops to reinforce the Spanish army in Lower Peru. General Olañeta ordered the contingent not to go. He then demanded that La Hera go with him to Chuquisaca to depose the president of the audiencia, General Rafael Maroto, a man whom Olañeta disliked and feared. La Hera refused to follow Olañeta's mutiny and a fight ensued between his small contingent and the army of Olañeta. The commander of Potosí, in view of Olañeta's superiority, had to surrender and was told to leave Upper Peru.[3]

After his victory in Potosí General Olañeta wrote a stinging letter to the president of the audiencia, General Maroto, requesting him to resign and depart from Upper Peru. Maroto wanted to negotiate.[4] Olañeta gave no answer and decided to advance with his army to Chuquisaca to force the president to leave. Before he left Potosí General Olañeta issued a proclamation to the people of the Perus, in which, for the first time, he announced publicly his intentions and reasons for rebellion and separation from the viceroy. He said to the people that he had been educated in the

Catholic religion and that he had been taught alway to obey the king and to remain faithful to him no matter what happened. He was a man of truth and liked frankness. Therefore he could no longer tolerate the vicious innovations that ill-minded people had introduced in their beloved nation. These elements had "spilled all the poison of their false philosophy" and by doing so had insulted religion and the king, which were "the most sacred objects." But fortunately he was going to eliminate those "partisans of the destructive system." He assured the people that those enemies would nevermore govern, and that his soldiers and he, General Olañeta, would work with great enthusiasm for the rights of religion and the crown. He would fight for them and he requested the people to support him in this task.[5]

Soon General Olañeta and the bulk of his army left for the capital. General Maroto abandoned the town in haste and fled north.[6] On February 11, 1824, the rebel general entered Chuquisaca in an impressive parade. He was received with flowers, perfumes, and hails for his army. The patricians of the town, who considered the Olañeta family as one of them, received the rebel general enthusiastically. At night a gala ball attended by all society was held in honor of General Olañeta.[7] The next day he proclaimed the new rules and laws of his government. Introducing the edicts, Olañeta stated that since the constitutional monarchy had been proclaimed he "had in secret shed tears" because of its fatal consequences. But he had been "chosen by Heaven" to correct this. He was willing to die together with his army for the cause of God and king. He wished only one thing of the people: that they obey strictly the new absolutist government. Therefore he was proclaiming five edicts and demanded absolute compliance. The constitution was abolished and the government would be as it had been in 1819, an absolute monarchy. All democratically elected officials would lose their posts with the exception of the cabildo. Any written or oral expression in favor of the constitution was to be considered subversive. All files of the recently abolished constitutional government were to be handed over to the audiencia. Everyone who had been a partisan of the absolutist regime would regain his position if he had lost one, and should receive indemnity. This edict was written by the two schemers, Casimiro Olañeta — who wrote all the edicts and correspondence of his uncle — and Manuel María Urcullu. Olañeta countersigned it.[8]

The general then proceeded to appoint his own supporters to the vital administrative jobs. His close relative, Colonel Guillermo Marquiegui, was named president of Charcas. Urcullu, Mariano Callejo, and José Santos Cavero, three members of the *dos caras* lodge, were named judges of the audiencia. Father Emilio Rodríguez was named chaplain of the rebellious army. Casimiro Olañeta became personal secretary to the general, a post he had held unofficially for more than a year. One of the general's brothers, Gaspar Olañeta, was appointed governor of Tarija. The rough General Aguilera, who operated in the open and isolated territory of east Charcas, joined the absolutist rebellion. Once his government was solidified, General Olañeta returned with his army to Potosí, and on February 21 issued the same edict of government there which he had proclaimed in the capital, adding two more articles to it. He forbade strictly any talk against the Roman Catholic religion and swore to punish those who did not comply with their religious duties. He decreed that on February 22 a High Mass with a *Te Deum* be celebrated in the principal church of Potosí, at which thanks should be given for the abolition of the constitution and the restoration of the absolutist government. All government employees and principal citizens were ordered to attend the event. In addition, all churches were to be illuminated for three days as a token of enthusiasm for the new order. Identical celebrations should take place in the other towns of Charcas.[9] The *dos caras* had won the first round and the secession of General Olañeta from the viceregal authority had been achieved. The "government of General Olañeta"[10] had started. It lasted fifteen months and constituted the prelude to the creation of Bolivia.

Meanwhile, news of the strange actions of General Olañeta had reached Lower Peru and the viceroy and his two able generals felt mystified.[11] General Olañeta had given two vague reasons for his march south. He had talked about the imminent danger of an Argentine invasion. This the general supported with supposed confidential information received from his spies in northern Argentina.[12] The viceroy found this news difficult to believe, since the Urdininea division had not moved during the critical period, and since there was even less reason for it to march at this time. Moreover, La Serna had sent a representative, General Baldomero Espartero, and a qualified assistant to Salta to negotiate a permanent truce with the northern provinces of Argentina. This mission had been well received; in addition, the mission had discovered that the information that Olañeta had got from his confidential agents, telling him that an Argentine offensive was near, had been falsified. It is probable that José Mariano Serrano and his associates had written the letter with this confidential information, with the same intention as the fraudulent letter from the regency of Urgel. Besides, Espartero and his secretary, José Domingo de Vidart, a Royalist native of Salta, had seen that the Urdininea division was in no position to undertake an offensive because of its small size and poor organization. They had not seen a single soldier between Humahuaca, a village near the border between the inner and lower provinces, and Salta.[13] For these reasons the viceroy was quite sure that Olañeta's indication of danger from the United Provinces was false. General Olañeta's second complaint was a protest against General Maroto, president of the Audiencia in Chuquisaca.[14] The trio, La Serna, Canterac, and Valdés, came to believe that Olañeta had engaged in his revolutionary action because he had disliked and feared General Maroto. La Serna was as yet unaware of the real nature of General Olañeta's rebellion and thought that petty rivalry was the cause. He decided to use tact and moderation, for he needed the army of Olañeta. It was agreed to send General Valdés into Charcas to meet General Olañeta and settle the differences amicably.[15] Valdés was delayed somewhat because of illness, but on February 17 he opened correspondence from Puno, with the rebel general, advising him to put aside personal quarrels and ambitions and consider the damage that anarchy in the Spanish army would produce. He requested the general to meet with him. A flow of letters between the two took place, with Valdés using restraint and reason, and Olañeta writing in very ambiguous terms, expressing some of his long-accumulated passions.[16] On February 26 the mutinous general proposed seven points which he deemed necessary for an understanding.

He insisted that the constitution be abolished in both Perus. General Olañeta then demanded that he be made commander of all the provinces of Río de la Plata and that he be responsible to the viceroy in Lima only in regard to political matters. In return he offered to support the Spanish army in Lower Peru with a minimum of four thousand men in its fight against Bolívar. All promotions of military and administrative personnel which he had decreed should remain valid. Once he agreed to these demands,

General Valdés could under no circumstances remain in Charcas but must retreat to Lower Peru. General Olañeta terminated his letter of demands by stating that he would send his private secretary, Casimiro Olañeta, to settle some minor details.[17] In summary, Casimiro Olañeta, who inspired and wrote all these communications of his uncle, demanded independence for the general. Since the general wanted the command of all the Viceroyalty of Río de la Plata, the Olañetas probably had the ambition of conquering the government of the free provinces from Charcas. This might be an explanation of why the general was appointed, in the fraudulent Urgel letter, viceroy of Buenos Aires, rather than of Lima. The youthful Casimiro Olañeta in his moment of success was even considering that Charcas was too small for his ambitions, and had begun to think in terms of the old Viceroyalty of Río de la Plata. So in Upper Peru another ambitious, provincial *caudillo* was in search of power in the United Provinces. Buenos Aires rightly feared the liberation of the inner provinces, which would only add more territory, power, and *caudillos* to the provincial forces and therefore prolong the vicious anarchy. Later Casimiro Olañeta acquired more maturity and adjusted his aspirations to his prospects of success. He came to limit his ambitions to Charcas.

On February 28 the general wrote another letter to Valdés in which, among other things, he told him that he had received with great rejoicing the good news that the Spanish armies had recaptured the port of Callao. He informed Valdés that he had ordered the celebration of a High Mass with a *Te Deum,* and the illumination of Potosí, to give thanks and express a general public enthusiasm for such a splendid victory of the armies of the king.[18] Olañeta well realized that with the capture of Callao the viceroy was more anxious than ever to come to a quick settlement with him, in order to move north and meet Bolívar. The day after the general wrote of his joy concerning the victory at Callao, General Valdés ordered the abolition of the constitution in the jurisdiction of the army of the south.[19] Valdés probably wished to undercut Olañeta since the general had used the constitution as the main pretext for his disagreement with the commanding trio. Valdés then continued to advance, always writing to the general with extreme moderation and tact. In Venta Media he met with Casimiro Olañeta and gave the young man his counterproposals. He would not agree to making the general independent and insisted that the line of authority must be as it had existed before Olañeta's secession. Olañeta would be military commander of Upper Peru, responsible to the commander of the army of the south and the viceroy. General Valdés would have the right to dispose of Olañeta's troops as he deemed necessary. Olañeta's appointments would be respected and General Maroto would not be returned as president of Charcas. Casimiro took the proposed terms with him to show them to his uncle and to study them. Still the rebel general refused to meet Valdés; he was trying to gain time, since he knew that time was in his favor. Valdés was in a hurry to come to a settlement as he continued to advance toward Potosí, Olañeta's headquarters and stronghold. Olañeta was unwilling to fight the approaching army.

But Valdés had come to realize that he did not possess superior and advantageous striking power. General Aguilera was ready to march on Cochabamba and thereby dangerously outflank him.[20] Valdés and the Olañetas met in the small village of Tarapaya, about fifteen miles from Potosí. Although General Olañeta had tried to avoid seeing Valdés, the close proximity of the invading army to Potosí had forced him to change his mind and accept Valdés' offer to talk things over personally. The rebel general was accompanied by his nephew. Some sharp negotiations took place, each side holding some good cards. Valdés was in a rush to come to an honorable settlement and depart north to join the army of Canterac. He was unwilling to lose time in a war between the two Spanish armies, and besides, he had daringly overextended his lines. The Olañetas knew all this very well. However, they felt unprepared to take up arms against Valdés, who was the ablest Spanish general in America. Moreover, Valdés' army was in combat formation on the very outskirts of Potosí. But the rebel general held the trump. He could sign away whatever advantages he had won in his secession as long as Valdés agreed to leave him and his army in Charcas, and would himself leave for the north. Once Valdés withdrew, the Olañetas could do again whatever they pleased. The final advantage lay with them.

On March 9, 1824, the two commanders signed an agreement known as the treaty of Tarapaya. General Olañeta would not be called upon to account for his secession. He would remain military commander of Upper Peru but responsible to General Valdés as commander of the army of the south. The final authority would be the viceroy. General Olañeta was required to furnish whatever

aid was needed in Lower Peru. Olañeta was not allowed to increase
the size of his army beyond the agreed maximum strength. General
Maroto would not be returned as president of Charcas and General
Aguilera was named in his place. Olañeta's appointments and promotions would remain valid. General La Hera would not be
reappointed as military commander of Potosí.[21] To show his good
faith Valdés, as soon as the treaty was signed, had his army turn
around and retreat with speed to Oruro, ordering his cavalry to
continue without interruption to Arequipa.[22]

From Oruro Valdés wrote a detailed letter to the viceroy, enclosing the Tarapaya agreement for his approval. Valdés stated
frankly that he was not pleased at all with his diplomatic achieve-
ment, but that because of the over-all circumstances it was the
best he could get. He felt that granting the command of extensive
Charcas to Olañeta was giving him too much power, and in view
of his unpleasant behavior it constituted approval of outright
insubordination. Valdés had learned that Olañeta and Aguilera
would have dispersed their forces to maintain active guerrilla
warfare in case no agreement would have been reached. And
Valdés believed that because of this plan "it would have been very
difficult to fight Olañeta," it would have required a large army and
much time. If he had decided to open war on Olañeta, the general
asked, ". . . and Bolívar would attack, with what troops would
we fight him?" Valdés reminded the viceroy that because of the
victory at Callao it was "necessary to *throw north* every possible
force."[23] The same day Valdés wrote a letter to Canterac, also
sending him the treaty plus a copy of his letter to their mutual
friend, the viceroy. To the commander of the army of the north
Valdés expressed identical opinions, adding that he had agreed to
the Tarapaya treaty only because he wanted to join him as soon
as possible in their march on Bolívar.[24] Valdés knew very well that
all depended on the good faith of Olañeta and evidently he decided
to take a chance. In General Olañeta's hands lay the fate of the
Spanish cause in the Perus, and the unscrupulous Casimiro Olañeta
was only too eager to take advantage of this situation.

With the remaining infantry units General Valdés decided on
a bold move from Oruro before returning north. He made up his
mind to march into the impregnable Ayopaya republic and defeat
the guerrilla Lanza who had recuperated from his narrow escape
at Falsuri and had again become aggressive. Lanza was diligently

taking advantage of the dissension in the Spanish army and had made some intrepid incursions around La Paz. Valdés, with a crack unit, climbed the rough mountains, narrow passes, and small valleys in search of the guerrilla commander. At Palca he surprised the partisan fighter and took him prisoner. It was the first time that this *republiqueta* had suffered a severe defeat in its own territory. General Valdés treated Lanza with great dignity and honor, acknowledging him as a brave enemy. This was quite in contrast with the behavior of General Aguilera in 1816, when this savage Spanish officer defeated the great guerrillas Padilla and Warnes and beheaded them, and exposed their heads in public.[25] The dignified treatment of Lanza by Valdés showed the honorable nature of this general. Later, General Sucre was very anxious to meet General Valdés to express personally his admiration and respect he felt for this enemy commander. Apparently Lanza took advantage of the general's generous treatment and immediately escaped to his mountain refuge.[26] Valdés' short campaign into Ayopaya had been so strenuous that the general collapsed with a severe illness upon his return. It became doubtful whether he would survive, and this naturally retarded his return to Upper Peru.

From the moment Valdés had left for Lower Peru General Olañeta began to ignore completely the stipulations of the Tarapaya treaty. He never fulfilled his verbal pledge to issue a public proclamation in which he would announce his reunion with the viceroy. He refused to submit to the army of the south and never dispatched to its headquarters correspondence, copies of his files, accounting reports, statistics of his units, or other matters which were part of the administrative routine. He kept his brother-in-law, Colonel Marquiegui, as president of Charcas, thereby assuming the political administration of Upper Peru. He ordered all provincial authorities and other employees to deal with him, General Olañeta, directly, instead of with the viceregal capital. On his stationery he used the letterhead "Commander of the Provinces of Río de la Plata." He moved his troops as he pleased and increased the strength of his units in complete disregard of article seven of the Tarapaya agreement. When requested to send troops to Lower Peru for defensive and offensive maneuvers, he only gave evasive answers and never sent the men.[27] One author states that he opened contact with most of the guerrilla units, requesting their allegiance.[28] The most perplexing of all moves was the departure of Casimiro Olañeta, as soon as the treaty of Tarapaya was approved, to the free provinces. Casimiro went to Buenos Aires and Montevideo on a secret mission, the motives for which remain unexplained.

Valdés and La Serna still hoped to bring Olañeta back into the ranks, although more and more they realized that he was being influenced by some outside elements. They needed him. General Valdés used every imaginable means to convince and influence the stubborn rebel general. He applied the same efforts in regard to General Aguilera. The proposed spring offensive had been postponed because of Olañeta's secession. Valdés asked the bishop of La Paz and high eccclsiastical officials in Chuquisaca to intervene and convince Olañeta that he was bringing doom to the Spanish cause. He thought that because of the general's deep Catholic feeling this might be of avail. General Olañeta ignored every effort.[29]

When Casimiro Olañcta had departed for Argentina he had left Urcullu and Usín with the general with strict instructions to maintain the rebellion at all costs. Casimiro later wrote that these two men worked very hard in fulfilling his orders.[30] By June, 1824, the viceroy and General Valdés realized the complete futility of further attempts at appeasement and decided to act sternly. This they should have done in January, when the secession had started. Then it might have saved the Spanish cause in the Perus, but June was far too late. Before undertaking any drastic steps against the rebel general the viceroy consulted the attorney of the audiencia and the advisory attorney to the viceregal office. Both concurred with the viceroy.

On June 4 Viceroy La Serna issued an ultimatum to General Olañeta. He offered the rebel general two choices. Either he could appear before him at Cuzco and be judged for a court-martial together with General Maroto and General La Hera, whom Olañeta had accused of disobeying him, or if General Olañeta preferred, he could leave for Spain to present his case to the King. La Serna gave Olañeta three days to make up his mind as to which of the two procedures he would accept. If the general wished to go to Spain he could take whatever officer or administrative official he wished with him to support his case. The viceroy would use every possible means to facilitate their voyage to Spain. Olañeta was given eight days to leave Potosí for Cuzco or Spain. He was to

hand over the army of Upper Peru to General Valdés or to whomever Valdés would appoint for the transfer. He assured him that
all officers and soldiers of the Olañeta army would retain their
rank, and their services to Olañeta would not be held against them.
The viceroy gave his personal word that Olañeta's family would be
protected and that nothing would happen to them. In the event
Olañeta refused to obey this ultimatum, the viceroy would feel it
necessary to order the commander of the army of the south, General
Jerónimo Valdés, to use his forces to arrest the rebel general.[31]

The viceroy appointed the intendant of Puno, Tadeo Garate,
a man of absolutist leanings and of personal influence with the
king, but an obedient public servant,[32] to implement the ultimatum
and render legal advice to Olañeta. On June 14 General Valdés
forwarded the ultimatum from Oruro along with a personal letter
of his own in which he enumerated the disobediences of Olañeta
since the Tarapaya agreement in polite terms. He terminated his
letter by saying that "you should remember that you are a Spaniard
. . . and that the only blood that should be shed must be in
defense of the King and the nation. This is my wish and it should
be yours, too."[33]

General Olañeta, who naturally refused to obey the ultimatum
of La Serna, gave his answer in a detailed letter. He stated that
La Serna was not the legitimate viceroy and that he recognized
only the King of Spain as his immediate superior. The general
said that he was enclosing two copies, one for Valdés and one
for La Serna, of a proclamation to the people of the Perus which
he had issued the same day. This long manifesto was written
by Manuel María Urcullu in the absence of Casimiro Olañeta.[34]
The proclamation is a detailed account of the rebel general's antagonism toward the commanding trio. He again emphasized his
fanatic absolutist and religious feelings and his hate for the
"representative system because it always has led the people to a
frightful abyss of crime and misfortune." He insisted that the
viceroy and his commanding generals belonged to the party which
wished confusion and wanted to "destroy all principles of morality
and honor."[35] The general disputed the legality of La Serna's
occupying the viceregal chair because he had usurped this post
from General Pezuela. After having become rulers of the Perus
the revolutionary Spanish generals had wanted to eliminate him,
General Olañeta, at all costs, for he had remained faithful to the

absolutist king and had been a friend of Pezuela's. The general
stated that he had signed the treaty of Tarapaya in good faith but
that General Valdés had ignored its stipulations. The viceroy had
named people who supported him to army and governmental positions, instead of consulting with General Olañeta about these
appointments. Furthermore, the Constitutionalists had requested
that Olañeta send troops which amounted to half of his army to
fight Bolívar. The real purpose of this order had not been to
strengthen their army but to debilitate his units.

Olañeta accused Valdés of opening a campaign on the guerrilla
Lanza for the sole reason of remaining in northern Charcas territory,
which was supposed to be under Olañeta's command. General
Valdés had concentrated his army in Oruro to check him. He even
went so far as to accuse bluntly the commander of the army of
the south of having offered twenty thousand pesos for his death.
The mutinous general of Charcas ended his long manifesto by
saying that he had decided to die for the king and the Catholic
religion rather than submit and accept the plans of the traitorous
and usurped government of La Serna and his aides. He assured
the people that he would fight if the Constitutionalists opened war
on him. General Olañeta was well aware that this was his declaration of war. The struggle between the Spanish armies in Charcas
had started, a combat that passed into the pages of history as the
"Separatist War"; the Argentine newspaper, *El Argos,* called it
"the battle between the liberals and serviles of Spain in Upper
Peru."[36] This fratricidal struggle was the direct cause for the
emergence of Charcas as an independent country.[37]

Six days after this manifesto, on June 26, 1824, General Olañeta
issued two more proclamations which showed that he had accepted
the fact that war had broken out between his Secessionist army
and the army of the south. He published a proclamation to his
own officers and soldiers. The general congratulated them for
having given him their unqualified support up to that point. He
assured his army that he had done everything possible to avoid
war, but that the other side had not shown good faith. Since it
had been decided "to fight for the sacred cause of King, religion,
and humanity," he requested them always to try to persuade their
brothers on the opposite side to join in their struggle for the glory
of the king. At the same time he issued a call to the officers and
soldiers of the army of Valdés. He asked them to leave their

army because they were fighting for a general and viceroy animated by personal ambitions. He asked them to come and join
his army, which was waging a sacred fight for "the sweet and
paternal government of the King."[38] By addressing the soldiers of
Valdés and tempting them to desert the army of the south, General
Olañeta had closed the door completely to a last-minute understanding. The war had started.

General Valdés had approximately five thousand men to battle
the Secessionists, with some good mountain artillery. It was neither
a superior army nor was it deficient. General Olañeta had one
thousand men less but he had a crack unit, mostly Upper Peruvians
who were accustomed to the difficult climate and terrain.[39] The
general was a rough soldier who insisted on stern discipline and
hard work. Among his officers he had two of the toughest men in
the whole Spanish army: the bloody and intrepid General Aguilera,
and Colonel José María Valdez, better known as Barbarucho, the
Barbarous. The latter's savage courage was proverbial. In 1821
he and some of his soldiers had worked their way into Salta
through impassable roads and had killed the great Argentine
*montonero* leader, Güemes. Such officers as Francisco López and
Carlos Medinaceli were of great sagacity and later were among
the founders of the Bolivian army.[40] Indeed the absolutist Secessionist army became the nucleus upon which the army of the new
republic was built. This Royalist background must be considered
when evaluating the Bolivian army, which became the force of
power and misfortune in Bolivian history. López and Medinaceli
shifted allegiance to Sucre's army in the last weeks of the War of
Independence. Olañeta had a better and tougher army, but Valdés'
was larger and better equipped. Olañeta was a good fighter but his
troops feared him. Valdés was more prepared in the military
sciences and his soldiers loved him. Considering all these factors,
the armies were equally balanced.

Valdés was with his army in Oruro. Olañeta was situated
with some of his units in Potosí. The bulk of his army, under
Colonels Marquiegui and Valdez (Barbarucho), was stationed in
Chuquisaca. General Aguilera had moved slowly from Santa Cruz
toward Cochabamba but without occupying it. General Valdés
left Oruro with his army in late June, 1824, toward Vilcapugio.
Here he was informed that the Olañeta army was split between
Potosí and Chuquisaca. Therefore the advancing general decided

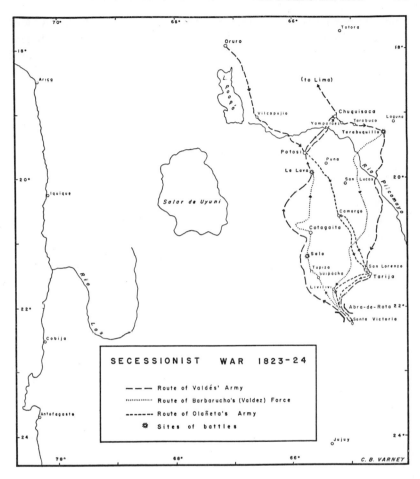

SECESSIONIST    WAR    1823-24

— — —   Route of Valdés' Army

................   Route of Barbarucho's (Valdez) Force

— — — —   Route of Olañeta's    Army

✳   Sites   of   battles

C. B. VARNEY

to change his route and, instead of marching straight on Potosí, to go through the Chayanta province and cut in between the two towns, thereby separating the Secessionist units. This was an effective move because General Olañeta realized that he was being outflanked and that his army was in danger of being cut in two. He evacuated Potosí and retreated toward Tarija by the way of Cinti. As all the retreating armies from Potosí had done before, he, too, took with him the accumulated riches of the Casa de Moneda and the silver banks. In addition, he seriously damaged the mint.[41] Colonel Marquiegui and Barbarucho (Valdez) followed Olañeta's move and left Chuquisaca, taking the road toward Laguna where General Aguilera had concentrated a unit. General Valdés occupied Chuquisaca and dispatched his second in command, General José Carratalá, to occupy Potosí. The Constitutionalist general was received by the inhabitants with the usual routine. The old days of the auxiliary invasions had returned to the Imperial City: armies entered gloriously and left in defeat. This time it was the Constitutional army and the Absolutist forces instead of the auxiliaries and the Royalists.

General Valdés named a new president of the audiencia, General Antonio Vigil, and appointed new personnel at the audiencia. On July 11, 1824, after three days in Chuquisaca, General Valdés left the capital in pursuit of Barbarucho, with a force of about one hundred men. General Valdés advanced with tremendous speed and on July 12 he saw the vanguard of Colonel Valdez at a place called Tarabuquillo. General Valdés decided on a daring move. He ordered his army to halt and then he, one aide-de-camp, and two volunteers[42] galloped toward the enemy's rear guard and shouted to them to halt. Valdés then addressed the Secessionist soldiers and asked them to do everything possible to stop this war among brothers. The general's unprecedented courage had an astounding effect, and the whole battalion constituting the rear and twenty-five other soldiers gave in and were ready to follow General Valdés. Barbarucho, who had been at the head of his retreating column, was informed of what was happening, and rushed back with his nearby soldiers and opened fire on Valdés. The horse of General Valdés and that of his aide collapsed. The two volunteers were wounded. When Barbarucho had commanded his soldiers to fire they had obeyed him because they feared the rough colonel, but they also loved their old commanding general and therefore they had all spontaneously pointed their guns at the horses instead of at Valdés. Not one single soldier of Barbarucho had thought in that split second of shooting the general. He and his aide and volunteers ran back to their lines and the general, furious at the outrageous act, ordered a general attack. A fierce battle ensued and lasted from noon until darkness, when Barbarucho, whose unit was starting to disintegrate under the heavy firing power of the Constitutionalists, slipped into the dark of the night and took to the hills.[43] Barbarucho had suffered heavy casualties and Valdés had lost quite a few men, too.[44]

Valdés then advanced southward, crossing rough mountain

terrain and dangerous rivers. At Laguna he met an Aguilera unit commanded by Colonel Ignacio Rivas who, with his soldiers and officers, abandoned the Secessionist side and joined the army of General Valdés.[45] The general, aware of the dubious character of Aguilera, decided to open negotiations with him by correspondence, with the intent of convincing him to stay aloof from the war. As Aguilera was undecided as to who would win this battle between the Spanish armies he accepted the bid to remain inactive.[46] He intended to await the final outcome. In his march south General Valdés was unable to locate Barbarucho, who had disappeared with his remaining army after his escape from the battlefield of Tarabuquillo.

The Constitutionalist general, José de Carratalá, had remained with his small unit in Potosí. Then, on July 14, at seven o'clock in the morning, while Carratalá was sleeping in his room at the Casa de Moneda, a commando unit led by Colonel Marquiegui and Colonel Pedro Arraya, a renegade guerrilla leader, made its way to Potosí. Arraya worked his way into the room of Carratalá unnoticed and forced him, in his pajamas, to come with him. He was taken out of Potosí as a prisoner of the Secessionists. It was a bold raid. When Carratalá's soldiers saw that their commander had disappeared, they dispersed and left for Oruro.[47] Marquiegui and Arraya took Carratalá to San Lorenzo, near Tarija, and handed him over to Eustaquio Méndez, another famous guerrilla, who espoused the cause promising the greatest benefit[48] and at the time was fighting for Olañeta. Apparently many of the guerrillas who had survived the 1816 campaign had become as *dos caras* as many *doctores* and Royalist officers—Lanza being an exception. Barbarucho, who had evaded General Valdés successfully, had decided to turn north and make an attack on Potosí. He reached the town on July 18, but to his surprise found it without Loyalist troops. He then realized, or was informed, that his colleagues, Marquiegui and Arraya, had already achieved what he intended to do. He took advantage of the situation and entered the Imperial City, raided it, and then the next day departed for the south again.[49]

General Valdés, unaware of what had happened in Potosí, continued his advance south in the direction of Tarija, where he believed Olañeta to be. On July 26 he reached San Lorenzo and to his great surprise found Eustaquio Méndez, who now had turned enemy, holding as prisoner Valdés' highest officer, Carratalá, who the general thought was in Potosí. Méndez had no desire to fight Valdés and he switched sides again, joining the Valdés army and turning Carratalá, whom his fellow ex-guerrilla, Arraya, had entrusted to him, over to the general.[50] The Constitutionalist commander continued his advance and occupied Tarija without incident.

General Olañeta had retreated toward a little place called Libilibi, not far from today's border between Bolivia and Argentina. Here he was joined by Marquiegui and Barbarucho.[51] In the absence of active participation by the Aguilera unit, the reunion of the Secessionist forces at Libilibi constituted their whole army. From Tarija General Valdés dispatched the freed Carratalá with over five hundred troops, wounded soldiers, and heavy equipment, back to Potosí in order to reoccupy and hold this vital fortress.[52] Valdés himself decided to advance with the rest of his unit in pursuit of Olañeta and force him to engage in battle. The Secessionist army abandoned Libilibi and retreated farther south. Valdés overtook them at a place called Abra Rota.[53] It was August 1, 1824, and it was getting dark. Valdés decided to wait until morning to battle the enemy. During the dark of the night General Olañeta decided on an escape. He split up his army, ordering each unit to take a different road. He sent Colonel Marquiegui and his brother, Gaspar Olañeta, with the heavy equipment and luggage to march farther south toward the free provinces. Barbarucho was ordered to go north to Suipacha and, if possible, to Potosí; Carlos Medinaceli was to go to Cotagaita, the great fortress protecting Charcas from the south; and Colonel Francisco Ostria was to go to Cinti to stir up the dense population in this vineyard region. General Olañeta himself would march back to Tarija.[54] It was Olañeta's plan, as Valdés had warned the viceroy earlier, to fight a sort of guerrilla warfare. All units slipped out undetected. When morning arrived, the surprised General Valdés realized that the enemy had left. He spent some bad hours trying to figure out the tracks of the horses and the footprints; they were all over and led in all directions. He finally detected the different routes the enemy had taken. Valdés decided to follow the route of the most abundant and marked tracks, which led south, thinking that they belonged to Olañeta himself. This was a mistake because he had pursued the Marquiegui contingent. On August 5, 1824, at Santa Victoria, Valdés reached the column of Marquiegui and Gaspar Olañeta, which was moving very slowly because of the heavy equipment.

The Secessionists surrendered without a fight. Valdés treated his prisoners with friendliness and great tact, as was his custom.[55] The Loyalist general then turned around and took the road north.

August 5, 1824, the day on which Valdés achieved his victory at Santa Victoria, was a day filled with misfortune for the Constitutionalist army. This same August 5, General Olañeta surprised Tarija and reoccupied it, taking prisoner the garrison left behind by Valdés. On the very same day Barbarucho too achieved a great victory. In his march north he had learned that Valdés had sent Carratalá back to Potosí with a great contingent of Loyalist soldiers, and he decided to surprise them. On that night Carratalá had halted at a place called Salo, or Chacapa.[56] He was unaware of the danger and thought that the Olañeta army was far away to the south. Carratalá and his unit had put their rifles away and had let the horses graze while they were preparing to rest. Suddenly, Barbarucho and his soldiers, with loud screaming resembling an Indian ambush, fell upon the surprised Constitutionalists. It was all over in a matter of seconds and no one had time to run for his rifle. In one stroke the Carratalá contingent had been captured along with its heavy equipment and some valuable armaments. General Carratalá had had the bad luck of falling twice into the enemy's hands without having had the opportunity to fight on either occasion.[57] But that was not all; the Loyalists suffered other reverses on that fateful August 5. General Aguilera had made a move to throw his army into the fight on the side of Olañeta. He broke off negotiations and moved west, taking the wealthy agricultural town of Totora, where he took prisoner the small Constitutionalist garrison. From there he dispatched Colonel Francisco López to Laguna to capture the unit of Colonel Rivas, who had deserted to General Valdés. On August 5 López surprised Rivas and his army and took all of them prisoners. Rivas was sent to Aguilera, who put him immediately before a firing squad, together with two associates.[58] In all it was a very good day for the Secessionists, only somewhat spoiled by Valdés capture of Marquiegui and Gaspar Olañeta and their soldiers.

On this same August 5, so eventful in the Separatist War in Upper Peru, about one thousand miles north of the Charcas battlefield, two armies were camping close to each other, unaware that on the next day, August 6, 1824, they would clash ferociously. It was the army of General Simón Bolívar and the Spanish army of the north under General Canterac. August 6, 1824, was the day of the great battle of Junín which brought defeat to the Spanish power in Lower Peru. It was the day on which General Valdés and his army of the south were supposed to have been north with Canterac. Bolívar would not have dared to attack the united Spanish army. On August 5 when General Olañeta was winning many victories with his Secessionists, he did not know that many miles north of his position in Tarija the fateful result of his wrongdoing would be a matter of hours. And more than one thousand miles south, in Buenos Aires, over two thousand miles from the battlefield of Junín, was Casimiro Olañeta, scheming as ever.[59] His great intrigue to bring defeat to the Spanish armies by introducing rebellion in their midst was being fulfilled on this August 6. But in those days communications were slow, and no one knew for some time afterwards what had happened on those two days in August. General Valdés was happy about his capture of Marquiegui; General Olañeta was happy about his capture of Tarija; Barbarucho was happy about his capture of Carratalá; General López was happy about his capture of Rivas. Far away north, General Canterac was confused about the position of Bolívar; General Bolívar was wondering whether to attack Canterac. Far away south Casimiro Olañeta was having a good time in Buenos Aires. All were unaware that the climax was at hand.

General Valdés was soon informed of the various misfortunes of his Loyalist army in Charcas, although the news of Junín had yet to arrive. The bad news was exaggerated by some misinformation about the movement of Aguilera, who, it was said, had taken Chuquisaca and was throwing the bulk of his great unit into the fight, advancing with the purpose of capturing Potosí and Oruro. This was not true. Aguilera was still hesitating and had stopped about ten miles from the capital, again taking a wait-and-see attitude. But Valdés' situation was quite grave. He was isolated with his army far south, while the Secessionists occupied the road north, including the strong fortress of Cotagaita. This citadel blocked any advance to Potosí. The Loyalist general decided to take a chance and try to break through to the Imperial City. He outflanked Tarija to his left and then swung back east, advancing straight toward Cotagaita, occupied by Barbarucho. The Secessionist colonel, Medinaceli, was close by in Suipacha.

At Cotagaita Valdés decided on a desperate plan. He com-

manded General La Hera to maintain Barbarucho in check by
making a flanking movement which would look as if La Hera
wanted to surround Cotagaita. In the meantime Valdés, with the
bulk of his army, would move to the left into the *despoblado*, a
desert-like region, and then swing back northeast toward Potosí.[60]
It was a daring move since he was ready to sacrifice part of his
army in order to disorient the enemy, and then march into the
*despoblado*, which no army had yet crossed. La Hera fulfilled
his mission but his unit was torn to pieces and he himself was
severely injured. Valdés by this time had gone into the *despoblado;*
the wounded La Hera and his surviving soldiers rushed into the
*despoblado*, too, and evidently were able to catch up with Valdés.
Barbarucho and Medinaceli decided to pursue them, but then
hesitated. A violent disagreement between the two Secessionist
officers took place and as a result Medinaceli turned around.[61]
Apparently Barbarucho wanted to go into the *despoblado*, while
Medinaceli was opposed to it. Barbarucho went after Valdés, but
the Loyalist commander had won enough time and swung to his
right again, out of the *despoblado* into the royal road *(camino real)*
that led to Potosí. He had successfully by-passed powerful Cotagaita. On August 16, 1824, General Valdés reached the abandoned
mine of Lava, about thirty miles from Potosí. It was a cold night,
the troops were tired and Valdés felt good since he had just heard
that Aguilera had not occupied Chuquisaca and that Potosí was
also unoccupied. It was decided to make a halt and use the mine
shaft for sleeping, protected from the biting cold of the cordillera.

Late at night Barbarucho, with about six hundred soldiers,
reached Lava and decided on a frontal attack early in the morning.
The Constitutionalists had seen Barbarucho's arrival and prepared
for the battle. On August 17, as soon as dawn broke, the opposing
forces clashed with savage impact: the Loyalists, well situated in
the mine, and the Secessionists, throwing one line after another
against the shafts and hills with the hope of taking the mine by
assault. Both factions collided with the cry of "Long live the King."
The fratricidal war had reached its summit.

But the Constitutionalists were well entrenched in the mine
which turned out to be an unexpected fortress. Barbarucho's
frontal assaults were savage and courageous, but militarily un-
feasible and senseless. Then the attacking colonel decided to throw
his whole army in one great wave against the shafts with the hope

of forcing his way in. Just as he was ready to attack, the calvary of General Valdés, led by General Valentín Ferraz, stormed from behind the hills and surrounded the entire army of Barbarucho. A severe fight ensued and the Secessionists lost many soldiers. Their situation was hopeless and everyone, including Barbarucho, surrendered. The Secessionists had lost half of their army and the remaining three hundred all became prisoners of the Constitutionalists.[62] The captured men, as well as the Loyalists, were convinced that General Valdés could court-martial and condemn Barbarucho to death because of his unbecoming behavior at Tarabuquillo when he opened fire upon the general while he was negotiating a truce. Instead Valdés received Barbarucho with great courtesy and was personally interested in seeing that he received immediate medical attention and a thorough rest. The Loyalists had lost very few soldiers, but one casualty was the sad loss of a close friend of General Valdés, General Cayetano Ameller, who was mortally wounded in this battle.[63] All injured soldiers of both sides were rushed to Potosí for treatment.

General Valdés stationed his victorious army at Puno, a village in the neighborhood of Potosí, giving the command to General Ferraz. He decided to go to Chuquisaca with a small unit and have a personal talk with General Aguilera, who was still waiting and watching. In the meanwhile General Olañeta had advanced north with the hope of recapturing Potosí, but when he reached Cinti he was informed of the defeat and complete capture of the Barbarucho contingent.[64] He decided to halt his advance and remain at Cinti. But the defeat at Lava had seriously demoralized the Secessionist army and some officers began to open secret conversations with General Ferraz at Puno, offering to desert Olañeta. Ferraz, in the absence of his superior, General Valdés, was unwilling to assume any responsibility in this matter. This was a serious mistake since by it the Constitutionalists lost their last chance to terminate the Separatist War.[65] A few days later the mutinous officers of General Olañeta abandoned their idea of desertion because of an unexpected turn of events.

The Constitutionalist commander had entered Chuquisaca without any incident and soon left the capital in search of Aguilera. On August 25 General Valdés was in Yamparáez, a village near Chuquisaca, when finally the news of the great catastrophe of Junín reached him, along with an urgent request to move his army of the south out of Charcas into Lower Peru to aid the Spanish armies retreating before the advancing Bolívar. Immediately, he wrote General Olañeta a letter in which he informed him of the bad news from the north. Valdés told Olañeta that their war was terminated and that he and his army would rush to Lower Peru. He named General Olañeta absolute commander of the Spanish armies in Upper Peru. The next day Valdés reaffirmed his order and suggested that Olañeta reorganize his troops in order to be ready for an invasion from Lower Peru or even the United Provinces. He hoped that General Olañeta would not hesitate to send his northern contingents, such as those stationed in La Paz, to Lower Peru if needed. The Loyalist general suggested that Olañeta shift the bulk of his army to Oruro and La Paz and have ready plenty of ammunition in case the defeated Spanish army in Lower Peru would have to retreat into Upper Peru. Valdés wrote that he would free all Secessionist prisoners he had taken, including Barbarucho, and he hoped that General Olañeta would reciprocate in the same way. He asked Olañeta to send the freed Constitutionalist prisoners straight to Lower Peru since they were needed there. Valdés thought that the most important part of his army's equipment that had fallen into Olañeta's hands at Salo should be forwarded to him, but that Olañeta should keep all heavy apparatus.[66] General Valdés dispatched Colonel Vicente Miranda to take the letter to Olañeta personally.

Without awaiting Olañeta's reply, General Valdés immediately began his march north. On August 28, 1824, he evacuated the capital and two days later left Potosí. In the first days of September the Constitutionalist army traveled via Oruro and La Paz into Lower Peru. General Olañeta answered Valdés in vague terms, telling him that he was satified with his appointment as over-all commander of Upper Peru and that he would fight as any other Spaniard against the Colombian invaders. These were his official replies, yet in his talk with the personal representative of General Valdés, Colonel Miranda, he expressed other views. He said that it was too bad that the soldiers of Barbarucho at Tarabuquillo had missed their chance to kill General Valdés. Moreover, the rebel general expressed frankly his joy over General Canterac's great defeat at Junín. Miranda communicated these words to Valdés. Furthermore, on September 1, General Olañeta issued from Cotagaita several victorious proclamations in which he announced that

Valdés' army was routed and fleeing north. He then sent instructions to the local civil authorities, as the royal executive of the provinces of Río de la Plata.[67]

On September 5, 1824, Olañeta entered Potosí, which had already been occupied by an advance Secessionist patrol, in great pomp. The usual reception was given to the victorious general. The *potosinos* had lost count of the innumerable receptions they had given to triumphal invading armies. Here at Potosí General Olañeta had his army diary published, in which he glorified his great campaign. He did not say a word about the battle of Junín, but rather stated that his victorious army had so severely defeated the Constitutionalists that they had fled Upper Peru, abandoning Chuquisaca and Potosí and other towns without a fight. He accused General Valdés of brutality and said that he had forced the prisoners, including Barbarucho, to walk to La Paz. Olañeta added that Valdés had then condemned Barbarucho to death, leaving the impression that Colonel Valdez had been killed.[68] This was absolutely not true since Barbarucho later reappeared in the war. He was the last Spanish officer to surrender to the Bolivarian army in the Perus. After Olañeta had re-established his government as it had been before the invasion of General Valdés, he started to move north. He was in Oruro on October 2, 1824, when, through General Juan Antonio Alvarez de Arenales, now governor of Salta, he received a letter from Bolívar, who had proclaimed General Olañeta as a liberator.[69]

The war had taken a new turn. The great intrigue had been successful but the schemers had not expected that the ambitious Simón Bolívar, hardly known in Upper Peru in 1823, would appear on the scene as a liberator. And this Venezuelan general, of honest and thorough Patriot convictions, proclaimed the fanatic absolutist, General Pedro Antonio de Olañeta, as a liberator, a small liberator, not as great as Bolívar, but a true liberator. The strange war in Charcas was becoming stranger. The government of the "liberator," General Olañeta, had begun.

*Chapter 7*

# "LIBERATOR" AND TRAITOR

T THE BEGINNING OF 1824 THE SITUATION of Bolívar and his army was far from encouraging. The Peruvian army and republic had completely disintegrated. At this critical time Bolívar was in the little village of Pativilca, north of Lima. He realized very well that in view of the defeats, defections, and outright treason in the Peruvian army, he and his Colombian expeditionary force would be unable to resist the combined attack of the two Spanish armies under Canterac and Valdés. Therefore, on February 13, 1824, he outlined to General Sucre a precise plan of retreat to the north into the department of Trujillo.[1] He hoped that there he could hold out until reinforcements from Colombia arrived. Bolívar's correspondence from January through March was pessimistic. On February 16 he thought that his only wish was to keep his army "intact, and conserve ourselves at all costs; the year must not end with our not remaining in Peru." Nine days later he wrote to Francisco de Paula Santander that if the reinforcements did not come, "I shall order General Sucre and the army of Colombia to withdraw, and, as for myself, I shall go to the devil." On March 14 Bolívar was in Trujillo, pessimistic as ever, and asking frantically for more troops from Colombia to save him. The prospects about everything were bleak and Bolívar was only too frank in making it known. On April 9 he said to Sucre that he believed that without help from Colombia they could not hold out for more than three or four months. A few days later Bolívar received the amazing news of the rebellion of General Olañeta and that the Spanish army of the south under General Valdés had gone

into Upper Peru, instead of coming north to join the Canterac
army. On April 14 he wrote an exuberant letter to Sucre. His
whole spirit seemed to have picked up, and he thought that in
view of this unexpected turn of events the Colombian army should
prepare for an offensive in May against Canterac.[2] Certainly General Olañeta had done more for the hard-pressed Colombian army
than anyone else.

As more and more details reached the Bolivarian headquarters
the Colombian general began to prepare for the great attack. Yet
General Bolívar did not fully understand the underlying motive
of the Olañeta secession. He thought that perhaps the Spanish
general had embraced the cause of liberty, and that Olañeta would
join the Patriot army. Bolívar was quite convinced that General
Olañeta had become a Patriot.[3] Therefore on May 21, from Huaraz,
he wrote the Secessionist general his first letter.

Bolívar expressed his satisfaction that General Olañeta had
parted ways with "the hateful party that until today has oppressed
this unfortunate part of the world." Bolívar told Olañeta that he
was convinced that the general had taken this step because of his
convictions and belief in the cause of freedom. Bolívar then expressed his distaste for the Spanish constitution, which he classified
as "a monster of undefinable forms." He thought that the constitutional government of Spain was a regime of many heads, and all
with tyrannical dispositions. Bolívar felt, too, as he indicated to
Olañeta, that the infamous constitution "had trampled the church
[and] the throne." He then told the Spanish general in Upper
Peru that he ought to embrace the cause of liberty and freedom
because it was the cause that was destined to win. Bolívar confided
to Olañeta that he would start an offensive south against the Spanish
army in Lower Peru, and if Olañeta would maintain the rebellion
it would mean that he would have done an invaluable service to
the Patriot cause. Then, Bolívar added that he would consider
Olañeta and his army as *beneméritos del Perú y de la América*. At
the same time Bolívar astutely reminded his correspondent that
should the Patriot army be defeated then General Olañeta would
not be compromised, because he could say that he had served the
King faithfully. Bolívar implied to Olañeta that by continuing his
secession he had nothing to lose. But he added that he was absolutely convinced that his army could not be defeated. The Colombian leader suggested that General Olañeta thoroughly consider

the whole situation of America and that undoubtedly he would come to the conclusion that the Spaniards had not a single chance. Bolívar then added several reasons why he was sure that the cause of freedom would soon win. The commander of the United Army terminated his eloquent and diplomatic letter by suggesting to General Olañeta that he should send a confidential delegate to his headquarters in Lower Peru and personally see the great strength and enthusiasm of the Patriots.[4]

It is not to be believed that Bolívar was expressing a deep-seated political conviction in this letter, but rather that he was wooing General Olañeta.[5] He was anxious to see the rebellion continued because it would bring victory within easy grasp. This indeed is what happened. Although the letter was written on May 21, 1824, it took four months to reach Olañeta. The letter went via Chile to General Arenales, governor of Salta, who forwarded it to Olañeta.[6] When it reached Olañeta on October 2 in Oruro, the army of Bolívar had already severely defeated the Spanish army of the north under Canterac at Junín on August 6, and General Olañeta had won the Separatist War.

Seven days after the victory of Junín, Bolívar issued a proclamation to the people of Peru announcing the good news to them. Bolívar told the people that "two great armies harass the Spanish in Peru, the United Army [under Bolívar] and the army of the brave Olañeta." Bolívar then announced to the people that "Olañeta and his illustrious companions are worthy of American gratitude." The commander of the United Army declared General Pedro Antonio de Olañeta a liberator.[7] Seemingly, in the absence of an answer from Olañeta to his letter of May 21 (which was not the fault of Olañeta since he did not get the letter until October), Bolívar made it appear that General Olañeta had thrown his lot with the army of freedom. Although Bolívar, under the impact of the first news, thought that the rebel general had joined him, on November 26 he expressed to General Andrés Santa Cruz a different opinion. He said that it was his belief that General "Olañeta would never be a Patriot and will be always more *godo* than the enemy." But on the same day he wrote to General Sucre that he regarded "it as certain that Olañeta can never be a friend of these Spaniards, but a conjecture is not a fact; hence, you must always have eyes in the back of your head."[8] It seems quite clear that Bolívar was undecided about Olañeta's intentions. This is understandable. What really mattered at this moment for the United Army was that Olañeta continue his secession and therefore deprive the hard-pressed Spanish army of reinforcement and an escape route. As long as Olañeta did this Bolívar was satisfied with the obscure actions of the general.

The first important step was to defeat the remainder of the Spanish army in Lower Peru. In view of Canterac's defeat the viceroy, La Serna, had put himself at the head of the Spanish army and had fused the decimated army of the north and the army of the south, worn out from its campaign in the Separatist War. General Sucre, who had been given the task of defeating the Spanish army in Lower Peru by Bolívar, started a brilliant campaign in southern Lower Peru, a campaign which culminated in the artfully executed battle of Ayacucho on December 9, 1824. The whole Spanish army surrendered to Sucre; among the captives were Viceroy La Serna, Generals Canterac, Valdés, Carratalá, and Ferraz, all veterans of long campaigns in Upper Peru, and many others. The only force left was the small garrison of Callao and the large army of General Olañeta in Upper Peru. After Ayacucho only Charcas remained to be freed, the same land where the War of Independence had started sixteen years before. But strangely enough, the victorious United Army did not even know whether the Spanish commander of Upper Peru had joined them or was still fighting for the King. The curious drama of Upper Peru was about to start. Would Olañeta receive the victorious Sucre as a companion-in-arms or would he meet him as a foe? And what about Upper Peru: Did it belong to the United Provinces, to Lower Peru, or did it wish separation? Sucre had just won a great battle but an even greater task awaited him.

General Olañeta answered Bolívar's letter of May 21 on October 2 in vague terms. He told Bolívar that he agreed with his judgment about the constitution. Olañeta then added that La Serna had usurped the viceregal chair from Pezuela. The Separatist general assured Bolívar that because of his military victory he was the ruler of Upper Peru and that he was "convinced that I am working for the benefit of America." Olañeta said he thought "a solid system" was the solution to all the problems that had beset America. What did Olañeta mean by a solid system? Vagueness was a quality of Olañeta's correspondence, written by his understudies. Then he asked Bolívar to review all the events in Peru and Tierra Firme and the evident conclusion would be that the "vices of a popular government are only too obvious." Indeed, this was a stimulating thought to submit to Bolívar, and really the only clear sentence in the whole letter. Olañeta ended his letter by saying that "I wish we could make our sentiments uniform, and give a day of rejoicing to America and humanity."[9] Really a strange correspondence between the great Patriot, Bolívar, and the fanatic Absolutist, General Pedro Antonio de Olañeta. The rebel general did not say a word about sending a confidential representative to Bolívar's headquarters as the letter had suggested. What about Casimiro Olañeta, might his uncle not want to send him? What had happened to this master schemer, originator of the idea of rebellion?

Casimiro Olañeta had left for Buenos Aires and Montevideo as soon as the treaty of Tarapaya was signed, but the exact date of his departure is unknown. Casimiro was accompanied by an assistant, a mysterious priest. They were able to go into the free provinces with the help of a pass personally written by Governor Arenales of Salta.[10] Governor Arenales was the ex-guerrilla leader who, although born in Spain, embraced the revolutionary cause as early as 1809. After the defeat of Rondeau he went into northern Argentina, distinguishing himself as a brave and patriotic soldier. Arenales represented one of the purest and most honest partisans of the War of Independence. In his probity and integrity he resembled General Sucre closely. Arenales was the very antithesis of Casimiro Olañeta. The *dos caras* Casimiro said that Arenales helped him to get into the free provinces because he had been his confidential agent, forwarding to the governor of Salta restricted information about the Spanish army. Casimiro wrote that "nothing happened in Peru that I did not write to Arenales; the intentions of my uncle, the situation of the army of liberation, its strength, and whatever was important."[11] Obviously, this is a gross exaggeration, yet Casimiro admits to having served as a spy for Arenales. A fine game the *dos caras* Patriot and Royalist played: Casimiro as secretary to his uncle, the Spanish commander in Upper Peru, spied for Arenales, the Patriot governor of Salta, and José Mariano Serrano, the secretary and aide of Governor Arenales,[12] was accused of having spied for General Olañeta. Each one of the comrades spied for his friend's superior. This means that Casimiro and José Mariano exchanged information. Indeed the two great schemers, Casimiro

Olañeta and José Mariano Serrano, today considered the fathers of Bolivia, were a fine pair of unscrupulous operators with not an iota of political conviction or ethics.

Casimiro Olañeta had no difficulty in obtaining a pass into the free provinces. In Salta he met Serrano and his friends[13] and from there continued to Tucumán and Córdoba. No one disturbed Casimiro, and the safe-conduct pass of Arenales opened the gates to all cities and provinces in Argentina to him. In Córdoba he probably went to visit his alma mater and found out that his old teachers, Dean Funes, was in Buenos Aires and held the position of confidential agent of Colombia and of Bolívar to the United Provinces.[14] Undoubtedly, Casimiro made it a point to take advantage of this. According to Olañeta, in July he was in Buenos Aires and in August in Montevideo.[15] The next known record of the young schemer is that in December he was back in Cochabamba at the headquarters of his uncle.

What was Casimiro doing in the free provinces? He said, as did José María Paz, that he had been sent to purchase arms for the Secessionist army.[16] He had eighteen thousand pesos with him to pay for the weapons. This sounds reasonable, since General Olañeta needed arms for his army and the only place he could get them was through Buenos Aires. Upper Peru was an isolated region with roads only from Buenos Aires and Lima, and the rebel general was fighting against Lower Peru. Casimiro's companion, the mysterious priest, was supposed to continue to Spain to take important messages to the court. General Valdés thought that Casimiro himself was going to Spain, and he suggested to the viceroy that he speed information to Madrid to apprehend this "perverse and revolutionary Doctor Casimiro Olañeta."[17] Valdés was right when he called him perverse, but revolutionary was hardly correct. The nephew of General Olañeta was doing many other things besides looking for arms. Everything he did is obscure and René-Moreno, the only one ever to have exposed Casimiro, concluded after searching for more facts, that Casimiro Olañeta was engaged in "mysterious errands."[18]

He did not go to Spain and he did not get arms, and it may be assumed that he kept the eighteen thousand pesos for himself or split with his companion, the priest. In 1826, once Bolivia had been created, many of the Upper Peruvian emigrants to the free provinces returned to their home soil. The majority had been honest and convinced Patriots who had suffered as many as sixteen years of hardship in foreign lands. These people knew Casimiro Olañeta very well and spoke of him as *"colla doscaras disfrazado de patriota faroleante."*[19] Some of them tried to expose Casimiro[20] and one of them, a conscientious citizen of Santa Cruz by the name of Manuel Castro, together with his friends, stopped Casimiro one night in Chuquisaca and demanded that he publicly account for what had happened to the eighteen thousand pesos.[21] Another Patriot, under the pseudonym of El Mosquetero, published in Salta a frank attack against Casimiro Olañeta, and he, too, wondered where the eighteen thousand pesos had gone.[22] Casimiro was unable to defend himself in a convincing way. He said he gave the money to the priest, who might have spent it. Then, he added that this companion was supposed to have gone to Spain as a courier, but that he had stayed in the United Provinces, probably to spend the eighteen thousand pesos. After this Olañeta wrote that he went to see this man, whose name he never gave, to fetch the documents which the priest was supposed to have taken with him to Spain, so that he might send them to the court.[23] If Casimiro went to get the letters from the priest, why did he not demand the eighteen thousand pesos? This was a considerable amount of money, about thirty to forty thousand dollars.[24] René-Moreno rightly asks if Casimiro gave him the money, and this is hardly understandable, why did he not demand a receipt; one does not give so much cash to anyone without any proof.[25] Furthermore, if the priest kept the money, why did Olañeta not do anything: sue him, investigate where he went, identify him by name, and take other steps that anyone would immediately undertake in such circumstances? It seems clear that Casimiro simply took the money for himself. The mystery about this affair is that he did not claim that he returned the money to his uncle, since in 1826 General Olañeta was already dead. Young Olañeta was not only unethical in political dealings but also in finances.

El Mosquetero and the newspaper, *Mensajero Arjentino*,[26] also accused Casimiro of having entered into negotiations in Montevideo with a Brazilian agent with the intention of offering the great productive eastern part of Charcas to the Brazilian empire.[27] Casimiro denied this vehemently in March, 1826, and said that the only time he met the Brazilian agent was in the theater.[28] A month later, in April, he again denied this charge in a letter to the

editor of the Bolivian newspaper, *El Condor*. Here he took a
different line of defense by writing that he knew that the governor
of Mato Grosso had invited his uncle, General Olañeta, to invade
Mato Grosso. Casimiro said that General Olañeta was enthusiastic
about this project, but that Manual María Urcullu intervened and
persuaded the general not to undertake such a "wild plan." The
master schemer said that all this took place in July, 1824, while
he was in Buenos Aires; therefore, he did not have anything to
do with this matter.[29] Yet only a month earlier Casimiro admitted
that in August, 1824, in Montevideo, he had met a Brazilian agent.
This sparse information points to another intended great intrigue.

Young Olañeta had something else to worry about since a great
new army was advancing toward Upper Peru. Casimiro Olañeta
decided it was high time to contact Bolívar. He took advantage of
the fact that Funes was in Buenos Aires, and he talked to this
venerable old man extensively.[30] Casimiro said that he wrote a
letter to Bolívar, from Buenos Aires, through Funes.[31] Apparently
Funes never forwarded the letter to Bolívar, but rather told him
what Casimiro had said, for there is no letter from Casimiro Olañeta
to Bolívar written in Buenos Aires in the practically complete
collection of correspondence to Bolívar. Funes, however, did refer
to Casimiro in a letter to Bolívar.[32] It can be inferred that Casimiro
wrote favorably to Bolívar about his uncle and tried to convince
the Colombian leader of the Patriot sentiments of General Olañeta.
At least that is what Bolívar understood.[33] He also informed Bolívar
of the split in the Spanish army and suggested to him to advance,
since this was the opportune time for an offensive. The news of
the great southern push had not yet reached Casimiro Olañeta in
distant Buenos Aires.[34]

This is all that is known about the strange doings of the rebel
general's secretary in the free provinces. Casimiro, with his usual
disregard for the truth, said that he returned to Upper Peru because
Bolívar wanted him to go back to aid the Patriot cause.[35] However,
no letter of Bolívar written in 1824 to Casimiro Olañeta exists in
the correspondence of the Liberator. Indeed, in December of
1824 Bolívar could not even remember the name of this "relative
of Your Lordship who recently resided in Buenos Aires," as Bolívar
put it in a letter to General Olañeta.[36] René-Moreno, who became
so disgusted with the lies and exaggerations of Casimiro Olañeta,
wrote that Casimiro always gave the appearance of discussing

matters with heavy documentation, but that he always added that either a friend of his had the documents, or that he had mislaid them, or that he would publish them later, or some other excuse. Instead Olañeta gave long quotations in Latin or cited Lamartine, Hugo, Goethe, Shakespeare, Dante, Cicero, and others. He never presented documents of any kind. René-Moreno rightly said that Casimiro's defenses, expositions, writings, debates, and letters to editors are "documented argumentations without documents."[37] It is probable that Casimiro returned to Upper Peru at his own volition at the end of August or beginning of September to rejoin his uncle.

His first task was to make a journey to the Ayopaya republic to meet the guerrilla Lanza and persuade him to join ranks with General Olañeta.[38] The ascent of the *dos caras* Doctor Olañeta, neatly dressed in his black suit, white shirt, black tie, and black hat, into the rough *montonera* republic to confer with the rugged, harsh, and unpolished guerrillas must have been a strange sight.[39] Casimiro was able to convince the plain Lanza that his uncle was fighting for the Patriots, and the guerrilla leader accepted the false assurance of the young Olañeta in good faith. Lanza was deceived by a smooth manipulator and talker, and he admitted it later to Bolívar, while apologizing for his naïveté.[40] By then he had learned from experience, and in February of the year 1825 Lanza was the only one to warn Sucre about Casimiro Olañeta, and to advise him not to trust this dangerous man. Sucre ignored Lanza and three years later paid dearly for it, because then Casimiro Olañeta betrayed the victor of Ayacucho and had him expelled from Bolivia, or as Casimiro wrote to a friend, ". . . I kicked him from his sultanic throne." In this same letter he called Sucre "*el carajillo.*"[41] Unfortunately, General Lanza had to die defending Sucre, killed by bullets for which Casimiro was indirectly responsible.

All this happened in April, 1828. In 1824 Lanza was duped because he was honest but not overly intelligent. Sucre had heard in Cuzco after the victory of Ayacucho that in the mountains Lanza was being called "Doctor," and therefore he appointed him president of La Paz.[42] "Doctor" Lanza nearly ruined the finances of La Paz because of stupidity,[43] and Sucre had to admit to Bolívar that Lanza was "a mule" and that he was "an animal with two feet plus honesty" but one "who did not even know how to talk."[44] René-Moreno wrote that the best way to describe Lanza was with three *b*'s, standing for *"benemérito,* battler, and brute."[45]    It is understandable that the slick Casimiro had an easy time of convincing the man with the three *b*'s. But this "brute mule," once fooled by Casimiro, had enough intelligence to see through him. If Sucre had listened to this "animal with two feet" in 1825, Bolivia's history might have been different. On December 23, 1824, Casimiro was back in Cochabamba with his uncle. On this day the nephew wrote a confidential letter to Bolívar, since he knew that the day before General Olañeta had received a letter from the Liberator and had immediately answered it. Casimiro wanted to show Bolívar that he was more important than his uncle.

It should be recalled that Bolívar took the initial step and wrote to General Olañeta, for the first time from Huaraz on May 21, or more than two months before the battle of Junín. In his letter the Liberator congratulated Olañeta for his secession. The rebel general did not receive this letter until October 2. On October 6 Bolívar decided to write a second letter to General Olañeta, offering him friendship and hoping that the general would be an integral part of the new order in America. He suggested that the general open negotiations with General Sucre who had been authorized to deal with him. Again not having received an answer to his letter, Bolívar decided to write a third time on December 15, six days after the victory of Ayacucho, repeating his earlier thoughts and saying that he had heard indirectly from a young relative of the general in Buenos Aires, who had expressed the opinion that General Olañeta was honest in his Patriot convictions. Bolívar thought that this was encouraging and again congratulated the general for his secession and offered him a solid future with the liberating army. He then added that Olañeta should settle the details of integration of his army with Sucre. Nine days later, on December 24, Bolívar received the long-delayed answer of General Olañeta to his first letter. Although this answer was full of ambiguous statements, Bolívar immediately took his pen to write Olañeta his fourth letter, expressing joy for the general's good words. Bolívar wrote that "the victory of Ayacucho will never let us forget what we owe you; more than ever we should thank you for the opportune diversion of the Spanish army that you have undertaken in Upper Peru." Bolívar repeated that Sucre had the authority to sign an agreement with him. On December 22 General Olañeta answered Bolívar's communication with a short letter, saying only that General Valdés

had left behind many foci of subversion which had required his
close attention. He had finished this unpleasant clean-up campaign, and he was determined and ready to move up to the Desaguadero River in order to open negotiations with Sucre. Olañeta
dispatched an identical letter to Sucre, with whom he was supposed
to negotiate.[46]

The next day Casimiro Olañeta wrote, unknown to his uncle,
a confidential letter to Bolívar. He asked the Liberator to honor
his confidence and not divulge this letter. In it Casimiro hinted to
Bolívar that he was the power behind his uncle and that he had
been responsible for General Olañeta's secession. He said that he
was a partisan of the Patriots and that he had long been persecuted
by the Royalists. He repeated his favorite phrase that it did not
matter which road one takes as long as one reaches or works for
the same goal. He added with strong emphasis that "I belong
entirely to the revolution." Casimiro politely informed Bolívar
that "as secretary and friend of General Olañeta I am informed
of many details which it is impossible to confide in a letter," and
he wrote that it would be too hazardous to enumerate them because
it might endanger his plan. Casimiro did not even hint what his
plan was, but in this intelligently calculated letter he seemingly
wished to maintain the great Bolívar in a state of suspense. Then
he wrote that the army of General Olañeta would belong to Bolívar,
but because of many difficulties this could not yet be openly announced. And he hinted that a serious split had developed in the
midst of the Secessionist army, between those favoring union with
Bolívar and those opposed to it. He did not write what the attitude
of his uncle was, but he stated that Patriot elements, or as he identified them, the liberal elements (liberal within the Absolutist army!),
were decided to join Bolívar. Naturally he gave the impression
that he, Casimiro Olañeta, was the leader of this liberal faction
and he recommended especially Manuel María Urcullu, whom he
called the auditor of the Olañeta army. He ended his letter with
extravagant eulogies such as, "What a day it will be when all
Americans united will sing around the tree of liberty hymns of
gratitude to our liberator. It looks as if it is very near."[47] Casimiro
Olañeta and Manuel María Urcullu were ready to sing songs of
gratitude to Bolívar, yet it had not been long since Casimiro,
defending Manuel María before the audiencia, spoke of the "infamous revolutionaries," and Urcullu was damning the Patriot cause

in every part. Was Casimiro ready to betray his uncle and join Bolívar, or was he honestly trying to gain time to convince the rebel general to come to terms with the United Army? All was enigmatic and Sucre was quite baffled. It would have been easier to fight an open war than to solve the riddle of Upper Peru.

Even before the battle of Ayacucho Sucre had received authorization from the commander of the United Army, General Bolívar, to draw up a treaty of defense, or an alliance, or any other feasible agreement with General Olañeta, which would integrate the army of Olañeta within the United Army.[48] Sucre immediately informed General Olañeta of his delegated power and apparently asked him to set up the machinery for an agreement.[49] This was before the successful battle of Ayacucho and the problem of Olañeta and Upper Peru was still secondary. But with the victorious battle of December 9, 1824, when nearly the whole Spanish army was captured, the Upper Peruvian theater required firsthand attention. In the capitulation of Ayacucho the defeated viceroy and the commander of the army of the south, General Valdés, wanted to include the army of Olañeta in the stipulations of the surrender, but Marshal[50] Sucre refused this because he said that he considered the army of Olañeta an integral part of the liberating forces.[51] As strange as it may sound, Sucre probably did this to prove to General Olañeta that they really meant it when he and Bolívar had declared Olañeta to be an ex officio member of the United Army because of his secession.

But in the absence of any concise answer by the rebel general the matter became a riddle. Marshal Sucre felt not at all enthusiastic about starting his campaign in Charcas. Three days after the victory of Ayacucho Sucre asked Bolívar to be relieved of any further task. Eleven days later Sucre thought that the whole problem of Charcas was too "delicate" for him. On December 25 he repeated the same thought because he "did not want to become involved in this mess that prevails in Upper Peru.[52] General Bolívar was unwilling to let Sucre go, since he was his best general. Bolívar simply ignored Sucre's complaints, and it was Sucre who had to solve the confusion of Charcas. When Marshal Sucre complained about the complex situation of Charcas, he had in mind not only the strange and puzzling behavior of General Olañeta, but also other factors. To whom did Charcas belong: to Buenos Aires, to Peru, or to the Upper Peruvians? On January 8, 1825, Sucre wrote to Bolívar that he had heard that Arenales of Salta was ready to move into Charcas[53] and he, Sucre, felt that a clash of interests would take place, and he added, ". . . this is what I am most afraid of." Sucre reminded Bolívar that if he moved into Upper Peru he would be in a country "that is not part of Peru and does not wish to belong to it, but seems to want to belong to itself." He prophetically wrote in the next line that he could foresee "that we shall get ourselves into a maze of trickery."[54]

But Marshal Sucre was not excused, and Bolívar paid no attention to his beloved general's desire to retire.[55] Sucre unenthusiastically accepted his new task with his usual resignation and conscientiousness. On New Year's Day of 1825 he began his new campaign or diplomatic maneuver. First, he wrote a letter to General Olañeta in which he expressed the line of policy that had been adopted to deal with the rebel general, considering him a new member of the Bolivarian army. He told him that he was sending his personal aide, Colonel Antonio Elizalde, to draw up an agreement with the Olañeta army. Next, he wrote a letter to General Aguilera in which he expressed identical sentiments as those stated to Olañeta and asked Aguilera to join the United Army which was beginning its march into Upper Peru. The same day he wrote another letter to the great guerrilla leader, Lanza, who had joined the Olañeta army. Since he had heard that Lanza was a qualified man he named him president of La Paz and requested him to march to La Paz and prepare the city for the entrance of the Bolivarian army, ten thousand strong. Another letter was sent to the ex-guerrilla leader, Pedro Arraya, who had joined the Secessionist army, to whom he also wrote that he was starting his march with the Bolivian army into Upper Peru. The same January 1 he dispatched other letters to the municipalities of La Paz, Cochabamba, Chuquisaca, and Potosí, informing them of the forthcoming entrance of the United Army into Charcas with the sole object of "guaranteeing its liberty."[56] After Ayacucho General Valdés and General Canterac had smilingly told Sucre that it was now his turn to try to figure out General Olañeta. They thought that he would not be more successful than they had been.[57] To Lanza, Sucre frankly stated that "the uncertain behavior of General Olañeta in the meanwhile embitters my heart." Marshal Sucre then decided to wait for the return of Colonel Elizalde and see what he brought back from the headquarters of General Olañeta.

As the first days of the new year of 1825 passed, it became more and more apparent that General Olañeta had decided to fight rather than to accept the offer to become a member of the Bolivarian army. On December 16, 1824, after the Spanish disaster of Ayacucho, the Audiencia of Cuzco had named General Pío Tristán, commander of Arequipa, the new viceroy. But this last viceroy in Spanish America lasted less than one month, and Pío Tristán submitted without a fight to the Ayacucho surrender terms. Not so General Olañeta; although he had had an active correspondence with the United Army he was unwilling to come to terms, but was determined to create confusion and keep the United Army guessing.

On January 4, 1825, General Olañeta issued from Oruro two more of his famous proclamations. He spoke to the people of both Perus, accusing the defeated army of Viceroy La Serna of treason and incapacity when it capitulated at Ayacucho. He told all the inhabitants that such a small defeat would never destroy his enthusiasm and determination. It was his firm intention that should the new viceroy, Pío Tristán, surrender, the Spanish army in Upper Peru would never do the same and in the end final victory would be theirs, because they defended the sacred cause of the king and religion. A similar proclamation was addressed to his soldiers and officers.[58] Four days later he wrote two letters to the new viceroy, Pío Tristán, unaware that he was ready to lay down arms. Olañeta told him that he was not at all surprised at the defeat of the army of La Serna; it merely constituted the culmination of his many crimes. He assured the viceroy that he had a good army and with it could keep the Colombian units in check until he could get reinforcements from Spain via Tarapacá. In the second letter he emphatically stated that he would never surrender but would fight to the last man.[59] Indeed these words by General Olañeta were sincere in view of his refusal later to surrender. He was determined to fight the United Army of Bolívar and Sucre, but he needed time to obtain more ammunition and weapons. He wished to repeat the same strategy used with General Valdés the year before.

Therefore, on January 13 Olañeta concluded a four-month truce with Colonel Elizalde, Sucre's personal representative. It was stipulated that until General Olañeta could consult "with whom it should be done"—strange words, indeed—about the feasibility of joining the Bolivarian cause, a temporary truce would be signed

which would last four months. The United Army was to remain
north of the Desaguadero River and the Secessionist army south
of it. The guerrilla army of General Lanza would be allowed to
stay in its *montonera* republic of Ayopaya. Article four provided
that the region of Tarapacá, which formed the northern coastal
Atacama Desert that was part of the province of Arequipa (Lower
Peru), would remain in the hands of the Secessionist army.[60] This
was the crucial article of the La Paz treaty because General Olañeta,
after the departure of the army of General Valdés, had occupied
the Tarapacá region in order to have access to the Pacific coast,
his only exit from isolated Upper Peru.[61] This reflected clearly the
general's plan, expressed confidentially to the viceroy, that he
wanted to wait until he could get reinforcements. He needed Tarapacá and was unwilling to give it up although it was an integral
part of Lower Peru. The draft of the treaty of La Paz was quite
favorable to the Absolutist commander and it provided him with
the necessary respite. Would Marshal Sucre accept this draft and
be caught in the trap? The treaty of La Paz represented the same
line of policy that General Olañeta had adopted when he signed
the treaty of Tarapaya, but Marshal Sucre was in a much more
favorable position than General Valdés had been. General Olañeta
repeated another feature of his Separatist War. After Tarapaya
he had sent his nephew, Casimiro, to the free provinces to purchase
arms, and as soon as the La Paz treaty was drawn up, he again
dispatched Casimiro to try once more to acquire arms and ammunition, but this time he sent him to Iquique in Tarapacá to establish
contact with the island of Chiloé, the only other remaining Spanish
strong point. He hoped to get aid from Chiloé. Casimiro was to
be accompanied by another individual, General Pablo Echeverría.

This general had been Spanish commander of Puno and had
accepted the capitulation of Ayacucho.[62] In view of the stipulations
of the surrender terms Echeverría had requested the new Bolivarian
commander, General Rudecindo Alvarado, to let him return to
Spain. Almost all the Spanish officers had gone back to their homeland from the port of Quilca, but Echeverría asked Alvarado to
grant him permission to return home via Buenos Aires since his
family resided in Oruro.[63] Alvarado had no objection to the request
of the Spanish general, and kindly gave him five hundred pesos to
finance his trip because Echeverría was short of funds. All Royalist
officers had given their word of honor not to take up arms against

Patriots again. This had been a stipulation of the surrender terms of Ayacucho which the Royalists, including Echeverría, had accepted under oath. As soon as Echeverría had entered Upper Peru he broke his word of honor and his oath and had joined the army of General Olañeta, offering to procure arms from Chiloé and even Brazil for the rebel general.[64] Therefore General Olañeta decided to send his nephew and Echeverría to the port of Iquique in Tarapacá to try to get ammunition, giving them ten thousand pesos to pay for the purchase. As soon as General Olañeta had signed the truce treaty of La Paz and forwarded it to Marshal Sucre for his signature, Casimiro and Echeverría left for the coast. But before Casimiro departed he committed his first large-scale treason.

On January 12, a day before the treaty of La Paz was signed by the rebel commissioner, and only a few days before his departure for Tarapacá, Casimiro Olañeta wrote two letters to Marshal Sucre. One was official correspondence in which he expressed his usual Patriot sentiments, and told the Marshal that he would be very happy and anxious to meet the victor of Ayacucho, and that "It would be the happiest moment of my life." Casimiro then suggested that Sucre personally meet his uncle to work out a peaceful solution. It was a harmless letter in the usual flowery style of Casimiro Olañeta.[65] He then wrote a second letter, longer, and marked confidential. Here he re-emphasized that it was he who had convinced his uncle to rebel in order to create a split in the Spanish army. He added that his uncle was signing the truce treaty only in order to gain time and get the necessary reinforcements. The traitor then told Marshal Sucre that his uncle's army was only four thousand men strong and was of low morale because they were unable to get the necessary food, since Lanza occupied the fertile valleys of La Paz. Besides, Casimiro said that the soldiers had not received their pay and were bady equipped. He gave Sucre the impression that Colonels Arraya and Medinaceli were ready at any moment to desert his uncle and proclaim the Patriot cause. The rebel general's nephew declared that he was completely sure that should Marshal Sucre cross the Desaguadero River the Olañeta army would disintegrate because of "desertion, hunger, exhaustion, and lack of any enthusiasm to serve the tyrants any longer."

The most amazing aspect of this letter of treason is that in it Casimiro vaguely admitted another act of treason. In confusing words he said that he had informed General Arenales, the governor of Salta, of all this through a confidential agent of his. Was this agent Serrano? But then, even more vaguely, he wrote that he had worded the letter so that Arenales' ambition would not jeopardize Sucre's plan. This seems to mean that in this letter to Sucre he hinted that he preferred the marshal to General Arenales. Since the letter to Arenales in Salta has not been located, it can be assumed that to the governor of Salta (whose secretary, Serrano, was another *dos caras*) he wrote just the opposite: that he would prefer United Provinces' hegemony to that of the Bolivarian regime. This is the first hint that Casimiro had already begun to play the Patriots against each other.

Casimiro told Sucre that after a career of "constant persecution by the Spaniards, of exiles, prison terms, confiscations, and even death sentences," he would make his last effort for the liberty of his fatherland. He said, "I am intending to join you as a parliamentarian and never return to the territory of the tyrants whom I have served with the only purpose of making permanent the discord that I have introduced and that I have maintained until the end." Then Casimiro offered his services to the marshal by writing, "Please have the goodness to reward me by admitting me as a simple soldier in your cavalry unit until the end of the war. My fatherland demands my sacrifice and I am ready to make it in order to enjoy liberty in the midst of my family." He wrote Sucre that he was enclosing a *dictamen,* a memorandum which unfortunately has been lost.[66] Its existence might even magnify the treason of Casimiro. Underneath his signature he added a note stating that Sucre should forgive his bad handwriting,[67] but because of the fear of being discovered writing this letter, he had worked in haste. This is a monstrous case of treachery and lies.[68] Marshal Sucre answered the correspondence of Casimiro in an elegant tone, saying, "Receive, my dear Doctor, the expression of my cordial friendship."[69] Probably Casimiro did not receive this communication as he had already deserted. But before departing to the enemy's side, he first sacrificed the life of a Spaniard to make himself more acceptable to the Patriots.

After General Olañeta had signed the treaty of La Paz and forwarded it to the United Army's headquarters, Casimiro and General Echeverría left for the region of Tarapacá in order to secure arms from the port of Iquique. Neither the rebel· general nor Echeverría was aware that Casimiro was ready to commit treason. Showing no sign of his forthcoming switch to the enemy, Casimiro departed with Echeverría. When they reached the village of Tarapacá, capital of the region, Casimiro overpowered his fellow companion, took away his documents and money, and handed him over to the local authorities with an order to send him as a prisoner to Arequipa, capital of the province to which the *partido* of Tarapacá belonged.[70] Casimiro then took the road to Puno, evidently carrying with him the ten thousand pesos. Somewhere on the road from Tarapacá to Puno another *dos caras* friend of Casimiro, Mariano Calvimontes, joined him on his trip to Puno. Calvimontes was another politically dishonest individual who had changed allegiance continually since 1811.[71]

It was on the morning of February 3 at Puno, Lower Peru, that General Rudecindo Alvarado, in poor health, left the city for a journey south. Several days earlier Marshal Sucre had arrived in Puno with the Bolivarian army. He had given Alvarado permission to undertake his trip. About ten miles from the city limits, which Alvarado must have reached in the late morning, he suddenly met a man who he was amazed to learn was General Olañeta's nephew, Casimiro. Alvarado stopped him and in harsh terms asked him what he was doing. He then found out that the young man had deserted his uncle and was on his way to meet the marshal. Horrified by such treachery, Alvarado left Casimiro standing in the road and departed without further words. "I must confess that I felt disgusted by this surprise [encounter] and I did not hide it, and I interrogated this person with no courtesy because of his abandonment of his uncle and benefactor; finally, I turned around and continued on my way," is what Alvarado wrote in his diary.[72] Although Marshal Sucre had a poor opinion of General Alvarado and did not recommend him highly to Bolívar because he lacked ability,[73] Alvarado, who had never met Casimiro before, immediately realized his bad character, which most people were unable to do. Casimiro and his companion, Calvimontes,[74] after their unpleasant encounter with the Patriot general continued their trip, probably reaching Puno around noon of February 3.

Casimiro went directly to meet the victor of Ayacucho, who was highly impressed by the young man. The first thing Casimiro told Sucre was to stop the shipment of arms to Iquique as quickly as possible. He handed over the papers he had taken away from

Echeverría.[75] It is quite certain that he did not give Sucre the ten thousand pesos; undoubtedly he kept them for himself. With the money he took from the Buenos Aires mission, plus the Tarapacá funds, Casimiro had become a rich man. He had probably further enriched himself when he was the confidential secretary of his uncle and when Urcullu, his associate, was the auditor of the Secessionist forces. The night of February 3 Sucre rushed a letter to Bolívar, requesting him to stop the arms that General Olañeta might receive via Iquique. The marshal then added, "This Don Olañeta, who is very patriotic and looks as if he has talent, I shall appoint as general auditor of the army [United Army] which is the best position I have available for him here: he has been *oidor* of the Audiencia of Chuquisaca [*sic*].[76] In summary, I will treat him with all distinction, since besides meriting it, they tell me that he has great influence in all the province [*sic*, for Upper Peru or Charcas]."[77] The marshal's faithful private secretary, José María Rey de Castro, who was with Sucre when Casimiro met the liberator of Peru for the first time, tells that Sucre was indeed quite impressed with the young man. He states that the facility of words, the relaxed attitude, and the great energy of Casimiro Olañeta captivated everyone, and "it was impossible to resist the sympathy which he inspired in all of us."[78] The marshal felt enthusiastic about this new addition to his army. He liked Casimiro Olañeta and was aware that he needed the young man in his coming campaign in Upper Peru. Casimiro at his side was worth many divisions. But the marshal, with his honesty and correctness, was unaware of the true character of the man he had hired. Three years later he realized his mistake and confided it to Bolívar,[79] but then Sucre could not say that no one had warned him. Undoubtedly Rudecindo Alvarado expressed to Sucre his feelings about Casimiro. And another good Patriot who had just been tricked by Casimiro hurried a frank warning to Sucre.

Marshal Sucre was quite worried about the supposed war material that General Olañeta might get via Iquique. As he rushed a letter to Bolívar to ask him to stop the shipment, he also wrote a letter immediately to guerrilla General Lanza and requested him to send some of his partisan units into Tarapacá to stop or intercept the shipment for General Olañeta. He informed Lanza that he knew the arms were on their way because Casimiro Olañeta, who had joined him, had informed him of it.[80] On February 6 Lanza responded to the letter and wrote Sucre that already half of a division of his *montonero* army had left for Tarapacá to fulfill the requested mission. In the next paragraph Lanza warned Sucre about Casimiro by stating that "this individual, who realizes the desperate situation of General Olañeta, had had the temerity to desert to our side: as I know his character I am well acquainted with the shrewdness of both [uncle and nephew]." Lanza thought that Casimiro's desertion was motivated by a "perfidious project." The guerrilla general said that he wished that Marshal Sucre would realize and comprehend the character of this man. He then added, "I take the liberty to suggest that you ought to send Doctor Olañeta to a distant country," because it would be "very prudent and would be a very welcome precautionary step."[81] Yet the marshal ignored this sensible and timely advice from a man whom he later called an animal.

Casimiro did not leave Sucre's side until the victorious army entered Chuquisaca. From his desk as auditor, but more so as informal adviser to Sucre, Casimiro ingeniously directed the fall of his uncle. The marshal and his Bolivarian army did not have to fire a single shot. Casimiro, probably through his agents, convinced his *dos caras* aides, Urcullu in Chuquisaca and Usín in Potosí, to prepare the rebellion against his uncle.[82] He convinced Colonels Arraya and Medinaceli to change allegiance at the proper moment; General Olañeta trusted Urcullu, Usín, Arraya, and Medinaceli blindly. With the aid of these men the rule of General Olañeta began to collapse under the impact of the intrigues of his nephew. In April the general died from a shot fired by Medinaceli's rebel unit. Casimiro was indirectly responsible for the death of his uncle, who had done so much for him. To his credit is the fact that through the successful play of intrigues by Casimiro, a bloody campaign was averted, thus saving many lives. Strangely, Casimiro never adopted this line of defense when, in the late thirties, he was severely criticized for his unbecoming behavior in 1824-1825.[83]

Yet not only the death of his uncle can be attributed to him, but also that of his companion to Tarapacá, General Echeverría, whom he deceived in such an underhanded fashion As Echeverría had broken his word of honor and his oath never to take up arms again against the Patriots, Marshal Sucre was infuriated and ordered the prefect of Arequipa to put him before a firing squad. "He is perfidious, ungrateful, and very infamous, and has despised the generosity with which he has been treated . . . he must die for a thousand reasons . . . I repeat, he must be shot without delay," ordered Marshal Sucre.[84] Later Sucre repented of his harsh action in view of the personal imploring on the part of Echeverría's wife. The marshal rushed words to suspend the execution, but the letter was delayed and reached Arequipa too late. Sucre was deeply moved by this unfortunate incident.[85] But it was Casimiro who had betrayed Echeverría, and who therefore was as much responsible for the death of this Spanish general as Echeverría was himself.

In 1840 the Ecuadorian politician, Francisco Mariano de Miranda, when exposing Olañeta's betrayal of Santa Cruz, wrote him an open letter in which he told Casimiro, "Abusing the confidence of your uncle, the Spanish general, Olañeta, who favored you with the position of his secretary, you sold him vilely to his enemies and handed him over to death, making yourself the political Judas of the apostolate which surrounded the last remains of Spanish power in America" Miranda then continued in even stronger terms, ". . . in view of your subsequent treasons you can be classified as a traitor par excellence and an assassin." He compared him with Brutus.[86] Casimiro was unable to answer the grave charges of Miranda satisfactorily. He could only say, "After the battle of Ayacucho I honorably left my uncle in the village of Paria [near Oruro] in order to join General Sucre in Puno. I did not desert treacherously and infamously; I left him with his explicit permission and knowledge, which he expressed in a letter I think I have in my files and which I published in 1826 to answer similar charges."[87] Casimiro talked of his *Exposición* of 1826, of which only two copies —one complete and another incomplete—exist today in the National Library of Bolivia. When René-Moreno wrote his monograph on Casimiro Olañeta he knew of only the incomplete copy, which belonged to him. He wrote then, "The letter mentioned does not appear in any of the eight pages [of the *Exposición*] that in this moment lie before me."[88] Casimiro had not published this letter in the 1826 *Exposición*. Nowhere in the twelve pages of the complete copy is the letter to be found, or even a mention of it. When Casimiro wrote that he thought that he had it in his files he was giving his usual "documented defense without documents."

Alvarado and Lanza exposed Casimiro in 1825, but Sucre needed the young Olañeta in his forthcoming campaign. The Ecuadorian,

Miranda, the Guatemalan, Antonio José de Irisarri, and the Chilean, Juan García del Río, also unmasked the powerful Bolivian politician.[89] René-Moreno sketched fragmentarily the true career of this man in pages not published. In print he classified Olañeta as "perverse."[90] Bolivian historians who continue to glorify Casimiro Olañeta are exemplified by one biographer who writes that the name of Casimiro Olañeta means "liberty, justice, disinterest, patriotism, action, and fire."[91] Only the contemporary Bolivian historian, Humberto Vázquez-Machicado, has placed this glorified man in his proper perspective; he pleads that the "myth of Olañeta needs to be revised, reduced to its true place, role, and size. . . . Let us tear down this absurd historical web and weave with the real thread the positive truth."[92]

Sucre and Casimiro Olañeta were ready to march into Charcas to defeat General Pedro Antonio de Olañeta and then reorganize Charcas. But who was going to be the father of the new nation: Antonio José de Sucre or Josef Casimiro Olañeta?

## *Chapter 8*

# FROM PUNO TO CHEQUELTE

*E*VEN BEFORE CASIMIRO OLAÑETA had joined Marshal
Sucre in Puno at noon on February 3, 1825, the
commander of the United Army of liberation had come to the
conclusion that there was little choice but to move his army into
Upper Peru and fight the Separatist general. On January 19 Sucre
had decided to leave Cuzco and advance with his army toward
Upper Peru in campaign formation.[1] This sudden decision had
been taken in view of accumulated evidence that General Olañeta
was not going to come to terms. The marshal had read the warlike
proclamations of General Olañeta to the people of the Perus and
to his own army; he had been informed of the letters to Pío Tristán
and other communications Olañeta had written to the various
Spanish pockets that held out and refused to accept the Ayacucho
surrender, inciting them to go on fighting.[2] Then he received the
perfidious letter of Casimiro Olañeta, in which the young man
informed Sucre of the real intentions of his uncle to gain time in
order to strengthen the Separatist army for the eventual attack on
the Patriots. Naturally this communication shed new light on the
strange behavior of General Olañeta. But what had infuriated
Sucre more than anything else was that the Spanish general had
dispatched Colonel Valdez, alias Barbarucho, on a raid into the
province of Puno, across the Desaguadero River, in order to seize
fifty thousand pesos of tribute money. Seemingly Barbarucho failed
in this bold attempt.[3]

Marshal Sucre felt little disposed to let this provocative act
pass without informing Olañeta of his displeasure. On his way from

**161**

Cuzco to Puno, in the little village of Santa Rosa, he wrote a stringent letter to Olañeta, amounting to an ultimatum. He told the rebel general that he had had confidence in his good faith and therefore had not protected the Desaguadero border. Sucre told Olañeta that he was surprised and indignant when he was informed of the raid of Colonel Valdez. He added that it was "painful to use our arms against soldiers with whom we offered to share our laurels." Yet the marshal did not close the door completely and did not make this letter a declaration of war. He told the Spanish general that he was still willing to forget all past abuses and offer peace and friendship to him once more. But if General Olañeta was unwilling to accept this offer, the "ray of Ayacucho will put terror among the ungratefuls." Sucre gave Olañeta twelve days to make up his mind, but demanded that he evacuate La Paz and Oruro and concentrate his army in Potosí, while the Bolivarian unit would occupy northern Charcas. Then an assembly of the people of Charcas should decide about the future of their provinces. He terminated this letter by reminding the general that the United Army had begun its advance.[4]

But Marshal Sucre's letter was ignored and General Olañeta never answered it. He was beset by problems even more pressing than the advance of the Bolivarian army. His own regime was beginning to crumble. Casimiro Olañeta, his nephew and secretary whom he loved so much, had laid a careful plan of subversion; and early in the morning of January 14, four days before Sucre sent his qualified declaration of war, the Royalist garrison of Cochabamba revolted and proclaimed the cause of freedom and arrested those who wished to remain faithful. The turncoat commander of the Cochabamba rebellion was Colonel Antonio Saturnino Sánchez; he said that he had decided to join "the sacred cause of our liberty." Immediately the newly-converted Patriots, who had suddenly become so fond of the principle of liberty and freedom, organized a revolutionary army and were ready to advance east and south from Cochabamba.[5] The marshal received the good news on January 26 and he immediately dispatched another letter to the rebel general, telling him that this was conclusive proof that the people of Upper Peru, as well as Olañeta's own army, were more than willing to join the side of the Patriots. He hoped that General Olañeta would realize the futility of continuing to oppose the generous offer of the Patriots, and he reiterated the wish that the general would join the army of freedom. At the same time he warned Olañeta not to undertake any punitive moves against Cochabamba.[6]

Marshal Sucre expected Olañeta to evacuate La Paz in view of the events of Cochabamba.[7] Realizing that the enemy in Cochabamba would outflank him, that is precisely what he did. On January 28 the Spanish Separatist army departed in haste from La Paz, taking the road to Oruro. The next day the guerrilla leader, Lanza, with his Ayopaya unit, entered La Paz and proclaimed the cause of freedom.[8] The rebel general was retreating quickly with between one thousand and fifteen hundred men,[9] losing nearly three hundred soldiers who deserted.[10] Olañeta had to by-pass Oruro because the turncoat ex-guerrilla leader, Colonel Arraya, had come out for the Bolivarian cause and wanted to stop the Spanish general on the outskirts of the town. Olañeta and Barbarucho were able to avoid Arraya. It was Casimiro Olañeta who had convinced Arraya, before he left for Puno, to rebel at the opportune moment. But Arraya missed his chance to apprehend Olañeta.[11] The Spanish general hastily marched south in order to reach the safety of the fortress of Potosí. There he stopped and was ready to reorganize his decimated army. Barbarucho and Colonel Medinaceli, whom he trusted, remained at his side. But Medinaceli was working hand in hand with Casimiro and was waiting for the chance that Arraya had missed. Barbarucho could not be bought, and he was loyal to the last.[12]

In view of General Olañeta's retreat to southern Charcas Marshal Sucre advanced leisurely with his liberating army toward the Desaguadero River. He left Cuzco on January 19, was in Sicuani on the twenty-third, and entered Puno, the last Lower Peruvian town before the river, on February 1. There he stopped for several days. Two days later, on February 3 at noon, he was joined by Casimiro Olañeta, and the next day the Bolivarian army departed for La Paz. On February 4 the army was in the little village of Acora on the shores of Lake Titicaca. The next day the advancing army camped in Ilave and then continued its march under torrential rain. Even so it was a victorious march. In the densely populated villages along the shores of the lake the army was received with zealous sympathy. Each of these indigenous villages had built triumphal arches and the inhabitants in their colorful vestments surrounded the Bolivarian army, singing gay songs and

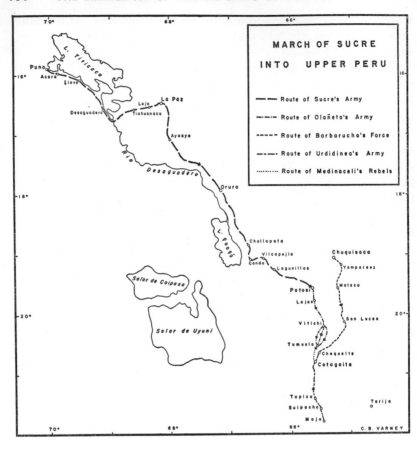

dancing to the rhythm of Aymara music. Casimiro Olañeta was proudly riding next to the adored young marshal. On February 6, the army crossed the Desaguadero River in the delicate but elegantly built rafts of totora reeds. The marshal then called his army to a halt so that he might leisurely view the ruins of Tiahuanacu. Later, in Laja, a delegation of distinguished citizens of La Paz was waiting to greet the marshal. As he approached La Paz they met more and more people who had hiked all the way from the city, mostly out of curiosity, to see the advancing army. On February 7 the Bolivarian army reached the outskirts of La Paz, seeing from the cold Alto the city lying below. Everyone was overwhelmed by the breath-taking view, especially by the majestic beauty of the eternally snow-covered Illimani towering mightily over the canyon at the bottom of which lay La Paz. The army was welcomed thunderously and the way from the Alto down into the center of the city was marked by triumphal arches. From the balconies in the main streets hung sumptuous tapestries. In the main square the young marshal, surrounded by lovely ladies, listened to lengthy eulogies. The shy Sucre smiled modestly and blushed. Only the people of Quito, after his victory of Pinchincha, had given him a similar welcome, but then he had had to share it with Bolívar, who was never too shy to enjoy these adorations. Even the rough guerrilla veterans of the Ayopaya *republiqueta* participated in the welcome of the Bolivarian army. During the night and the entire next day the marshal and his officers were feted by many banquets and parties.[13]

After the festivities had calmed somewhat, on February 9, 1825, Marshal Sucre, as commander of the United Army of liberation, issued his famous decree which is the very cornerstone of Bolivia's independence. He began by telling the people of Charcas that the purpose of the entrance of the Bolivarian army into Upper Peru was to free them from the Spanish rule, but under no circumstances to intervene in the domestic affairs of the provinces. But the decree emphasized that it was necessary that the provinces should be governed by some authority. It stated that Upper Peru had belonged to the Viceroyalty of Buenos Aires but that this region now lacked a government that was representative of all its provinces, and therefore the inner provinces had no possibility of turning to Buenos Aires. The decree explained that any final solution for the provinces should be based on an understanding of the provinces of Charcas with the government of Lower Peru and with whatever government there was in the Río de la Plata. Because of all these complications Upper Peru would be under the authority of the commander of the United Army of liberation, until an assembly of legally chosen Upper Peruvians had decided what the provinces wanted to do. Sucre ordered that this assembly should start its deliberations on April 29 in Oruro. The army of liberation would accept the resolution of this body. The commander forbade strictly any intervention by his army in the proceedings of the assembly. There were seven articles detailing the procedure of election of the delegates to the congress. The decree was signed by Antonio José de Sucre and Agustín Geraldino, his personal secretary, in

La Paz on February 9, 1825.[14] It has passed into the annals of history as the decree of February 9. This was, then, the basic document out of which came the assembly which declared the independence of Upper Peru.[15]

As the decree was signed by Sucre and elaborated without the knowledge of Bolívar, the marshal should be called the father of Bolivia. Yet Bolivian historians as well as foreign authors assume that the real author of the decree was Casimiro Olañeta. It is said that Casimiro, as soon as he joined Sucre in Puno, convinced him to write this proclamation.[16] Urcullu, the chronicler and *compadre* of Casimiro, was the first to attribute authorship of the decree to Casimiro.[17] Because of Olañeta's inspiration in the writing of the famous February 9 decree, this Upper Peruvian politician is today considered as father of Bolivia. Casimiro Olañeta himself wrote that, "In Acora [the village on Lake Titicaca] I inspired the great philosopher and marshal, Sucre, with the idea of independence of the provinces of Upper Peru, and the foundation of a new republic, which came to be called *Boliviana* by the assembly of deliberation to which I belonged."[18] These claims would indeed make sense in view of Olañeta's ability to scheme and plot, and would be the logical final result of his great intrigue. If Casimiro had been able to convince his uncle to rebel and bring doom to the Spanish cause against heavy odds, it might, as Casimiro stated, have been easy work to "inspire" the young marshal who was then at a loss about what to do with the inner provinces.

However, this decree was written by Marshal Sucre alone, and it was the product of his own judgment. René-Moreno, in his unpublished essay on Casimiro Olañeta, has assumed that he could not have written or inspired it. Humberto Vázquez-Machicado, using the René-Moreno essay, elaborated and expanded his thesis.[19] Yet neither author had conclusive proof. Both writers based their deductions mostly on a thorough study of the intimate letters of Sucre to Bolívar, in which it is apparent that before the marshal arrived in Puno he had already reached the conclusion that Upper Peru wished to be on its own, and that therefore an assembly should decide its fate. This can be further corroborated by the letter of the marshal to General Olañeta from Santa Rosa, a message which virtually constituted an ultimatum. It should be recalled that in this Santa Rosa ultimatum the marshal requested the rebel general to retreat to Potosí and said that an assembly should decide the future of the provinces of Charcas. The letters of Sucre show that he conceived the idea of an assembly himself, before he reached Puno on February 1, 1825. Furthermore, because of a newly published source, unavailable to René-Moreno and Vázquez-Machicado, one can show definitely by a simple process of chronology that Casimiro Olañeta had nothing to do with the decree of February 9.

It can be established that Sucre finished the decree on the night of February 2 at Puno, because the marshal wrote on February 3 to his friend and superior, Bolívar, "Last night, thinking about the business of Upper Peru, I arranged the ideas into the enclosed decree to be published upon my arrival in La Paz, if it looks feasible then."[20] The marshal thus says specifically that he wrote the decree on the night before, February 2, and was sending a copy to Bolívar. Urcullu assumed that Casimiro Olañeta arrived in Puno on February 1, and from this reference almost all Bolivian historians and the Peruvian, Paz Soldán, have said that Olañeta joined Sucre on the first of the month.[21] In the absence of other definite indication, René-Moreno and Vázquez-Machicado accept this date. If Casimiro was with the marshal on the first, then it would be very conceivable that he could still have inspired the decree, even taking Sucre's earlier ideas into consideration. Here then lies the weakness of the René-Moreno-Vázquez-Machicado deduction. But if Casimiro arrived in Puno on the first, where is the proof? Sucre never specified the exact date when the young man joined him; the marshal's secretary, Rey de Castro, does not cite a date and neither does Colonel Burdett O'Connor, who was with Sucre. But it was General Alvarado who gave more details than anyone else about the arrival of Casimiro at Puno. It should be recalled that when Alvarado left Puno for a trip to Argentina he encountered Casimiro Olañeta about ten miles from town, as he was going toward Puno to join Sucre. General Alvarado in his memoirs does not tell the day of his departure from Puno. Yet Sucre, in his letter of February 3, the same one in which he enclosed a copy of the draft of the decree for Bolívar, wrote the Liberator that "Alvarado has left *this morning* from here."[22] It seems then, that Alvarado left Puno on the morning of February 3 and that after riding three leagues (about ten miles), he encountered Casimiro who was on his way to meet Sucre. Alvarado probably encountered Olañeta in the late morning and by then Casimiro still had to walk or ride ten miles more. Therefore he should have reached Puno about noon on February 3. If this is the case, Casimiro Olañeta was not even present at the time the decree was written. It had already been drafted the night before his arrival at Puno, when he and Sucre met for the first time.[23]

Sucre said that he had a long talk with Casimiro Olañeta on February 3, which coincides with the date of arrival.[24] Whether Olañeta told him about the wishes of Charcas to become independent on this day remains a matter of speculation. Sucre does not mention anything specifically. Casimiro might have done it, but at the same time it is not very probable that Sucre, who had just met the young man, showed him the draft of the decree which he had written the night before. On February 4 the army was in the little village of Acora, and again Sucre and Casimiro had a long conference about the problem of Upper Peru. Casimiro told Sucre, according to a letter from Sucre to Bolívar, that the people of Charcas had come to dislike the United Provinces and that it would be very difficult to join the inner provinces to Buenos Aires. Casimiro insisted that Upper Peru wanted either independence or union with Lower Peru, but he thought that men of judgment in Charcas wanted to join Lower Peru if the capital would be in Cuzco.[25] This more or less coincides with what Olañeta himself wrote when he said that he influenced Sucre in Acora. Olañeta was correct in the fact that he and Sucre debated the question of Charcas seriously and extensively in the village of Acora. And Olañeta wrote this in 1839, which meant that he recalled this little village very well fourteen years later, probably because of the serious discussion they had on this day.[26]

When, on February 9, Sucre published his decree, Olañeta naturally assumed that the conversation in Acora had been the basis for the decree. It seems that both Sucre and Olañeta had the same idea, that of granting independence to Upper Peru. Naturally Olañeta's adherence to this proposal was motivated by personal ambitions; Sucre honestly felt that it was the proper solution. Although Sucre was the sole author of the decree, Casimiro Olañeta was indeed the most powerful personality in the emergence of Bolivia, because of his masterful intrigues in 1824 and 1825 and his great influence on the Upper Peruvian intelligentsia. Actually, both Olañeta and Sucre are the fathers of the nation; the one because of shrewd intrigues and scheming, the other because of an honest, forceful, and clear policy. But before the decree could be implemented the army of General Olañeta had to be defeated.

General Olañeta remained passively in Potosí while Sucre stayed in La Paz, laying the foundation for a free Charcas. The tension between the two opposing armies had relaxed somewhat. The marshal was in no hurry and was hoping that the Separatist army would collapse by itself, therefore avoiding useless bloodshed. The marshal was quite worried about the eagerness of the new Patriots of Cochabamba to march against Olañeta via Chuquisaca. He said to Bolívar that if this Cochabamba contingent clashed with Olañeta it might be defeated, and in addition, "one should never trust a contingent which has just deserted." Sucre felt quite relieved when the Cochabamba troops turned around and retreated to the city.[27] The new commander of Oruro, Colonel Carlos María Ortega, taking things into his own hands, had threatened Olañeta with a strong letter. When Sucre was informed of this he reprimanded Ortega severely. But the colonel continued to be insubordinate, showing no sympathy toward Sucre's policy of moderation. The marshal wrote him a blistering letter, and called Ortega an "insolent" officer. He said to the colonel, "I do not know where you have learned to be disorderly. In the last few days I have noticed that you have been very ostentatious and I am very tired of it . . . . I want more exactness, less of the show of authority and noise in which you are now engaged."[28]

The marshal was extremely particular that the United Army behave properly; he wanted it to be a model of good conduct and organization. He gave strict orders that perfect harmony must obtain between the troops and the people of Charcas. He threatened that any soldier or officer who abused the people would be "severely punished or even condemned to death." He told his officers that when they traveled they should never ask or demand aid from the people except from those specified in their travel orders. If any soldier or officer abused his authority the municipalities should put a pair of shackles on him and send him straight to the superior headquarters of the United Army. The marshal was also concerned about good clothing and food for his army. As soon as he reached La Paz he requested that three thousand comfortable overcoats be made because of the severe cold. He stated in an order that "the food should be good, abundant, and nutritious," and that even the "horses should be treated with great care and special neatness."²⁹ The marshal wanted to see that the army of liberation was worthy of its title. But above anything else, Sucre wanted to avoid further bloodshed. His favorite phrase was that he wanted to economize American blood, and that anyone who saved even "one single drop of American blood" had rendered an "important service to humanity."³⁰ With this in mind he addressed letters to practically all the officers of the army of General Olañeta, offering them all kinds of guarantees and positions with their same ranks in the United Army of liberation.

In the meantime Casimiro Olañeta was working actively from his desk, trying to persuade many of his Upper Peruvian Royalist friends to desert the cause of his uncle. Sucre's moderation and correctness and Casimiro's ability for scheming were quite a successful combination. On February 12 the Royalist garrison of the rich village of Vallegrande, belonging to the Aguilera unit, joined the Sucre army.³¹ The marshal had wooed Aguilera in three long and detailed letters, but Augilera was undecided.³² When Vallegrande deserted, Aguilera surrendered to the new turncoat officers who sent him as a prisoner to La Paz.³³ On February 14 the garrison and city of Santa Cruz followed the example of Vallegrande,³⁴ and joined the Bolivarian army. It must be said that Aguilera himself did not change allegiance, but surrendered. On February 22 the Separatist colonel, Francisco López, Spanish commander of Chuquisaca, defected to Sucre.³⁵ This event made the marshal extremely happy, as it occurred in the capital. He hurried a letter of gratification to López, saying that "the army of liberation and I give you our thanks for having joined our ranks." At the same time he ordered López to see to it that General Olañeta did not try to march east with the intention of making an escape into Brazil. He also wrote López not to get overly enthusiastic and march on Potosí to fight Olañeta, but rather to remain in Chuquisaca.³⁶

General Olañeta waited tensely in Potosí to see what Sucre would do, and when he intended to leave for Potosí. He dispatched the daring Barbarucho across the mountain range into the Altiplano to gather information about the United Army. He also called together a war council of his trusted officers, including the malicious Medinaceli. The main issue before the council was whether to surrender or fight until the last. No one wished to surrender except Colonel José de Mendizábal; all wished to go on to the last and, in case of final defeat, avoid falling into the hands of Sucre or the turncoats.[37] Medinaceli, who was in communication with Casimiro, was still waiting for the opportune moment to apprehend the general and hand him over to Sucre. At the council meeting he vociferously insisted on fighting to the last man. General Olañeta was unaware of Medinaceli's treason. If his army collapsed completely he wanted to make his way to the Arenales unit in Salta and surrender to him.[38] Strangely enough, Governor Arenales, the long-time Patriot veteran, was a friend of General Olañeta.[39] Olañeta's home was in Salta; besides his wife he had many friends there. The general was set to hold out until the very last, and then go alone to meet Arenales.

One of the first things General Olañeta did in Potosí was to issue another proclamation, trying to create the impression that he had not cooperated with Bolívar. The Liberator had published Olañeta's first letter written from Oruro on October 2, in which the Separatist general showed sympathy with the Bolivarian cause. The general now accused Bolívar of having made changes in the letter which made him, General Olañeta, appear to have worked in association with the Liberator. However, it seems that the version published by Bolívar was the correct one, and that Olañeta was the one who changed the letter.[40] Olañeta published Bolívar's version in the proclamation and next to it, his own.[41] In the original, the letter was addressed to "Simón Bolívar, Liberator of Colombia and Dictator of Peru," but in the revised letter it read only to "General Simón Bolívar." In the Olañeta version many additional sentences and phrases such as "my love for the King and Spain," and "dignity of the throne" are added. In the Bolívar rendition Olañeta wrote that he thought that "a solid system" was the appropriate solution to all the problems of America; the Separatist general changed this to say that the "monarchial system" was the one he believed in. And the final sentence in which General Olañeta wrote in grand style, "I wish we could make our sentiments uniform, and give a day of rejoicing to America and humanity," was changed to ". . . give a day of rejoicing to *Spain*, to America and humanity."[42] The general had given a completely different meaning to the letter by the few changes and additions. In October the general had negotiated with the Liberator because he wanted to undermine the cause of the Constitutionalists, whom he hated. Later this letter was embarrassing to him since the hateful trio, La Serna,

Canterac, and Valdés, had been eliminated. He now wanted to deny any show of sympathy with Bolívar.

The proclamation of General Olañeta in itself was of little importance, except to show that the general was determined to fight the Bolivarian army with the same intensity he fought the Constitutionalist army. He would not spare any means, even if dishonest, to damage the enemy. When his army was in a position inferior to the powerful unit of Sucre and victory was out of the question, he decided to try terrorist methods and even to poison Marshal Sucre. After a long search for the appropriate man to undertake this distasteful job, he finally located a Swiss mercenary soldier and adventurer who had fought with the Lanza guerrilla unit.[43] The man's name was Paul Ecles; he was about forty years old, quite illiterate, tall, robust, and blond,[44] indeed a rare specimen in those regions. Ecles was willing to undertake the task. He was provided with some arsenic poison in a small capsule and was supposed to make his way to the Bolivarian headquarters, and then at the appropriate moment slip into the kitchen and drop the capsule in the pot in which the chocolate to be served to Sucre was boiling. The marshal was known to be fond of chocolate and consumed it regularly at every meal. Ecles was also asked to try to poison his ex-commander, General Lanza.[45] Once his main purpose of killing the marshal was achieved, he was to collect from some Spaniards in La Paz his reward of sixteen thousand pesos. But in case Ecles might fail the general was still on the lookout for another person whom he could persuade, for another sixteen thousand pesos, to kill Sucre.[46] Ecles left for his mission and took the road to Oruro. What advantage General Olañeta could see in killing Sucre and Lanza is hardly understandable, except that the Spanish general wanted to go down in defeat causing as much trouble and damage as possible.

By the middle of March the marshal felt that he was ready to move with his army toward Potosí In more than a month in La Paz he had carefully and diligently reorganized his United Army. Since his entrance into Upper Peru eighteen hundred Upper Peruvians had been added to the army, all of them from units which had deserted General Olañeta. Sucre now commanded sixty-one hundred men, while Olañeta had only thirteen hundred left. The Bolivarian cavalry outnumbered the Separatists by six to one.[47] Sucre's precise instructions to all the commanders during the months of February and March show that he wanted to march on Potosí with a powerful army and force the Spanish general to evacuate the city without a battle, by impressing him with the superior might of the United Army. Finally, after many days of delay, the army left La Paz on March 12 for Oruro, where Colonel Ortega had gathered three thousand soldiers.[48] The marshal left the Colombian division in La Paz to continue its rest from the hard campaign in Lower Peru. Only the Peruvian and new Charcas units were called upon to advance on Olañeta, and the tough but humorous Irishman, Burdett O'Connor, was put in charge of this combined Peruvian army.

The Irish commander led the march to Oruro while the marshal, accompanied by the two *dos caras,* Casimiro Olañeta and Mariano Calvimontes, followed at a distance. At the Altiplano village of Ayoayo Sucre was nearly killed when his horse stumbled and fell, almost crushing its rider.[49] Fortunately, the marshal only smashed his left hand. When O'Connor reached Oruro on March 14, a day ahead of Sucre, he was met by a strange, tall, blond man in a military jacket who could not speak either Spanish or English, but who gave O'Connor a small capsule and some documents signed by General Olañeta. O'Connor, to his amazement, after having finished reading the letters carefully, realized that they were instructions to poison Marshal Sucre and General Lanza, plus letters addressed to four Spaniards in La Paz to pay a reward after the death of Sucre. The blond soldier was, of course, Ecles, who had repented his action and decided to surrender. The Irish commander rushed the news to Sucre, who immediately requested Casimiro Olañeta and O'Connor to subject Ecles to a long questioning in order to find out more details. Ecles acted confused; he could speak only German, and his questioners were unable to locate anyone who spoke that language. Sucre decided to make Ecles understand that he should immediately leave the Perus and return home. The marshal gave him enough money to make his way back to Switzerland.[50] At the same time he wrote to La Paz, ordering the arrest of the four Spaniards.[51] But Sucre was extremely perturbed about the Ecles affair and wrote a letter to General Olañeta, saying, "It is impossible to believe that a man like you who boasts about moral and religious principles can even think of such a horrible attempt. . . . Such a crime can only fit into an evil and corrupted heart, and speaking frankly, I never thought you were capable of this." Then Sucre warned Olañeta that he had given strict orders that if any officer of the United Army was murdered or poisoned he would take Spanish hostages and put them before a firing squad.[52]

On March 19, 1825, the powerful United Army left Oruro, toward its great targets, Potosí and General Olañeta. But before the departure the marshal requested one of his staff officers of the Oruro garrison to go in search of a spacious house with a large hall in which to hold the meeting of the forthcoming assembly of the deputies of Charcas who would decide the future of the Upper Peruvian provinces. Sucre said that this place must be "clean and decent."[53] The marshal intended to make a flanking movement by taking the road to Chuquisaca and occupying the capital before Potosí, if this became necessary. In this way he wanted to force the Spanish general to evacuate Potosí and retreat south instead of east toward Brazil. From Chuquisaca Sucre thought that he could march south faster, on better roads, than Olañeta, and therefore cut off his retreat.[54] But he said that this was a flexible plan and depended on the movements of Olañeta, and that he would make his final decision of whether to march directly on Potosí or to go via Chuquisaca once he crossed the cordillera and had reached Vilcapugio. He wrote the commander of Chuquisaca, Colonel López, that should Olañeta leave for the capital he should evacuate the town rather than risk a battle.[55] The Bolivarian army advanced on the high Altiplano along the shores of Lake Popo and made its first stop at Challapata. Here Colonel O'Connor remained somewhat longer than Sucre in order to integrate a new Upper Peruvian unit. Sucre and Casimiro Olañeta went ahead toward the next village of Condo, eighty-five miles from Oruro and the last stop before crossing the Cordillera de los Frailes. At Condo most of the army units would concentrate for a final review and then begin their powerful push toward Chuquisaca and Potosí[56]

On their way from Challapata to Condo on the dry and desert-like Altiplano, with whistling winds and biting cold, a serious conversation took place between Sucre and Casimiro about the future of Charcas. What was said remains a matter of speculation. Probably Casimiro, in view of a closer acquaintance with Sucre than before, felt more confident and insisted on the need of making the Charcas provinces independent of Argentina and Lower Peru. In Acora Olañeta had given the impression that Upper Peru might wish to join Lower Peru, but now he emphasized this solution less and less. It is quite possible that Sucre listened attentively but remained noncommittal and left the final decision to the forthcoming assembly called by him. But then even if this body would declare independence it would not be effective until the approval of the United Provinces and Lower Peru was granted according to the stipulations of the February 9 decree. There were three conflicting sovereignties in Charcas in 1825: first the wishes of Upper Peru, second the congress of Lower Peru, and third the congress of the United Provinces.[57] Even a fourth one might be added, the will of the United Army of liberation under Sucre.[58] Perhaps Olañeta asked Sucre to intervene in the future deliberations of the Upper Peruvian congress and throw his weight in favor of independence or to use the army of liberation to oppose the claims of sovereignty by Argentina and Lower Peru over Charcas. Undoubtedly the marshal politely refused such drastic action and wished to leave unchanged the ambiguity of the decree of February 9. All this is pure speculation, for the only thing known is that an important talk took place on the road from Challapata to Condo, and that Casimiro Olañeta was troubled; he wanted to dramatize the need for an independent Upper Peru. He left Sucre's side, reined his horse about, and galloped back toward Challapata.

After having finished his administrative task in Challapata, O'Connor left the village to catch up with the marshal. To his surprise he found Casimiro Olañeta on the road, alone, waiting for him. Casimiro rushed to the colonel and said that he wished to talk to him and ask him a question. O'Connor, always friendly and affable, was only too glad to have Casimiro Olañeta ride along with him on the dusty trail. Casimiro told the Irishman that he and Sucre had talked about the future of Charcas and the decree of February 9, and whether the provinces should join Argentina or Lower Peru or become independent. After this Casimiro, with his bouncing enthusiasm and shrewd mind, asked O'Connor, "I wish to know your opinion, Colonel, in regard to this matter which is so important to us." Casimiro had great ability to make other people believe at the right moment that their judgment was vital, thus stimulating their egos. O'Connor was only too glad to tell Casimiro his ideas, and stated that since he was actively engaged in this campaign in Upper Peru he had with him many maps of the country and had studied them carefully. Before coming into

Upper Peru, he had made it a point to become acquainted with the history and problems of the provinces in order to have a good background. He told Casimiro that if the country was as rich from Challapata south to the Argentine border as it was from the Desaguadero to Challapata, a road which he had just covered, "I don't see why it should be added to Lower Peru or to Argentina." O'Connor said that as soon as Casimiro heard this answer he spurred his horse with great enthusiasm and galloped away toward Condo.

Indeed O'Connor must have been somewhat surprised at such odd behavior, but then he gave it little thought. The Irish colonel reached Condo at night and immediately went to see Sucre to let him know of his arrival. O'Connor had completely forgotten his strange conversation with Casimiro several hours before, but when he entered the room everyone got up and ran to embrace the perplexed colonel, calling him the "founder of a new republic."[59] O'Connor seemingly took it as a joke, and later when he served Bolivia with great distinction[60] never insisted on being called the inspirer of the republic. Casimiro Olañeta was making sure that Sucre would not turn his back on the idea of ultimate independence for Charcas, and on the long road from Puno to Potosí the young man, more than anyone else, exercised great influence over Sucre. This little episode of Casimiro Olañeta and the Irish colonel, Burdett O'Connor, shows the great charm, warmth, and outward expression of sincerity and enthusiasm Casimiro was able to exhibit to convince people. The conversation of the Altiplano once more indicates that Casimiro and Sucre stand as the coauthors of Bolivia.

From Condo the army began to cross the steep Cordillera de los Frailes by the way of Vilcapugio on March 24, reaching Lagunillas two days later.[61] There Sucre issued a proclamation to the army of Olañeta, telling it that its commander, General Olañeta, was a rebel to the Spanish cause and a traitor to the American cause. He asked them to desert and come over to the army of liberation.[62] In view of the possibility that General Olañeta might abandon Potosí at any moment it was decided to advance straight on the Imperial City. On the night of March 28 the powerful United Army camped in the alfalfa fields on the outskirts of Potosí where the many mules of the silver mines grazed. A patrol unit under the revolving turncoat, Colonel Arraya, dared to make its way into the city and found out that General Olañeta had evacuated with his reduced army at eleven o'clock that morning, in a state of complete confusion. Arraya and his soldiers, because of the late hour, decided to camp in the middle of the main square. Around one hundred of Olañeta's soldiers had deserted and hidden in the town in order not to have to go south with him.[63] Olañeta had taken with him about sixty thousand pesos in gold from the Casa de Moneda.[64] The next day the whole Bolivarian army entered Potosí, and its inhabitants were somewhat taken by surprise since they had had no previous information of the proximity of the Sucre contingents. They had missed their chance to prepare the usual grandiose reception for a victorious army. But some quickly improvised festivities were organized to honor the young Venezuelan commander.[65] Sucre was none too enthusiastic about Potosí; he thought that the town was full of *godos,* and was much too cold.[66]

Olañeta had decided to continue the war and had told Sucre on March 22 that even if everyone was against him he would go down fighting because his honor and his fidelity to the king demanded it.[67] For him only two choices existed: either to die or give himself up to his friend, Arenales. The Spanish general dispatched Medinaceli to the fortress of Cotagaita while he had the resourceful Barbarucho take the road to Chuquisaca with five hundred men, to ransack some of the rich villages in the valley. The bold Royalist colonel even undertook one of his surprise raids into the capital to obtain funds.[68] Olañeta himself left Potosí with about four hundred soldiers for the next village south, known as Vitichi, a center of goatherds where cordovan leather was manufactured by the villagers.[69] Near the abandoned mine of Lava, well-remembered from the Separatist War, the general was nearly captured by some of his deserters. From Vitichi he dispatched his aide, Colonel Antonio Hebia, to reinforce the troops of Medinaceli at Cotogaita and guard against the approaching force of Arenales from Salta.[70] But on March 30 Medinaceli finally decided that it was time to give his stab in the back. He had promised the *dos caras* since January to finish with the general at the right moment, but for some unknown reason he had postponed it.[71] If Medinaceli wanted the honor of capturing Olañeta and handing him over to Sucre, it was now or never. On this March day Medinaceli proclaimed the Bolivarian cause in Cotagaita.[72] Hebia, who was on his way to reinforce Medinaceli, was informed of the treason in Tumusla, and he immediately turned around and raced back to Vitichi to consult with Olañeta about this critical situation. The Spanish general decided to advance on Cotagaita to battle the traitor while he was moving north toward Vitichi to apprehend Olañeta. The armies met on April 1 in the afternoon at Tumusla, a village situated on Tumusla Creek, about seventy miles south of Potosí.[73] One distinguished author writes that Olañeta had seven hundred men while Medinaceli commanded only three hundred soldiers, but this is undocumented and is hardly possible.[74] Olañeta was severely defeated and wounded, and Medinaceli affirmed that he surrendered to him. The next day, on April 2, Medinaceli informed Sucre in a short statement that the general had died of the wounds he had received in the battle.[75] So came to an end the career of the great and most complex Spanish general, who brought doom to the Spanish cause in the Perus but refused to come to terms with the Patriots, preferring to die for the king.

Olañeta had infuriated everyone including the affable Sucre, who the day of the battle of Tumusla had said that General Olañeta was "the most abominable delirium of Spanish despotism."[76] A German author even thinks that Olañeta had wanted to conquer all South America, while an Argentine editor dismisses all this and says that the general was an "imbecile who lived without honor and died without glory."[77] The Chilean, Gonzalo Bulnes, wonders if it will not "be difficult for posterity to concede to this man the rehabilitation and admiration that is due to everyone who serves in one or another camp, under different banners, for a great cause or the sovereignty of his homeland, because Olañeta did not frankly join one or the other side." Mariano Torrente, the best Spanish historian of the War of Independence, says that Olañeta's tragic death was proof of his innocence and that he was the unfortunate victim of some malicious advisers.[78] General Olañeta was never considered a traitor at the court and when the king was informed of the great defeat of Ayacucho, in the royal cedula of May 28, 1825, he named General Olañeta the new viceroy.[79] It was not known then in Spain that the general had died nearly two months before in defense of the crown. The general's great ambition to become viceroy, of which his nephew had so dishonestly taken advantage, had finally come true. This time the assignment was genuine, but too late, for the general already rested in his grave, probably in the frozen ground of Tumusla.[80] He was a victim of his fanatic loyalty to the crown and of treason by two Upper Peruvians whom he had always trusted, Casimiro Olañeta, the creator of Bolivia, and Carlos Medinaceli, future general of the Bolivarian army.[81] Only a year later Sucre had to admit to a close friend that Medinaceli and Arraya were "very bad" people.[82]

The battle of Tumusla still remains a mystery. Urcullu, who was on his way to talk to General Olañeta, affirmed that only a single shot was fired, by an unknown soldier, with the intent of murdering the general.[83] Urcullu's statement seems correct, especially in view of Medinaceli's laconic letter giving no details of the battle but simply saying, "The action was decided at seven o'clock [and] General Olañeta has just died at this moment [April 2]."[84] Where are the surrender terms, and the account of how many soldiers perished in the battle? Medinaceli never elaborated and Sánchez de Velasco, another chronicler of this war and probably a witness, said that Sucre, when informed of the death of Olañeta, was annoyed and suspected foul play.[85]

As soon as Marshal Sucre entered Potosí he had talk with Urcullu, who probably had come up from Chuquisaca.[86] During the invasion of the Bolivarian army Urcullu had outwardly taken a neutral attitude, but had maintained good relations with General Olañeta, who trusted him until the very last and relied heavily on his advice.[87] At the same time he was in intimate contact with Casimiro Olañeta and the turncoats of Chuquisaca. Sucre took advantage of Urcullu's good standing with General Olañeta and requested him to go and seek the general, convince him of the futility of further resistance, and offer him fair surrender terms.[88] Sucre had received information from Medinaceli through the *dos caras*, Usín, that the Spanish colonel was definitely planning to switch allegiance and fight General Olañeta any day.[89] The marshal was convinced that Medinaceli was serious and he wrote to Bolívar, "I am hopeful that Medinaceli will catch Olañeta and send him to me."[90] But Sucre was also afraid that the traitorous colonel might fail in his attempt and therefore decided to stay as short a time as possible in Potosí and depart for a position near Medinaceli in case the colonel needed help. The marshal promised Medinaceli that he would leave Potosí on April 2, but he was delayed by administrative matters.[91]

On the next day the advance units under O'Connor departed

in the late morning for their campaign to the south and Sucre was ready to follow on April 4. About ten miles from town O'Connor was stopped by a messenger of Medinaceli, who informed him of the victory of Tumusla and the death of Olañeta. O'Connor then halted his advance and turned around to return to the city, leaving his army at Lava. Having told the Irish colonel the good news, the messenger went ahead to inform Sucre of the happy events of Tumusla. He reached Potosí around noon when Sucre had just finished his lunch and retired for a short rest. José María Rey de Castro, the marshal's faithful and diligent personal secretary, rushed to Sucre's room with the news.[92] Sucre was not overly pleased by Olañeta's death because he had wanted to capture the general alive and convince him of his wrong attitude toward the United Army "and show him how generous *we are,*" as he told Bolívar. He suspected that some foul play had taken place.[93] Casimiro Olañeta rushed to Sucre's side, and when informed of the news gave the appearance of deep pain, and it is said that he was shaken because of his uncle's death.[94] Apparently Casimiro was also a good actor. Marshal Sucre dispatched a letter to Medinaceli to congratulate him on his victory. At the same time he wrote another letter to the colonel, ordering him to see to it that the widow of General Olañeta be treated with great respect and that anyone who insulted her should be severely punished. In a third letter the marshal asked Medinaceli to congratulate, in his name, all the soldiers and officers who had fought at Tumusla against Olañeta.[95]

The only remaining Spanish force in the Perus was the unit of Barbarucho, who had taken the road to Chuquisaca and then disappeared. Sucre estimated that Barbarucho had with him between four and five hundred men.[96] The marshal decided that O'Connor could handle the situation and therefore commanded the Irish colonel to go in search of Valdez. Sucre gave O'Connor precise instructions, especially that he should take all precautionary steps because Barbarucho was the boldest and most cunning officer that the Spanish army had. The marshal had great respect for the ability of the venturesome Valdez and he was unwilling to suffer a defeat by the last small Spanish unit just at the end of the war. O'Connor had thirteen hundred men with him while Medinaceli's force was estimated at around seven hundred men, made up mostly of the defeated Olañeta contingents. Medinaceli was ordered to obey the command of O'Connor. Therefore the Irish colonel had two thousand soldiers as compared with the five hundred of Barbarucho.[97] The marshal then wrote a letter to the enemy colonel in which he said that "a courageous officer always should be treated with respect," but that Valdez' situation was completely hopeless and that to surrender would be no shame but would shorten the war and save lives. He offered the same terms to Valdez as had been negotiated at Ayacucho.[98] The problem was how to get the letter to Barbarucho since everyone was at a loss as to where he was. O'Connor, carrying the letter with him, departed on April 4 along the road to Potosí to Cotagaita, and in Lava joined his army which he had left behind.

Barbarucho had been in Yamparáez, near Chuquisaca, on March 30, and then had begun to move south, apparently to rejoin General Olañeta.[99] On April 2, the day of the death of his beloved commander, Valdez was in Mataca and in the last three days had lost half of his troops by desertion. The last Spanish colonel wished to continue to San Lucas with the probable purpose of making his way to the Argentine border.[100] Yet his small force was disintegrating completely and the colonel then decided to swing east and go to the fortress of Cotagaita and surrender. On April 7 he reached the royal highway at a place called Chequelte by Sucre and Urdininea, and Vichacla by O'Connor, situated somewhat south of Tumusla and north of Cotagaita.[101] Here at Chequelte Valdez met Colonel Urdininea of the advance guard of the little Arenales expedition that was coming up from Salta. Days earlier Urdininea had deserted the Argentine army and joined the Bolivarian army.[102] Valdez surrendered to the enigmatic Urdininea who had switched from one ally to the other. Urdininea then dispatched Valdez with some guards to Potosí to present him to Sucre. A few miles north Barbarucho met O'Connor who was still searching for him and his nonexistent army. The Irish colonel was astounded when he suddenly saw Barbarucho as a prisoner, going to meet Sucre, and he felt somewhat annoyed at his failure, but took it in good humor.[103] About midnight of April 8 Sucre received the news of the surrender of Barbarucho at Chequelte,[104] and the next morning, April 9, he issued a proclamation to all the authorities of Upper Peru, informing them of the capture "of the last enemy that remained in Peru." He stated that with this surrender he was declaring "the absolute and final end of the war."[105] The same morning of April 9 a High Mass with a *Te Deum* was celebrated with all the authorities in attendance to give thanks for the successful end of the war in the Perus.[106]

From the Desaguadero River to Chequelte the powerful army of liberation had not fired a single shot at the enemy. The Spanish army had disintegrated by itself, by the mere presence of the Bolivarian army in Charcas and by the successful schemes of the *dos caras* who had found many officers ready to abandon the lost Spanish cause. The war came to an end after sixteen long years and the schemers emerged as the real victors. The next step was to make their land independent of Lima and the United Provinces, and to become its masters. In Marshal Sucre they had found a credulous man who was willing to cooperate with the Upper Peruvian *doctores* because he trusted their sincere patriotism.

# Chapter 9

## THE TURNCOAT ASSEMBLY

*7*HE DECREE OF FEBRUARY 9, 1825, calling for an assembly to determine the future of the four provinces of Upper Peru, also embodied the electoral procedure for choosing its deputies. The five provinces, La Paz, Santa Cruz, Potosí, Chuquisaca, and Cochabamba, contained the colonial *partidos*. Article two of the decree stipulated that each *partido* would elect one deputy to the assembly. The election procedure was simple and provided that in the capital of each *partido* the *cabildo* and all property owners who had an annual income of three hundred pesos or more should form a local assembly and elect the deputy representing the *partido*. The qualifications for a deputy were that he must be at least twenty-five years old, have a minimum income of eight hundred pesos a year, and have resided in the *partido* no less than four years. The assembly of the *partido* must then certify the election of its delegate.[1] This electoral law was part of the decree of February 9, written by Sucre alone. It was an uncomplicated system and fairly liberal for the time, and it brought the election down to the provincial level with no extravagant property qualifications.

Unfortunately, this amateurish and unsophisticated procedure was later changed and elaborated into a much more complex electoral system, seemingly written by an expert in political procedure. It was still part of the February decree and simply constituted an amendment or elaboration of the original and basic decree worked out by Sucre. The provision for one delegate from each *partido* was changed from one to three, according to the

183

relative importance of the provinces. In this way each *partido* in Potosí was to name three delegates while the provinces of La Paz and Cochabamba were given only two each for their *partidos*, and Chuquisaca and Santa Cruz were awarded one. This might have been an improvement had it not been for the fact that Potosí, the most strongly Royalist province, had the largest representation, while more populous Cochabamba and the valleys of Chuquisaca, strongholds of the guerrilla forces, were not adequately represented in comparison. The system of electing the representatives to the assembly was made much more complicated by indirect election. First parochial elections were to be held within each parish; all citizens with the prescribed income could vote for four electors. After this all the parish electors within a *partido* would meet in the capital of the *partido* and elect from their midst a certain number of electors representing them. These new electors would then go to the capital of the province where all the electors of the *partidos* would assemble and elect the stipulated number of deputies allowed to that province. The qualifications were changed so that representatives had to be residents of the province as a whole rather than of the various *partidos*. In all, it was a thrice-removed election: parish, *partido*, and province, and although the number of deputies was based on the *partido*, the final selection was made from the entire province.[2] In this way the preponderance of the small villages and populated country-side with its plain people of grass-roots ideas and guerrilla habits was eliminated as the predominant factor in the election, which enabled the *dos caras* elements to be elected deputies. It is easy to deduce that this electoral law probably was elaborated by the two Upper Peruvian aides who accompanied Sucre from Puno to Potosí, Casimiro Olañeta and Mariano Calvimontes. Olañeta's experience on the audiencia made him an expert in these political refinements, a trait which Sucre lacked completely.

The assembly met on July 10 in Chuquisaca, and not on April 29 in Oruro as stipulated in the February decree. This delay was due to a number of factors, especially the sudden coolness of Bolívar toward the idea of calling the assembly until the delicate question of Argentina's right of control over Charcas had been more thoroughly studied. A further reason was that the province of Potosí, which would send the largest delegation to the assembly, was in the enemy's hands until the first days of April; thus an election in this department was not permitted on the specified days but only in late April.[3] The meeting of the assembly was postponed several times, and on June 3 Marshal Sucre gave up the idea of holding it in Oruro, because too many delegates had protested that the climate and high altitude of the city were not propitious for an intensive debate. He decided that the assembly should be held in Chuquisaca on June 24. The original idea of holding the meeting in Oruro would have taken the debate away from the oppressive Royalist environment of the capital, a strong point of the *dos caras* faction. Perhaps the *dos caras* were responsible for engineering the transfer, but more probably the bad climate of Oruro was an honest impediment to holding the meetings there. Further delay because of the lack of a quorum was responsible for the sessions not starting until July 10, 1825.[4]

Whether the forty-eight delegates were elected in strict accordance with the law remains an unanswered question, because of the absence of primary material, especially on the provincial level. The electoral law was restrictive in nature and the huge department of Santa Cruz could send only two delegates because in the large *partidos* of Cordillera and Chiquitos not a single man could be found who qualified for the position of deputy. These *partidos*, because of their universal illiteracy, were unable even to name the necessary electors.[5] Some irregularities did take place in La Paz, but the facts were suppressed by the assembly.[6] But the marshal did his utmost to hold honest elections. He wrote to the commanders of the provinces to watch for any irregularities and he made them personally responsible for seeing that the electoral law was strictly obeyed. To the commander of Cochabamba he said that "the election must be free so that the people have no complaint." He wrote his officers to punish severely and dismiss any provincial or parochial officials who exerted pressure in the elections.[7] When the meetings were at last ready to start, Sucre left Chuquisaca with his army so that the assembly might deliberate far away from the United Army; thus, no one could say that Sucre had intervened in the proceedings.[8] He was sincere in the belief that the Upper Peruvian delegates should decide the future of their lands without advice from outsiders. On July 1, after delaying his trip many times because the assembly had continually postponed its inauguration, the marshal and his army left Chuquisaca for Cochabamba.[9] Everything was ready for the great inauguration.

Finally, the long-awaited assembly was opened on July 10 in the city of Chuquisaca, capital of the old Audiencia of Charcas. The meetings were held in the assembly hall of the famous old house of studies known as the Universidad Pontificia y Real de San Francisco Xavier. This institution of higher learning was the intellectual center, not only of the extensive territory of the Audiencia of Charcas, but of the huge Viceroyalty of Río de la Plata. From these very halls sixteen years earlier had come the cry of independence; the university was the cradle of subversion which produced such leaders as Mariano Moreno, Bernardo Monteagudo, Juan José Castelli, the Zudañez brothers, and all the great generation of 1809. After many years of war the struggle had come to an end and again the halls of the university served as host to an assembly convened to decide the future of Charcas. These men were different from those of the generation of 1809, who had given their lives for the cause they upheld.

Thirty-nine delegates were present at the inauguration, and nine had not yet arrived in the capital.[10] In their midst were such *dos caras* as Casimiro Olañeta, Manuel María Urcullu, Angel Mariano Moscoso, and José Mariano Serrano. Almost all the other delegates were obscure people who were unknown in the annals of the War of Independence, and who probably were subservient to the will of the *dos caras*. Of the forty-eight delegates only two had the distinction of being veterans of the war. Miguel Lanza and José Miguel Ballivián were delegates from La Paz and their records, especially that of Lanza, were unblemished.[11] Most of the delegates held the doctoral degree from the university in which they were again seated, this time not to study, but to decide the fate of their provinces. A careful investigation of the records of the university and the tax records—since each graduate had to pay a specific fee—reveals that thirty of the forty-eight representatives graduated from the University of San Francisco.[12] But since the university archives as well as the tax records are incomplete, it can be assumed that of the eighteen nongraduates it is possible that a few also might have studied at the university. The preponderance of the university in preparing the environment for the War of Independence is an established and known fact. The influence of the University of San Francisco in the emergence of Bolivia is less known, but is indisputable. There is no relationship, however, between the revolutionary and idealistic generation of 1809 and the *dos caras* generation of 1825. It was an assembly of insincere *doctores* who never had the welfare of the people at heart, but who were motivated by hopes of personal gain. Casimiro Olañeta, José Mariano Serrano, and Manuel María Urcullu, the prototypes of this class, became the leaders of the assembly.

The first part of the day was dedicated to voting on the credentials of all the delegates and determining whether they were the legally elected deputies of their *partidos*. A preparatory commission had already examined the certifications of the delegates and found them all in perfect order. The assembly accepted the recommendations of the commission and the thirty-nine delegates present were seated. The same procedure was followed with the rules, which also were accepted as presented by an advance committee. Following this routine, the delegates elected José Mariano Serrano, the famous *dos caras* who had resided in Salta during the war, president of the assembly.[13] Serrano had been named provisional president of the assembly by Marshal Sucre before his departure, in order that someone might act as leader in the opening moments of the first day.[14] This act by Sucre was enough to gain the permanent presidential chair of the assembly for Serrano. José María Mendizábal of La Paz, who was a priest and former Royalist, and who had been associated with the Holy Office,[15] was named vice-president. Manuel María Urcullu was chosen to write down and edit the minutes of the assembly's deliberations.[16] But Urcullu was careful not to write down the heated debates, thus presenting a distorted picture at times.[17] Doctor Angel Moscoso and Doctor Ignacio Sanjinés were elected as secretaries to aid President Serrano in his manifold duties. These people, chosen unanimously, were apparently selected by the dominant *dos caras* faction beforehand. It should be noted that Casimiro Olañeta was not elected to any post, which was in keeping with his professed policy of handling matters from behind the scenes. Sucre realized that Olañeta was unofficial leader of the assembly; a fact he made known to Bolívar.[18]

The next act was for the executive delegates to take the oath of office, and as no precedent existed, it was decided that the president was to be sworn in by the vice-president, and that then the vice-president was to take the oath from the newly sworn president. Serrano and Mendizábal were asked to swear that they would uphold the Catholic religion, fulfill their duties as delegates to the assembly, and keep secrecy when this was demanded by vote. The secretaries took the same oath before the president. After this Serrano delivered his inaugural speech. It was a baroquely pompous speech.[19] The president said:

Where is the fatal monster surrounded by injustice, ambition, and fanaticism which has converted these provinces into a city of tyranny, a place of bloodshed, and a symbol of slavery? Where is the iniquitous power which desolated our lands, burned our villages, put our families in mourning, and dared to think that its ominous power was eternal? I ask these questions and then receive this pleasant answer, that from the Gulf of Darién to the Amazon, from the Amazon to the Rimac, from the Rimac to the Desaguadero, from the Desaguadero to the Maule, from the Maule to the Plata, the free people in one ardent and respectful cry respond that Bolívar and Sucre have destroyed forever the Lion of Iberia and have wrested from its terrible clutches the lands of the Perus and made unshakable the cherished liberties in all the continent of Columbus.

The subsequent words of the president were as bombastic as his beginning sentences; he neither delineated a plan for the future nor defined the purpose of the Assembly. The president terminated his address by asking the delegates that they always "conserve the purity of the fire of liberty, confirm the hatred for the tyrant and tyranny and behave with order, justice, and constancy in order to build the happiness of our constituents and their descendants."[20] The hypocrisy of Serrano's words reflected that of his past career.

After concluding his speech the president declared the assembly of the Upper Peruvian provinces officially inaugurated. It was then decided to name a commission of five delegates to go to the cathedral to give thanks and ask for divine inspiration. The committee left the assembly room, crossed the spacious plaza where they were joined by the various town guilds, and then entered with solemn dignity into the huge cathedral, an impressive monument made of solid stone but "without defined style."[21] A High Mass was celebrated and the "Doctoral Doctor," Pedro Brito,[22] delivered from the impressive pulpit of the Holy Spirit a majestic religious and patriotic sermon. At the moment of the elevation of the Host a deafening artillery discharge, accompanied by the ringing of the bells of the many churches of Chuquisaca, rang through the calm air of this festive day. The religious ceremony finished, the commission, still accompanied by the guilds and surrounded by many curious onlookers, returned to the halls of the university where the president proclaimed open house for the many spectators. Distinguished citizens of the capital took this opportunity to express to the assembly and its president their best wishes for success. Serrano was busy expressing his gratitude and assuring the enthusiastic citizens that they could be confident that the fate of their homeland was in qualified hands.[23]

After the public demonstration had come to an end the assembly gathered to listen to the speech which Marshal Sucre had left to be read. It was a substantial speech and, in contrast to Serrano's address, candid, mature, and honest. The marshal outlined to the assembly the reasons for which he had issued the February 9 decree. He thought that although it might appear that by issuing a call for the assembly he had usurped some power, this was a necessity because of the "complicated circumstances." He explained why the meeting of the assembly had to be postponed from April until July, and he hoped that it was justified. In the last part of the message the marshal said that he must account to the legislators for the record of his short period of military government, from the time he crossed the Desaguadero River until the opening of the assembly. He outlined his administrative actions, detailing his fiscal policy first. He emphasized that he had avoided any collection of taxes to support his army, and furthermore, he had strived to eliminate or reduce the abusive emergency war taxes levied by the Spaniards. Step by step the marshal told the legislators how, in the period of five months while he was fighting Olañeta, he had democratized the government of the Upper Peruvian provinces on a sound basis. The marshal was honest; indeed he was much too humble. He really did much more than he told the legislators, but his modesty restrained him from presenting more details.[24] At the end of his administrative account Sucre told the assembly that he was sorry he had been unable to provide any public service during his short government, but that he had studied many possibilities for building schools and colleges, and he hoped that the new government would take advantage of his preliminary steps. He terminated his speech by saying:

> This is, gentlemen, my simple report of my operations since I passed the Desaguadero; it is written with the frankness of a soldier and my conduct has been submitted to your judgment. If you should approve I shall repose happily in

the future; but if your kindness attributes to me some services to your fatherland, I say that they are not mine but are of the legislators of Colombia, to whom I owe my principles; to the Liberator, Bolívar, who has been my torch, and to the United Army, which is the protector of the good cause.[25]

What the response was to this simple and straightforward speech from the Upper Peruvian *doctores,* with their love for subtle words, was not written in the record.[26] But as soon as the speech had been read, Casimiro Olañeta stepped to the rostrum to deliver his address. Casimiro is today recognized as the greatest orator that Bolivia ever produced. He swayed the masses with empty phrases full of patriotic ardor. His gestures, intonation, sharp look, and imposing figure, in addition to his immaculate dress, were all designed to help his oratory. He never spoke from a prepared draft, and every word was completely spontaneous.[27] Unquestionably, Olañeta was the best orator in the hall. President Serrano's words were pompous but not persuasive, while Olañeta was pompous but convincing for Olañeta spoke the language of his audience.[28] He spoke at the level of the lower class one moment,[29] while the next, he would address the aristocracy with the words and ease of a distinguished gentleman. Casimiro Olañeta was an orator and a demagogue. The record does not transcribe Olañeta's first speech to the assembly, but says only that the energetic and youthful speaker asked the delegates to possess great moral fortitude in order to face the heavy task confronting them.[30]

After the speechmaking Serrano announced that the marshal had left with him the insignia of investiture of the president of the department (Chuquisaca) in order that the assembly could elect the president, who would assume office during the days of deliberation. In this way Sucre wished to remove any suspicion that he wanted to interfere in the discussions through the president of the department. The delegates were delighted by this show of propriety, but as it was late in the day and everyone was hungry and tired, it was decided to postpone the election until the next day. The inaugural day had concluded and probably the spirit of festivity, which the *Gaceta de Chuquisaca* in its first number thought was an expression of "the patriotic enthusiasm" and resulted in a "revolution of gaiety," continued into the early morning. The gaiety was due less to a sense of patriotism than to the fact that in Chuquisaca responsibilities were easily sacrificed for enjoyment, and such an unusual occasion as the inauguration of an assembly to determine the destiny of its land was enough cause for everyone, foe and friend, to join in the festivities.

The final process of the birth of a new nation had started and the members of the assembly were well aware of the importance of the moment. Yet these men who had come to debate about the future of Charcas, with the exception of one or two, did not deserve this honor. They were opportunists who had usurped the seats belonging to the veterans of the sixteen-year war; these demagogues had successfully veiled their records of allegiance to the king. They had come to the halls of the university to debate their own personal future with complete disregard for the welfare of Charcas and its people. It was hardly the place to present a clean record and express an intense preoccupation with the progress of Upper Peru, as Sucre did, and ask the *dos caras* to judge his record. The marshal had done more in five months than these people, once in power, would do in five decades. To the *chuquisaqueños* July 10, 1825, simply meant one more day of holiday and festivities, another of many days of rest and merriment on their calendar.

The next two meetings of July 11 and 13 were of a preparatory nature. The assembly chose General Andrés Santa Cruz, whom Sucre had left in charge until the assembly could name a president, as the executive of Chuquisaca, thus respecting the choice of the marshal.[31] Santa Cruz, the eminent *dos caras* general, had been elected a deputy from La Paz, but he had refused to accept the honor because he considered himself a Lower Peruvian, and despised his native upper provinces.[32] Three more late delegates had joined the meetings,[33] and after the election of Santa Cruz as executive of the department it was decided to appoint several committees to do preliminary work. Among these was one which was requested to draft a dignified answer to the address of the marshal.

Then came the touchy problem of how to proceed in the proper way in discussing and elaborating the crucial issue before the assembly, the future status of Charcas. After long discussion it was decided that this problem should not be referred to a committee but should be debated before the whole assembly. Some delegates had wished to name a committee which would study the problem and then present its findings and suggestions to the entire body. Once this proposal had been defeated, one delegate suddenly rose and questioned the propriety of debating this vital issue until the missing delegates from Santa Cruz had arrived. The delegate won his point and the assembly decided to dismiss the meetings until the eighteenth, five days later, with the hope that the representation from Santa Cruz would have arrived by then. But before suspending the meetings the delegates entered into a great debate about how they should be addressed. Finally, modesty won over ambitious titles, and it was voted that they should be called *Señor,* but that President Serrano must be addressed as *Excelencia,* because this term had been used by Sucre in his communications to the assembly. The executive members of the assembly, such as the secretaries, should be given the title of *Señoría.* It was also decided by majority vote to employ two aides, and someone suggested that a janitor should be hired—an idea which everyone thought was good. A certain Juan de Díos Campusano was proposed for the job and was accepted as suitable, and the delegates voted to give Juan a salary of twenty-five pesos a month. After this they went into a five-day recess.[34] It is said that the real reason for this recess was not the absence of the Santa Cruz members, but to allow time for backstage political maneuvering.[35]

The assembly again convened on July 18 and began to consider the vital problem of the future organization and jurisdiction of Charcas. Serrano was the one who opened the debate; he stepped down from the presidential chair and asked Vice-President Mendizábal to preside. The president, who had resided many years in the United Provinces and who had been the author of the declaration of independence of 1816 at the Congress of Tucumán, now came out for the separation of Upper Peru from other political jurisdictions, which meant Argentina and Lower Peru. Serrano gave powerful geographic and ethnological reasons why the inner provinces should become independent. He stressed the fact that the long anarchy reigning in the lower provinces certainly was not conducive to reunion. Apparently, Serrano, in this first speech in favor of separation and the creation of an independent nation, hinted that the most powerful reason to justify separation was the necessity for proper political balance among the new nations in South America. By this Serrano implied that if the inner provinces would join either the United Provinces or Lower Peru, it would mean the strengthening of one at the expense of the other, and would cause serious disturbances. Indeed, this later became the single most important and immediate reason for the separation of Charcas. It was a realization that Upper Peru must become a buffer between the Bolivarian nations and Argentina. If Serrano outlined this point with clarity, which is doubtful, he showed excellent foresight and put the separation of Charcas upon a sound and practical premise. This realization of the balance of power politics was recognized by Argentina and Peru, and therefore they did not deter the independence of these provinces. The record also states that the president took issue with some of the objections that might arise against separation, but the recorder did not tell what these objections were. Serrano finished his speech by indicating that he had expressed his sincere convictions, but that if the assembly should decide against separation the provinces should join Argentina rather than Peru.[36] The long residence of the president in the lower provinces undoubtedly impelled this preference.

The next speaker was Casimiro Olañeta who, although he did not occupy any distinguished position, had taken the liberty to deliver a speech on the inaugural day. He was again the first to rush to the rostrum after the president. Serrano and Olañeta were the two giants of the assembly. Casimiro, too, as was natural, came out decisively in favor of separation, and he explained with great ardor to his attentive audience that the provinces possessed all the ingredients for independent life. The young man said that Charcas not only had the economic wealth necessary for a successful new country, but that it also could produce "great men for the administration and state leadership." By saying that in Upper Peru leaders would emerge that could guide the destiny of the new nation, Olañeta was indirectly referring to his own ambition. He wanted independence for Charcas because in this way he would become its leader. If the provinces should join either Argentina or Peru, Olañeta's aspirations for political leadership would be considerably diminished, since his influence in Buenos Aires and Lima was negligible. In this second speech to the assembly Casimiro showed the personal ambition which was the guiding motive in his fight for separation since 1823. Politely but firmly Olañeta argued against the president's assertion that if separation was voted down the provinces should vote for union with Argentina. To Olañeta there was no other solution than separation permissible.

With Serrano and Olañeta taking the lead in favoring separation, the final decision of the assembly was a foregone conclusion.[37]

Although the creation of a separate and independent Upper Peru was inevitable, the *dos caras* leaders had no intention of rushing the final vote through the assembly. They wished to give an outward appearance of a long, thoughtful, and democratic debate. Serrano, who in addition to his presidential position served as the incognito editor of the *Gaceta de Chuquisaca*,[38] wrote in his newspaper that the organization of the provinces was an "enormous task" which had to be discussed, "thinking thoroughly about the most minute and imperceptible combinations." The editor thought that the assembly did not want to "construct a building on a base of sand."[39] These were mere words. Most of the delegates wished separation because the new country they advocated would be under their leadership, and they wanted to perpetuate the old system. As one honest Bolivian writer says, the only ones who would harvest fruits from separation and independence "were the *doctores* and *godos*," and these were the ones who played the game of "intrigue in the assembly of 1825."[40] But as *doctores intrigantes* they had to talk and debate, even though they were in unanimous agreement, and because they debated, Serrano wrote that he thought that this august assembly "should be the school where the democratic government could learn to combine the elements of their existence."[41] Although not all the delegates wished separation, the number of those opposed was so small that it had no voice or influence.

Again in the next session of July 21 the two giants, Serrano and Olañeta, monopolized the rostrum and spoke in favor of separation. It became an oratorical contest between the two, each wanting to impress the assembly with his superior knowledge and more intense patriotic feelings. In the previous session Serrano had spoken for separation, but had said that union with Argentina was the second-best solution. Then Olañeta had taken issue with the president's weakened attitude for separation. In this fifth session Serrano thought that Olañeta had implied some shortcomings that might be the consequence of an independent Charcas. Had Casimiro Olañeta really done this? The records do not say a single word, but give the impression that young Casimiro had insisted all the way through that separation was necessarily the only acceptable solution. Yet Serrano by implication accused Casimiro Olañeta of having given a vague speech and having used double talk, from which he inferred that the young man had hinted that an independent Charcas would create such problems as defense, lack of a governmental bureaucracy, antagonism of the United Provinces, and the impossibility of defending itself against the ambitions of the Holy Alliance. Serrano proceeded to debate each of these objections, and then outlined in detail many more reasons why he thought the provinces should not join Argentina or Peru. Serrano concluded his long speech by requesting the delegates to realize that the independence of Upper Peru was the most feasible solution, but that they should depart from the United Provinces in a spirit of brotherhood, just as two brothers who depart from their parents' house, each one to take care of his own family, but always remain good brothers and desire each other's mutual happiness. As soon as Serrano finished Olañeta demanded the floor, refuted Serrano's accusation, and demanded more strongly than ever the separation of the provinces. Then with great emotion he asked the delegates and the people of Charcas to recall the long abandonment of Charcas by the United Provinces during the war, leaving them to fight the Spanish forces alone. Here Olañeta hit a sore spot, the great obstacle that made it impossible for Argentina to demand the provinces at this time, since Charcas had liberated itself and defeated the Spanish forces by its own efforts.[42] Not even the Bolivarian army had had to shoot a single rifle against the enemy. The Serrano-Olañeta oratory was getting ridiculous, since each one tried to outdo the other and appear more patriotic before the assembly of ex-*godos*.

Finally, after Olañeta had concluded, the delegate from La Paz, Eusebio Gutiérrez, asked to be recognized as the next speaker. In a vigorous speech he opposed separation and insisted that the provinces should join Lower Peru. Unfortunately the record does not detail this first speech of a minority member, whom Argüedas calls "upright, cautious, and observing,"[43] but says only that Gutiérrez thought that the provinces "lacked political virtues, true patriotism, civic enterprise, and elements of security" necessary to become an independent nation. How the delegates received the speech of Gutiérrez remains a matter of speculation since Urcullu did not record it.[44] The fact that the speaker came from La Paz is a powerful reason for his wanting union with Lower Peru. La Paz was always more inclined toward Lima, Cuzco, and Arequipa than Chuquisaca, and the city was a geographical part of the Titicaca basin. Gutiérrez was followed by one of the most disreputable *doctores* of Charcas, Angel Mariano Moscoso, who with his three brothers represented the most vicious *dos caras* mentality.[45] Delegate Moscoso took issue with Gutiérrez and thought that the provinces had every imaginable element required for a successful independent life. He insisted that Charcas had not only the physical and political attributes but also possessed intellectual maturity which was a great asset for separation. With the Moscoso speech finished, the fifth session came to an end; thus far, only the home delegates from Chuquisaca had spoken, with the exception of the challenging speech by Gutiérrez. Olañeta and Serrano were willing to let many more days of debate pass before the final vote.

The next day the delegates assembled for their sixth session and again the whole day was dedicated to the debate.[46] The first speaker produced a somewhat unexpected surprise. Vice-President Mendizábal, a deputy from La Paz, born in the United Provinces and graduated from the University of San Francisco Xavier in theology, came out against separation and favored union with Lower Peru. Mendizábal thought that Charcas lacked enough resources, especially a good seaport, and that the two Perus complemented each other and would make a powerful nation.[47] But Mendizábal was not intellectually honest, and he by no means presented his case with the forcefulness and dedication of his fellow delegate, Gutiérrez. The vice-president said that this was only a suggestion and oratorical exercise and that in the end he might vote against union with Lower Peru and come out in favor of separation. Seemingly Mendizábal was unfolding his acquired Upper Peruvian mentality of never committing himself to a given principle, but toying with all causes and ideas. Mendizábal suggested that a commission be appointed to study the resources of the provinces and compare them with the probable expenditures. The vice-president thought that by comparing income with expenditures it would be possible to find out whether the inner provinces possessed the necessary economic resources to become an expanding nation.

Again Olañeta demanded the floor, and in strong terms assailed the assertion of Gutiérrez that Charcas did not have the necessary civic spirit and patriotism to qualify as an independent nation. He then thought that Mendizábal's objections were groundless and that the vice-president's request for a commission to study the economy of the provinces was impractical since the fiscal administration had not yet been organized. Casimiro was wrong in this assertion and he knew it, because Marshal Sucre had thought that this issue would come up and on June 30, the day before his departure from Chuquisaca, had sent to Serrano a letter with an enclosure listing the income and expenditures of each of the provinces in great detail. The marshal noted that deficit financing could be expected as long as the interest on the loans negotiated by the Spanish authorities were honored.[48] Probably because of the unpromising picture of the marshal's financial account, Olañeta and Serrano suppressed the document.

Gutiérrez again took the floor, reaffirmed his position, and added that the capital of the Perus ought to be in Cuzco or Arequipa, since Lima was too far from Charcas. Gutiérrez had been preceded by half a century in this idea by the great intendant of Potosí, Pino Manrique, an outstanding personality of the eighteenth-century Enlightenment,[49] who had asked the crown to transfer the capital of the viceroyalty to Cuzco, thus bringing unity to the two Perus.[50] René-Moreno thought that if Pino Manrique's advice had been followed, an independent Upper Peru would have never emerged.[51] But Gutiérrez' speech was a voice in the desert. He was followed by Doctor José Mariano Enríquez, a delegate from Potosí, who spoke in favor of an independent Charcas, but suggested that the Bolivarian army should guarantee the sovereignty of the new nation for a certain time and see to it that anarchy and civil war would not develop. Delegate Manuel Mariano Centeno from Cochabamba concurred and insisted that the protection of the Bolivarian army would be needed for a long time. With this speech another session came to an end, without any hint of when the delegates would vote on the vital issue of separation or union with Argentina or Peru. The two delegates from Santa Cruz had not yet arrived and seemingly no vote would be taken until they had reached Chuquisaca and expressed their opinions.

The next day the discussion was continued.[52] The assembly voted down the motion of Mendizábal to have a committee study the economic and fiscal potentials of Charcas. A large number of delegates stepped to the rostrum and all of them spoke in favor of separation. Of these, Manuel Antonio Arellano, the delegate from Potosí, gave the most chauvinistic oration by implying that the people of Charcas were of superior quality and therefore could not belong to another nation. Dionicio de la Borda, the delegate from Cochabamba, thought that because the provinces had belonged to the Viceroyalty of Río de la Plata when the war started was no reason that they should now belong to the United Provinces, since the colonial demarcations were a product of an authority which had vanished with defeat. Borda was followed by Manuel Montoya, the delegate from Potosí, who placed the need for separation and an independent Upper Peru upon a pragmatic basis. He felt that Charcas should become an independent nation because this was the most politically expedient move in the touchy game of international politics. Montoya said that he thought that the provinces had all the necessary ingredients to become an independent state. But even more important, Charcas needed to become a separate nation, for if the provinces should join Lower Peru the enmity of the United Provinces would be aroused and Argentina would not rest in her effort to detach the provinces from Peru. Should Charcas join the United Provinces exactly the same would happen with Peru. In either case the provinces would suffer constant fear of an attack by one of their neighbors. The only way to avoid this dilemma was not to join either of them, but to create an equilibrium between Peru and Argentina. This argument was sound and realistic.[53] What Montoya did not foresee was that if they were independent, the provinces would always be an easy prey for Argentina or Peru.[54] Not until 1842 did Bolivia consolidate her independence, because she had to fight constant efforts at reintegration by Peru and Argentina.

The eighth session[55] was a continuation of the previous meetings. One by one the delegates delivered their speeches, insisting on separation and repeating old arguments. Delegate José Ignacio Sanjinés, secretary of the assembly and another *doctor* of Charcas,[56] thought that Upper Peru possessed a sufficient quantity of all the elements—animal, vegetable, and mineral—to become an independent nation. He finished his speech with a farsighted warning: Should the upper provinces join one of their neighbors it would later be impossible to separate from this union, if they found it detrimental to their well-being. But if they became an independent nation and later realized that this was the wrong step, it would be easy to join Argentina or Peru. What the delegate from Potosí suggested was that they would lose nothing if they tried separation as an experiment. The next speaker, Isidoro Trujillo, also came from Potosí; he thought that they should become independent but leave a provision for the possibility of federation with their neighbors. Manuel María García, a delegate from Potosí, stated that the reasons expounded by Montoya in the previous session were correct and that he concurred with them. This was the day for the populous delegation from Potosí to monopolize the rostrum, since García was followed by another *potosino,* Manuel Anselmo de Tapia, who also believed that the policy of a buffer state between Peru and Argentina was the only practicable solution for Charcas, because otherwise the provinces would be exposed to constant trouble.

The next, and last, speaker was again President Serrano, who harangued the assembly with a detailed speech.[57] He said that it was absurd that the provinces should join Lower Peru because that country had a constitution full of "great vices," such as provision for a unicameral legislature. The president then went into much detail about this constitution, the gist of his objection being that the executive was subservient to the legislature. He thought, too, that a United States of Peru was hardly possible, and that there was a great difference between the mentality of the people of the United States of America and those of the Perus. Serrano thought that the provinces possessed an adequate port in Cobija (between Antofagasta and Tocopilla), which could be built up at some expense. After this the president continued to debate all the objections that had been brought against separation during the many days of discussion. He concluded his address by saying, with great foresight, that the only real danger in the creation of a new country was anarchy, but that this could be avoided by the self-denial and patriotism of its leaders. And since the provinces had before them an example in the United Provinces of what anarchy could do, it was hardly imaginable that they would want to imitate this neighbor.

This was the last speech in the long and colorless debate on the future of Charcas. It was decided that the issue had received enough discussion, and someone moved that in view of the overwhelming feeling in favor of separation and independence of the provinces the debate should be terminated, and a commission appointed to write the Declaration of Independence. The proposal was seconded and passed with a great majority. The commission was named without opposition and the delegates appointed were Serrano, Olañeta, Urcullu, and José María Dalence from Chuquisaca, Manuel Mariano Centeno from Cochabamba, and Vice-President Mendizábal and José María de Azín from La Paz. Each one of them was a *dos caras* and had received his degree from the University of San Francisco Xavier. The two veterans of the war, Lanza and Ballivián, never had voiced their opinions and the record does not transcribe a single speech or suggestion by them.

While the commission was drawing up the Declaration of Independence, the assembly dealt with some minor matters. On August 1 it held its first secret meeting because the credentials of the missing Santa Cruz delegates had been submitted and there was an accusation that they had been elected by fraud. In its secret meeting the assembly reviewed the credentials and no conclusion was reached, but it was decided that the Santa Cruz delegates should be given their seats.[58] In its public sessions of August 1 and 3 the assembly discussed vehemently a proposal presented by Casimiro Olañeta and supported by Urcullu, that the delegates should draw a salary. It was finally voted that the members should receive a salary of two thousand pesos a year and that those from La Paz and Santa Cruz, because of the distance, should be given an additional two hundred pesos for travel expenses. But it was stipulated that those who drew another salary of over two thousand pesos should not be eligible for the pay. The new law also said that it was left up to the honesty of the delegates to declare their other income; thus they themselves would have to decide whether they could draw their salary as members of the assembly.[59]

On August 3, 1825, in the assembly's tenth session, the commission finished its task of writing the Declaration of Independence, but because of the continued absence of the delegates from Santa Cruz the great moment when the provinces would declare themselves independent was again postponed.[60] This session and the next on August 4 dealt with the touchy problem of how to enter into negotiations with Bolívar.[61] This last session was partially secret and it was decided to name a commission in the near future that would meet with Bolívar and request his approval of the separation. Several projects were presented by Vice-President Mendizábal, including one to name the new country "Bolívar," with the purpose of stimulating Bolívar's ego and thus making it hard for him to reject Upper Peru's separation.[62] Its approval, although unopposed, was delayed until the Declaration of Independence was officially voted upon and passed.

On August 6, the day of the first anniversary of Junín, a year after the provinces were in the midst of the Separatist War, the delegates assembled for the great moment in order to vote and proclaim that separation of Charcas from any other jurisdiction and its creation as a sovereign nation.[63] This act should have taken place earlier but not until this day had the delegate from Santa Cruz, Antonio Vicente Seoane y Robledo, son of the last Spanish governor of Santa Cruz,[64] arrived in the assembly. After giving an official welcome to Seoane, Serrano informed him of what they had discussed and done in the previous meetings. Seoane then gave a short speech in which he said that he was in favor of separation and independence of the provinces and that Santa Cruz had fought valiantly for the Patriot cause during the whole war. A thunderous applause was given to the delegate who had come from the faraway east.

Finally, the high point was reached. The president announced that he would step down from the presidential chair while voting was held on whether separation, union with the United Provinces, or union with Lower Peru was the wish of the provinces. Serrano thought that as he had been a most active member in the discussions, someone more impartial, who had not engaged in the long debate, should take his place in order to count the votes. General Miguel Lanza, the great guerrilla leader and only veteran of distinction in the assembly, was invited to take over the presidency during this sublime moment. Lanza deserved this honor, which was the only honestly patriotic act of the assembly of turncoat *godos*. Were the revolving *dos caras*, afraid that Lanza would vote against separation, playing up to him by asking him to preside in this great moment? Lanza announced the first choice to be voted on: that the departments of Upper Peru join the United Provinces. One by one each of the forty-seven delegates announced his vote of "*no.*" Not a single delegate voted in favor of this proposition. This was the sterile harvest that the Plata provinces reaped for their years of blunders and abandonment. Then Lanza, in his hoarse and unpolished military voice, read the second proposition to be voted on: that the provinces of Charcas join the republic of Lower Peru. Again the loud sound of "*no*" echoed in the gilded hall, but when the president called the name of Eusebio Gutíerrez from La Paz, for the first time, in a clear voice, the word "*si*" was heard. The hope that separation would be approved by a unanimous decision was spoiled by Gutíerrez' unwavering conviction. Again the word "*no*" resounded, and then there was a tense moment when Lanza called the name of José María Mendizábal, the vice-president, who in his initial speech had favored union with Peru, but who had said that he was not sure whether this was an honest and patriotic conviction. Mendizábal, in his orotund style, clearly said "*no*." Historical imagination allows one to say that a loud cheer rang through the long, narrow hall. But one more "*si*" was heard when the other delegate from La Paz, Juan Manuel Velarde, joined his colleague Gutiérrez in voting in favor of the union of the Perus. The final vote was forty-five to two.

The great moment came when Lanza announced the third proposition: that "the departments of Upper Peru declare themselves a sovereign state independent from all other nations in the old and new world." It was a foregone conclusion that this would carry by an overwhelming majority, but even so it was a tense moment. The great intrigue of Casimiro Olañeta, José Mariano Serrano, and Manuel María Urcullu was to come to its victorious fulfillment. All but two of the delegates clearly and proudly pronounced "*si*." By a vote of forty-five to two the independence of Upper Peru was declared on Saturday, August 6, in the beautiful assembly hall of the University of San Francisco Xavier. Not a single chronicler has written in detail what happened on this memorable day.[65] It is unknown whether the assembly, after the vote, had a period of great rejoicing and applause. The record says that after the vote the secretary, Moscoso, rushed to the rostrum and read the Declaration of Independence written by the committee appointed for this task. It is said that the author was José Mariano Serrano,[66] who in 1816 had written a similar document, the declaration of independence of the United Provinces. The document, even the patriotic historians admit, was defective in style and even in grammar.[67] It was a pompous and bombastic piece of literature[68] which started by saying, "That the lion of Iberia, furiously jumping from the columns of Hercules to the empires of Montezuma and Atahualpa, has for many centuries torn to pieces the unfortunate body of America and nourished itself from the substance of the continent." The many lines following were an absurd explanation of the plight of Charcas during the War of Independence. The declaration categorically affirmed that no other region in America had been exploited and tyrannized as thoroughly as Upper Peru,

and that Spain even "profaned the altars and attacked the dogma
and insulted the worship." This sounded exactly like one of General
Olañeta's separatist and absolutist proclamations. But after all,
those were written by Casimiro Olañeta and Urcullu, two members
of the commission which wrote the Declaration of Independence.
The document is replete with references to Sparta, *Indostan,* Manco-
Capac, *Ylotas, Nijeros, Ojandalam, Caribes;* and such phrases as
"dessicated hand of Iberia; a nervous and great manifestation of
solid fundamentals; ferocious lands; torrents of tears." René-Moreno
stated irritably that Serrano knew how to write only "miserable
ballads" which echoed hideously from Churuquella, a steep hill,
at the foot of which is Chuquisaca. The echo then came back
saying, "The Serranos, the great Olañetas, the Urcullus . . . history
and the heavens are full of them and the acumen which is held
by their skulls." And René-Moreno added that Serrano was not
the father of the nation but the father of the "rhymed adulation."[60]

The document was divided into two parts, with a preamble,
and the main body which began saying, "We have arrived by unanimous vote in determining the following DECLARATION," and then
contained the proclamation of independence and separation of the
Upper Peruvian provinces. The crucial paragraph was a monstrous
sentence of two hundred and ninety words without even so much
as a semicolon. There are again such phrases as "the immense
weight of our responsibility with heaven and earth; imploring
full of submission and respectful ardor; the paternal assistance of
the Holy Maker of the orb; the miserable power of King Ferdinand
VII, corroborated a thousand times with the blood of his sons."
The decisive sentences read:

> The provinces of Upper Peru erect themselves into a sov-
> ereign state independent from all nations in the old world
> as well as in the new. The departments of Upper Peru,
> strong and united in this just and magnanimous resolution,
> protest to the whole earth that their irrevocable will is to
> govern themselves, and be governed by a constitution, laws,
> and authorities chosen by them and which they believe is
> more conducive to the future happiness of their [new] nation.

This proclamation was signed by all forty-eight delegates, including
the two from La Paz who originally had voted for union with Lower
Peru. They decided, or were persuaded, to put their signatures

on the great document in order to make the final record of independence and separation unanimous.

Indeed, it was a queer document, this Declaration of Independence. One Bolivian author, devoid of historical perspective, says that the deputies of the assembly were all "animated by the most intense civic fervor." Yet this same writer has to admit that the proclamation of independence "denotes poor concepts and [has] a profusion of *rimbombante* phrases, which can be attributed to the level of culture of those who wrote it."[70] This document, written by Serrano with the help of Olañeta, Urcullu, and other *doctores,* is a perfect expression of the dual characters of the alumni of the University of San Francisco Xavier. Their leader, Casimiro Olañeta, who in 1825 was sparing no ink to embellish Sucre, in 1828 defamed the marshal. In 1829 he repeated the same procedure with Santa Cruz; he wrote him that he "did not know that any man could deny his blood" for such a just and virtuous man as he. Olañeta told the new president of Bolivia that he would prove his friendship by being willing to give his life for this just man. Then he asked Santa Cruz to have many children because Bolivia needed virtuous descendants from such an upright man.[71] In 1840, when Olañeta had left the defeated general, he calumniated Santa Cruz in many pamphlets, calling him among other things a "master of intrigues" and possessor of a "hypocritical patriotism."[72] This same Casimiro Olañeta, who turned against every president and his own benefactors, and who died peacefully in bed at an advanced age, wrote in 1838 an essay entitled *Quam dulce est pro Patria mori.*[73] Olañeta was the incarnation of this assembly which declared the independence of Bolivia. It was not a reunion of civic-minded men, but of opportunists without honesty or political conviction.

The leftist Bolivian writer, Alipio Valencia Vega, writes that the actions of the delegates of the first assembly created Bolivia because they wished to perpetuate their own reactionary, egotistic class, "and Casimiro Olañeta appears as the spokesman of this aspiration."[74] Carlos Montenegro, the intellectual father of modern radical Bolivian nationalism, believed that the assembly produced only a "fraud of the republican spirit," and that of the forty-eight delegates only Lanza and Ballivián represented the real epic as well as the people's will and desire for independence.[75] But Lanza and Ballivián were submerged by the great wave of the Olañetas, Urcullus, Serranos, Moscosos, and the many *doctores* of Chuquisaca

who were "a fearful and lazy cast"[76] that did absolutely nothing
for the good of the masses of Charcas. General Lanza in the midst
of these *dos caras* was only the sad picture of a "truncated epic."[77]
Yet Serrano wrote in his newspaper that one "should bless the
authors of the Declaration of Independence of Upper Peru" because
of their abnegation, patriotism, and unimpeachable character.[78]
To René-Moreno, Serrano and the other great *dos caras* wished to
compare themselves "to the skyline of the southern constellation,"
as pure and as bright, untouchable and beautiful as those stars.[79]

The emergence of Bolivia was a product of sixteen long years
of revolution, war, and intrigues. It was a conclusion which should
have been achieved by the generation of 1809, the veterans of the
war, the mestizos, the masses of Indians, the honest *criollos* such
as Sucre, and the patriotic Spaniards such as Arenales. But these
were betrayed by the dishonest class which usurped the concepts of
1809 and turned them to its own advantage. Herein lies one important factor of the many misfortunes of the future history of Bolivia.
The creation of the Republic of Bolívar is meritorious, but its
immediate creators deserved to be despised rather than praised.
The glory and credit belong to those who were absent from the
assembly and innocent of the great intrigue. Unquestionably, Casimiro Olañeta in his own way was a great leader and genius in
politics and scheming—but he was dishonest. Yet he was the greatest and most important of all Bolivian leaders and politicians. The
creation of Bolivia is in part the story of Casimiro Olañeta.

After sixteen years of striving, Upper Peru became an independent nation, but the Declaration of Independence and the
separation were no final guarantee of lasting sovereignty; at this
point began the seventeen years of hardship which attended the
implementation of Bolivia's independence. In this second period
Casimiro Olañeta exhibited even less scruples. This period, too,
is in part the history of Josef Casimiro Olañeta. On Saturday,
August 6, 1825, Bolivia began her life as an independent nation;
she was at the threshold of a terrible and frightening history.

# NOTES*

CHAPTER 1

1. See Lewis Hanke, *La villa imperial de Potosí* (Sucre, 1954), pp. 32, 57.
2. Royal cedula, Valladolid, April 20, 1551, in Roberto Levillier, *Audiencia de Charcas* (Madrid, 1918), I, 503-504.
3. Bautista Saavedra, *Defensa de los derechos de Bolivia en el litigio de fronteras con la república del Perú* (Buenos Aires, 1906), I, 10.
4. Lib. 2°, Tit. XV, Ley XXXVI.
5. Royal cedulas of June 12, 1559, in Ricardo Mujía, *Bolivia-Paraguay* (La Paz, 1914), Anexos, I, 244-246, 303-305; Alfredo Jáuregui Rosquellas, "La Audiencia de Charcas," *BSGS*, XXX, nos. 316-319 (1933), 9-10; concise information about the five different names by which Chuquisaca (today Sucre) is known is available in Charles W. Arnade, "A Sojourn in Sucre," *Michigan Alumnus Quarterly Review*, LX, no. 10 (1953), 64-70.
6. René-Moreno, *Notas* (2d ed.), p. 202.
7. *Colección de arengas en el foro i escritos del doctor don Mariano Moreno* ... (London, 1836), p. xliii.
8. Ignacio de Castro, *Relación de la fundación de la Real Audiencia del Cuzco en 1778* ... (Madrid, 1795), *passim.*
9. *Real ordenanzas para el establecimiento e instrucción de intendentes de exército y provincia en el Virreinato de Buenos Aires* (Madrid, 1782), *passim;* see also Guillermo Céspedes, "Lima y Buenos Aires. Repercusiones económicas y políticas de la creación del Virreinato del Plata," *Anuario de Estudios Americanos* (Seville), III (1946), 669-874.
10. René-Moreno, *Notas* (2d ed.), p. 325.
11. Guillermo Francovich, *El pensamiento universitario de Charcas* (Sucre, 1948), p. 32.
12. See Luis Paz, *La Universidad Mayor Real y Pontificia de San Francisco Xavier* (Sucre, 1914), chap. vii; "Homenaje al tercer centenario de la fundación de la Universidad de San Francisco Xavier," *BSGS*, XXI, nos. 233-245 (1924), *passim.*

*See pages 243-245 for abbreviations relating to archives and to frequently cited books, journals, and unpublished essays.

13. Jaime Mendoza, "La Universided de Charcas y la idea revolucionaria," *USFX*, VII, no. 23 (1940), 225-282.

14. René-Moreno, *Ultimos días*, p. 175, n. 1.

15. Montenegro, *Nacionalismo*, p. 1; Boleslao Lewin, *Tupac Amaru, el rebelde* (Buenos Aires, 1943), chaps iii, iv.

16. Montenegro, *Nacionalismo*, chap. i; Carlos Ponce Sanginés and Raul Alfonso García, eds., *Documentos para la historia de la revolución de 1809* (La Paz, 1953), I, 46-55; Humberto Vázquez-Machicado, "El pasquinismo sedicioso y los pródromos de la emancipación en el Alto Perú," *BSGS*, XLV, no. 442 (1955), 373-381.

17. *Ibid.*, p. 383; Francovich, *op. cit.*, p. 81.

18. René-Moreno, *Ultimos diás*, pp. 61-63.

19. Ancelmo Natein [pseud. for Vicente Pazos Kanki], "Reflexiones políticas escritas vaxo el titulo de Instinto Comun por el ciudadano Tomas Payne y traducidas abreviadamente por Ancelmo Natein, indigena del Perú. Impreso en Londres por cuenta de su mismo traductor," in BNB, *Manuscritos de Chuquisaca*, I, no. 10, 16 fols. (The original was located in 1953 in BNB but efforts to determine if it really has been printed and where have remained futile; no copy is known to exist.)

20. [Vicente Pazos Kanki], *Compendio de la historia de los Estados Unidos de América* (Paris, 1825), 422 pp.

21. See Bernardo Monteagudo, *Obras políticas* in Ricardo Rojas, ed., *Biblioteca argentina* (Buenos Aires, 1916), VII, 39-41, 183-188.

22. See René-Moreno, *Ultimos días, passim;* see also Manuel Giménez Fernández, "Las doctrinas populistas en la independencia de Hispano-América," *Anuario de Estudios Americanos* (Seville), III (1946), 553.

23. George H. Sabine, *A History of Political Theory,* revised ed. (New York, 1950), p. 249; cf. Lewin, *op. cit.*, chap. v.

24. See René-Moreno, "D. Mariano Alejo Alvarez y el silogismo altoperuano de 1808," in *Notas*, 2d ed., pp. 1-86.

25. Mariano Alejo Alvarez, *Discurso sobre la preferencia que deben tener los americanos en los empleos de América. . .* (Lima, 1820), 26 pp.

26. See René-Moreno, *Ultimos días,* chaps. v-ix.

27. Extensive research in regard to the happenings in Charcas at the turn of the century has been done by René-Moreno and is available in his *Ultimos días, Documentos inéditos, Notas, Más notas, Nuevas notas,* and *Bolivia y Argentina.*

28. "Testimonio de la Real Cedula, Real Despacho i obrados de obedecimiento en La Plata concernientes a la exaltación del Señor Don Fernando VII (1808)," in René-Moreno, *Ultimos días,* pp. 164, 177-180.

29. *Ibid.*, pp. 115-146.

30. Biographical reminiscences of Ramón García Pizarro by people who knew him are transcribed in René-Moreno, *Más notas,* index, p. 307.

31. René-Moreno, *Ultimos días,* pp. 146-162.

32. Interesting descriptions of Moxó are available in René-Moreno, *Más notas,* index, p. 308, and in *Ultimos días, passim;* a concise biography of Moxó, containing some of his private papers, is Rubén Vargas Ugarte, *Don Benito María de Moxó y de Francolí* (Buenos Aires, 1936).

33. Benito María de Moxó y Francolí, *Pública i solemne rogativa que el Iltmo. Señor Arzobispo de la Plata hizo . . .* (Buenos Aires, 1808), p. 16.

34. See René-Moreno, *Ultimos días,* p. 164.

35. Audiencia de La Plata [Charcas] to the Viceroy Santiago de Liniers. La Plata, October 26, 1808, in René-Moreno, *Documentos inéditos,* p. xiv.

36. Real acuerdo de la Audiencia de Charcas, La Plata, September 18, 1808, in *ibid.*, p. xxv.

37. See *ibid.*, p. xxv *et seq.*; cf. René-Moreno, *Ultimos días*, pp. 201-218, plus notes.

38. Ussoz y Mozí was born in South America but was taken to Spain as a baby. He was educated in Spain. In July, 1809, José Felix Campoblanco took the place of José de la Iglesia.

39. "Discurso que pronunció . . . Benito María de Moxó . . . el día 27 de septiembre de 1808," in René-Moreno, *Documentos inéditos*, p. lvi.

40. Benito María de Moxó to the Audiencia of Charcas, La Plata, September 28, 1808, in *ibid.*, p. lxv.

41. Benito María de Moxó, "Exhortación al venerable clero," La Plata, September 25, 1808, in *ibid.*, p. lxii.

42. See "Vista reservada del Fiscal [Audiencia de Charcas]," La Plata, February 7, 1809, in *ibid.*, pp. lxxxviii-cv.

43. Lib. 3°, Tit. I, Ley I.

44. René-Moreno, *Ultimos días*, p. 385, n. 1.

45. René-Moreno, *Más notas*, p. 37.

46. [Benito María de Moxó], "Carta pastoral . . . con ocasión del arribo del Señor don José Manuel de Goyeneche, Brigadier de los Reales exércitos y diputado etc.," La Plata, November 10, 1808, partially reproduced in René-Moreno, *Ultimos días*, p. 389, n. 1.

47. Ramón García Pizarro to the Audiencia of Charcas, La Plata, October 25, 1808, in René-Moreno, *Documentos inéditos*, pp. lxvi-lxvii.

48. Benito María de Moxó, *Obras patrióticas*, 2d part, pp. 92-94, as cited by René-Moreno, *Ultimos días*, pp. 441-442.

49. Paz, *Historia*, I, 580.

50. Benito María de Moxó to Manuel Goyeneche, La Plata, November 16, 1808, as transcribed in René-Moreno, *Ultimos días*, p. 445, n. 1.

51. See José Presas, *Memorias secretas de la Princesa del Brasil actual Reina viuda de Portugal* (Bordeaux, 1830), p. 29.

52. See all the other correspondence between President Pizarro and the Audiencia of Charcas (four letters) on November 12, 1808, in René-Moreno, *Documentos inéditos*, pp. lxvii-lxix.

53. See Real acuerdo de la Audiencia de Charcas, La Plata, November 12, 1808, in *ibid.*, pp. lxix-lxx.

54. These four proclamations are all dated Rio de Janeiro, August 19, 1808, and are in *ibid.*, pp. lxxii-lxviii.

55. *Ibid.*, pp. lxxvi-lxxvii.

56. The primary sources of this meeting are Real acuerdo, *op. cit.* (n. 53), and the reports by the *fiscal* of the Audiencia of Charcas, Miguel López Andreu, La Plata, February 6, March 6, 1809 in René-Moreno, *Documentos inéditos*, pp. lxxxviii-cxx; cf. René-Moreno, *Ultimos días*, p. 455, n. 1.

57. See Presas, *op. cit.*, p. 32. Goyeneche was also accused of working for Napoleon. That would mean he represented Seville, Carlota, and the French. For a discussion of this see Paz, *Historia*, II, chap. xxviii. It is doubtful that Goyeneche worked for the French, but it is unquestionable that he was the agent for Seville and Carlota at the same time.

58. Cf. Pedro Vincente Cañete, "Dictamen a pedimiento del excmo. Sr. Virrey," Potosí, May 26, 1810, in *Gazeta Extraordinaria de Buenos-Ayres* (July 3, 1810).

59. [Ramón García Pizarro] to Rodrigo de Souza Cautinho, La Plata, December 26, 1808, in René-Moreno, *Documentos inéditos*, p. cxx; the letter of

Moxó is of November 23 and is cited by René-Moreno, *Ultimos días*, p. 457; cf. Vargas Ugarte, *op. cit.*, 45, 64-65.

60. See the two reports of the *fiscal* cited in n. 56.

61. Francisco de Viedma to José Manuel Goyeneche, Cochabamba, January 25, 1809, in René-Moreno, *Documentos inéditos*, pp. cxx-cxxi.

62. See reports of the *fiscal* of February 6 and March 6, 1809, *op. cit.*, pp. xcv, cvii, cix.

63. René-Moreno, *Ultimos días*, p. 385, n., p. 416; Mariano de Vedia y Mitre, *La vida de Monteagudo* (Buenos Aires, 1950), I, 49-50.

64. For a complete list of the radicals see Adolfo Durán, *Apéndice a los documentos inéditos publicados en la obra de G. René-Moreno* (Buenos Aires, 1909), pp. 5-6.

65. Cf. "Relato de Doña Martina Lazcano," in René-Moreno, *Más notas*, p. 120.

66. There has been a long controversy in Bolivia and Argentina about whether Monteagudo was born in Chuquisaca or Tucumán. For further information see Valentín Abecia, *Historia documental, la cuna de Monteagudo* (Sucre, 1905), 25 pp.; René-Moreno, "Monteagudo," in *Nuevas notas*, pp. 285-354; the best biography is Mariano de Vedia y Mitre, *La vida de Monteagudo* (Buenos Aires, 1950), 3 vols., see his Vol. I, chaps. ii-iv. Seemingly Monteagudo was born in Tucumán in 1789.

67. René-Moreno, *Ultimos días*, p. 467, n.

68. Cf. Pedro Vicente Cañete, "Espectáculo de la verdad," in René-Moreno, *Documentos inéditos*, pp. cxxxi-clii. This essay by Cañete, a shrewd royal *criollo* official and partisan of Pizarro, is one of the most valuable primary sources for the events in Chuquisaca in 1808-1809.

69. The minutes of these important cloister meetings remained lost until 1955 when they were located in the library of the University of Montevideo and the Museo Histórico Nacional in Montevideo, Uruguay, among the papers of Jaime Zudañez. They were published for the first time in "Documentos históricos," *BSGS*, XLV, no. 442 (1955), 420-427.

70. Benito María de Moxó to Gerónimo Cardona y Tagle, La Plata, April 9, 1809, in René-Moreno, *Documentos inéditos*, pp. cxxii-cxxvii.

71. See "Expediente que contiene la carta del M. R. Arzobispo ... presentada a este Superior Tribunal," La Plata, April-May, 1809, in *ibid.*, pp. cxxii-cxxxi.

72. Cf. René-Moreno, "El oidor Ussoz y Mozí," *Nuevas notas*, pp. 271-283.

73. Cañete, "Espectáculo," p. cxlv.

74. *Ibid.*, pp. cxl, cxliv-cxlv.

75. "El proceso contra los oidores," La Plata, May 26, 1810, in Durán, *op. cit.*, p. 54.

76. See the judicial defense of the president's contentions in Cañete, "Espectáculo," p. cxlv; cf. "Reepresentación [*sic*] del Señor M. A. Tardio ante el Exmo. Sr. Virrey, en Agosto 26 de 1809," in Samuel Oropeza, *El 25 de Mayo de 1809. Otro documento histórico* (Sucre, 1894), pp. 5-33.

77. "Relato de doña Martina Lazcano," in René-Moreno, *Más notas*, p. 128.

78. *Ibid.*, p. 112; "Carta del Arzobispo Moxó a la Audiencia de la Plata explicando los motivos que le obligaron a salir de la ciudad en la noche del 25 de Mayo," Moromoro, May 28, 1809, in Vargas Ugarte, *op. cit.*, pp. li-liii.

79. See Juan Antonio Alvarez de Arenales to Baltasar Hidalgo de Cisneros, Plata, August 10, 1809, in Durán, *op. cit.*, p. 32; "Auto revolucionario de la Real Audiencia ... reasumiendo el mando político y militar del distrito ... ," Plata, May 26, 1809, in *BSGS*, IX, nos. 97-100 (1908), 43.

80. Uriburu, *Historia, passim.* This is an excellent book with transcriptions of important documents taken from the archives of Arenales. Unfortunately, the book goes only as far as 1820. A second volume was intended but never published.

81. See the documents entitled "Emisarios, correos, agentes, etc., de la Audiencia Gobernadora," June, 1809, in René-Moreno, *Documentos inéditos,* pp. 47-49; Moxó to the audiencia, Moromoro, May 28, 1809, certification of Moxó against Arenales, [Chuquisaca], February 6, 1810, in Vargas Ugarte, *op. cit.,* pp. xv-xviii, li-liii.

82. "El proceso contra los oidores," La Plata, May 26, 1810, in Durán, *op. cit.,* pp. 62-66.

83. Samuel Velasco Flor, *Foro boliviano* (Sucre, 1877), p. 7.

84. The only copy of this dialogue, ten fols. long, is available in the CR at the BNB. It is partially transcribed in Vedia y Mitre, *op. cit.,* I, pp. 56-67; see also Francovich, *op. cit.,* pp. 78-79; cf. *infra,* n. 89.

85. Most of the documents dealing with the 1809 revolution in La Paz have been brought together in Carlos Ponce Sanginés and Raúl Alfonso García, eds., *Documentos para la historia de la revolución de 1809* (La Paz, 1953-1954), 4 vols. The various declarations of the apprehended revolutionaries all point to the crucial importance of the Michel mission.

86. See Luis F. Jemio, *Biografías de Pedro Domingo Murillo y José Antonio Medina* (La Paz, 1909).

87. Usually in the standard textbooks Pedro Domingo Murillo is considered the leader of the La Paz rebellion, which he was only nominally. A careful reading of the great bulk of documents contained in the 4 volumes cited in n. 85 shows the priest, Medina, as the real leader of the revolution; see also Paz, *Historia,* II, pp. 89-95.

88. The authorship of the proclamation of the Junta Tuitiva of La Paz remains in dispute. It was known as the official manifesto of the Junta Tuitiva. But diligent research by the competent Bolivian philosopher, Guillermo Francovich, has led to the discovery of the original proclamation in manuscript form in the National Archive of Argentina, which is reproduced in facsimile form in his *El pensamiento universitario de Charcas,* pp. 144-145. The document is entitled "Proclama de la ciudad de la Plata [Chuquisaca] a los valerosos habitantes de la ciudad de la Paz." It has no signature, no date, and no place of origin. But it is believed that it was written in Chuquisaca as can be deduced from the title of the manuscript. Mr. Francovich believes that its author was Bernardo Monteagudo, as it is much like the dialogue between Atahualpa and Ferdinand VII (see *supra,* n. 84). It is thought that Michel took it with him to La Paz and the junta used it as its official proclamation. Again we have here a good indication that Chuquisaca was the headquarters of the radical generation of 1809 and that the revolution of La Paz was prepared in Chuquisaca. Historians from La Paz disagree with this thesis, see Manuel M. Pinto, *La revolución de la intendencia de la Paz en el virreynato del Río de la Plata, con la ocurrencia de Chuquisaca* (Buenos Aires, 1909).

89. Juan Antonio Alvarez de Arenales, "Estado general que manifiesta el nuevo alistamiento de milicias urbanas de la ciudad de la Plata [Chuquisaca]," Plata, June 25, 1809, located in the personal library of General Blanco Galindo, Cochabamba, Bolivia; cf. Uriburu, *Historia,* p. 24 (he speaks of 1300 men).

90. "Expediente sobre el cumplimiento del auto de la Audiencia para que el intendente de Potosí no venga a Chuquisaca a sostener, como lo dice, cirtas [sic] providencias violentas del Presidente Pizarro," May 26 to June 26, 1809, in René-Moreno, *Documentos inéditos,* pp. 27-41.

91. Woodbine Parish, *Buenos Aires y las provincias del Río de la Plata* . . ., translated and edited by Justo Maeso (Buenos Aires, 1852-1853), II, 216.

92. "Medidas tomados de la Audiencia gobernadora para recibir en paz y honor al presidente Nieto . . .," Plata, September 27, 1809, proclamation of Vicente Nieto, Jujuy, November 8, 1809, proclamation of Juan Antonio Alvarez de Arenales, Plata, October 13, 1809, Vicente Nieto to the Audiencia of Charcas, Cuchiguasi, December 21, 1809, all available in René-Moreno, *Documentos inéditos*, pp. 73, 88-89, 91; also see René-Moreno, "Relato de doña Martina Lazcano," *Más notas*, p. 120.

93. Vicente Nieto to José Manuel Goyeneche, Jujuy, November 10, 1809, in René-Moreno, *Documentos inéditos*, pp. 90-91; René-Moreno, "El oidor Ussoz y Mozí," *Nuevas notas*, p. 273.

94. Gabriel René-Moreno, who for long years diligently collected documents about the events in Chuquisaca in 1808-1809 all over Latin America and Europe, was unable to determine what happened to the *oidores*. He found evidence that Ussoz y Mozí was expelled from Chuquisaca, see *ibid.*, pp. 271-283. Uriburu, *Historia*, p. 26, tells that Ballesteros and Arenales were sent to Lima together.

95. Vedia y Mitre, op. cit., I, 78-146; Angel Sandoval, "Don Jayme de Zudañez," *BSGS*, XXIX, nos. 310-311 (1931), 133-141.

96. Uriburu, *Historia*, pp. 27-29.

97. Joaquín Gantier, *Doña Juana Azurduy de Padilla* (La Paz, 1946), pp. 58-60; Ramallo, *Guerrilleros*, pp. 19-25.

98. Many authors, and nearly all Bolivian historians, affirm that the movement of May 25, 1809, in Chuquisaca marked the real beginning of the War of Independence in Spanish America. See especially Luis Arce, "Iniciativa y comienzos de la guerra de la independencia sud-americana," in *Cuarto Congreso Científico, 1° Pan-Americano, septima sección, ciencias sociales, historia americana* (Santiago, 1908), pp. 4-60.

CHAPTER 2

1. [Urcullu], *Apuntes*, p. 93, is the first to give the number 102. All other authors copy Urcullu; see Luis M. Guzmán, *Historia de Bolivia*, 3d ed. (Cochabamba, 1896), p. 23; Mitre in his *Belgrano*, 5th ed., II, 379, copies Urcullu too.

2. [Urcullu], *Apuntes*, p. 93, gives the exact number of nine, without specifying any names. And again all other Bolivian historians, and also Mitre, *loc. cit.*, repeat Urcullu. Further, [Urcullu], *loc. cit.*, states that none surrendered and here, too, all Bolivian historians proudly repeat Urcullu, Yet Manuel José Cortés, *Ensayo sobre la historia de Bolivia* (Sucre, 1861), p. 93, makes an exception and says that two became Loyalists, but he does not name them. It is probable that Miguel Lanza, Eustaquio Méndez, Juana Azurduy de Padilla, Juan Antonio Alvarez de Arenales, and a certain Mercado survived the war. Only Lanza became a prominent figure in the creation and consolidation of Bolivia. This chapter will make it clear that desertion and shifting allegiance to the enemy was frequent among the partisan forces.

3. See Mitre, *Belgrano*, II, chap. xxxiii.

4. Today known as Padilla.

5. The rebellion in this strategic region of Chayanta (today in the department of Potosí) remains very confusing and obscure, see Mitre, *Belgrano*, II, 397. It seems that such leaders as Betanzos, Zarate, Cardoso, Fuentes, Umaña, and maybe Monroy operated from there, see Camacho, *Historia*, p. 151. There

is an interesting document about some unknown guerrilla warfare around Oruro in ANB, *ACh* (EC, 1818), no. 2, 59 fols.

6. Very interesting information is available in a curious manuscript sketching the history of Tarija during the war, "Fragmento q. pasa el Gov.$^{no}$ y Municipalidad de Tarixa p.$^a$ q. se de ala prensa adornado en estilo, Tarija, y Sep.$^e$ 2 de 1826," ANB, *MG*, Vol. XIV, no. 19; cf. Bernardo Trigo, *Las tejas de mi techo* (La Paz, 1939), pp. 89-96; Paz, *Historia*, Vol. II, chaps. xix-xxii; Tomás O'Connor D' Arlach, *El Coronel José Eustaquio Méndez* (Tarija, 1893), 25 pp.

7. See Arenales to San Martín, Vallegrande, August 7, 1814, and Sauses, September 4, 1814, in Uriburu, *Historia*, I, 285-294.

8. See Julio Díaz A., *Vida . . . del General José Miguel Lanza* (La Paz, 1927), 49 pp.; Victor Santa Cruz, "El guerrillero Lanza . . . ," *Revista Militar* (La Paz), no. 154 (1950), 137-144.

9. The original manuscript version of the Vargas diary was found in *CR* in the BNB, and was used for this chapter. Subsequently it was partially published by Gunnar Mendoza, "Una crónica desconocida . . . ," *USFX*, XVI, nos. 37-38 (1951 [*sic*, published in 1954]), 199-301. Mr. Mendoza introduced the diary (pp. 199-254) with a solid discussion about guerrilla warfare in Upper Peru, hereafter cited as Mendoza, *Introducción*. Later the University of San Francisco Xavier in Sucre published the whole diary, plus Mr. Mendoza's introduction and notes in a *separata*. It was published in 1954 and not 1952, as the title page reads, since the diary was not located until 1953. This *separata*, due to a small printing, is hard to locate. The diary will be cited hereafter as *Diario*, folios.

10. *Diario*, fols. 156-157v.

11. The information given by most historians in regard to the Ayopaya faction is erroneous when compared with the precise, eyewitness account of guerrilla Vargas in his diary. For example, historians speak of a great battle on August 20, 1816, by Chinchilla at Charapaya (José Macedonio Urquidi, *Compendio de la historia de Bolivia*, 4th ed., Buenos Aires, 1944, p. 141; Paz, *Historia*, II, 377). Yet the entry for August 20, 1816, in the diary (*Diario*, fols. 47v.-48), mentions Charapaya but does not speak of a battle. Again, such a chronicler as [Urcullu], *Apuntes*, pp. 86, 88, from whom most modern accounts are drawn, speaks always of Lanza in 1816 and 1817 when really Lanza had left in 1815. The most detailed biography of Lanza is Luis S. Crespo, *José Miguel García Lanza* (La Paz, 1928), 144 pp. Yet seemingly it is written with imaginary sources. Lanza's whole career during the War of Independence is written inaccurately. With the discovery of the diary of a soldier of the Lanza faction Crespo's book, which does not cite sources, has become worthless; see *infra*, n. 40.

12. ANB, *ACh* (EC, 1812), no. 2, fol. 1.

13. *Diario*, fol. 157v.

14. The fallacy of Lanza's being in Ayopaya might have been detected in Manuel Trelles, *Cuestiones de límites entre la república Argentina y Bolivia* (Buenos Aires, 1872), pp. 195-209, documents by Miguel Lanza requesting pay for his services in the United Provinces.

15. Mendoza, *Introducción*, p. 210.

16. Francisco de Viedma, "Descripción geográfica . . . de la provincia de Santa Cruz . . . ," in Pedro Angelis, ed., *Colección de obras y documentos relatives a la historia . . . de las provincias del Río de la plata* (Buenos Aires, 1836), III, 24.

17. *Ibid.*, III, 21-23.

18. Alcides D'Orbigny, *Voyage dans l'Amérique Méridional* (Paris, 1835-

1847), II, 466.

19. *Diario*, fol. 44.

20. Rigoberto Paredes, *Provincia de Inquisivi, estudios geográficos, estadísticos y sociales* (La Paz, 1906), p. 109-113.

21. It might be that further information about Vargas could be found in church records, if such exist, in the village of Moosa.

22. Mendoza, *Introducción*, p. 242.

23. *Diario*, fol. 100v.

24. *Ibid.*, fol. 101.

25. "Toda la vesindad desente" (*ibid.*, fol. 101v.).

26. Vargas says, "Lo más era que la misma madama de Lira, doña María Martínez, se empeñaba por la salud de Moreno" (*ibid.*, fol. 101v.).

27. It looks as if this meeting was held in the priest's house since the diary reads, "Todo esto se hablava en la casa del señor Cura" (*ibid.*, fol. 102).

28. *Ibid.*, fol. 103.

29. Identified here as "Sargento Mayor don Pedro Marquina" (*ibid.*, fol. 103v.).

30. *Ibid.*, fol. 104.

31. See Urquidi, *Rectificaciones*, p. 140.

32. *Diario*, fol. 104v.

33. *Ibid.*, fol. 105.

34. Moreno and Miranda were from Cuzco, cf. *ibid.*, fols. 294v.-295.

35. *Ibid.*, fols. 105v.-106.

36. *Ibid.*, fols. 106v.-107.

37. Mendoza, *Introducción*, p. 236.

38. *Diario*, fol. 107v.

39. Captain Carlos Bolaños, Major Juan Gonsales, Lieutenant Manuel Patiño, County Commissioner (*subdelegado*) José Manuel Arana, Lieutenant Gregorio Andrade (*ibid.*, fol. 108).

40. *Ibid.*, fol. 109. One example alone can prove the uselessness of Crespo's biography of Lanza, *op. cit.* He said Eusebio Lira joined the Lanza unit in October, 1823 (p. 64). This is six years after Lira's death.

41. See Mendoza, *Introducción*, pp. 235-236.

42. *Diario*, fol. 111.

43. *Ibid.*, fols. 116-156.

44. Gabriel René-Moreno was never subject to the blindness of chauvinism. Two contemporary historians, Humberto Vázquez-Machicado and Gunnar Mendoza, follow the unbiased path that characterized René-Moreno.

45. Urquidi, *Rectificaciones*, p. 38.

46. The document that comes closest to the diary of Vargas is the "Autobiografía del Teniente Coronel don Manuel Ascencio Padilla," in Miguel de los Santos Taborga, *Documentos inéditos para la historia de Bolivia* (Chuquisaca, 1891), pp. 167-203, also published in *BSGS*, III-IV, nos. 33-38 (1901-1902). This autobiography was really a report from Padilla, dated Laguna, June 24, 1815, to his superiors. It lacks the intimacy of Vargas' words, is much shorter, and is a kind of glorification of Padilla's own personality.

47. See Mendoza, *Introducción*, p. 261, n. 11.

48. See Gustavo Adolfo Otero, "El factor regional en la independencia de Bolivia," *Kollasuyo*, I, no. 2 (1939), 21-23.

49. Cf. Camba, *Memorias*, I, 317.

50. Interesting are the words of Marquina to his soldiers: ". . . entra Marquina, manda formar a toda la gente y dice: 'Muchachos: ya conoséis el caracter de los Yndios: conoséis lo crueles que son, que son crueles por condición natural:

si caso logran pescar a uno de vosotros, no less dejará hueso sano: conoséis que no entienden rasón alguna, ni tienen un poco de conmiseración con sus semejantes'" (*Diario*, fol. 124).

51. ANB, *ACh*, (EC, 1812), nos. 9, 10, 12; BNB, *CR*, Catálogo Corbacho, no. 316.

52. See Alipio Valencia Vega, *Julián Tupaj Katari* (Buenos Aires, [1948]), p. 15.

53. René-Moreno, *Ultimos días*, p. 55.

54. The movement of Cáceres is not very well known and has not been studied thoroughly, see Luis Paz, *Estudios históricos de Monseñor Miguel de los Santos Taborga* (La Paz, 1908), pp. 155-157; Muñoz, *Guerra*, pp. 220-221; Manuel de Odriózola, *Documentos históricos del Perú* (Lima, 1863-1877), III, 49-160; Nicanor Aranzaes, *Diccionario histórico del departmento de La Paz* (La Paz, 1915), pp. 156-157.

55. "Documentos de la independencia, proclamas en Quichua," *BSGS*, XVI, nos. 173,175 (1915), 44-56.

56. The contemporary Bolivian leftist writer, Alipio Valencia Vega, in his *Desarollo del pensamiento político en Bolivia* (La Paz, 1953), p. 50, is the only writer who clearly says that the Indian was a mobile force used by both contingents.

57. Roberto Alvarado, *Tres esquemas de historia* (no place, 1950), p. 28.

58. *Diario*, fol. 40v.

59. Gabriel René-Moreno, "Expediciones e invasiones," *Revista de Artes y Letras* (Santiago), V (1885), 484-489.

60. See Jáuregui Rosquellas, "La Audiencia de Charcas," 1-53.

61. *Diario*, fol. 40v.; cf. Mendoza, *Introducción*, p. 229.

62. M. A. Padilla to General Rondeau, Laguna, December 21, 1815, in Mallo, *Administración*, p. 27.

63. Humberto Guzmán, *Estéban Arze, caudillo de los valles* (Cochabamba, 1948), p. 64.

64. See Archivo General de la Nación (Argentina), *Partes oficiales y documentos relativos a la guerra de la independencia argentina*, 2nd ed. (Buenos Aires, 1900-1903), 4 vols., *passim*.

65. See Arturo Rawson, *Argentina y Bolivia en la epopeya de la emancipación* (La Paz, 1928), p. 133.

66. "En verdad, el vínculo formal de dependencia que liga la facción con respecto al Río de la Plata, es patente" (Mendoza, *Introducción*, p. 231).

67. Cf. Uriburu, *Historia*, *passim*.

68. Mostly published in the *Gaceta de Buenos Aires*.

69. *Gaceta de Buenos Aires*, no. 53 (1816).

70. Mitre, *Belgrano*, II, 407; Paz, *Historia*, II, 312.

71. See *infra*, chap. iii.

72. *Supra*, n. 62.

73. See Urquidi, *Rectificaciones*, pp. 34-35; José María Marquiegui, *Resumen histórico del Ckollansuyo, Charcas hoy Bolivia* (Sucre, 1938), pp. 75-76.

74. *Diario*, fol. 156.

75. *Ibid.*, fols. 156v.-157v.

76. See *Ibid.*, fols. 157v.-158; the fact that Lanza killed Chinchilla is something completely new in the annals of Bolivian history and it is doubtful that the patriotic historians will permit this event to enter into the standard histories or textbooks, cf. Urquidi, *Compendio*, p. 141; Luis M. Guzmán, *Historia*, p. 27.

77. *Diario*, fol. 158.

78. *Ibid.*, fol. 156v.
79. Gabriel René-Moreno, "La nueva constitución i el militarismo en Bolivia," *El Independiente* (Santiago). no. 2398, December 9, 1871.

CHAPTER 3

1. René-Moreno, *Biblioteca boliviana*, no. 207, p. 49.
2. The original documents which indicate this switch belonged to the collection of E.O. Rück, now located in the National Library of Bolivia in Sucre. According to Alfredo Jáuregui Rosquellas they were stolen but then recovered. Dr. Rosquellas has published some of them in "Documentos inéditos," *BSGS*, XLIII, nos. 427-428 (1948), 182-192. He promised to publish the rest of the documents in future numbers of the *BSGS*, along with a revelation of how the documents were stolen, but this promise was not fulfilled. Yet the documents published in *ibid.* are sufficient proof that this switch was made. See, too, Rigoberto Paredes, "Ligeros datos sobre la fundación de Bolivia," *BSGS*, XXXII, nos. 337-339 (1937), 141, n. 1; Paz, *Historia*, II, 113-114; Camba, *Memorias* I, 29; cf. Eduardo Aramayo, "Resumen . . . de documentos secretos . . . ," *BSGS*, XXXIV, nos. 344-346 (1939), 86-101.
3. Ernesto Díez-Canseco, *Perú y Bolivia, pueblos gemelos* (Lima, 1952), pp. 9-10.
4. Cf. Jaime Mendoza, "La creación de una nacionalidad," *BSGS*, XXVI, nos. 268-269 (1926), 1.
5. As cited by Jesús Arocha Moreno, *Las ideas políticas de Bolívar y Sucre en el proceso de la fundación de Bolivia* (Caracas, 1952), p. 10.
6. This event is brilliantly sketched in René-Moreno, *Ultimos días*, chaps vi-ix.
7. *Carta pastoral de . . .don Benito de Moxó y Francolí* (Buenos Aires, 1807), as cited by *ibid.*, p. 106, n. 1.
8. Benito de Moxó, *Manifiesto proclamatorio*, as cited by *ibid.*, p. 98, n. 1.
9. The contemporary Bolivian historian, Humberto Vázquez-Machicado, has an unpublished essay entitled "Los origenes socio-históricos de la nacionalidad boliviana," in which he considers Potosí as the crucial city of Charcas. According to Vázquez-Machicado, Potosí held the divergent regions of Charcas together.
10. Alfredo Jáuregui Rosquellas, "Juan José Castelli," *BSGS*, XLIII, nos. 429-430 (1949), 341.
11. BNB, *C-RM, Manuscritos de Chuquisaca, 1624-1903*, II, no. 21, III, nos. 1, 4, 6, V, nos. 9, 19; cf. Nicanor Mallo, "Tradiciones, cosas de aquellos tiempos," *BSGS*, XXXVII, nos. 371-373 (1941), 57.
12. Moxó to Castelli, La Plata [Chuquisaca], December 11, 1810, in *BSGS*, XLIV, nos. 433-434 (1950), 49-50.
13. Juan José Castelli to the Junta de Buenos Aires, Potosí, December 16, 1810, as cited by Julio César Chaves, *Castelli el adalid de mayo* (Buenos Aires, 1944), p. 191; Omiste, *Memoria, 1810*, pp. 33-34.
14. This intimate account of the behavior of the auxiliaries is sketched in *ibid.*, p. 30. The work of Omiste is of great value since he relied on the account of witnesses who still survived. See [Roberto Prudencio], "Modesto Omiste," *Kollasuyo*, II, no. 18 (1940), 52-55.
15. La junta provincional guvernativa de las provincias del Río de la Plata . . . a todos los habitantes de esta ciudad de la Plata [Chuquisaca], La Plata, January 5, 1811, in *BSGS*, XLIV, nos. 433-434 (1950), 57.
16. La excma. junta . . . , La Plata, February 8, 1811, in *ibid.*, 60-61;

Chaves, *op. cit.*, pp. 203-213.

17. *Ibid.*, pp. 228-231.

18. See Bartolomé Mitre, *Historia de San Martín*, 2d ed. (Buenos Aires, 1890), I, 217; Paz, *Historia*, II, 143, n. 1. Many Bolivian historians and the Argentine, Chaves, *op. cit.*, chap. xxii, accuse Goyeneche of breaking the armistice.

19. Omiste, *Memoria, 1811*, pp. 30-34. René-Moreno, in his *Biblioteca boliviana*, no. 2239, p. 563, believes that Omiste's second work (*Memoria, 1811*) is even better than his work about 1810.

20. Omiste, *Memoria, 1811*, pp. 9-11, is the only chronicler of this incident.

21. *Ibid.*, pp. 30-34.

22. *Ibid.*, p. 35.

23. The record of the investigation has not been located.

24. Juan Martín Pueyrredón a la Junta Gubernativa de estas Provincias, Campo Santo, October 4, 1811, in Muñoz, *Guerra*, p. 227.

25. Omiste, *Memoria, 1811*, pp. 36-37. Because of his extreme anti-Catholicism Omiste came to accept Pueyrredón's conclusion. This is very strange, since Omiste throughout his two works emphasizes the resentment of the *potosinos* against the auxiliaries, because of the latter's monstrous behavior. Paz, *Historia*, II, 158, n. 1, wonders what reasoning Omiste used to come to such an illogical conclusion. Paz takes issue with Omiste with sound reasoning, and there is every reason to believe that Paz's idea is correct.

26. See Mario J. Buschiazzo, "La Casa de Moneda en Potosí," *BSGS*, XXXV, nos. 359-361 (1940), 270-275.

27. Cf. René-Moreno, *Notas*, p. 207.

28. Pueyrredón a la Junta, *op. cit.*, pp. 230-232.

29. Omiste, *Memoria, 1811*, p. 45.

30. Pueyrredón a la Junta, *op. cit.*, p. 232.

31. "Es fragmento q. pasa el gov.no . . . de Tarixa a la prensa . . . ," Tarija, September 2, 1826, ANB, *MI*, XIV, no. 19, fol. 1.

32. *Ibid.*, fol. 1.

33. Bernardo Trigo, *Las tejas*, p. 97.

34. The case of Tarija is one of the most perplexing. As stated above, the people of Tarija joined the auxiliary army with great enthusiasm and cooperated decisively in the battles of Cotagaita and Suipacha (see Luis Pizarro, *Tarija, apuntes histórico-geográficos*, Sucre, 1936, p. 106; Bernardo Frías, *Historia del General D. Martín Güemes y de la provincia de Salta*, Salta, 1902-1911, III, 527). After the defeat of Huaqui the revolutionary junta (?) of Tarija issued a chauvinistic manifesto inciting the people of Tarija to arm and rush north to aid the routed Argentine army (Paz, *Historia*, II, 148-149). Then suddenly an antiauxiliary army feeling became prevalent and it is said that the town fought the defeated army with a loss of four hundred men (*supra*, n. 33). The document cited (*supra*, n. 31) might be the key to this change of sentiment. Probably, when the manifesto was published the disgruntled warriors had not returned to their native town. It might also be that the three people who signed the manifesto (Paz never cites from where he took the document) do not represent an official body. There is one more point that adds to the confusion. Pueyrredón, in his report home, considered Tarija as friendly territory. Seemingly the fury of Tarija was directed more against Díaz Vélez, who came through the town first, than against Pueyrredón, who came later.

35. Cochabamba had rebelled against Goyeneche and had proclaimed for a second time its allegiance to Buenos Aires. The local guerrilla leaders, especially Estéban Arze, were responsible for this second pronouncement. At

the approach of Goyeneche, Cochabamba refused to surrender and the Royalist general defeated the *cochabambinos* in the outskirts of the town. Entering the city, the victor had to confront and fight a legion of Cochabamba women, who in an act of extreme heroism wished to show their enmity for the general. Many of the women were killed. Goyeneche, usually of moderate temper, unleashed for several days a reign of terror that even surpassed that of Castelli. In this way Goyeneche foolishly aided the cause of the Patriots, which had suffered because of the terror of the Argentine expedition. Yet the history of Goyeneche's entrance, the women's fight, and his reign of terror has not been treated in an impartial study. The versions existing are generally exaggerated. But undoubtedly the Royalists committed a blunder of great magnitude (cf. Urquidi, *Rectificaciones,* pp. 28-29).

36. The first edition (Buenos Aires, 1855), 4 vols., is extremely rare, but it is a beautiful edition. The second edition (La Plata [Argentina], 1892), 3 vols., is less rare but still not easy to find. The third edition is available in the collection of the Biblioteca Ayacucho (Madrid, n. d.), Vol. XVI, but this is a defective edition. Citations will refer to this third edition because of its easy availability. The other two editions have been consulted to insure correctness. Cf. René-Moreno, *Más notas,* p. 208, n. 1.

37. See Vicente F. López, *Historia de la república argentina,* new ed., (Buenos Aires, 1913), IV, 373.

38. Paz, *Memorias,* p. 215.

39. For a detailed account of the campaign of Vilcapugio and Ayohuma see Mitre, *Belgrano,* II, chaps, xxii-xxiii.

40. This whole incident is sketched by Paz, *Memorias,* pp. 216-220, who was an eyewitness.

41. *Op. cit.,* II, 177.

42. Publicación Oficial [Gobierno de la Provincia de Santiago del Estero], *El Coronel Lorenzo Lugones* (Buenos Aires, 1896), 57.

43. San Martín to Godoy Cruz, no place given, August 24, 1816, in Mitre, *Belgrano,* II, 282, n. 34; see Alfredo Villegas, "Un documento de San Martín con referencias históricas," *Anuario de Historia Argentina,* V (1943-1945), 354-355, 367-369.

44. Other sources are "Memorias del General Rondeau," in Andrés Lamas, *Colecciones de memorias y documentos para la historia y la geografía de los pueblos del Río de la Plata* (Montevideo, 1849), pp. 2-88; Gregorio Aráoz de la Madrid, *Memorias,* Biblioteca Ayacucho, LX (Madrid, n. d.); also in the memoirs of General Rudecindo Alvarado unlocated by this author (cf. *infra,* chap. vii, n. 72).

45. Paz, *Memorias,* p. 281, writes, ". . . en que se hacía el *lavatorio* del dinero" [italics mine]. The word *lavatorio* is translated as *washing,* which hardly makes sense. Could it be that it is a colloquialism for counting? The word *lavatorio* is used in the first and second editions too.

46. Tomás Tejerina, Lorenzo Lugones (cf. *supra,* n. 42), José María Paz.

47. This is told by [Urcullu], *Apuntes,* pp. 80-81. Neither José María Paz, who was in Chuquisaca, nor La Madrid mentions it in his memoirs; cf. Paz, *Memorias,* pp. 290-292; cf. Valentín Abecia, "Introducción," in Ramallo, *Guerrilleros,* p. 13.

48. René-Moreno, *Más notas,* p. 206, feels sorry that José María Paz was not present when the excesses of Castelli occurred. He might have left a more precise and honest picture.

49. The battle is also known as the battle of Viloma or Wiluma, see Rodríguez Casado and Calderón Quijano, eds., *Memoria de gobierno del Virrey*

*Abascal* (Seville, 1944), II, 278.

50. Cuartel General en marcha, December 7, 1815, in Ramallo, *Guerrilleros,* pp. 144-145.

51. In *ibid.,* pp. 145-151; also published in Mallo, *Administración,* pp. 27-28.

52. The biography by Ramallo in *Guerrilleros* does not give much detail about the early background of the guerrilla, Padilla; cf. Samuel Velasco Flor, *Vidas de bolivianos célebres* (Potosí, 1871), pp. 13-14.

53. Valentín Abecia, "Introducción," in Ramallo, *Guerrilleros,* p. 13.

54. [Urcullu], *Apuntes,* p. 85; Mitre, *Belgrano,* II, 282.

55. This campaign is sketched in Araoz de la Madrid, *Memorias,* pp. 121-174, yet the colonel loved to glorify his actions.

56. Bolivian school texts consider the La Madrid contingent as the fourth auxiliary army, see Antonio Díaz Villamil, *Curso elemental de historia de Bolivia,* 3d ed. (La Paz, 1949), II, 51-52; Camacho, *Historia,* p. 164.

57. Mariano Zorreguieta, *Apuntes históricos de Salta en la época del coloniaje,* 2d ed., (Salta, n. d.), pp. 115, 119.

58. René-Moreno, "Expediciones e invasiones," pp. 484-489.

59. Gabriel René-Moreno has an unpublished work about the last expeditionary force under the command of Colonel Urdininea, who in 1828 became the third president of Bolivia, and whom he calles *pies de plomo.* The work is in the possession of Dr. Humberto Vázquez-Machicado. See also *El Correo de las Provincias* (Buenos Aires), 17 numbers, November 19, 1822, to April 10, 1823.

60. The relations between Upper Peru and the United Provinces, especially the reasons for letting Charcas fight alone after 1817, are superbly sketched in two books by René-Moreno, *Más notas* and *Nuevas notas.*

CHAPTER 4

1. Cf. *USFX,* no. 17 (1938), pp. 56-122. These are several articles referring to the date of the foundation of Chuquisaca.

2. José María Dalence, *Bosquejo estadístico de Bolivia* (Chuquisaca, 1851), p. 110; Juan José Segovia, a *criollo* lawyer in Chuquisaca at the turn of the century, believed that the town had about 18,000 inhabitants at that time (see Gabriel René-Moreno, *Bolivia y Argentina, notas biográficas y bibliográficas* (Santiago, 1901), p. 218.

3. See Gabriel René-Moreno, "La Audiencia de Charcas," *Revista Chilena,* VIII (1877), 93-142.

4. Antonio Alcedo, *Diccionario geográfico-histórico de las Indias Occidentales* (Madrid, 1786-1789), *passim.*

5. Naturally the classic work dealing with Chuquisaca is René-Moreno, *Ultimos días.*

6. Alberto Baldivieso, *Enfermedades altoperuanas* (Sucre, 1929), p. 1.

7. See Gustavo Adolfo Otero, *Figuras de la cultura boliviana* (Quito, 1952), pp. 199-201.

8. René-Moreno, *Ultimos días,* p. 118.

9. Humberto Vázquez-Machicado, *La sociología de Gabriel René-Moreno* (Buenos Aires, 1936), p. 8.

10. "Melgarejo y el melgarejismo," *Selecciones Bolivianas* (La Paz), II, no. 6 (1953), 35-41. Tristán Marof [pseud. of Gustavo A. Navarro] has written a humorous novel in which he ridicules the society of Chuquisaca, *La ilustre ciudad, historia de badulaques* (La Paz, 1950).

11. "Los feudales criollos en el poder," *Revista de la Federación de*

*Estudiantes de Chuquisaca,* I, nos. 1-2 (1945), 111-131.

12. *Nacionalismo,* pp. xvii-xxiii.

13. "Casimiro Olañeta, progenitores y ambiente social en que nació," *La Razón* (La Paz), November 20, 1949, literary supplement.

14. *Ibid.*

15. René-Moreno, "Fragmentos;" see René-Moreno, *Bolivia y Argentina,* pp. 271-272.

16. Guillermo Francovich, *La filosofía en Bolivia* (Buenos Aires, c. 1945), p. 79.

17. ANB, *EP* (May 5, 1792), escribano: Aramayo, fol. 288; ANB, *EP* (March 11, 1796), escribano: Callejas, fol. 257.

18. Capitán José Andrews, *Viaje de Buenos Aires a Potosí y Arica en los años 1825 y 1826* (Buenos Aires, 1920), pp. 140-141; ANB, *EP* (1800), escribano: Pimentel, fol. 290; ANB, *EP* (1801), escribano: Valda, fols. 244, 278.

19. "Lista de los individuos casados residentes en la Plata y a quienes se conminó el ir a reunirse con sus consortes," ANB, *ACh* (1787), unclassified document.

20. ANB, *EP* (May 5, 1792), escribano: Aramayo, fol. 288; ANB, *EP* (April 30, 1796), escribano: Valda, fol. 268.

21. ANB, *EP* (November 14, 1788), escribano: Callejas, fol. 813; ANB, *EP* (May 5, 1792), escribano: Aramayo, fol. 288; ANB, *EP* (January 22, 1795), escribano: Callejas, no fol.; ANB, *EP,* (April 30, 1796), escribano: Valda, fol. 268; ANB, *EP* (March 20, 1800), escribano: Callejas, fol. 591.

22. ANB, *ACh* (EC, 1801), no. 170, fol. 20; ANB, *EP* (April 19, 1797), escribano: Navarro, fol. 140; ANB, *EP* (February 19, 1800), escribano: Pimentel, fol. 290; ANB, *EP* (July 20, 1801), escribano: Valda, fol. 243; ANB, *EP* (July 30, 1801), escribano: Valda, fol. 277.

23. ANB, *EP* (1796), escribano: Navarro, fol. 496; ANB, *EP* (April 19, 1797), escribano: Navarro, fol. 46, 140; *infra,* n. 24.

24. ANB, *ACh* (EC, September 9, 1797), no. 129, 4 fols.; ANB, *EP* (1791), escribano: Navarro, fol. 480; ANB, *EP* (1797), escribano: Navarro, fol. 140.

25. "Certificación de óbito de doña Rafaela Güemes . . . ," *Archivo de la parroquia de Santo Domingo,* Libro de defunciones, 1787-1845, fol. 32 v.; "Testamento otorgado por doña Rafaela Güemes . . . ," ANB, *EP* (January 22, 1795), vol. 303, fols. 5-9.

26. Birth certificate signed by Jph. Antº de Sn Alberto, Arzº de la Plata, April 7, 1795, and located in the *Archivo de la parroquia de Santo Domingo* (Sucre, Bolivia). Reproduced in entirety in unpubl. diss. (University of Florida, 1955) by Charles W. Arnade, "The Creation of the Republic of Bolivia," chap. iv, n. 30.

27. Frías, *Historia,* I, 152-153; Joaquín Gantier, "Casimiro Olañeta, educación y primeras impresiones," *La Razón* (La Paz), December 18, 1949, literary supplement.

28. Later when Olañeta came back through Córdoba in 1824 as a Royalist agent, Funes wrote about it to the secretary of Bolívar but without telling him that he had known him as a student. Seemingly Funes did not remember this young insignificant student of 1809-1812, Funes to Pérez, no place, July 1, 1824, in BNB, *C-RM* (Copia de borradores autógrafos y cartas oficios originales de los papeles de Funes existentes en la Biblioteca Nacional de Buenos Aires).

29. Damaso Uriburu, *Memorias* (Buenos Aires, 1934), p. 30.

30. See *infra,* n. 31, p. 11 of the *Exposición.*

31. Olañeta, *Exposición,* pp. 1-2. Olañeta wrote this when someone, under

the pseudonym of El Mosquetero, circulated a strong attack on him. The pamphlet by El Mosquetero has never been located, although such authorities as Gabriel René-Moreno, Humberto Vázquez-Machicado, Gunnar Mendoza, and this author have searched diligently. Olañeta's *Exposición* is extremely rare and only one copy is available, located in the National Library of Bolivia. It has not been included in Gustavo Adolfo Otero, ed., *Folletos escogidos de Casimiro Olañeta* (La Paz, 1939), 197 pp., although it is one of the most interesting writings of Olañeta. More information is available in René-Moreno, *Biblioteca boliviana*, no. 1464; René-Moreno, "Fragmentos;" *El Condor de Bolivia* (Chuquisaca), no. 1, November 12, 1825, no. 16, March 16, 1826.

32. "La victoria de Salta me puso en aptitud de marchar a mi país nativo. Preso en Jujui por el Jeneral Belgrano sin mas crimen que mi apellido sufrí cuanto a la desgracia y la maldad pudieron inventar para aflijirme. Después de una atroz conducta, logré pasar a Chuquisaca" (Olañeta, *Exposición*, p. 2).

33. ANB, *ACh*, Expedientes de abogados y practicantes juristas, XIII, no. 13, fol. 252, contains the diploma.

34. Luis Paz, *La Universidad*, p. 233.

35. *Ibid.*, p. 262. The best study of Vicente Cañete is Gunnar Mendoza, *El doctor don Pedro Vicente Cañete* (Sucre, 1954); cf. René-Moreno, *Biblioteca peruana*, II, 563-567.

36. ANB, *ACh*, Expedientes de abogados, fol. 243.

37. See López, *Historia*, VII, 17-18; Ramallo, *Guerra*, pp. 12-13.

38. ANB, *ACh*, Expedientes de abogados, fols. 244-253.

39. *Ibid.*, fol. 253.

40. *Ibid.*, fols. 257v., 260.

41. "Conjuez de la Audiencia, Agente Fiscal en lo civil, y en la Protecturía de los naturales, y en la Defensuría general del Jusgado de Censos" (*ibid.*, fol. 264v.).

42. José Cabrera (Abogado del Reino y Escribano de esta Audiencia), Mariano José Calvo (Abogado y Escribano de esta Audiencia), Melchor Higueras (primer Notario de esta Curia metropolitana, Escribano de S. M., de Govierno, y Notario Eclesiástico), Mariano Moscoso (Escribano de S. M. y de los Jusgados de Censos, y primera instancia), Tomás Delgadillo (Escribano de S. M. y actuario de los juzgados constitucionales de prim? y segunda elección de esta corte) (*ibid.*, fols. 262v.-265).

43. *Ibid.*, Higueras, fol. 264.

44. *Ibid.*, Delgadillo, fol. 264v.

45. ANB, *ACh* (EC, 1820), no. 72, fol. 116.

46. Olañeta, *Exposición*, p. 2.

47. Joaquín Gantier, "Los Olañeta, el abogado y el militar," *La Razón*, January 29, 1950, literary supplement.

48. "Su afición a conspirar y destruir el orden existente se mantenía a gran parte de su ineptitud para crear ni organizar nada. La incoherencia de sus actos el día de hoy es precursora de su inconsecuencia el día de mañana. Su gusto por la palabra solo cedía en ardor a su propension incontenible a conspirar" (unpublished first draft notes of Gabriel René-Moreno belonging to Humberto Vázquez-Machicado).

49. Cf. Alfonso Crespo, "Perfil de Casimiro Olañeta," *Kollasuyo*, IX, no. 65 (1947), 3-11.

50. Cf. Charles W. Arnade, "Una figura mediocre en el motín del 18 de abril de 1828," *BSGS*, XLV, no. 441 (1954), 74-100.

51. This is one reason why so little is known about Casimiro Olañeta and why no biography of Olañeta has been written. The work of Félix Reyes

Ortiz, *Biografía del Dr. Casimiro Olañeta* (La Paz, 1860), 53 pp., is a short and useless essay. Gabriel René-Moreno's unpublished monograph on Olañeta is still the best work. The personal library of Mr. Andrés Santa Cruz Sch., grandson of the great general, in La Paz, has some holograph letters of Casimiro Olañeta.

52. See René-Moreno, *Biblioteca boliviana*, index under Olañeta; Otero, ed., *Folletos*.

53. In Bolivia Olañeta is known as "el Talleyrand criollo." In a holograph letter of Casimiro Olañeta to Angel Moscoso, La Paz, October 2, 1828 (BNB, CR, no. 441), Olañeta wrote, "Quiero hacerme el elogio de decir a V. q$^e$ Tailleran no havría echo más."

54. Olañeta, *Exposición*, pp. 2-5.

55. *Ibid.*, p. 3.

56. *Ibid.*, pp. 3-5.

57. *Ibid.*, p. 2.

58. See Paz Soldán, *Historia*, I, 110.

59. Gamarra and Olañeta still had long careers of intrigue before them. Each one wanted to match his devilish wits with the other. And each one dragged his respective country into this long personal struggle. When conditions required it, they would embrace each other, but soon would draw their daggers from behind. Finally Gamarra died on Bolivian soil in 1841, as a victim of his own intrigue and that of Casimiro. It was Casimiro who had started this long rivalry in 1820, when he denounced young Gamarra, then giving the appearance of wishing to help him.

60. ANB, *ACh* (EC, 1822), no. 110; ANB, *ACh*, Expedientes de abogados, fol. 263.

61. ANB, *ACh* (EC, 1824), no. 35, 11 fols.

62. Reyes Ortiz in his eulogistic biography of Casimiro Olañeta, *op. cit.*, p. 53, calls Olañeta a genius. The Chilean historian, Ramón Sotomayor Valdés, in his *Estudios históricos de Bolivia* (Santiago, 1874), p. 145, says of Olañeta, "Su intelijencia era grande, pero no profunda." Gabriel René-Moreno talks about his "ineptitude to organize or create anything" (*supra*, n. 48). This author disagrees with René-Moreno and Sotomayor Valdés, Casimiro Olañeta was a genius in his own way.

63. "Personaje notable en nuestra accidentada Historia este don Casimiro. Graduado doctor en la Universidad de Charcas, supo ser el espécimen más perfecto de tal grado y clase intelectual en lo que tuvo de malo y de perverso" (Humberto Vázquez-Machicado, "Papeles inéditos de Gabriel René-Moreno," unpublished essay).

64. Cf. Gabriel René-Moreno, *Elementos de literatura preceptiva* (Santiago, 1891).

65. René-Moreno, *Biblioteca boliviana, passim;* René-Moreno, *Biblioteca peruana, passim;* and other historical works of René-Moreno.

66. "Fragmentos."

67. [Urcullu], *Apuntes*, p. 150, note.

68. René-Moreno in his "Fragmentos" has pointed out those mistakes. His evaluation is reproduced and expanded in Humberto Vázquez-Machicado, *Blasfemias*, pp. 15-58.

69. See *infra*, chaps. vii and viii.

70. The biographic information is taken from some hastily written notes intended for a future biographic study by Samuel Velasco Flor, found in BNB, CR, no. 387. Seemingly Mr. Velasco Flor had some documents of Urcullu and also had obtained much information from Mrs. Urcullu. Mr. Velasco Flor

wrote these notes in February, 1866. The descendants of Urcullu do not possess any papers of their illustrious forefather. A university file for Urcullu, such as that of Olañeta, has not been located.

71. From the badly scribbled notes of Velasco Flor it looks as if Urcullu became the President of the Academy ("irijió la Academia de Practicantes juristas en clase de Censor i de Jue Pte.").

72. Certification by the royal notary, Melchor Higueras [Chuquisaca], October 25, 1823, as copied by Velasco Flor, *op. cit.* (unpublished).

73. *Ibid.*

74. See Ramallo, *Guerrilleros,* pp. 158-164.

75. *Ibid.,* p. 157; certification by Pedro Cabero [Chuquisaca], April 10, 1820, in BNB, *CR,* no. 387, fol. 3.

76. *Ibid.;* "En las veces que la ciudad ha sufrido ataques por los Insurgentes, con la misma voluntad ha peleado en defensa del Rey, y del nombre Español" (certification by Francisco Maruri, La Plata, April 14, 1820, in BNB, *CR,* no. 387, fol. 3v.).

77. Proclamation by the commander of the Spanish forces in Peru, no place, February 29, 1816, in *ibid.,* fol. 1.

78. Certification, *op. cit.,* fols. 3v.-4.

79. "Reclamo de los Señores Enrique Calvo y M! Mª Urcullu sobre la vara de Regidor," ANB, *ACh* (EC, 1819), no. 12, fol. 6.

80. See ANB, *ACh,* Expedientes de abogados, XI, no. 26 (for José Mariano Calvo); Velasco Flor, *Foro boliviano,* p. 11.

81. ANB, *ACh* (EC, 1819), no. 12, fol. 1.

82. *Ibid.,* fol. 26 (written by Urcullu).

83. *Ibid.,* fol. 3v.

84. *Ibid.,* fol. 2.

85. As a reward for his efficient campaigns General de la Pezuela became viceroy of Peru after the battle of Sipe Sipe. His assistant, General Juan Ramírez, who had occupied Chuquisaca after the battle of Sipe Sipe, became acting commander of the Upper Peruvian army. Ramírez assumed his command on November 12, 1816. Later General La Serna, fresh from Spain, became commander of the Spanish army in Upper Peru, and Ramírez became president of the Audiencia of Quito.

86. La Plata, April 17, 1816, in ANB, *ACh* (EC, 1819), no. 12, fols. 20-21.

87. *Ibid.,* fol. 43.

88. Proclamation of Rafael Maroto, La Plata, February 18, 1819, in BNB, *CR,* no. 387, fols. lv.-2.

89. It must be said that in 1828 Urcullu remained loyal to President Sucre (Francisco Ignacio Bustos, "Diario de los acontecimientos desde el 18 de abril [1828] . . . ," unpublished, original in Archivo Nacional Argentino, *Bolivia: representantes diplomáticos,* 1827-53, copy available in Archivo y Biblioteca de la Universidad de San Francisco Xavier, Colección depositada en el rectorado (Manuscritos Abecia-Arana). Olañeta organized the plot against Sucre from behind the scenes and later insulted him; see Arnade, "Una figura mediocre," p. 78, n. 20.

CHAPTER 5

1. The material about the Aguilera revolt has come exclusively from the ANB and is contained in the *legajos* of the *MI* and the *MG* for the year 1828.

2. "América," *El Argos* (Buenos Aires), nos. 18, 19, March 20, 24, 1824.

3. Torata, *Separatista,* III, 150.

4. *Ibid.,* II, 158-159.

5. See John Miller, *Memorias del General Miller*, [translated by General Torrijos] (London, 1829), II, 186.

6. Cf. Miller, *op. cit.*, II, 184-185.

7. See Torata, *Separatista*, I, II, III, III doble, IV, *passim*.

8. Camba, *Memorias*, I, 467-471.

9. José Canterac, Gerónimo Valdés, El Marqués de Vallehumbroso, Ignacio Landazuri, Ramón García, Ramón Gómez de Bedoya, Mateo Ramírez, Andrés García Camba, Francisco Narváez, Francisco Ortiz, Antonio Tur, Agustín Otermín, Fulgencio de Toro, José Ramón Rodil, Pedro Martín, Antonio Seoane, Manuel Bayona, José García, Valentín Ferraz.

10. [Nineteen officers] to the Viceroy [Joaquín de la Pezuela], Aznapuquio, January 29, 1821, in Torata, *Separatista*, II, 305-310.

11. Joaquín de la Pezuela to José Canterac [and others], Lima, January 29, 1821 (3 letters), José Canterac and others to Pezuela, Aznapuquio, January 29, 1821, in Torata, *Separatista*, II, 310-312 (nos. 2, 3, 4, 5).

12. Confirmation of La Serna, July 29, 1821, in Torata, *Separatista*, IV, 286.

13. "América," *El Argos* (Buenos Aires), no. 19, March 24, 1824.

14. For a complete analysis of the event of Aznapuquio see the invaluable volumes of Torata, *Separatista;* for an interesting analysis see "América," *El Argos* (Buenos Aires), nos. 15, 18, 19, March 10, 20, 24, 1824.

15. Pedro Olañeta to La Serna, Potosí, February 21, 1824, Pedro Olañeta to the King, Potosí, March 6, 1824, Pedro Olañeta to the King, La Plata, May 21, 1824, in Torata, *Separatista*, IV, 372-373, 381-385.

16. Cf. Torata, *Separatista*, III, 480-490 (biographic sketches of Pezuela).

17. Miller, *op. cit.*, II, 183; Benito Pérez Galdós, *Episodios nacionales,* tercera serie: *Zumalacárregui* (Madrid, 1929); Manuel Ovilo y Otero, *Historia de las cortes, de las armas, de las letras y artes españoles* (Madrid, 1851-1853), 7 vols., *passim*.

18. See Ricardo Palma, *Tradiciones peruanas* (Barcelona, 1893), I, 328.

19. See Bernardo F. Escudero, *Diario de la última campaña del Ejército Español en el Perú en 1824 . . . ,* in Torata, *Separatista*, III doble, 44, 47-49.

20. Gabriel René-Moreno has made an excellent and detailed study of the abandonment of the inner provinces by the United Provinces. It is available in his *Más notas* and *Nuevas notas*.

21. Gerónimo Valdés, "Exposición," in Torata, *Separatista*, I, 65, 72, 80; cf. Torata, *Separatista*, IV, 59, 86-88, 234; Torrente, *Historia*, III, 511; cf. Beltrán, *Logia*, p. 14; Charles W. Arnade, "Una figura mediocre," p. 85, n. 60; Olañeta, *Exposición*, pp. 4-5.

22. See Velasco Flor, *Foro boliviano*, pp. 8-13.

23. Beltrán, *Logia*, is the first to have realized the possible formation of a lodge, yet he has misinterpreted it and has called it a patriotic lodge (p. 6), which it was not. Beltrán Avila, a patriotic historian, was blind to the true nature of this lodge. He underestimates the influence of Olañeta and assumes that Usín was the moving spirit (p. 16). But Usín was a minor figure who perhaps deserves some study, but the name of Usín is missing in crucial documents.

24. Plans to write a separate chapter about the influence of the Upper Peruvian exiles in the creation of Bolivia had to be given up because of lack of original documents. Seemingly René-Moreno also intended a study about the doings of the exiles but encountered similar difficulties. His unpublished "Fragmentos" has two or three interesting pages about them.

25. The name of Serrano does not appear in any documents citing the participants of the 1809 rebellion. The Bolivian author, Adolfo Durán, *Apéndice*

*a los documentos inéditos,* p. 6, has gathered the names of the participants of the rebellion and comes to the same conclusion. José Mariano Serrano was among the members of the University cloister of 1809 and he signed the minutes of the famous January 12, 1809, meeting (*supra,* chap. i, n. 69). But this is not conclusive proof of anti-Royalist feeling. As a matter of fact, the resolution of January 12 was strongly pro-Spanish. As long as no more documentary evidence is available, Serrano cannot be considered a member of the generation of 1809. See also Velasco Flor, *Vidas,* p. 10; ANB, *ACh,* Expedientes de abogados, XV, no. 43; José Mariano Serrano, *Breves pinceladas sobre algunos puntos interesantes a mi honor* (Sucre, 1842), 11 pp.; José Macedonio Urquidi, *Figuras históricas* (Cochabamba, 1916), pp. 50-74; Agustín Iturricha, "El Doctor José Mariano Serrano . . . ," *BSGS,* XXXI, nos. 327-332 (1937), 21-42; Valentín Abecia, "Los fundadores de la república, José Mariano Serrano," *BSGS,* XXVI, nos. 274-278 (1926), 214-217.

26. Cf. René-Moreno, *Biblioteca boliviana,* nos. 396, 458, pp. 103, 118-119.

27. "Serrano era un dos caras de la peor especie" (René-Moreno, "Fragmentos").

28. *La Prensa* (Buenos Aires), May 26, 1936, numero de gala, reproduced in "El Doctor José Mariano Serrano fué redactor del acta de la independencia según su propia declaración," *BSGS,* XXXII, nos. 333-336 (1937), 36-38; Juan de Ermita, "El Doctor José Mariano Serrano y el acta de la independencia argentina," *BSGS,* XXXIII, no. 343 (1938), 117-122; cf. Serrano, *Breves pinceladas, op. cit.,* p. 11; Urquidi, *Figuras,* p. 54.

29. *El Argos* (Buenos Aires), no. 89, November 5, 1823; *El Teatro de la Opinion* (Buenos Aires), no. 27, November 21, 1823; René-Moreno, "Fragmentos." This is a disputed fact.

30. Urdininea can be studied in René-Moreno, *Notas* and *Nuevas notas, passim;* besides René-Moreno has unpublished notes called "Escuadrón de Urdininea, apuntes no utilizados o sobrantes" (belonging to Humberto Vázquez-Machicado); see Julio Díaz A., *Los generales de Bolivia* (La Paz, 1929), pp. 56-62; José María Pérez de Urdininea, *Manifiesto refutando el mensaje presentado por el gran Mariscal de Ayacucho al Congreso de Bolivia* (Chuquisaca, 1828), 4 pp., in BNB, *C-RM.*

31. [José Mariano Serrano], "Un boliviano," *El Fénix de Lima,* no. 1 (1827); cf. Paredes, "Ligeros datos," 142. It is strange that Serrano published an article in the *Fénix,* which was a yellow sheet whose purpose it was to discredit Bolivia. Serrano was then Bolivian minister to Peru. Seemingly he conspired with this country against the Sucre government in Bolivia. In the article in the *Fénix* he stated that there was founded, in 1820 in Tucumán, a patriotic lodge of the exiles with the purpose of separating Upper Peru from Buenos Aires.

32. Cf. Olañeta, *Exposición,* pp. 4-5; cf. José Mariano Serrano, "Comunicado," *El Condor de Bolivia,* no. 16, March 16, 1826.

33. Olañeta, *Exposición,* pp. 3-5.

34. See especially "Extracto del diario de las operaciones del ejército español en la campaña sobre el Desaguadero . . . " (Cuzco, 1824), in Torata, *Separatista,* IV, 246-270; the basic works of Torrente and Camba give good descriptions; see also Paz Soldán, *Historia,* I, 121.

35. "El Jeneral Gamarra escribió reservadamente al Dr. Leandro Uzín, pidiendole noticias ecsactas de la situación y disposición del Jeneral Olañeta . . . . interiorisado en las cosas, le dimos noticias de los planes y fuerzas con que contaban los españoles" (Olañeta, *Exposición,* p. 4).

36. "América," *El Argos* (Buenos Aires), no. 19, March 24, 1824.

37. The connection of the Urdininea and Santa Cruz expeditions is recounted in a seven-page, small-print footnote in René-Moreno, *Nuevas notas,* p. 166, n. 1.

38. See José Domingo de Vidart to José Santos de Hera, Salta, December 13, 1823, in Torata, *Separatista,* I, 129; *El Correo de las Provincias* (Buenos Aires), no. 3, December 15, 1822 (these are statistics of the Urdininea division).

39. René-Moreno, "Fragmentos."

40. See correspondence of Sucre to Bolívar, May 27, 1823-January 5, 1824, in O'Leary, *Cartas,* I, 33-140, especially Sucre to Bolívar, Lima, May 27, 1823, pp. 33-46.

41. José Domingo de Vidart to José Santos de Hera, Salta, December 13, 1823, in Torata, *Separatista,* I, 129; the Urdininea case is contained in *El Republicano* (Buenos Aires), no. 8, January 25, 1824. See René-Moreno, *Nuevas notas,* p. 172.

42. *El Correo de las Provincias* (Buenos Aires), nos. 1, 2, 3, 4, 6, 7, 8, 12, 13, supplement to 13, 14, 16, 17, November 19, 1822-April 10, 1823.

43. Pedro Antonio de Olañeta to the King, Potosí, March 6, 1824, La Plata, May 21, 1824, in Torata, *Separatista,* IV, 372-373, 381-385.

44. See Pedro Antonio de Olañeta to Jerónimo Valdés, Potosí, February 26, 1824, Pedro Antonio de Olañeta to the King, La Plata, May 21, 1824, Pedro Antonio de Olañeta to Manuel Ramírez, Potosí, June 8, 1824, in Torata, *Separatista,* IV, 365-387.

45. *El Depositario de Cuzco,* no. 103 [or 100?], November 25, 1823, in Torata, *Separatista,* IV, 500-504; also in Beltrán, *Logia,* p. 39.

46. Pedro Antonio de Olañeta to the King, La Plata, May 21, 1824, in Torata, *Separatista,* IV, 283 and n. 2; cf. Torata, *Separatista,* IV, 390, 393-394; "Vindicacioń del General Olañeta al papel escrito en Cuzco por el General D. José de la Serna" [Cuzco, February 27, 1824], in *El Argos* (Buenos Aires), no. 37, May 22, 1824.

47. La Serna to the Minister of War, Cuzco, March 20, 1824, in Torata, *Separatista,* IV, 115-116; cf. Torata, *Separatista,* IV, 86-88, I, 83; Beltrán, *Logia,* p. 40.

48. Antonio Ballestero y Beretta, *Historia de España* (Barcelona, 1934), VII, 194.

49. Olañeta, *Exposición,* p. 6.

50. [Urcullu],*Apuntes,* pp. 127-128; cf. Manuel Ramírez to Jerónimo Valdés, La Plata, May 15, 1824, in Torata, *Separatista,* I, 131.

51. "Una carta escrita de Yotala al Jeneral Olañeta cuya copia mostré a los padres muy patriotos Clement Enríquez y Manuel Padín y al Coronel Fermín de la Vega fue el orijen de la revolución. Yo les aseguré que el fin que me proponía era la division de los españoles para lograr el triunfo de la libertad" (Olañeta, *Exposición,* p. 5). The letter has never been located. Ramallo, *Guerra,* p. 36, gives a somewhat different explanation, holding the Argentine lodge responsible for the falsification, but his chronological interpretation is wrong since he has them doing it in late 1824.

52. Mariano Guillén to Valdés, Oruro, June 21, 1824, in Camba, *Memorias,* II, 566.

53. "Por los papeles públicos me impuse a fondo de la destrucción del sistema constitucional español. Conocía el caracter de mi tío, sus ideas, y el odio a los liberales. Tampoco se me ocultaba la disposición de la Serna, Valdés y sus satélites. Aproveché las circunstancias, e invité al Jenerel Olañeta a un rompimiento con el virrey. Destruimos la constitución, y empesó la guerra entre ellos" (Olañeta, *Exposición,* p. 5).

54. Jerónimo Valdés to Mariano Guillén (transcribing a letter of Antonio

de la Riva), Oruro, June 21, 1824, Mariano Guillén to Valdés, Oruro, June 21, 1824, in Camba, *Memorias*, II, 565-566.

55. "Carta del capitán de navío Jacinto de Vargas al Ministro de Marina, sobre las andanzas de Olañeta en Montevideo," AGI, Papeles de estado Buenos Aires, 79, as cited by Humberto Vázquez-Machicado, "La delegación Arenales en el Alto-Perú," *Revista de Historia de América*, no. 10 (December, 1940), pp. 96-97, also cited by Beltrán, *Logia*, pp. 42-43.

56. Jerónimo Valdés to Mariano Guillén (transcribing a letter of Antonio de la Riva), Oruro, June 21, 1824, in Camba, *Memorias*, II, 565.

57. La Serna to Canterac, Cuzco, June 12, 1824, in Torata, *Separatista*, IV, 159; Beltrán, *Logia*, p. 14, mentions that the private confessor of General Olañeta, Father Emilio Rodríguez, played a significant role in the lodge, influencing the general decisively. Yet this priest is not named in documents consulted, although he is mentioned by René-Moreno in his "Fragmentos."

58. Urquidi, *Rectificaciones*, p. 42; cf. Crespo, *Lanza*, pp. 62-63.

59. Olañeta, *Exposición*, pp. 4-5.

CHAPTER 6

1. Camba, *Memorias*, II, 133.

2. Jerónimo Valdés, "Exposición," in Torata, *Separatista*, I, 88.

3. P. A. Olañeta to the Viceroy, Challapata, December 27, 1823; P. A. Olañeta to La Hera, Potosí, January 22, 1824; Convenio hecho entre los Sres. Mariscales de Campo, D. Pedro Antonio de Olañeta y D. José Santos de la Hera, Potosí, January 22, 1824, and P. A. Olañeta to José de la Serna, Potosí, January 28, 1824, in Torata, *Separatista*, IV, 252-257.

4. P. A. Olañeta to Rafael Maroto, Potosí, January 29, February 4, 1824, Rafael Maroto to P. A. Olañeta, La Plata, January 27, 1824, Yotala, February 1, 1824 (2 letters), La Plata, February 7, 1824 (2 letters), in Torata, *Separatista*, I, 148-156.

5. "El General Olañeta a los pueblos del Perú," Potosí, February 4, 1824, in Torata, *Separatista*, I, 156-157; also in Camba, *Memorias*, II, 187-189, also in *El Argos* (Buenos Aires), supplement to no. 14, March 8, 1824.

6. P. A. Olañeta to Rafael Maroto, Pilcomayo, February 10, 1824, La Plata, February 13, 1824, Rafael Maroto to P. A. Olañeta, Moromoro, February 11, 1824, Ocuri, February 19, 1824, Rafael Maroto to La Serna, Moromoro, February 12, 1824 (2 letters), in Torata, *Separatista*, I, 148-156.

7. Ramallo, *Guerra*, pp. 30-42, gives a very detailed picture of Olañeta's reception. Unfortunately he does not tell the source of his information, but it seems that his imagination played an important role in this description.

8. "Proclama de Olañeta estableciendo el sistema absoluto," La Plata, February 12, 1824, in *El Argos* (Buenos Aires), no. 26, April 17, 1824, also in Torata, *Separatista*, IV, 358 (but without any signature).

9. Beltrán, *Logia*, pp. 30-31, 58-61; Ramallo, *Guerra*, p. 40; Torata, *Separatista*, IV, 361-362.

10. Lecuna, *Documentos*, I, chap. i.

11. See triangular correspondence of La Serna, Canterac, and Valdés in Torata, *Separatista*, II, IV (index).

12. P. A. Olañeta to La Serna, Challapata, December 25, 1823, in Torata, *Separatista*, IV, 352.

13. José Domingo de Vidart to José Santos de la Hera, Salta, December 13, 1823, in Torata, *Separatista*, I, 128-131.

14. Cf. P. A. Olañeta to La Serna, La Paz, September 27, 1823 (2 letters), in Torata, *Separatista*, IV, 342.

15. La Serna to Jerónimo Valdés, Cuzco, February 10, 1824 (2 letters), in Torata, *Separatista*, IV, 82.

16. Jerónimo Valdés to P. A. Olañeta, Puno, February 17, 1824, in Torata, *Separatista*, I, 159-164; see correspondence between Olañeta and Valdés in Torata, *Separatista*, I, IV (index); cf. "La diplomacia de los papeles entre los generales realistas," in Beltrán, *Logia*, chap. iii.

17. P. A. Olañeta to Jerónimo Valdés, Potosí, February 26, 1824, in Torata, *Separatista*, IV, 365-368.

18. P. A. Olañeta to Jerónimo Valdés, Potosí, February 28, 1824, in Torata, *Separatista*, IV, 370-371.

19. Decree, Oruro, February 29, 1824, in Torato, *Separatista*, I, 168-169.

20. [Jerónimo Valdés] to La Serna, Oruro, March 13, 1824, in Torata, *Separatista*, IV, 280-282.

21. The treaty is available in Torata, *Separatista*, I, 184-185; Camba, *Memorias*, II, 432-434; Ramallo, *Guerra*, pp. 46-47; Beltrán, *Logia*, pp. 53-54 (condensed version).

22. Jerónimo Valdés, "Exposición," in Torata, *Separatista*, I, 71.

23. [Jerónimo Valdés] to La Serna, Oruro, March 13, 1824, in Torata, *Separatista*, IV, 281-282 (italics in the original).

24. Jerónimo Valdés to Canterac, Oruro, March 13, 1824, in Torata, *Separatista*, IV, 279-280.

25. See Gantier, *Doña Juana Azurduy de Padilla, passim;* Miguel Ramallo, *Batalla del Pari* (Tarija, 1911), 18 pp.

26. The action of Valdés at Palca and subsequent doings of Lanza remain obscure. Valdés, in Torata, *Separatista*, I, 71, gives few details; Ramallo, *Guerra*, p. 48, says that Lanza remained a prisoner of Valdés until the battle of Ayacucho. Sánchez de Velasco, *Memorias*, pp. 126-127, says that Lanza escaped. Sánchez is probably correct. Lanza operated in Bolivia before Sucre's arrival and occupied La Paz in advance of Sucre's army.

27. See all the detailed correspondence in Torata, *Separatista*, I, IV (index), during the period of March to June. For a synopsis, although deficient and confusing, see Beltrán, *Logia*, chaps. iii and iv; Camba, *Memorias*, II, chaps. xxv and xxvi; Ramallo, *Guerra*, pp. 48-53.

28. Beltrán, *Logia*, p. 68. The relationship of the guerrillas with Olañeta remains a mystery. It is possible that some guerrillas cooperated with Olañeta since by then everybody realized that the support of Olañeta meant the continuation of dissension in the Spanish army and therefore would aid the Colombian advance from the north.

29. See the correspondence of P. A. Olañeta from March to June, 1824, in Toranta, *Separatista*, I, IV (index); cf. Valdés, "Exposición," in Torata, *Separatista*, I, 73.

30. Olañeta, *Exposición*, p. 4.

31. "Bando contra Olañeta," Cuzco, June 4, 1824, in Torata, *Separatista*, I, 199-201, and in Camba, *Memorias*, II, 579-582.

32. Cf. Camba, *Memorias*, II, 215.

33. Jerónimo Valdés to P. A. Olañeta, Oruro, June 14, 1824, in Torata, *Separatista*, I, 209.

34. P. A. Olañeta to Jerónimo Valdés, Potosí, June 20, 1824, in Torata, *Separatista*, IV, 389-391; Camba, *Memorias*, II, 228, attributes the manifesto to C. Olañeta. This is extremely doubtful since in June, July, and August of 1824 C. Olañeta was in Buenos Aires and Montevideo (C. Olañeta, "Articulo comunicado," *El Condor de Bolivia*, Chuquisaca, no. 19, April 26, 1826). It was written by Urcullu, see René-Moreno, *Nuevas notas*, p. 157.

35. "Manifiesto del General Olañeta a los habitantes del Perú," Potosí, June 20, 1824, in Torata, *Separatista*, IV, 391-398 (with good notes by the editor, Conde de Torata, son of General Valdés). Also published in *El Argos* (Buenos Aires), no. 64, August 21, 1824.

36. "América," *El Argos* (Buenos Aires), no. 15, March 10, 1824.

37. Bolivian historians do mention the war very incidentally but do not give it much importance. See [Urcullu], *Apuntes*, pp. 127-145; Cortés, *op. cit.*, pp. 87-91; Ramón Sotomayor Valdés, *op. cit.*, pp. 38-39; Camacho, *Historia*, pp. 169-173; Enrique Finot, *Nueva historia de Bolivia* (Buenos Aires, 1946), pp. 175-176; Argüedas, *Fundación*, pp. 216-222; Luis M. Guzmán, *Historia*, pp. 40-43; Paz, *Historia*, II, 586-600; Urquidi, *Compendio*, pp. 153-154; Manuel Ordoñez López and Luis Crespo, *Bosquejo de la historia de Bolivia* (La Paz, 1912), pp. 181-182; Muñoz, *Guerra*, nothing; Pedro Kramer, *Historia de Bolivia* (La Paz, 1899), nothing; Pinilla, *Creación*, p. 79, n. 1; Miguel Pacheco Loma, *Resumen de la historia de Bolivia* (Oruro, 1948), p. 324; Demetrio F. de Córdova, *Historia de Bolivia* (Sucre, 1911[?]), nothing; Díaz Villamil, *op. cit.*, II, 90-92; Sánchez de Velasco, *Memorias*, pp. 128-146; Lecuna, *Documentos*, I, cxxi, cxxxiii; Manuel Sanzetena, *Bolivia en su período de grandeza* (Oruro, 1948), pp. 14-15; Julio Díaz A., *Sucre, organizador y conductor de ejércitos* (La Paz, 1950), p. 83.

38. Cuartel general en marcha, June 26, 1824 (two proclamations), in Torata, *Separatista*, I, 200-211, also in Camba, *Memorias*, II, 444-447.

39. Cf. Ramallo, *Guerra*, pp. 54-55; Torrente, *Historia*, III, 464.

40. Histories of the Bolivian army are extremely deficient; the standard one is Julio Díaz A., *Historia del ejército de Bolivia* (La Paz, 1940).

41. See Torrente, *Historia*, III, 464; Valdés, "Exposición," in Torata, *Separatista*, I, 74.

42. *Ibid.*, III, 465, mentions two aides-de-camp; Ramallo, *Guerra*, p. 58, mentions two aides-de-camp and four soldiers. This is seemingly incorrect since Valdés, "Exposición," in Torata, *Separatista*, I, 74-75, speaks of one aide-de-camp and two volunteers.

43. For an account of the battle see Torrente, *Historia*, III, 465-466; Ramallo, *Guerra*, pp. 57-60 (some errors); Camba, *Memorias*, II, 231; and the interesting document entitled *Diario de operaciones del ejército real del Perú, en campaña que ha sostenido contra los constitucionales, el año de 1824* (Potosí, 1824), as reproduced in Ramallo, *Guerra*, pp. 95-103. The original copy is available in the Biblioteca de la Sociedad Geográfica Sucre. This diary is very biased in favor of the Secessionists. Hereafter cited as *Diario de operaciones*.

44. As in any battle each side said the other had heavier casualties. Cf. *Diario de operaciones*, pp. 96-97.

45. *Ibid.*, p. 97.

46. Jerónimo Valdés to Francisco Aguilera, Oruro, June 18, 1824 (2 letters), Yamparáez, July 11, 1824, Culpina, July 24, 1824 (2 letters), in Torata, *Separatista*, IV, 308-309, 317-322.

47. Ramallo, *Guerra*, p. 62, says that the soldiers left for Oruro. Olañeta's diary and Torrente's history do not mention anything about the Constitutionalist soldiers; Camba, *Memorias*, II, 232, says the soldiers remained in town; this is probably not so, because Barbarucho found Potosí empty (*Diario de operaciones*, p. 97).

48. Today Eustaquio Méndez is recognized in Bolivia, especially in Tarija, as a great hero. He is known as the "Moto Méndez." See Bernardo Trigo, *Las tejas*, pp. 320-330; O'Connor D'Arlach, *El Coronel, passim*. Yet apparently

his apotheosis is undeserved, since his behavior is extremely questionable on close examination.

49. *Diario de operaciones,* p. 62. Torrente and Camba evidently have ignored this attack.

50. This is acknowledged in the Secessionist diary (*Diario de operaciones,* pp. 97-98).

51. When the unit of Colonel Rivas of the Aguilera army deserted to the Loyalists, Colonel Marquiegui had been in serious danger of being apprehended by the deserters, with the aid of the army of General Valdés (Torrente, *Historia,* III, 465).

52. Ramallo, *Guerra,* p. 66, says he had six hundred soldiers with him; Olañeta's, p. 99, says seven hundred men.

53. Ramallo, *Guerra,* p. 66, calls it "Abra de Quenta;" Camba, *Memorias,* II, 233, calls it "Abra de Queta;" *Diario de operaciones,* p. 98, calls it "Abra rota," which seems more probable.

54. This division is taken from *Diario de operaciones,* p. 98; Torrente, *Historia,* III, 467, has the army separate into three units. But since the *Diario de operaciones* is a primary record of Olañeta himself his division should be considered correct.

55. "Me he conducido con la mayor generosidad respecto a los oficiales y soldados prisioneros que he tomado" (Jerónimo Valdés to P. A. Olañeta, no date, no place, because of partial destruction of the last part of the letter, in Torata, *Separatista,* IV, 323); cf. Torrente, *Historia,* III, 467.

56. Pedro Cortez to Capitán Gral. de Buenos Aires, Tupiza, August 16, 1824, in *El Argos* (Buenos Aires), no. 72, September 11, 1824 (Cortez calls the place Chacapa).

57. Carratalá later, by bribing his guards, was able to escape (P. A. Olañeta to Jerónimo Valdés, Cinti, August 30, 1824, in Ramallo, *Guerra,* pp. 82-83).

58. Valdés, "Exposición," in Torata, *Separatista,* I, 75; cf. Ramallo, *Guerra,* p. 69.

59. Casimiro Olañeta, "Artículo comunicado."

60. Pedro Cortez to Gobᵒ de Buenos Aires, Tupiza, August 16, 1824, in *El Argos* (Buenos Aires), no. 72, September 11, 1824; cf. Camba, *Memorias,* II, 234; Ramallo, *Guerra,* p. 70.

61. This information is not given in any of the sources that describe the war, but appears in an article, "Alto Perú," *El Argos* (Buenos Aires), no. 78, September 29, 1824.

62. See Jerónimo Valdés to La Serna, Campo de batalla en la Lava, August 17, 1824, in Torata, *Separatista,* IV, 322; Olañeta in his *Diario de operaciones,* 101, admits this loss.

63. Jerónimo Valdés to P. A. Olañeta, Puna, August 19, 1824, in Torata, *Separatista,* IV, 322-323; see also Torrente, Historia, III, 470-471; Camba, *Memorias,* II, 235.

64. Cf. *Diario de operaciones,* p. 101.

65. Cf. Torrente, *Historia,* III, 472.

66. Jerónimo Valdés to P. A. Olañeta, Yamparáez, August 25, 26, 1824, in Torata, *Separatista,* I, 222-223, IV, 225-226.

67. Vicente Miranda y Cabezón to Jerónimo Valdés, Puna, August 31, 1824, in Camba, *Memorias,* II, 460-462; see letters and proclamations of P. A. Olañeta from August 23 to September 1, 1824, dated in Cinti, Cazón, and Cotagaita, in Torata, *Separatista,* I, 183, IV, 400-405 (document no. 267 is misdated and should read, Cotagaita, September 1, 1824, instead of August 25).

68. *Diario de operaciones,* pp. 101-102.
69. See *infra,* chap. vii.

CHAPTER 7

1. Bolívar to Sucre, Pativilca, February 13, 1824 (because so many editions of the letters of Bolívar are available, the citations will be only of the letters and not the books from which they were taken); cf. Vicente Lecuna, *Crónica razonada de las guerras de Bolívar* (New York, 1950), III, 377-379.
2. Bolívar to Sucre, Pativilca, February 16, 1824, Trujillo, April 9, 1824, Otusco, April 14, 1824, Bolívar to Santander, Pativilca, February 25, 1824 (translation taken from Lecuna and Bierck), Bolívar to Bartolomé Salom, Trujillo, March 14, 1824.
3. Bolívar to Martín Jorge Guise, Huamachuco, April 28, 1824.
4. Bolívar to P. A. Olañeta, Huaraz, May 21, 1824.
5. Cf. Lecuna, *Crónica,* III, 423.
6. See P. A. Olañeta to Juan Alvarez de Arenales, Oruro, October 2, 1824, in Lecuna, *Documentos,* I, 2.
7. Proclama, Huancayo, August 15, 1824, in Vicente Lecuna, *Proclamas y discursos del Libertador* (Caracas, 1939), p. 290.
8. Bolívar to Santa Cruz, Chancay, November 26, 1824, Bolívar to Sucre, Chancay, November 26, 1824 (translation taken from Lecuna and Bierck).
9. P. A. Olañeta to Bolívar, Oruro, October 2, 1824, in Lecuna, *Documentos,* I, 4-5.
10. "Su correspondencia y el pasaporte que me dío para Buenos Ayres, llamándome patriota distinguido, ecsisten en mi poder orijinales" (Olañeta, *Exposición,* p. 8); René-Moreno, *Nuevas notas,* p. 559, n. 1.
11. Olañeta, *Exposición,* p. 8.
12. See Iturricha, "El Doctor José Mariano Serrano," 32; see Humberto Vázquez-Machicado, "La delegación Arenales," 87-123.
13. Ramallo, *Guerra,* p. 36.
14. Cf. Gregorio Funes to Bolívar, Buenos Aires, July 19, 1824, in O'Leary, *Memorias,* XI, 120-121.
15. "Artículo comunicado."
16. *Exposición,* p. 6; see Beltrán, *Logia,* p. 69.
17. Jerónimo Valdés to La Serna, Oruro, June 23, 1824, in Torata, *Separatista,* IV, 311.
18. "Fragmentos;" there is a *legajo* (*supra,* chap. v, n. 54) located in Seville concerning the activities of Casimiro Olañeta in Buenos Aires and Montevideo.
19. René-Moreno, *Nuevas notas,* p. 559, n. [1].
20. *El Condor de Bolivia* (Chuquisaca), no. 1, November 12, 1825; no. 16, March 16, 1826; no. 19, April 6, 1826.
21. René-Moreno got this information from an old citizen of Chuquisaca, witness of the event ("Fragmentos").
22. See *supra,* chap. iv, n. 31.
23. Olañeta, *Exposición,* p. 6.
24. J. Villasana Haggard, *Handbook for Translators of Spanish Historical Documents* (Oklahoma City, 1941), p. 106.
25. "Fragmentos."
26. The editors of the *Mensajero Arjentino* were Juan Cruz Varela, Agustín Delgado, Valentín Alsina, and Francisco Pico. No. 1 was published on November 18, 1825, and it ended its career on July 9, 1827. It was a government organ.

27. See Olañeta, *Exposición*, p. 11; Olañeta, "Artículo comunicado;" the *Mensajero Arjentino*, no. 24, was not consulted, but the facts are inferred from Olañeta's reply in *El Condor*.

28. Olañeta, *Exposición*, p. 11.

29. "Artículo comunicado."

30. Olañeta, *Exposición*, p. 7.

31. See C. Olañeta to Bolívar, Cochabamba, December 23, 1824, in Lecuna, *Documentos*, I, 8.

32. Cf. Gregorio Funes to Bolívar, Buenos Aires, July 19, 1824, in O'Leary, *Memorias*, XI, 122.

33. Bolívar to P. A. Olañeta, Lima, December 15, 1824.

34. Cf. C. Olañeta to Bolívar, Cochabamba, December 23, 1824, in Lecuna, *Documentos*, I, 8.

35. Olañeta, *Exposición*, p. 7.

36. Bolívar to P. A. Olañeta, Lima, December 15, 1824.

37. *Nuevas notas*, pp. 290-291.

38. [Urcullu], *Apuntes*, pp. 143-144.

39. Unfortunately the diary of drummer Vargas for these last years of fighting has been lost. He might have detailed in an unsurpassed style and manner the appearance of the stiff-collared *doctor* from Chuquisaca in their midst.

40. Miguel Lanza to Bolívar, n. p., December 13, 1824, as cited by René-Moreno in his "Fragmentos," and said to be located in the Paz Soldán archive.

41. C. Olañeta to José Mariano Armaza, Chuquisaca, April 27 [1828], in the private library of Andrés Santa Cruz in La Paz, Bolivia.

42. Sucre to Bolívar, Potosí, January 29 [*sic* for March 29,] 1824, in O'Leary, *Cartas*, I, 294-295.

43. Sucre to Ministros del Tesoro Público de la Paz, Chuquisaca, June 15, 1825, ANB, *MI*, VIII, no. 63.

44. Sucre to Bolívar, Potosí, January 29 [*sic*], 1824, *op. cit.*

45. "Fragmentos."

46. Bolívar to P. A. Olañeta, Sanaica, October 6, 1824, Lima, December 15, December 24, 1824, P. A. Olañeta to Bolívar, Cochabamba, December 22, 1824, P. A. Olañeta to Sucre, Cochabamba, December 22, 1824, in Lecuna, *Documentos*, I, 6-7.

47. C. Olañeta to Bolívar, Cochabamba, December 23, 1824, in *ibid.*, I, 8-10.

48. T. De Heres to Sucre, Sanaica, October 6, 1824, in O'Leary, *Memorias*, XXII, 507-508.

49. This letter has not been located, but cf. Sucre to P. A. Olañeta, Cuzco, January 1, 1825, in Lecuna, *Documentos*, I, 39; P. A. Olañeta to Sucre, Cochabamba, December 22, 1824, in Lecuna, *Documentos*, I, 7.

50. After Ayacucho Sucre was made a marshal (O'Leary, *Memorias*, XXII, 606).

51. Sucre to P. A. Olañeta, Cuzco, January 1, 1825, in Lecuna, *Documentos*, I, 39.

52. Sucre to Bolívar, Huamanga, December 12, 1824, Andahuaylas, December 23, 1824, Abancay, December 25, 1824, in O'Leary, *Cartas*, I, 265-266.

53. For a detailed exposition and background of the Arenales expedition see Gabriel René-Moreno, *Ayacucho en Buenos Aires* (Madrid, n. d.), 303 pp.; Humberto Vázquez-Machicado, "La delegación Arenales."

54. Sucre to Bolívar, Cuzco, January 8, 1825, in O'Leary, *Cartas*, I, 279.

55. See Rufino Blanco-Fombona, *Cartas de Bolivar*, Biblioteca Ayacucho, LIX (Madrid, 1921), p. 279, n. 2.

56. Sucre to P. A. Olañeta, Sucre to Francisco Aguilera, Sucre to J. M. Lanza, Sucre to Pedro Arraya, Cuzco, January 1, 1825, in Lecuna, *Documentos,* I, 39-43.

57. Sucre to Bolívar, Cuzco, January 15, 1825, in O'Leary, *Cartas,* I, 283.

58. Paz Soldán, *Historia,* I, 292-293.

59. P. A. Olañeta to Pío Tristán, Viacha, January 8, 1825 (2 letters), in *ibid.,* I, 385-386; cf. P. A. Olañeta to Rudecindo Alvarado [Viacha, January 8, 1825], in *ibid.,* I, guide, p. 66, no. 843.

60. Treaty available in Lecuna, *Documentos,* I, 12-13; in Torata, *Separatista,* IV, 408-409.

61. See Camba, *Memorias,* II, 365.

62. Sucre to the Prefect of Arequipa, Chuquisaca, May 11 [1825], in ANB, *MI,* VIII, no. 66.

63. "Justicia ejecutada en el Brigadier Echeverría," *La Estrella de Ayacucho* (Arequipa), no. 7, April 23, 1825. The name Echeverría in documents is also spelled Echavarría and Echevarría, cf. René-Moreno, *Nuevas notas,* p. 561, n.

64. Cf. Sucre to the Prefect of the Department of Arequipa, Sicuani, January 23, 1825, in Lecuna, *Documentos,* I, 63.

65. Casimiro Olañeta to Sucre, La. Paz, January 12, 1825, in Paz Soldán, *Historia,* I, no. 19, p. 384.

66. C. Olañeta to Sucre, La Paz, January 12, 1825, *reservado,* in Paz Soldán, *Historia,* I, no. 19, pp. 384-385.

67. The handwriting of Casimiro Olañeta is very awkward, and there are very few holograph letters by him. The private library of Mr. Andrés Santa Cruz has some of these rare letters. Casimiro had the habit of writing without any margins, in small letters, and with a cramped style.

68. This letter was brought to light by the Peruvian historian, Paz Soldán, who located it, bought this priceless manuscript, and published it in its totality in his history. Seemingly most Bolivian historians are not acquainted with this letter or refuse to admit its existence.

69. Sucre to C. Olañeta [Santa Rosa], no date, in Lecuna, *Documentos,* I, 71-72.

70. This interesting and little known fact is in "Justicia ejecutada en el Brigadier Echeverría."

71. Cf. Tomás O'Connor D'Arlach, ed., *Recuerdos de Francisco Burdett O'Connor* (Tarija, 1895), pp. 109-110; cf. Chaves, *Castelli,* p. 211.

72. *Recuerdos históricos,* in Ministerio de Educación de la Nación, Dirección General de Cultura [Argentina], *Selección de documentos del Museo Histórico Nacional* (Buenos Aires, 1952), I, 185.

73. Sucre to Bolívar, Puno, February 1, 1825, in O'Leary, *Cartas,* I, 299.

74. Strangely, Alvarado does not mention Calvimontes, who O'Connor said accompanied Casimiro Olañeta (*supra,* n. 71).

75. Sucre to the Prefect of Arequipa, Chuquisaca, May 11 [1825], in ANB, *MI,* VIII, no. 66.

76. Sucre is mistaken; Casimiro Olañeta was never an *oidor* of the audiencia. He occupied the position of *fiscal* of the various offices. Cf. Vázquez-Machicado, *Blasfemias,* p. 36, in which he severely criticizes Alfredo Jáuregui Rosquellas of Chuquisaca for transcribing the error of Sucre, when Jáuregui at one time was director of the National Archive where the Audiencia records are located. See Alfredo Jáuregui Rosquellas, *Antonio José de Sucre . . . .* (Cochabamba and La Paz [1928]), p. 110.

77. Sucre to Bolívar, Puno, February 3, 1825, in O'Leary, *Cartas,* I, 301.

78. "Recuerdos del tiempo heroico," as reproduced in *USFX,* XII, nos. 29-30

(1943-1944), 83.

79. Sucre to Bolívar, Chuquisaca, April 27, 1828, in O'Leary, *Cartas,* II, 249.

80. This letter has not been located. Lecuna published the Sucre files from December, 1824, to February 3, 1825 (*Documentos,* I, 14-82). This author has located all the letters of Sucre of 1825, starting with February 10. The letters between February 3 and 10, the days of Sucre's march toward La Paz, are still missing.

81. Lanza to Sucre, La Paz, February 3, 1825, in ANB, *MI,* III, no. 11.

82. Sucre to Leandro Usín, Oruro, March 16, 1825, Chuquisaca, May 28, 1825, in ANB, *MI,* VIII, no. 63; Sucre to M. M. Urcullu, Chuquisaca, May 20, 1826, in BNB, *CR,* no. 387; Sucre to Bolívar, Ilave, February 5, 1825, in O'Leary, *Cartas,* I, 303; Beltrán, *Logia,* pp. 132-133.

83. For all his defense pamphlets see René-Moreno, *Biblioteca boliviana,* index.

84. Sucre to the Prefect of Arequipa, La Paz, March 8, 1825, in ANB, *MI,* VIII, no. 66.

85. Sucre to the Prefect of Arequipa, Chuquisaca, May 10 [1825], in ANB, *MI,* VIII, no. 66.

86. *Carta del Dr. Francisco Mariano de Miranda al Dr. Casimiro Olañeta* (Quito, 1840), pp. 3-4.

87. C. Olañeta, *Mi defensa o conclusión* (La Paz, May 28, 1839), p. 11.

88. René-Moreno, "Fragmentos;" in 1826 four numbers of a newspaper named *El 25 de Mayo* were published in Chuquisaca. No copies are known to exist. The paper is mentioned in *El Condor,* no. 32, July 6, 1826.

89. See *Biblioteca boliviana,* index.

90. *Biblioteca peruana,* II, no. 1137 (132), 495.

91. Reyes Ortiz, *op. cit.,* p. 53.

92. "Papeles inéditos de Gabriel René-Moreno" (unpublished).

CHAPTER 8

1. Cf. Sucre to Bolívar, Cuzco, January 19, 1825, in O'Leary, *Cartas,* I, 286-287.

2. Cf. Rudecindo Alvarado to Sucre, Puno, January 10, 1825, in Paz Soldán, *Historia,* I, appendix, no. 19, p. 386; Sucre to Bolívar, Cuzco, January 15, 1825, in O'Leary, *Cartas,* I, 283; cf. Sucre to the Prefect of Cuzco, Quiquijana, January 21, 1825, in Lecuna, *Documentos,* I, 59.

3. Little is known about the invasion of Barbarucho except what is cited in the letter of Sucre to Olañeta, *infra,* n. 4; cf. Sucre to Rudecindo Alvarado, Cuzco, January 3, 1825, in Lecuna, *Documentos,* I, 47.

4. Sucre to P. A. Olañeta [Santa Rosa], January 24, 1825, in Lecuna, *Documentos,* I, 68-70.

5. Antonio Saturnino Sánchez to Sucre, Cochabamba, January 15, 1825, in *Gaceta del Gobierno* (Lima), February 24, 1825; J. M. Lanza to Sucre, La Paz, February 6, 1825, Yanacachi, January 18, 1825, in ANB, *MI,* III, no. 11; cf. José Macedonio Urquidi, *La última revolución de Cochabamba* (Cochabamba, 1943).

6. Sucre to P. A. Olañeta, Ayaviri, January 26, 1825, in Lecuna, *Documentos,* I, 73; cf. Sucre to Bolívar, Ayaviri, January 26, 1825, in O'Leary, *Cartas,* I, 292.

7. Sucre to J. M. Lanza, Lampa, January 27, 1825, in Lecuna, *Documentos,* I, 73-76.

8. J. M. Lanza to Sucre, La Paz, January 30, 1825, in *El Sol del Cuzco* (Cuzco), no. 7, February 12, 1825; J. M. Lanza to Sucre, La Paz, January 31, 1825, February 1, 1825, in ANB, *MI*, III, no. 11.

9. The exact number in Olañeta's army is hard to determine. Sucre's letters speak of different strengths at different times (cf. Lecuna, *Documentos*, I, chap. ii; ANB, *MI*, VIII, no. 63).

10. Sucre to Javier Aguilera, La Paz, February 9, 1825, in ANB, *MI*, VIIII, no. 66; J. M. Lanza to Sucre, La Paz, February 1, 1825, in ANB, *MI*, III, no. 11.

11. Sucre to Bolívar, Ilave, February 5, 1825, in O'Leary, *Cartas*, I, 303.

12. Cf. Gonzalo Bulnes, *Ultimas campañas de la independencia del Perú, 1822-1826* (Santiago, 1897), pp. 626-628.

13. José María Rey de Castro, "Recuerdos del tiempa heroico," *USFX*, XII, nos. 29-30 (1943-1944), 83-86.

14. Lecuna, *Documentos*, I, 94-96.

15. See René-Moreno, *Ayacucho en Buenos Aires, passim;* Arocha Moreno, *Las ideas políticas, passim;* Pinilla, *Creación, passim.* S. Pinilla is not the author of this book; see Enrique Finot, "Dos obras apócrifas de la literatura boliviana," *La Razón* (La Paz), November 6, 1945.

16. For a detailed discussion of the attitude of Bolivian writers about the authorship of the decree of February 9, see Vázquez-Machicado, *Blasfemias, passim.*

17. [Urcullu], *Apuntes,* p. 150.

18. C. Olañeta, *Mi defensa o conclusión,* p. 11.

19. *Blasfemias, passim.*

20. Sucre to Bolívar, Puno, February 3, 1825, in O'Leary, *Cartas,* I, 302.

21. [Urcullu], *Apuntes,* p. 150; Paz Soldán, *Historia,* II, 5.

22. Sucre to Bolívar, Puno, February 3, 1825, in O'Leary, *Cartas,* I, 302 (italics not in the original).

23. The assumptions of René-Moreno and Vázquez-Machicado, based on studies of Sucre's letters, prove therefore to be correct. The Bolivian historian who later literally wrote that Vázquez-Machicado was "nuts" because of his analysis, looks quite foolish himself in view of this conclusive proof, see Alfredo Jáuregui Rosquellas, "La fundación de Bolivia," *BSGS*, XXXVIII, nos. 383-385 (1942), 155. It must be stated that Enrique Finot, *Nueva historia de Bolivia,* which is the best one-volume history of Bolivia, accepts completely the theory of Vázquez-Machicado and has eliminated the old myth that Casimiro Olañeta was the real author of the February 9 decree (p. 181, n. 1).

24. Sucre to Bolívar, Puno, February 3, 1825, in O'Leary, *Cartas,* I, 301-302.

25. Sucre to Bolívar, Ilave, February 5, 1825, in O'Leary, *Cartas,* I, 304.

26. "Posteriormente se dijo que el decreto del 9 de febrero, lo expidió Sucre por consejos de don Casimiro Olañeta, por entonces joven, incapaz de sugerir ideas de determinaciones a un personaje de la talla del vencedor de Ayacucho, como era el de precipitar la formación inesperada de una república. Olañeta en la exposición que publicó en 1826 [*sic*], en la que enumera sus servicios a la causa de la independencia no menciona ese hecho, que pudo haber sido considerado por el como un timbre de gloria" (Paredes, "Ligeros datos," 146).

27. Sucre to Bolívar, Puno, February 3, 1825, in O'Leary, *Cartas,* I, 301; Sucre to the Comandante Jeneral de la división de Cochabamba, La Paz, February 11, 1825, in ANB, *MI*, VIII, no. 63.

28. Sucre to Carlos María Ortega, La Paz, February 28, 1825, March 1, 1825, in ANB, *MI*, VIII, no. 63.

29. Sucre to the President of Cochabamba, Chuquisaca, June 11, 1825,

Sucre to the Comandante Jeneral de la división de Cochabamba, La Paz, February 11, 1825, Sucre to the President of Potosí, Chuquisaca, June 20, 1825, Sucre to O'Connor, no date, no place, in ANB, *MI*, VIII, no. 63.

30. Sucre to Commander Michel, Oruro, March 16, 1825, in ANB, *MI*, VIII, no. 63.

31. Sucre to the Ministro de Estado en el Departamento de la Guerra del Perú, La Paz, March 2, 1825, Sucre to the Secretario de Estado del Despacho de Guerra, La Paz, March 8, 1825, in Lecuna, *Documentos*, I, 115, 122; Sucre to the Prefect of the Department of Cuzco, La Paz, March 2, 1825, in *El Sol del Cuzco*, no. 13, March 26, 1825; Sucre to Pedro José Antelo, La Paz, March 1, 1825, in ANB, *MI*, VI, no. 31.

32. Sucre to Aguilera, Cuzco, January 1, 1825, in Lecuna, *Documentos*, I, 40-41; Sucre to Aguilera, La Paz, February 22, 1825, in ANB, *MI*, VIII, no. 66; Sucre to Aguilera, La Paz, February 22, 1825, in ANB, *MI*, VIII, no. 63; cf. Sucre to the Ministro de Estado, La Paz, March 2, 1825, in Lecuna, *Documentos*, I, 115.

33. Sucre to the Secretario del Despacho de la Guerra etc., La Paz, March 8, 1825, in Lecuna, *Documentos*, I, 122. Much more material about the Vallegrande movement, and especially about Aguilera, is located in ANB, *MI*, VI, no. 31.

34. Sucre to the Secretario del Despacho de la Guerra, La Paz, March 8, 1825, in Lecuna, *Documentos*, I, 122; Sucre to the Municipality of Santa Cruz, La Paz, March 5, 1825, Sucre to José Menacho, La Paz, March 5, 1825, in ANB, *MI*, VIII, no. 63.

35. Sucre to the Ministro de Estado en el Departmento de Guerra, La Paz, March 8, 1825, Sucre to the Secretario de Estado del Despacho de la Guerra etc., La Paz, March 8, 1825, in Lecuna, *Documentos*, I, 120, 122; Sucre to the Prefect of the Department of Cuzco, La Paz, March 2, 1825, in *El Sol del Cuzco*, no. 13, March 26, 1825; Sucre to Francisco López, La Paz, March 5, 1825, in ANB *MI*, VIII, no. 63; Sucre to the Municipality of Chuquisaca, La Paz, March 5, 1825, in ANB, *MI*, VIII, no. 63; cf. Francisco López to Carlos María Ortega, Plata Libre [Chuquisaca], February 25, 1825, February 27, 1825, in Lecuna, *Documentos*, I, 110-112.

36. Sucre to Francisco López, La Paz, March 5, 1825, in ANB, *MI*, VIII, no. 63.

37. Torrente, *Historia*, III, 514; Camba, *Memorias*, II, 367; Pinilla, *Creación*, p. 113; cf. Conde de Torata, "Prólogo," *Separatista*, IV, li.

38. Juan Martín Leguizamón, *Límites con Bolivia* (Salta, 1872), p. 59, n. 1.

39. *Ibid.*, p. 39.

40. The version published by Bolívar is the same as the one published later by General Valdés' son in his *Separatista*, I, 225-227. Yet this is not conclusive proof because the Count of Torata might have gotten the letter from Bolívar's publication, rather than from his father's archive. However, Bolívar had no reason to doctor the letter, while General Olañeta did have.

41. This proclamation had never been known; it was located, attached to a letter from the commander of Oruro [Colonel Ortega] to Sucre, Oruro, February 28, 1825, in ANB, *MI*, III, no. 12. Evidently Ortega got hold of a copy of the proclamation and forwarded it to Sucre. No other copy is known to exist.

42. Pedro Antonio de Olañeta, *Conducta del General disidente Don Simón Bolívar en sus comunicaciones con el General Realista Don Pedro Antonio de Olañeta* (Potosí, February 22, 1825), in ANB, *MI*, III, no. 12.

43. Sucre to [Lanza], Caracollo, March [14 or 15, damaged], 1825, in

ANB, *MI,* VIII, no. 63.

44. Rey de Castro, "Recuerdos," 88.

45. *Idem;* O'Connor, *Independencia,* p. 62; Sucre to [Lanza], Caracollo, March [14 or 15, damaged], 1825, in ANB, *MI,* VIII, no. 63.

46. Sucre to P. A. Olañeta, Oruro, March 16, 1825, in O'Leary, *Memorias,* XXIII, 77-78.

47. Sucre to the Secretario de Estado del Despacho de la Guerra [Colombia], La Paz, March 8, 1825, in Lecuna, *Documentos,* I, 121-123; also see Lecuna, *Documentos,* I, 121; Sucre to Bolívar, Condo, March 24, 1825, in O'Leary, *Cartas,* I, 321.

48. Sucre to Ortega, many letters during February and March in ANB, *MI,* VIII, no. 63; cf. Sucre to the Secretario de Estado del Despacho de la Guerra [Colombia], La Paz, March 8, 1825, in Lecuna, *Documentos,* I, 121-123.

49. Sucre to Bolívar, Sicasica, March 13, 1825, in O'Leary, *Cartas,* I, 317-318.

50. O'Connor, *Independencia,* pp. 162-163; Rey de Castro, "Recuerdos," 88, has a somewhat different version, stating that Ecles went to see Colonel Ortega, commander of Oruro, rather than O'Connor.

51. Sucre to the President of La Paz [Lanza], Caracollo, March [14 or 15], 1825, in ANB, *MI,* VIII, no. 63.

52. Sucre to P. A. Olañeta, Oruro, March 16, 1825, in O'Leary, *Memorias,* XXIII, 77-78.

53. Sucre to Rufino Martínez, Oruro, March 16, 1825, in ANB, *MI,* VIII, no. 63.

54. Sucre to the Ministro de la Guerra del Perú, Oruro, March 18, 1825, in Lecuna, *Documentos,* I, 133-135.

55. Sucre to Francisco Sánchez [*sic* for López], Oruro, March 15, 1825, in ANB, *MI,* VIII, no. 63.

56. O'Connor, *Independencia,* p. 164; Sucre to the Ministro de la Guerra del Perú, Oruro, March 18, 1825, in Lecuna, *Documentos,* I, 133; Sucre to Bolívar, Condo, March 24, 1825, in O'Leary, *Cartas,* I, 321.

57. René-Moreno, *Nuevas notas,* p. 511.

58. Jaime Mendoza, "Advenimiento de la nacionalidad boliviana," *Revista del Instituto de Sociología Boliviana* (Sucre), I, no. 1 (1941), 6.

59. O'Connor, *Independencia,* pp. 164-165.

60. See Gabriel René-Moreno, "Vida del Jeneral José Ballivian," *Anales de la Universidad* (Santiago), LXXXVIII (1894), 414.

61. Sucre to Francisco López, Oruro, March 15, 1825, in ANB, *MI,* VIII, no. 63.

62. Lagunillas, March 26, 1825. This proclamation is seemingly available only in Rey de Castro, "Recuerdos," 91.

63. [Urcullu], *Apuntes,* p. 151; Sánchez de Velasco, *Memorias,* p. 151; Sucre to the Prefect of Arequipa, Potosí, March 29, 1825, in Manuel de Odriózola, *Documentos históricos del Perú,* VI, 265.

64. Sucre to Carlos Medinaceli, Potosí, April 1, 1825, in ANB, *MI,* VIII, no. 63.

65. Rey de Castro, "Recuerdos," 92.

66. Sucre to Bolívar, Potosí, April 3, 1825, in O'Leary, *Cartas,* I, 324.

67. This letter of Olañeta to Sucre is unlocated, but Sucre cites it in Sucre to Carlos Medinaceli, Potosí, April 1, 1825, in ANB, *MI,* VIII, no. 63.

68. Francisco López to Sucre, Tarabuco, April 1, 1825. April 2, 1825, [Chuquisaca], April 9, 1825, in BSGS, XXIII-XXV, nos. 255-267 (1925), 81-84, 86.

69. Hesperiophylo [pseud.], "Descripción histórica y corográfica de las provincias de Chichas y Tarija," *Mercurio Peruano*, II, no. 39, May 15, 1791, 36.

70. Torrente, *Historia*, III, 514; Torata, "Prólogo," *Separatista*, IV, p. lii, believes that Torrente is the most accurate source for these last days of the campaign; cf. Sucre to Bolívar, Potosí, January 29 [*sic* for March 29], 1825, in O'Leary, *Cartas*, I, 293.

71. Emilio Medinaceli, "Tumusla, batalla que selló la independencia de Bolivia," *El Diario* (La Paz), January 11, 1953, literary supplement; cf. René-Moreno, *Nuevas notas*, p. 493.

72. Emilio Medinaceli, "Tumusla," calls his article a "historical rectification" and says that his distinguished forefather proclaimed the Patriot cause on March 25, not 30, yet he gives no documentary proof of this. The unpublished letter of Sucre to Medinaceli, April 1, 1825, in ANB, *MI*, VIII, no. 63, indicates that Medinaceli did not switch until March 30, but that he wrote a letter to Olañeta on March 29, probably telling the general that he was shifting. From where did Emilio Medinaceli get March 25? Does he think he can justify his forefather's treason by making it five days earlier? Medinaceli's action was one of the most unethical of the war. In the letter of Sucre to the Minister of War of Peru, Potosí, April 3, 1825, in Lecuna, *Documentos*, I, 143, Sucre wrote explicitly that Medinaceli shifted to the Patriots on March 30.

73. René-Moreno, *Nuevas notas*, p. 493.

74. William Bennet Stevenson, *Memorias*, Biblioteca Ayacucho, XV (Madrid, no date), 259; cf. Sucre to Bolívar, Potosí, January [*sic* for March] 29, 1825, *op. cit.*

75. Carlos Medinaceli to Sucre, Tumusla, April 2, 1825, in Emilio Medinaceli, "Tumusla."

76. Sucre to Carlos Medinaceli, Potosí, April 1, 1825, in ANB, *MI*, VIII, no. 63.

77. Carlos Matzenauer, *Bolivia in Historischer, Geografischer und Kultureller Hinsicht* (Vienna, 1897), p. 24; *El Tiempo* (Buenos Aires), July 9, 1828.

78. Bulnes, *op. cit.*, p. 629; Torrente, *Historia*, III, 511.

79. In Camba, *Memorias*, II, 213-214.

80. No available sources indicate whether Olañeta was taken home to Salta to be buried.

81. See Díaz A., *Los generales*, pp. 128-133.

82. Sucre to León Galindo, Chuquisaca, July 7, 1826, in Carlos Blanco Galindo, ed., *Cartas del General Antonio José de Sucre* (La Paz, 1918), p. 45; cf. Sucre to León Galindo, Potosí, October 7, 1826, in *ibid.*, p. 104.

83. [Urcullu], *Apuntes*, pp. 151-152.

84. Carlos Medinaceli to Sucre, Tumusla, April 2, 1825, in Emilio Medinaceli, "Tumusla."

85. Sánchez de Velasco, *Memorias*, p. 152. The assumption that there was no fight at Tumusla has quite valid grounds in view of the absence of primary material that sketches the battle.

86. See *supra*, chap. vii, n. 82.

87. Leguizamón, *op. cit.*, p. 59, n. 1.

88. [Urcullu], *Apuntes*, p. 151.

89. Sucre to Medinaceli, Potosí, April 1, 1825, in ANB, *MI*, VIII, no. 63.

90. Sucre to Bolívar, Potosí, January [*sic* for March] 29, 1825, in O'Leary, *Cartas*, I, 293.

91. Sucre to Medinaceli, Potosí, April 1, 1825, Sucre to the President of Potosí and Municipality of Chuquisaca, Potosí, April 2, 1825, in ANB, *MI*,

VIII, no. 63.

92. Rey de Castro, "Recuerdos," 92.

93. Sucre to Bolívar, Potosí, April 3, 1825, in O'Leary, *Cartas*, I, 323; Sánchez de Velasco, *Memorias*, p. 152.

94. *Idem.*

95. Sucre to Carlos Medinaceli, Potosí, April 3, 1825 (3 letters), in ANB, *MI, VIII*, no. 63.

96. Sucre to José María Urdininea, Potosí, April 3, 1825, in ANB, *MI*, VIII. no. 63; Sucre to Francisco O'Connor [Potosí, April 3, 1825], in ANB, *MI*, VIII, no. 63; Sucre to Bolívar, Potosí, April 3, 1825, in O'Leary, *Cartas*, I, 323.

97. Sucre to Francisco O'Connor [Potosí, April 3, 1825], in ANB, *MI*, VIII, no. 63.

98. Sucre to José María Valdez [Barbarucho], Potosí, April 4, 1825, in ANB, *MI*, VIII, no. 63.

99. Sucre to Medinaceli, Potosí, April 3, 1825, in ANB, *MI*, VIII, no. 63.

100. Sucre to José María Urdininea, Potosí, April 6, 1825, in ANB, *MI*, VIII, no. 63.

101. Sucre to José María Urdininea, Potosí, April 9, 1825, in ANB, *MI*, VIII, no. 63; *infra*, n. 105; O'Connor, *Independencia*, p. 167.

102. René-Moreno, *Ayacucho en Buenos Aires*, p. 101, n. 1. Much information is contained in a letter by Arenales to Sucre, Salta, February 6, 1827, in ANB (unclassified document).

103. O'Connor, *Independencia*, p. 167.

104. Sucre to José María Urdininea, Potosí, April 9, 1825, in ANB, *MI*, VII, no. 63.

105. Circular letter by Sucre, Potosí, April 9, 1825, in ANB, *MI*, VIII, no. 63.

106. Rey de Castro, "Recuerdos," 93 (Rey de Castro called the place of Valdez' surrender Chequeltani).

CHAPTER 9

1. In Lecuna, *Documentos*, I, 95.

2. See República de Bolivia, *Colección oficial de leyes, decretos* . . . (La Paz, 1834), I, 1 ff.; Pinilla, *Creación*, p. 111; Paz, *Historia*, II, 634; Sucre to the President of Potosí and the Municipality of Chuquisaca, Potosí, April 2, 1825, in ANB, *MI*, VIII, no. 63.

3. *Memoria que el jeneral en jefe del ejército libertador* . . . *presenta a la asamblea jeneral* . . . ([La Paz] Impr. del Ejército [1825]), pp. 4-5; Sucre to the President of Potosí and the Municipality of Chuquisaca, Potosí, April 2, 1825, in ANB, *MI*, VIII, no. 63.

4. Vázquez-Machicado, "Creación;" Sucre to the Presidente de la Junta Electoral de Oruro, Chuquisaca, June 11, 1825; Sucre to the President of Cochabamba, Chuquisaca, June 3, 1825, in ANB, *MI*, VIII, no. 63; see letters of Sucre to Bolívar during the month of June, in O'Leary, *Cartas*, I, 348-366.

5. José Vázquez-Machicado, "La nacionalidad boliviana" (unpublished).

6. Cited by Vázquez-Machicado, "Creación."

7. Sucre to Carlos Antonio Ortega, La Paz, February 22, 1825, Sucre to Antonio Saturnino Sánchez, La Paz, February 22, 1825, in ANB, *MI*, VIII, no. 63.

8. Sucre to Arenales, Chuquisaca, June 29, 1825, in ANB, *MI*, VIII, no. 65.

9. Sucre to the Governor of Oruro, Chuquisaca, June 25, 1825, Sucre to Andrés Santa Cruz, May 30, 1825, in ANB, *MI*, VIII, no. 63.

10. For the names of the delegates see *Libro mayor;* see also Urquidi, *Compendio,* p. 168.

11. See José María Santibáñez, *Vida del Jeneral José Ballivian* (New York, 1891).

12. Universidad de San Francisco Xavier (Sucre), *Libros de secretaría en que se asientan las asistencias, y fallas de los individuos de la Real Carolina Academia de practicantes juristas de esta corte;* ANB, *ACh,* Expedientes de abogados, 1775-1825; ANB, *ACh,* Caja Reales de La Plata, Libros mayores de contaduría; Velasco Flor, *Foro boliviano,* pp. 3-13; Valentín Abecia, *Historia de Chuquisaca* (Sucre, 1939), pp. 339-374; Luis Paz, *La Universidad,* pp. 390-398. The graduates of the University were: *Chuquisaca,* José Mariano Serrano, Casimiro Olañeta, Manuel María Urcullu, José María Dalence, Angel Mariano Moscoso; *Potosí,* Manuel José Calderón, Manuel Anselmo de Tapia, Manuel Martín Cruz, Manuel Argote, José Antonio Pallares, Manuel María García, José Mariano Enríquez, José Ignacio de Sanjinés, Rafael Monje; *Cochabamba,* Miguel José de Cabrera, José Manuel Pérez, Pedro Terrazas, Melchor Paz, Nicolás de Cabrera, Manuel Mariano Centeno, Dionicio de la Borda, Manuel Cabello, Francisco Vidal; *La Paz,* José María Mendizábal, José María de Asín, José Indalecio Calderón y Sangínez, Eusebio Gutiérrez, Fermín Eysaguirre; *Santa Cruz,* Antonio Vicente Seoane, Vicente Caballero.

13. *Libro mayor,* session 1 (July 10), pp. 1-2.

14. Vázquez-Machicado, "Creación."

15. René-Moreno, *Nuevas notas,* p. 658.

16. Thanks to Urcullu's pen the actions and discussions of the delegates were preserved and the originals are today deposited in a safe of the Banco Central in La Paz; cf. Pinilla, *Creación,* p. 177.

17. Cf. René-Moreno, *Nuevas notas,* p. 663.

18. See the letter of Sucre to Bolívar, Cochabamba, July 11, 1825, in O'Leary, *Cartas,* I, 371.

19. See Ignacio Prudencio Bustillo, "Letras bolivianas," *Kollasuyo* (La Paz), V, no. 50 (1943), 157.

20. *Libro mayor,* s. 1 (July 10), pp. 2-3; also reproduced in *BSGS,* XXIII-XXV, nos, 255-267 (1925), 2d part, 95-97.

21. *Bolivia en el primer centenario de su independencia* ([New York], 1925), p. 683; cf. Academia Nacional de Bellas Artes de la República Argentina, *Documentos de arte colonial sudamericano, Chuquisaca* (Buenos Aires, 1948), cuaderno IV, pp. xxxix-xl.

22. Mathías Terrazas to Sucre, La Plata, May 8, 1825, in ANB, *MI,* I, no. 5 (enclosure: Lista de el coro de esta Santa Yglesia Metropolitana de Charcas).

23. *Libro mayor,* s. 1 (July 10), p. 4.

24. In the more than one thousand letters located in the lost copybook of Sucre for the year 1825 a confirmation of the words of Sucre becomes only too evident.

25. This speech is available in Lecuna, *Documentos,* I, 283-292, but it is a faulty transcription; the original version is in *Memoria que el jeneral en jefe . . .* available in BNB, *C-RM.*

26. "Acto continuo se leyó por uno de los representantes la esposición de la conducta política y militar del Excmo. Señor Jeneral en Jefe del Ejército Libertador del Alto Peru, Antonio José de Sucre, desde que pasó el Desaguadero hasta el 30 de junio. Este hombre prodijioso, este segundo Bolívar, que habló de los pueblos con acciones dignas de alto reconocimiento brilló más en ese día, que en sus espediciones bélicas y se presentó, más grande que fijando la suerte del nuevo mundo en el campo de Ayacucho! Solo ese jenio

pudo decir lo que había hecho, y hacer lo que el ha dicho!" (*Gaceta de Chuquisaca*, no. 1, Saturday, July 30, 1825, in BNB, *C-RM*).

27. See Gustavo Adolfo Otero, *Figuras de la cultura boliviana*, pp. 136-139.

28. Prudencio Bustillo, *op. cit.*, p. 157.

29. Cf. Joaquín Gantier, "La mujer en el motín del 18 de abril," *BSGS*, XLIV, nos. 438-440 (1952), 269-275.

30. *Libro mayor*, s. 1 (July 10), p. 4.

31. Sucre to Arenales, Chuquisaca, June 29, 1825, in ANB, *MI*, VIII, no. 65; Sucre to Santa Cruz, Chuquisaca, May 30, 1825, in ANB, *MI*, VIII, no. 68.

32. See Alfonso Crespo, *Santa Cruz* (Mexico City, 1944), pp. 64-65.

33. Francisco Pinedo (La Paz, July 11), José María Dalence (Chuquisaca, July 13), Miguel Fermín Aparicio (La Paz, July 13), in *Libro mayor*, s. 2 and 3 (July 11, 13), pp. 7-8.

34. See Pinilla, *Creación*, p. 184; *Libro mayor*, s. 2 (July 11), pp. 6-7.

35. See René-Moreno, *Nuevas notas*, p. 667; Argüedas, *Fundación*, p. 279.

36. *Libro mayor*, s. 4 (July 18), p. 11.

37. *Loc. cit.*; cf. Pinilla, *Creación*, p. 189.

38. See Montenegro, *Nacionalismo*, p. 48.

39. *Gaceta de Chuquisaca*, no. 2, Saturday, August 6, 1825.

40. Vázquez-Machicado, "Creación."

41. *Gaceta de Chuquisaca*, no. 2, *op. cit.*

42. *Libro mayor*, s. 5 (July 21), pp. 13-14.

43. Argüedas, *Fundación*, p. 283.

44. Cf. Pinilla, *Creación*, p. 190.

45. See Agustín Iturricha, *Historia de Bolivia bajo la administración del Mariscal Andrés Santa Cruz* (Sucre, 1920), p. 203.

46. *Libro mayor*, s. 6 (July 22), pp. 15-17.

47. Delegate Mendizábal was completely accurate in this line of reasoning, and nearly one century later the Spanish scholar, Carlos Badia Malagrida, in his superb study, *El factor geográfico en la política sudamericana* (Madrid, 1919), pp. 147-148, 206-208, 313-315, showed with a scientific and scholarly mind what Mendizábal had already suggested in Bolivia's first national assembly. Badia Malagrida's theory was debated with a powerful pen by the great Bolivian writer, Jaime Mendoza, in his *El factor geográfico en la nacionalidad boliviana* (Sucre, 1925).

48. Sucre to José Mariano Serrano, Chuquisaca, June 30 [1825] (enclosure missing), in ANB, *MI*, VIII. no. 61.

49. Gunnar Mendoza, *Pedro Vicente Cañete*, p. 22.

50. Juan del Pino Manrique, "Informe reservado . . . ," in *Revista Chilena*, VIII (1877), 207-234.

51. Gabriel René-Moreno, "El Alto-Perú en 1783 . . . ," in *Revista Chilena*, VIII (1877), p. 206.

52. *Libro mayor*, s. 7 (July 23), pp. 18-21.

53. "El discurso de Montoya, representante de Potosí, revela una visión bastante clara de lo que podríamos llamar la realidad internacional de entonces" (Vázquez-Machicado, "Creación").

54. See Charles W. Arnade, "La creación de Bolivia," in *Nuevo Mundo* (La Paz) (August-September, 1953), p. 22.

55. *Libro mayor*, s. 8 (July 28), pp. 21-24.

56. *Bolivia en el primer centenario de su independencia*, p. 410; Pinilla, *Creación*, p. 178.

57. *Libro mayor*, s. 8 (July 28), pp. 23-24.

58. República de Bolivia, *Libro menor de sesiones secretas . . .* (La Paz, no date), s. 1 (August 1), pp. 1-3.

59. See *Libro mayor,* s. 9, 10, 11 (August 1, 3, 4), pp. 26-31.

60. *Libro mayor,* s. 10 (August 3), pp. 29-30.

61. *Ibid.,* s. 11 (August 4), pp. 31-33.

62. See René-Moreno, *Nuevas notas,* pp. 65-68.

63. See Pinilla, *Creación,* pp. 197-201.

64. "Relación de méritos y servicios del Coronel don Antonio Seoane de los Santos," AGI (Seville), Audiencia de Charcas, 582 (E. 121, C. 2, L. 15), as cited by Vázquez-Machicado, "Creación," n. 118.

65. "Sensiblemente para la historia, el Libro Mayor de sesiones de la famosa asamblea, no registra los discursos íntegros de los oradores, sino extractos demasiado cortos, que no dan lugar a juzgar las piezas oratorias en su verdadero mérito" (Iturricha, "El Doctor José Mariano Serrano," 35).

66. Vázquez-Machicado, "Creación."

67. Pinilla, *Creación,* p. 199; Paz, *Historia,* II, 671; Arguedas, *Fundación,* p. 287; Vázquez-Machicado, "Creación."

68. In Lecuna, *Documentos,* II, 292-297.

69. *Biblioteca boliviana,* no. 458, p. 119; cf. Carlos Romero, "Gabriel René-Moreno," *Gesta Bárbara* (Potosí), segunda epoca, V, no. 10 (November, 1926), 1.

70. Luis Terán Gómez, "La emancipación política del Alto Perú," *Revista Militar* (La Paz), no. 154 (1950), p. 129.

71. C. Olañeta to Santa Cruz, Chuquisaca, November 11, 1829, December 11, 1829, in personal archive of Andrés Santa Cruz (La Paz).

72. Otero, ed., *Folletos,* pp. 77-78.

73. Signed: Casimiro Olañeta, La Paz, June 3, 1838, 3 pp., in BNB, *C-RM.*

74. *Desarollo del pensamiento político en Bolivia,* p. 53.

75. *Nacionalismo,* p. 52.

76. Vázquez-Machicado, "Creación."

77. Montenegro, *Nacionalismo,* p. 52.

78. *Gaceta de Chuquisaca,* no. 3 (August 27, 1825).

79. *Biblioteca boliviana,* no. 458, p. 119.

# ABBREVIATIONS

ARCHIVES

*ACh*     Audiencia de Charcas. Collection located in ANB.
ANB     Archivo Nacional de Bolivia.
BNB     Biblioteca Nacional de Bolivia.
*CR*     Colección Ernesto Rück. Collection located in BNB.
*C-RM*     Colección René-Moreno. Collection located in BNB.
EC     Expedientes coloniales. Subdivision of *ACh*.
*EP*     Registro de escrituras públicas de la ciudad de la Plata. Located in ANB.
*MG*     Ministerio de Guerra. Collection located in ANB.
*MI*     Ministerio del interior. Collection located in ANB.

BOOKS

Argüedas, *Fundación*
    Argüedas, Alcides. *La Fundación de la república*. La Paz, 1920.
Beltrán, *Logia*
    Beltrán Avila, Marcos. *La pequeña gran logia que independizó a Bolivia*. Cochabamba, 1948.
Camacho, *Historia*
    Camacho, José María. *Historia de Bolivia*. 14th ed. La Paz, 1952.
Camba, *Memorias*
    García Camba, Andrés. *Memorias*. Biblioteca Ayacucho. Vols. VI and VII (respectively Vols. I and II of *Memorias*). Madrid, no date.
Lecuna, *Documentos*
    Lecuna, Vicente. *Documentos referentes a la creación de Bolivia*. 2 vols. Caracas, 1924.
*Libro mayor*
    República de Bolivia. *Libro mayor de sesiones de la asamblea de representantes del Alto-Perú, instalada el 10 de julio de 1825*. La Paz, 1926.
Mallo, *Administración*
    Mallo, Jorge. *Administración del Jeneral Sucre*. Sucre, 1871.
Mitre, *Belgrano*
    Mitre, Bartolomé. *Historia de Belgrano y la independencia argentina* [several editions used].

Montenegro, *Nacionalismo*
  Montenegro, Carlos. *Nacionalismo y coloniaje.* 2d ed. La Paz, 1943.
Muñoz, *Guerra*
  Muñoz Cabrera, Juan. *La guerra de los quince años en el Alto-Peru.* Santiago, 1867.
O'Connor, *Independencia*
  O'Connor, Burdett. *Independencia americana.* Biblioteca Ayacucho. Vol. III. Madrid, no date.
Olañeta, *Exposición*
  Olañeta, Casimiro. *Exposición.* Sucre: Imprenta del Ejército [1826].
O'Leary, *Cartas*
  O'Leary, Daniel. *Cartas de Sucre al Liberatador.* Biblioteca Ayacucho. Vols. XXXVI and XXXVII, respectively Vols. I and II of *Cartas. Madrid,* no date.
O'Leary, *Memorias*
  O'Leary, Daniel. *Memorias.* Vols. XI, XXII, XXIII. Caracas, 1883.
Omiste, *Memoria, 1810*
  Omiste, Modesto. *Memoria histórica sobre los acontecimientos políticos ocurridos en Potosí en 1810.* Potosí, 1877.
Omiste, *Memoria, 1811*
  Omiste, Modesto. *Memoria histórica sobre los acontecimientos políticos ocurridos en Potosí en 1811.* Potosí, 1878.
Paz, *Historia*
  Paz, Luis. *Historia general del Alto Perú, hoy Bolivia.* 2 vols. Sucre, 1919.
Paz, *Memorias*
  Paz, José María. *Memorias póstumas.* Biblioteca Ayacucho. Vol. XVI. Madrid, no date.
Paz Soldán, *Historia*
  Paz Soldán, Mariano F. *Historia del Perú independiente.* 3 vols. Lima, 1868-1874.
Pinilla, *Creación*
  Pinilla, Sabino [sic]. *La creación de Bolivia.* Biblioteca Ayacucho. Vol. XVII. Madrid, no date.
Ramallo, *Guerra*
  Ramallo, Miguel. *Guerra doméstica.* Sucre, 1916.
Ramallo, *Guerrilleros*
  Ramallo, Miguel. *Guerrilleros de la independencia, los esposos Padilla.* La Paz, 1919.
René-Moreno, *Biblioteca boliviana*
  René-Moreno, Gabriel. *Biblioteca boliviana: catálogo de la sección de libros i folletos.* Santiago, 1879.
René-Moreno, *Biblioteca peruana*
  René-Moreno, Gabriel. *Biblioteca peruana. Apuntes para un catálogo de impresos.* 2 vols. Santiago, 1896.
René-Moreno, *Documentos inéditos*
  René-Moreno, Gabriel. *Ultimos días coloniales en el Alto-Perú. Documentos inéditos de 1808 y 1809.* Santiago, 1901.
René-Moreno, *Más notas*
  René-Moreno, Gabriel. *Bolivia y Perú, más notas históricas y bibliográficas.* Santiago, 1905.
René-Moreno, *Notas*
  René-Moreno, Gabriel. *Bolivia y Perú, notas históricas y bibliográficas.* 2nd ed. Santiago, 1905.
René-Moreno, *Nuevas notas*

René-Moreno, Gabriel. *Bolivia y Perú, nuevas notas históricas y bibliográficas.* Santiago, 1907.
René-Moreno, *Ultimos días*
René-Moreno, Gabriel. *Ultimos días coloniales en el Alto-Perú.* [text]. Santiago, 1896.
Sánchez de Velasco, *Memorias*
Sánchez de Velasco, Manuel. *Memorias para la historia de Bolivia.* Sucre, 1938.
Torata, *Separatista*
Torata, Conde de [Hector Valdés]. *Documentos para la historia de la guerra separatista del Perú.* 4 vols. Madrid, 1894-1898.
Torrente, *Historia*
Torrente, Mariano. *Historia de la revolución hispano-americana.* 3 vols. Madrid, 1830.
[Urcullu], *Apuntes*
[Urcullu, Manuel María]. *Apuntes para la historia de la revolución del Alto-Perú, hoi Bolivia por unos patriotas.* Sucre, 1855.
Uriburu, *Historia*
Uriburu, José Evaristo. *Historia del General Arenales.* 2d. ed. Vol. I. London, 1927.
Urquidi, *Rectificaciones*
Urquidi, José Macedonio, *La obra histórica de Argüedas, breves rectificaciones.* Cochabamba, 1923.
Vázquez-Machicado, *Blasfemias*
Vázquez-Machicado, Humberto. *Blasfemias históricas. El Mariscal Sucre, el doctor Olañeta y la fundación de Bolivia.* La Paz, 1939.

JOURNALS

*BSGS* *Boletín de la Sociedad Geográfica "Sucre".*
*USFX* *Universidad de San Francisco Xavier.*

UNPUBLISHED ESSAYS

René-Moreno, "Fragmentos"
René-Moreno, Gabriel. "Fragmentos biográficos de Casimiro Olañeta."
Vázquez-Machicado, "Creación
Vázquez-Machicado, Humberto. "La creación de la nacionalidad boliviana."

# BIBLIOGRAPHY

$\mathcal{A}$LMOST ALL THE WORK FOR THIS STUDY was done in Bolivian archives which possess an abundance of material that defies description, but unfortunately is badly preserved and practically unorganized. The most important document depository is the Archivo y Biblioteca Nacional de Bolivia. There is one director for both the library and the archives; both sections, under Bolivian law, are independent of each other, but they are located in the same building. (A move is scheduled in the near future.)

In the Biblioteca Nacional the splendid *Colección Gabriel René-Moreno* constitutes practically the whole library. A complete description of this collection, listing each item with excellent comments, is available in Gabriel René-Moreno, *Biblioteca boliviana: catálogo de la sección de libros i folletos* (Santiago, 1879), 880 pp.; Gabriel René-Moreno, *Primer suplemento a la biblioteca boliviana; epítome de un catálogo de libros y folletos, 1879-1899* (Santiago, 1900), 349 pp.; Gabriel René-Moreno, *Segundo suplemento a la biblioteca boliviana: libros y folletos, 1900-1908* (Santiago 1908), 348 pp. Everything cited in these bibliographic guides is part of the René-Moreno collection, with the exception of several items that are missing. An additional guide to supplement some works not listed by René-Moreno is available in Valentín Abecia, *Adiciones a la biblioteca boliviana de Gabriel René-Moreno* (Santiago, 1899), 440 pp. A great part of the René-Moreno library is the splendid newspaper collection which is listed in Gabriel René-Moreno, *Ensayo de una bibliografía general de periódicos de Bolivia, 1825-1905* (Santiago, 1905), 336 pp. All the newspapers cited are available in this collection with the exception of the rarest newspaper, *El Condor de Bolivia.* For more information about the René-Moreno collection the monograph by Gunnar Mendoza, *Gabriel René-Moreno, bibliógrafo boliviano* (Sucre, 1954), 76 pp., should be consulted. Two items not listed in the guides are the six volumes entitled *Prensa argentina, estractos sobre Bolivia y Bolívar* (handwritten) which René-Moreno collected with the intention of writing a study entitled "Bolívar y Bolivia." The existence of these manuscripts had passed unnoticed until I

247

located them. The other manuscript collection not noted is entitled *Manuscritos de Chuquisaca, 1624-1908;* it contains miscellaneous documents which René-Moreno possessed and had used in his research. They do not deal with any particular topic.

The next most valuable collection for this study in the National Library was the *Colección Ernesto Rück,* which is mostly miscellaneous manuscript material which Mr. Rück, a German who became the first director of the Bolivian archives, had gathered as his own personal collection. This depository is much smaller and is contained in a showcase. The manuscripts do not pertain to any specific subject. Seemingly Mr. Rück acquired whatever he felt was rare, without any intention of using it for a research project. The documents are listed in *Biblioteca de Ernesto O. Rück, catálogo* (Lima, 1898), 72 pp. (rare). Most of the material listed in the guide is available in the Rück collection, with some minor exceptions. Some manuscripts are not listed in the *catálogo.* For example, the fascinating diary of Drummer Vargas was found in the Rück library.

Another collection used incidentally was that of the Bolivian biographer, Velasco Flor, entitled *Manuscritos: archivo epistolar de Samuel Velasco Flor.* This reservoir is not well organized and has little to do with the topic of this study, but contains much information, since Mr. Velasco Flor had a wide circle of friends with whom he maintained a lively correspondence. No guide is available for this collection and it awaits classification.

Of much value is the collection of Bolivian newspapers from 1825 to the present, which is not part of the René-Moreno collection and which is in the process of being classified and cataloged. When finished it will complement the rich newspaper files of René-Moreno.

One of the problems which the National Library faces in the future is the desired integration of its collections into one organized whole, with a single guide. For example, it would be advisable that the René-Moreno newspaper collection and the newly cataloged newspapers should be integrated into one collection. The documents of the René-Moreno, Rück, and Velasco Flor collections, and other unused reservoirs in the library should be integrated with the manuscripts there.

In the National Archives is the great collection of the Audiencia of Charcas, including practically all the colonial records of Upper Peru. This large collection is divided into several sections of which the largest is the *Expedientes coloniales, 1552-1825.* This is a "loosely designated" division and contains "not only true criminal, civil, and administrative *expedientes,* but also correspondence, cedulas, reports, and all other kinds of documents which accumulated in the government offices." No index is available.

Of great use in determining the background of the turncoat Royalist leaders was the division entitled *Expedientes de abogados y practicantes juristas, 1688-1825,* which is the application file of students of the University of San Francisco Xavier and the graduate Carolina Academy. This collection was brought together by the director, Gunnar Mendoza, and a hastily written index is available. Other collections within the Audiencia of Charcas that were used were the *Caja reales de la Plata, libro mayores de contaduría* and *Registro de escrituras públicas de la ciudad de la Plata,* which are mostly notary and tax records of the city of La Plata (Chuquisaca), but sometimes contain information on other topics which cannot be obtained anywhere else. For a further description of these collections and others, see Juan de Zengotita, "The National Archive and the National Library of Bolivia at Sucre," *Hispanic American Historical Review*, XXIX (November, 1949), 649-676. This is an extremely well-written and accurate article.

For the national period the divisions are very easy to use because of a streamlined organization by the director. The documents are divided according to the administrative divisions of the government of Bolivia. Since in the first year of its existence, 1825-1826, only the Ministry of Interior was organized, all documents are available in the files of the *Ministerio del Interior*. Later the *Ministerio de Guerra* and the *Ministerio de Hacienda* were added. Within each ministry's files the documents are divided according to the departments—La Paz, Oruro, Cochabamba, Potosí, Chuquisaca, and Santa Cruz—following a chronological order. A typewritten guide of the *Ministerio del Interior* was available from the director. All three divisions were consulted. In 1953 the organization of the manuscripts of the national period had only reached the 1840's.

The library of the Sociedad Geográfica de Sucre is invaluable. The collection was severely damaged in the 1948 earthquake and since that time had never been reorganized. No description or catalog was available. The most valuable piece in this library is the complete file of *El Condor de Bolivia*, Bolivia's first newspaper, which is not available in the National Library or any other place in Bolivia. In my search and research in the society, I had some unusual experiences. No one knew where *El Condor* had been put after the earthquake, and after an intensive search I found it in a glass box underneath a skull. A card attached to the skull gave the information that it was Casimiro Olañeta's, which sometime in the past had been donated to the society. The present members of the society had lost track of this interesting historical relic of the great *dos caras*. Another day, in the same disheveled room, a beautiful little metal box caught my eye. In the excitement of the treasure hunt I had some difficulty in opening it. When I had at last succeeded in prying it open, I found quite a different kind of treasure from what I had expected. The box contained ashes; underneath them was a card saying that these were the remains of José Mariano Serrano. Apparently it had been years since anyone had opened the box. No one in the society seemed to have known of the box's historic content, and they congratulated me for having found the remains of the great Serrano, intellectual father of Bolivia.

The rich collection of the University of San Francisco Xavier was opened only in the last months of my stay in Sucre. Before that it was closed to the public, and it was said that the librarian had been exiled by the government and had taken the keys with him. When it was opened again it was found to be in a state of complete confusion, but the university appointed two able men to catalog it. Most of the library is composed of the private collections of two late citizens of Sucre, Messrs. Abecia and Arana, who were collectors of rare items. No catalog is available, but Abecia's *Adiciones* is nearly all in the library. Most of the material is duplicated in the National Library. Some volumes of the *Libros de secretaría en que se asientan las asistencias, y fallas de los individuos de la Real Carolina Academia de practicantes juristas de esta corte* were used for this study. Only the records for the period June 22, 1813, to September 25, 1819, could be located. The rest probably were burned in a fire that destroyed the university archive. The attendance records proved valuable in determining which of the founders of Bolivia attended the university and graduate academy. Some valuable unorganized and miscellaneous documents, mostly unknown letters to and from Sucre, were located in the rector's office.

The church records of Santo Domingo were used only in order to copy the birth certificate of Casimiro Olañeta, which Dr. Mendoza had located earlier, and the death certificate of his mother.

The personal archive of Andrés Santa Cruz in La Paz constitutes a most splendid collection. Mr. Santa Cruz estimates that he has from six to seven thousand documents that pertain to his distinguished forefather, Marshal Andrés Santa Cruz. Most of the material is family property, but Mr. Santa Cruz, in order to complement this, has occupied himself with acquiring originals or good copies of all material concerning the marshal. Unquestionably this is a great archive and no history of Santa Cruz and his time can ever be written without consulting it. Mr. Santa Cruz has compiled two excellent guides in which each one of the documents is listed according to chronology: "Lista alfabética, índice alfabético chronológico de cartas y oficios del Mariscal Andrés de Santa Cruz (originales, borradores, copiadores . . . )"; "Lista alfabética . . . de cartas y oficios al Mariscal Andrés de Santa Cruz . . . " (typewritten).

In the library of the University of San Andrés in La Paz some important miscellaneous manscripts are available. Most of these cover the year 1828. They are well preserved, thanks to the director, Humberto Vázquez-Machicado, and an excellent guide, "Catálogo cronológico de documentos manuscritos" (typewritten), provides a good description of each document.

In Cochabamba, Bolivia's second-largest city and most thriving center of the country, two archives are located, which apparently possess excellent material, but unfortunately are beyond the reach of the scholar. The departmental archive is in complete chaos, with documents piled to the ceiling, others thrown on the floor. No one knows what is in them and no inventory has ever been taken, nor has anyone used them. There seems to be invaluable material in this archive, including some from the colonial period. But at the present research is impossible. The personal library of the family Blanco Galindo, organized in its present form by the late General Carlos Blanco Galindo, ex-president of Bolivia, is a useful archive with some valuable material, especially of their forefathers, General León Galindo, aide of Marshal Sucre, and General Pedro Blanco, hero of the War of Independence. Later General Blanco, in association with Casimiro Olañeta, invited the Peruvian army to enter Bolivia in 1828 and overthrow Marshal Sucre. Blanco was made president of Bolivia by his Peruvian proteges, but was killed by Bolivian patriots. The Blanco Galindo family is reluctant to open its library to research; it is said that one of the reasons for this is the desire to protect the name of General Blanco. Although I did have an opportunity to make a hasty survey of the library, the diaries of General Blanco, which undoubtedly contain interesting information about the creation of Bolivia, were kept from sight.

Dr. Humberto Vázquez-Machicado has an excellent library in La Paz, with many books available in no other library. His many unpublished essays were of great help. He provided copies of documents of the Archivo Nacional de Argentina and the Archivo General de Indias. The unpublished guide of Dr. Vázquez-Machicado's brother, the late José Vázquez-Machicado, "Catálogo descriptivo del material del Archivo de Indias referente a la historia de Bolivia," three volumes, is a masterful piece of research.

The many archives in Bolivia will provide any scholar with a tremendous amount of material never used before by anyone.

## LIST OF ARCHIVES

    A. Biblioteca Nacional de Bolivia (Sucre).
        1. Colección Ernesto Rück.
        2. Colección Gabriel René-Moreno.
        3. Colección Velasco Flor.
        4. Colección de periódicos bolivianos.

    B. Archivo Nacional de Bolivia (Sucre).
        1. Audiencia de Charcas.
          a. Expedientes coloniales.
          b. Expedientes de abogados y practicantes juristas.
        2. Cajas reales de la Plata, libros mayores de contaduría.
        3. Registro de escrituras públicas de la ciudad de la Plata.
        4. Archivo del Ministerio del Interior.
        5. Archivo del Ministerio de Guerra.
        6. Archivo del Ministerio de Hacienda.

    C. Archivo y Biblioteca de la Sociedad Geográfica de Sucre.

    D. Archivo y Biblioteca de la Universidad de San Francisco Xavier.
        1. Libros de Secretaría . . . de la Real Carolina Academia.
        2. Colección Abecia-Arana.
        3. Colección depositada en el rectorado (Manuscritos Abecia-Arana).

    E. Archivo parroquial de Santo Domingo (Sucre).

    F. Archivo personal de Andrés Santa Cruz (La Paz).
        1. Correspondencia al Mariscal Andrés Santa Cruz.
        2. Correspondencia del Mariscal Andrés Santa Cruz.

    G. Biblioteca de la Universidad de San Andrés (La Paz).

    H. Archivo departmental de la provincia de Cochabamba (unorganized).

    I. Archivo personal de Blanco Galindo (Cochabamba) (restricted).

    J. Biblioteca personal de Humberto Vázquez-Machicado (La Paz).

    K. Archivo Nacional de Argentina.
      Bolivia: representantes diplomáticos (1827-1853)
          (copies supplied by Humberto Vázquez-Machicado).

## LIST OF REFERENCES

Books

Abecia, Valentín. *Adiciones a la biblioteca boliviana de Gabriel René-Moreno.* Santiago, 1899.
——. *Historia de Chuquisaca.* Sucre, 1939.
——. *Historia documental, la cuna de Monteagudo.* Sucre, 1905.
Academia Nacional de Bellas Artes de la República Argentina. Cuaderno IV: *Documentos de arte colonial sudamericano. Chuquisaca.* Buenos Aires, 1948.
Acosta, Nicolás. *Apuntes para la bibliografía periodística de la ciudad de La Paz.* La Paz, 1876.
Alcedo, Antonio. *Diccionario geográfico-histórico de las Indias Occidentales.* Madrid, 1786-1789.
Alvarado, Roberto. *Tres esquemas de historia.* No place, 1950.
Alvarado, Rudecindo. *Recuerdos históricos* in Ministerio de Educación de la Nación, Dirección General de Cultura [Argentina], *Selección de documentos del Museo Histórico Nacional.* Vol. I. Buenos Aires, 1952, 181-190.
Alvarez, Mariano Alejo. *Discurso sobre la preferencia que deben tener los americanos en los empleos de América [1811]* . . . Lima, 1820.
Andrews, Captain Joseph. *Journey . . . to Potosí . . . in the years 1825-1826.* 2 vols. London, 1827.
——. *Viaje de Buenos Aires a Potosí y Arica en los años 1825 y 1826.* Buenos Aires, 1920.
Aranzaes, Nicanor. *Diccionario histórico del departamento de La Paz.* La Paz, 1915.
Aráoz de la Madrid, Gregorio. *Memorias.* Biblioteca Ayacucho. Vol. LX. Madrid, n. d.
——. *Memorias.* 2 vols. Buenos Aires, 1895.
Archivo General de la Nación (Argentina). *Partes oficiales y documentos relativos a la guerra de la independencia argentina.* 2d ed. 4 vols. Buenos Aires, 1900-1903.
Argüedas, Alcides, *La fundación de la república.* La Paz, 1920.
Arocha Moreno, Jesús. *Las ideas políticas de Bolívar y Sucre en el proceso de la fundación de Bolivia.* Caracas, 1952.
Badia Malagrida, Carlos. *El factor geográfico en la política sudamericana,* Madrid, 1919.
Baldivieso, Alberto. *Enfermedades altoperuanas.* Sucre, 1929.
Ballestero y Beretta, Antonio. *Historia de España.* Vol. VII. Barcelona, 1934.
Beltrán Avila, Marcos. *Historia del Alto Perú en el año 1810.* Oruro, 1918.
——. *La pequeña gran logia que independizó a Bolivia.* Cochabamba, 1948.
*Biblioteca de Ernesto O. Rück, catálogo.* Lima, 1898.
Blanco-Fombona, Rufino. *Cartas de Bolívar.* Biblioteca Ayacucho. Vols. LIX, LXII. Madrid, 1921.
Blanco Galindo, Carlos (ed.). *Cartas del General Antonio José de Sucre.* La Paz, 1918.
*Bolivia en el primer centenario de su independencia.* [New York], 1925.
Bulnes, Gonzalo. *Ultimas campañas de la independencia del Perú, 1822-1826.* Santiago, 1897.
Caceres, Armando. *La primera campaña del General Arenales en el Valle Grande.* Buenos Aires, 1944.
Camacho, José María. *Historia de Bolivia.* 14th ed. La Paz, 1952.

Cañete y Domínguez, Vicente. *Guía de la provincia de Potosí.* 1787. Potosí, 1952.
Castro, Ignacio de. *Relación de la fundación de la Real Audiencia del Cuzco en 1778, y de las fiestas con que esta grande y fidelísima ciudad celebró este honor.* Madrid, 1795.
Chaves, Julio César. *Castelli el adalid de mayo.* Buenos Aires, 1944.
*Colección de arengas en el foro i escritos del doctor don Mariano Moreno* . . . . London, 1836.
Córdova, Demetrio, F. de. *Historia de Bolivia.* Sucre, 1911 [?].
Cortés, Manuel José. *Ensayo sobre la historia de Bolivia.* Sucre, 1861.
Crespo, Alfonso. *Santa Cruz.* Mexico City, 1944.
Crespo, Luis S. *José Miguel García Lanza.* La Paz, 1928.
Dalence, José María. *Bosquejo estadístico de Bolivia.* Chuquisaca, 1851.
Department of the Interior, Office of Geography. *Gazetteer No. 4: Bolivia.* Washington, 1955.
*Diario de operaciones del ejército real del Perú, en campaña que ha sostenido contra los constitucionales, el año de 1824.* Potosí, 1824.
Díaz A., Julio. *Historia del ejército de Bolivia.* La Paz, 1940.
——— *Los generales de Bolivia.* La Paz, 1929.
———. *Sucre, organizador y conductor de ejércitos.* La Paz, 1950.
———. *Vida . . . del General José Miguel Lanza.* La Paz. 1927.
Díaz Villamil, Antonio. *Curso elemental de historia de Bolivia.* 3d. ed. 4 vols. La Paz, 1945-1949.
Díez-Canseco, Ernesto. *Perú y Bolivia, pueblos gemelos.* Lima, 1952.
Díez de Medina, Fernando. *Thunupa.* La Paz, 1947.
D'Orbigny, Alcides. *Voyage dans l'Amérique Méridional.* 9 vols. Paris, 1835-1847.
Durán, Adolfo. *Apéndice a los documentos inéditos publicados en la obra de G. René-Moreno.* Buenos Aires, 1909.
Escudero F., Bernardo. *Diario de la última campaña del Ejército Español en el Perú en 1824 . . . ,* in Torata, Conde de, *Documentos para la historia de la guerra separatista del Perú.* Vol. III doble. Madrid, 1894-1898.
*Extracto del diario de las operaciones del ejercito español en la campaña sobre el Desaguadero.* Cuzco, 1824.
Finot, Enrique. *Historia de la literatura boliviana.* Mexico City, 1943.
———. *Nueva historia de Bolivia.* Buenos Aires, 1946.
Francovich, Guillermo. *La filosofía en Bolivia.* Buenos Aires, c. 1945.
———. *El pensamiento universitario de Charcas.* Sucre, 1948.
Frías, Bernardo. *Historia del General D. Martín Güemes y de la provincia de Salta.* 3 vols. Salta, 1902-1911.
Gantier, Joaquín. *Doña Juana Azurduy de Padilla.* La Paz, 1946.
García Camba, Andrés. *Memorias para la historia de las armas españolas en el Perú.* 2 vols. Madrid, 1846.
———. *Memorias.* Biblioteca Ayacucho. Vols. VI and VII (respectively Vol. I and II of *Memorias*). Madrid, no date.
Guzmán, Humberto. *Estéban Arze, caudillo de los valles.* Cochabamba, 1948.
Guzmán, Luis M. *Historia de Bolivia.* 3d ed. Cochabamba, 1896.
Haggard, J. Villasana. *Handbook for Translators of Spanish Historical Documents.* Oklahoma City, 1941.
Hanke, Lewis. *La villa imperial de Potosí.* Sucre, 1954.
Iturricha, Agustín. *Historia de Bolivia bajo la administración del Mariscal Andrés Santa Cruz.* Vol. 1 (and only one). Sucre, 1920.
———. *Leyes numeradas y compiladas de la república boliviana.* 2 vols. La Paz, 1912.

Jáuregui Rosquellas, Alfredo. *Antonio José de Sucre, heroe y sabio, mártir y santo.* Cochabamba and La Paz [1928].

———. *La ciudad de los quatro nombres.* Sucre, 1924.

Jemio, Luis F. *Biografías de Pedro Domingo Murillo y José Antonio Medina.* La Paz, 1909.

Junta de Historia y Numismática Americana [Argentina]. *Gaceta de Buenos Aires.* Reimpresión facsimilar. 6 vols. Buenos Aires, 1910-1915.

Kempff Mercado, Enrique. *Gabriel René-Moreno.* Washington, D. C. [1953].

Kramer, Pedro. *Historia de Bolivia.* La Paz, 1899.

Lamas, Andrés. *Colecciones de memorias y documentos para la historia y la geografía de los pueblos del Río de la Plata.* Montevideo, 1849.

Lecuna, Vicente. *Crónica razonada de las guerras de Bolívar.* 3 vols. New York, 1950.

———. *Documentos referentes a la creación de Bolivia.* 2 vols. Caracas, 1924.

———. *Proclamas y discursos del Libertador.* Caracas, 1939.

Lecuna, Vicente, and Bierck, Harold (eds.). *Selected Writings of Bolivar.* 2 vols. New York, 1951.

Leguizamón, Juan Martín. *Límites con Bolivia.* Salta, 1872.

Levillier, Roberto. *Audiencia de Charcas.* 3 vols. Madrid, 1918.

Lewin, Boleslao. *Tupac Amaru, el rebelde.* Buenos Aires, 1943.

López, Vicente F. *Historia de la república argentina.* New ed. 10 vols. Buenos Aires, 1913.

Loza, León M. *Bosquejo histórico del periodismo boliviano.* 2d ed. La Paz, 1926.

Machicado, José Santos. *Galería de hombres célebres de Bolivia.* Santiago, 1869.

Mallo, Jorge. *Administración del Jeneral Sucre.* Sucre, 1871.

Mariátegui, Francisco X. *Anotaciones a la historia del Perú independiente de Mariano F. Paz Soldán.* Lima, 1869.

Marof, Tristán. [pseud. of Gustavo A. Navarro]. *La ilustre ciudad, historia de badulaques.* La Paz, 1950.

Marquiegui, José María. *Resumen histórico del Ckollansuyo, Charcas hoy Bolivia.* Sucre, 1938.

Matzenauer, Carlos. *Bolivia in Historischer, Geografischer und Kultureller Hinsicht.* Vienna, 1897.

Mendoza, Gunnar. *El doctor don Pedro Vicente Cañete.* Sucre, 1954.

———. *Gabriel René-Moreno, bibliógrafo boliviano.* Sucre, 1954.

Mendoza, Jaime. *El factor geográfico en la nacionalidad boliviana.* Sucre, 1925.

———. *El Mar del Sur.* Sucre, 1926.

Miller, John. *Memoirs of General Miller* . . . . 2 vols. London, 1828.

———. *Memorias del General Miller* [translated by General Torrijos]. 2 vols. London, 1829.

[Miranda, Francisco Mariano de]. *Carta del Dr. Francisco Mariano de Miranda al Dr. Casimiro Olañeta.* Quito, 1840.

Mitre, Bartolomé. *Historia de Belgrano y la independencia argentina* [several editions used].

———. *Historia de San Martín.* 2d ed. 2 vols. Buenos Aires, 1890.

Monteagudo, Bernardo. *Obras políticas* in Ricardo Rojas (ed.). *Biblioteca argentina.* Buenos Aires, 1916. Vol. VII.

Montenegro, Carlos. *Nacionalismo y coloniaje.* 2d ed. La Paz, 1943.

Morales, José Agustín. *Los primeros cien años de la república de Bolivia.* 2 vols. La Paz, 1925.

Moscoso, Octavio. *Apuntes biográficos de los próceres mártires de la guerra de la independencia del Alto-Perú.* Sucre, 1885.

Moxó y Francolí, Benito María de. *Carta pastoral de* . . . *don* . . . . Buenos

Aires, 1807.
——. *Pública i solemne rogativa que el Iltmo. Señor Arzobispo de la Plata hizo* . . . Buenos Aires, 1808.
Mujía, Ricardo. *Bolivia-Paraguay*. 8 vols. (3 books and 5 *anexos*). La Paz, 1914.
Muñoz Cabrera, Juan. *La guerra de los quince años en el Alto-Perú*. Santiago, 1867.
O'Connor, Burdett. *Independencia americana*. Biblioteca Ayacucho. Vol. III. Madrid, no date.
O'Connor D'Arlach, Tomás. *El Coronel José Eustaquio Méndez*. Tarija, 1893 (rare).
——. (ed.). *Recuerdos de Francisco Burdett O'Connor*. Tarija, 1895.
——. *Tarija, bosquejo histórico*. La Paz, 1932.
Odriózola, Manuel de. *Documentos históricos del Perú*. 10 vols. Lima, 1863-1877.
Olañeta, Casimiro. *Exposición*. Sucre: Imprenta del Ejército [1826] (very rare).
——. *Mi defensa o conclusión*. La Paz, May 28, 1839 (rare).
——. *Quam dulce est pro patria mori*. La Paz, 1838 (very rare).
Olañeta, Pedro Antonio de. *Conducta del General disidente Don Simón Bolívar en sus comunicaciones con el General Realista Don Pedro Antonio de Olañeta*. Potosí, February 22, 1825 (very rare).
O'Leary, Daniel. *Cartas de Sucre al Libertador*. Biblioteca Ayacucho. Vols. XXXVI and XXXVII (respectively Vols. I and II of *Cartas*). Madrid, no date.
——. *Memorias*. Vols. XI, XXII, XXIII. Caracas, 1883.
Omiste, Modesto. *Crónicas potosinas*. 2 vols. La Paz, c. 1919.
——. *Memoria histórica sobre los acontecimientos políticos ocurridos en Potosí en 1810*. Potosí, 1877.
——. *Memoria histórica sobre los acontecimientos políticos ocurridos en Potosí en 1811*. Potosí, 1878.
Ordoñez López, Manuel, and Crespo, Luis. *Bosquejo de la historia de Bolivia*. La Paz, 1912.
Oropeza, Samuel. *El 25 de mayo de 1809. Otro documento histórico*. Sucre, 1894.
Otero, Gustavo Adolfo. *Figuras de la cultura boliviana*. Quito, 1952.
——. (ed). *Folletos escogidos de Casimiro Olañeta*. La Paz, 1939.
Ovilo y Otero, Manuel. *Historia de las cortes, de las armas, de las letras y artes españoles*. 7 vols. Madrid, 1851-1853.
Pacheco Loma, Miguel. *Resumen de la historia de Bolivia*. Oruro, 1948.
Palma, Ricardo. *Tradiciones peruanas*. Vol. I. Barcelona, 1893.
Paredes, Rigoberto. *Provincia de Inquisivi, estudios geográficos, estadísticos y sociales*. La Paz, 1906.
——. *Relaciones históricas de Bolivia*. Oruro, no date.
Parish, Woodbine. *Buenos Aires y las provincias del Río de la Plata, desde su descubrimiento y conquista por los españoles*. Translated and edited by Justo Maeso. 2 vols. in 1. Buenos Aires, 1852-1853.
Paz, José María. *Memorias póstumas*. 4 vols. Buenos Aires, 1855.
——. *Memorias póstumas*. Biblioteca Ayacucho. Vol. XVI. Madrid, no date.
Paz, José María. *Un proceso histórico, respuestas al proceso literario de Alcides Argüedas*. Sucre, 1922.
Paz, Luis. *Don José María Paz*. Tarija, 1891.
——. *Estudios históricos de Monseñor Miguel de los Santos Taborga*. La Paz, 1908.

————. *Historia general del Alto Perú, hoy Bolivia.* 2 vols. Sucre, 1919.
————. *La Universidad Mayor Real y Pontificia de San Francisco Xavier.* Sucre, 1914.
————. *Miguel de los Santos Taborga.* Sucre, 1906.
Paz Soldán, Mariano F. *Historia del Perú independiente.* 3 vols. Lima, 1868-1874.
[Pazos Kanki, Vicente]. *Compendio de la historia de los Estados Unidos de America.* Paris, 1825 (very rare).
Pérez de Urdininea, José María. *Manifiesto refutando el mensaje presentado por el gran Mariscal de Ayacucho al Congreso de Bolivia.* Chuquisaca, 1828 (very rare).
Pérez Galdós, Benito. *Episodios nacionales.* Tercera serie: *Zumalacárregui.* Madrid, 1929.
Pinilla, Sabino [*sic*]. *La creación de Bolivia.* Biblioteca Ayacucho. Vol. XVII. Madrid, no date.
————. [*sic*]. *Crónica del año 1828.* Cochabamba [1929].
Pinto, Manuel M. *La revolución de la intendencia de la Paz en el virreynato del Río de la Plata, con la ocurrencia de Chuquisaca.* Buenos Aires, 1909.
Pizarro, Luís. *Tarija, apuntes histórico-geográficos.* Sucre, 1936 (rare).
Ponce Sanginés, Carlos, and García, Raul Alfonso (eds.). *Documentos para la historia de la revolución de 1809.* 4 vols. La Paz, 1953-1954.
Presas, José. *Memorias secretas de la Princesa del Brasil actual Reina viuda de Portugal.* Bordeaux, 1830.
Pruvonena, P. [pseud. of José de la Riva Agüero]. *Memorias y documentos para la historia de la independencia del Perú y causa del mal éxito que ha tenido esta. . . .* 2 vols. Paris, 1858 (rare).
Publicación Oficial [Gobierno de la Provincia de Santiago del Estero]. *El Coronel Lorenzo Lugones.* Buenos Aires, 1896.
Ramallo, Miguel. *Batallas de la guerra de la independencia.* La Paz, 1930 (rare).
————. *Batalla del Pari.* Tarija, 1911 (rare).
————. *Guerra doméstica.* Sucre, 1916.
————. *Guerrilleros de la independencia, los esposos Padilla.* La Paz, 1919.
Rawson, Arturo. *Argentina y Bolivia en la epopeya de la emancipación.* La Paz, 1928.
*Real ordenanzas para el establecimiento e instrucción de intendentes de exército y provincia en el Virreinato de Buenos Aires.* Madrid, 1782.
René-Moreno, Gabriel. *Anales de la prensa boliviana, matanzas de Yañez, 1861-1862.* Santiago, 1886.
————. *Ayacucho en Buenos Aires.* Madrid, no date.
————. *Biblioteca boliviana: catálogo de la sección de libros i folletos.* Santigo, 1879 (rare).
————. *Biblioteca perunana. Apuntes para un catálogo de impresos.* 2 vols. Santiago, 1896 (very rare).
————. *Bolivia y Argentina, notas biográficas y bibliográficas.* Santiago, 1901.
————. *Bolivia y Perú, notas históricas y bibliográficas,* Santiago, 1900.
————. *Bolivia y Perú, notas históricas y bibliográficas.* 2d ed. Santiago, 1905.
————. *Bolivia y Perú, más notas históricas y bibliográficas.* Santiago, 1905.
————. *Bolivia y Perú, nuevas notas históricas y bibliográficas.* Santiago, 1907.
————. *Elementos de literatura preceptiva.* Santiago, 1891.
————. *Ensayo de una bibliografía general de periódicos de Bolivia, 1825-1905.* Santiago, 1905.
————. *Primer suplemento a la biblioteca boliviana; epítome de un catálogo de libros y folletos, 1879-1899.* Santiago, 1900.

——. *Segundo suplemento a la biblioteca boliviana: libros y folletos, 1900-1908.* Santiago, 1908.

——. *Ultimos días coloniales en el Alto-Perú.* [text]. 2 vols. in 1. Santiago, 1896 (rare).

——. *Ultimos días coloniales en el Alto-Perú. Documentos inéditos de 1808 y 1809.* Santiago, 1901 (limited circulation, 100 numbers).

República de Bolivia. *Colección oficial de leyes, decretos, órdenes, resoluciones* . . . Vol. I. Paz de Ayacucho [i.e. La Paz], 1834.

——. *Libro mayor de sesiones de la asamblea de representantes del Alto-Perú, instalada en 10 de julio de 1825.* La Paz, 1926.

——. *Libro menor de sesiones secretas de la asamblea de los señores diputados q. componen la asamblea general del Alto Perú instalada el 10 de julio de 1825* . . . . La Paz, no date.

Reyes Ortiz, Félix. *Biografía del Dr. Casimiro Olañeta.* La Paz, 1860.

Rodríguez, Casado, Vicente, and Calderón Quijano, José Antonio (eds.). *Memoria de gobierno del Virrey Abascal.* 2 vols. Seville, 1944.

Romero, Carlos V. *Apuntes biográficos del Coronel José Vicente Camargo.* Sucre, 1895.

Romero, Emilia. *Indice de los documentos de Odriozola.* Lima, 1946.

Saavedra, Bautista. *Defensa de los derechos de Bolivia en el litigio de fronteras con la república del Perú.* 2 vols. Buenos Aires, 1906.

Sabine, George H. *A History of Political Theory.* Revised ed. New York, 1950.

Sánchez de Velasco, Manuel. *Memorias para la historia de Bolivia.* Sucre, 1938.

Santibañez, José Maria. *Vida del Jeneral José Ballivián.* New York, 1891.

Santos Taborga, Miguel de los. *Documentos inéditos para la historia de Bolivia.* Chuquisaca, 1891.

Sanzetena, Manuel. *Bolivia en su período de grandeza.* Oruro, 1948.

Serrano, José Mariano. *Breves pinceladas sobre algunos puntos interesantes a mi honor.* Sucre, 1842 (rare).

Sotomayor Valdés, Ramón. *Estudios históricos de Bolivia.* Santiago, 1874.

Stevenson, William Bennet. *Memorias.* Biblioteca Ayacucho. Vol. XV. Madrid; no date.

Sucre, Antonio José de. *Convocatoria del Alto-Perú a una asamblea jeneral deliberante.* La Paz: Imprenta del Ejército, 1825 (very rare).

Sucre, Antonio José de. *Memoria que el jeneral en jefe del ejército libertador* . . . *presenta a la asamblea jeneral* . . . . [La Paz]: Imprenta del Ejército [1825] (rare).

Terán, Juan. *José María Paz, 1791-1854.* Buenos Aires, 1936.

Torata, Conde de [Hector Valdés]. *Documentos para la historia de la guerra separatista del Perú.* 4 vols. Madrid, 1894-1898.

Torrente, Mariano. *Historia de la revolución hispano-americana.* 3 vols. Madrid, 1830.

Trelles, Manuel. *Cuestiones de límites entre la república Argentina y Bolivia.* Buenos Aires, 1872 (rare).

Trigo, Bernardo. *Las tejas de mi techo.* La Paz, 1939.

Trigo, Heriberto. *Don Tomás, vida, obra y época de Tomás O'Connor D'Arlach.* Tarija, 1953.

[Urcullu, Manuel María]. *Apuntes para la historia de la revolución del Alto-Perú, hoi Bolivia por unos patriotas.* Sucre, 1855 (rare).

Uriburu, Damaso. *Memorias.* Buenos Aires, 1934.

Uriburu, José Evaristo. *Historia del General Arenales.* 2d ed. Vol. I [final one]. London, 1927.

Urquidi, José Macedonio. *Compendio de la historia de Bolivia.* 4th ed. Buenos Aires, 1944.

——. *Figuras históricas.* Cochabamba, 1916.

——. *La obra histórica de Arguedas, breves rectificaciones.* Cochabamba, 1923.

——. *La última revolución de Cochabamba.* Cochabamba, 1943.

Valencia Vega, Alipio. *Desarrollo del pensamiento político en Bolivia.* La Paz, 1953.

——. *Julián Tupaj Katari.* Buenos Aires, [1948].

Vargas, Tambor Mayor. *Diario de un soldado de la independencia altoperuana en los valles de Sicasica y Hayopaya.* Sucre, 1952 [sic for 1954].

Vargas Ugarte, Rubén. *Biblioteca peruana.* 6 vols. (?). Lima, 1935-1949.

——. *Don Benito María de Moxó y de Francolí.* Buenos Aires, 1936.

Vázquez-Machicado, Humberto. *Blasfemias históricas. El Mariscal Sucre, el doctor Olañeta y la fundación de Bolivia.* La Paz, 1939.

——. *La sociología de Gabriel René-Moreno.* Buenos Aires, 1936.

Vedia y Mitre, Mariano de. *La vida de Monteagudo.* 3 vols. Buenos Aires, 1950.

Velasco Flor, Samuel. *Vidas de bolivianos célebres.* Potosí, 1871 (rare).

——. *Foro boliviano.* Sucre, 1877 (rare).

Vidaurre, Enrique. *Potosí, cuartel general de los guerreros de la independencia,* La Paz, 1952.

Viscarra, Eufronio. *Biografía del General Esteban Arze.* 2d ed. Cochabamba, 1910 (rare).

Zinny, Antonio. *Gaceta de Buenos Aires desde 1810 hasta 1821. Resumen de los bandos, proclamas . . . .* Buenos Aires, 1875.

Zorreguieta, Mariano. *Apuntes históricos de Salta en la época del coloniaje,* 2d ed. Salta, no date.


ARTICLES

Abecia, Valentín. "Los fundadores de la república, José Mariano Serrano," *BSGS,* XXVI, nos. 274-278 (1926), 214-217.

——. "Observaciones a los capítulos de la historia de Bolivia de Monseñor Taborga," *BSGS,* VIII, no. 94 (1908), 159-173.

Alvarado, Roberto. "Los feudales criollos en el poder," *Revista de la Federación de Estudiantes de Chuquisaca,* I, nos. 1-2 (1945), 111-131.

"América," *El Argos* (Buenos Aires), nos. 15, 18, 19, March 10, 20, 24, 1824.

Aramayo, Eduardo. "Resumen . . . de documentos secretos . . . ," *BSGS,* XXXIV, nos. 344-346 (1939), 86-101.

Arce, Luis. "Iniciativa y comienzos de la guerra de la independencia sudamericana," *Cuarto Congreso Científico, 1º Pan-Americano, septima sección, ciencias sociales, historia americana* (Santiago, 1908), pp. 1-60.

Arnade, Charles W. "A Sojourn in Sucre," *Michigan Alumnus Quarterly Review,* LX, no. 10 (1953), 64-70.

——. "La creación de Bolivia," *Nuevo Mundo* (La Paz) (August-September, 1953), 18-22.

——. "Una bibliografía selecta de la guerra de la emancipación en el Alto-Perú," *Boletín de la Sociedad Geográfica y de Historia "Potosí",* XL, no 12 (1953), 159-169.

——. "Una figura mediocre en el motin del 18 de abril de 1828," *BSGS,* XLV, no. 441 (1954), 74-100.

Belgrano, Manuel. "Fragmento de memoria sobre la batalla de Tucumán (1812)," *Biblioteca Ayacucho,* XVI, 36-40.

Buschiazzo, Mario J. "La Casa de Moneda en Potosí," *BSGS,* XXXV, nos. 359-361 (1940), 270-275.

Cañete, Pedro Vicente. "Dictamen a pedimiento del excmo. Sr. Virrey," *Gazeta Extraordinaria de Buenos-Ayres*, July 3, 1810, pp. 1-10.
———. "Espectáculo de la verdad," in René-Moreno, *Documentos inéditos* pp. cxxxi-clii.
Céspedes, Guillermo. "Lima y Buenos Aires. Repercusiones económicas y políticas de la creación del Virreinato del Plata," in *Anuario de Estudios Americanos* (Seville), III (1946), 669-874.
Crespo, Alfonso. "Perfil de Casimiro Olañeta," *Kollasuyo*, IX, no. 65 (1947), 3-11.
"Documentos de la independencia, proclamas en Quichua," *BSGS*, XVI, nos. 173-175 (1915), 44-56.
"Documentos históricos," *BSGS*, XLV, no. 442 (1955), 420-427.
"El Doctor José Mariano Serrano fué redactor del acta de la independencia según su propia declaración," *BSGS*, XXXII, nos. 333-336 (1937), 36-38.
Ermita, Juan de. "El Doctor José Mariano Serrano y el acta de la independencia argentina," *BSGS*, XXXIII, no. 343, (1938), 117-122.
Finot, Enrique. "Dos obras apócrifas de la literatura boliviana," *La Razón* (La Paz), November 6, 1945.
Gantier, Joaquín. "Casimiro Olañeta," *La Razón* (La Paz), November 20, December 18, 1949; January 29, February 26, March 19, April 23, May 21, June 25, July 2, August 13, September 24, 1950; February 3, 1952, all in the literary supplements.
———. "La mujer en el motín del 18 de abril," *BSGS*, XLIV, nos. 438-440 (1952), 269-275.
Giménez Fernández, Manuel. "Las doctrinas populistas en la independencia de Hispano-América," in *Anuario de Estudios Americanos* (Seville), III (1946), 519-665.
Hesperiophylo [pseud.]. Descripción histórica y corográfica de las provincias de Chichas y Tarija," *Mercurio Peruano*, II, no. 39, May 15, 1791.
"Homenaje al tercer centenario de la fundación de San Francisco Xavier," *BSGS*, XXI, nos. 233-245 (1924), 1-203.
Iturricha, Agustín. "El Doctor José Mariano Serrano . . . ," *BSGS* XXXI, nos. 327-332 (1937), 21-42.
Jáuregui Rosquellas, Alfredo. "Crónica documental," *BSGS*, XLIV, nos. 433-434 (1950), 41-61.
———. "Documentos inéditos," *BSCS*, XLIII, nos. 427-428 (1948), 182-192.
———. "Juan José Castelli," *BSGS*, XLIII, nos, 429-430 (1949), 340-342.
———. "La Audiencia de Charcas," *BSGS*, XXX, nos. 316-319 (1933), 1-53.
———. "La fundación de Bolivia," *BSGS*, XXXVIII, nos. 383-385 (1942), 153-157.
"Justicia ejecutada en el Brigadier Echeverría," *La Estrella de Ayacucho* (Arequipa), no. 7, April 23, 1825.
Mallo, Nicanor. "Tradiciones, cosas de aquellos tiempos," *BSGS*, XXXVII, nos. 371-373 (1941), 53-57.
Marof, Tristán. [pseud. of Gustavo A. Navarro]. "Melgarejo y el melgarejismo," *Selecciones Bolivianas* (La Paz), II, no. 6 (1953), 35-41.
Medinaceli, Emilio. "Tumusla, batalla que selló la independencia de Bolivia," *El Diario* (La Paz), January 11, 1953, literary supplement.
Mendoza, Gunnar. "Una crónica desconocida de la guerra de independencia altoperuana," *USFX* (Sucre), XVI, nos. 37-38 (1951 [sic, 1954]), 199-301.
Mendoza, Jaime. "Advenimiento de la nacionalidad boliviana," *Revista del Instituto de Sociología Boliviana* (Sucre), I, no. 1 (1941), 5-13.
———. "El cuarto centenario de la fundación de La Plata," *USFX*, no. 17

(1938), 56-122.
——. "La creación de una nacionalidad," *BSGS,* XXVI, nos. 268-269 (1926), 1-15.
——. "La Universidad de Charcas y la idea revolucionaria," *USFX,* VII, no. 23 (1940), 225-282.
Olañeta, Casimiro. "Artículo comunicado," *El Condor de Bolivia* (Chuquisaca), no. 19, April 26, 1826.
Olañeta, Pedro Antonio. "A los pueblos del Perú," *El Argos* (Buenos Aires), no. 14, supplement, March 8, 1824.
Olañeta, Pedro Antonio [and Manuel Maria Urcullu]. "Manifiesto a los habitantes del Perú," *El Argos,* no. 64, August 21, 1824.
Olañeta, Pedro Antonio and Casimiro Olañeta. "Proclama estableciendo el sistema absoluto," *El Argos,* no. 26, April 17, 1824.
Otero, Gustavo Adolfo. "El factor regional en la independencia de Bolivia," *Kollasuyo,* I, no. 2 (1939), 21-23.
Padilla, Manuel Asencio. "Autobiografía," *BSGS,* nos. 33-38 (1901-1902).
Paredes, Rigoberto. "Ligeros datos sobre la fundación de Bolivia," *BSGS,* XXXII, nos. 337-339 (1937), 134-156.
Pino Manrique, Juan del. "Informe reservado del gobenador intendente de Potosí sobre la nueva real ordenanza de intendente del virreinato del Río de la Plata," *Revista Chilena,* VIII (1877), 207-234.
Prudencio Bustillo, Ignacio. "Letras bolivianas," *Kollasuyo,* V, no. 50 (1943), 156-168.
[Prudencio, Roberto]. "Modesto Omiste," *Kollasuyo,* II, no. 18 (1940), 52-55.
René-Moreno, Gabriel. "El Alto-Perú en 1783, documento histórico importante," *Revista Chilena,* VIII (1877), 206-207.
——. "El golpe de estado de 1861," *USFX,* XIV, nos. 33-34 (1946), 289-348.
——. "Expediciones e invasiones," *Revista de Artes y Letras* (Santiago), V (1885), 484-489.
——. "La Audiencia de Charcas," *Revista Chilena,* VIII (1877), 93-142.
——. "La nueva constitución i el militarismo en Bolivia," *El Independiente* (Santiago), no. 2398, December 9, 1871.
——. "Los archivos históricos en la capital de Bolivia," *Revista Chilena,* VI (1876), 111-141.
——. "Vida del Jeneral José Ballivián," *Anales de la Universidad* (Santiago), LXXXVIII (1894), 407-433.
Rey de Castro, José María. "Recuerdos del tiempo heroico," *USFX,* XII, XIII, XIV, nos. 29-34 (1943-1946).
Romero, Carlos. "Gabriel René-Moreno," *Gesta Bárbara,* segunda época, V, no. 10 (November, 1926), 1-4.
Sandoval, Angel. "Don Jayme de Zudañez," *BSGS,* XXIX, nos. 310-311 (1931).
Santa Cruz, Víctor. "El guerrillero Lanza . . . ," *Revista Militar* (La Paz), no. 154 (1950), 137-144.
Serrano, José Mariano. "Comunicado," *El Condor de Bolivia,* no. 16, March 16, 1826.
[——]. "Un boliviano," *El Fénix de Lima,* no. 1, July 23, 1827.
Tauro, Alberto. "Historia e historiadores del Perú," *Revista de Historia de América,* no. 27 (1949), pp. 1-43.
Terán Gómez, Luis. "La emancipación política del Alto Perú," *Revista Militar* (La Paz), no. 154 (1950), pp. 129-131.
Trostine, Rodolfo. "Las memorias y autobiografías en la historiografía argentina, 1810-1852," *Anuario de Historia Argentina,* V (1943-1945), 411-414.
Vargas Ugarte, Rubén. "Los archivos de la antigua Chuquisaca," *BSGS,* XXVII, nos. 297-299 (1930), 101-115.

Vázquez, Ismael. "Juana Azurduy de Padilla," *BSGS*, XXVI, nos. 274-278 (1926), 151-158.

Vázquez-Machicado, Humberto. "El pasquinismo sedicioso y los pródromos de la emancipación en el Alto Perú," *BSGS*, XLV, no. 442 (1955) 366-419.

———. "La delegación Arenales en el Alto-Perú," *Revista de Historia de América*, no. 10 (1940), 87-123.

Viedma, Francisco de. "Descripción geográfica y estadística de la provincia de Santa Cruz . . . ," in Pedro Angelis (ed.). *Colección de obras . . . relativas a la historia . . . del Río de la Plata*. Vol. III. Buenos Aires, 1836.

Villegas, Alfredo. "Un documento de San Martín con referencias históricas," *Anuario de Historia Argentina*, V (1943-1945), 345-377.

Zengotita, Juan de. "The National Archive and the National Library of Bolivia at Sucre," *Hispanic American Historical Review*, XXIX, (1949), 649-676.

UNPUBLISHED ESSAYS

Arnade, Charles W. "The Creation of the Republic of Bolivia," doctoral dissertation. University of Florida, 1955.

"Catálogo Corbacho" (typewritten), no pagination, 906 numbers and 7006 documents listed, in BNB.

Natein, Ancelmo [pseud. for Vicente Pazos Kanki]. "Reflexiones políticas escritas vaxo el titulo de Instinto Común por el ciudadano Tomás Payne y traducidas abreviadamente por Ancelmo Natein, indígena del Perú. . . ," in *C-RM*, BNB.

René-Moreno, Gabriel. "Escuadrón de Urdininea, apuntes no utilizados o sobrantes," belonging to Humberto Vázquez-Machicado (La Paz).

———. "Fragmentos biográficos de Casimiro Olañeta," belonging to Humberto Vázquez-Machicado (copy in author's library).

———. "Manuscritos de Chuquisaca, 1624-1908," 3 vols. (handwritten) in BNB.

———. (ed.). "Prensa argentina, estractos sobre Bolivia y Bolívar" (handwritten), 6 vols., in BNB.

Santa Cruz Sch., Andrés. "Lista alfabética, índice alfabético chronológico de cartas y oficios del Mariscal Andrés de Santa Cruz (originales, borradores, copiadores . . . )."

———. "Lista alfabética, indice alfabético chronológico de cartas y oficios al Mariscal Andrés de Santa Cruz (originales, borradores, copiadores . . . )."

Universidad Mayor de San Andrés (La Paz), "Catálogo cronológico de documentos" (typewritten).

Vázquez-Machicado, Humberto. "La creación de la nacionalidad boliviana."

———. "Los origenes socio-históricos de la nacionalidad boliviana."

———. "Papeles inéditos de Gabriel René-Moreno."

Vázquez-Machicado, José. "Catálogo descriptivo del material del Archivo de Indias referente a la historia de Bolivia." 3 vols., in possession of Humberto Vázquez-Machicado.

———. "La nacionalidad boliviana."

[Velasco Flor, Samuel]. "Manuel María Urcullu," sketchy notes in BNB.

NEWSPAPERS

*El Argos* (Buenos Aires), 1820-1825.
*El Condor de Bolivia* (Chuquisaca), 1825-1826.
*El Correo de las Provincias* (Buenos Aires), 1822-1823.

*El Depositario de Cuzco,* 1823.
*El Diario* (La Paz), 1953-1954.
*La Estrella de Ayacucho* (Arequipa), 1825.
*El Fénix de Lima,* 1827.
*Gaceta de Buenos Aires,* 1810, 1816.
*Gaceta de Chuquisaca,* 1825.
*Gaceta del Gobierno* (Lima), 1825.
*El Independiente* (Santiago), 1871.
*El Mensajero Arjentino* (Buenos Aires), 1825-1827.
*Mercurio Peruano* (Lima), 1791.
*La Razón* (La Paz), 1945-1952.
*El Republicano* (Buenos Aires), 1824.
*El Sol de Cuzco,* 1825.
*El Teatro de la Opinion* (Buenos Aires), 1823.
*El Tiempo* (Buenos Aires), 1828.

# INDEX

**263**